# SWAY

## UNRAVELLING
## UNCONSCIOUS BIAS

Pragya Agarwal

BLOOMSBURY SIGMA

LONDON · OXFORD · NEW YORK · NEW DELHI · SYDNEY

BLOOMSBURY SIGMA
Bloomsbury Publishing Plc
50 Bedford Square, London, WC1B 3DP, UK

BLOOMSBURY, BLOOMSBURY SIGMA and the Bloomsbury Sigma logo
are trademarks of Bloomsbury Publishing Plc

First published in the United Kingdom in 2020

A catalogue record for this book is available from the British Library
Library of Congress Cataloguing-in-Publication data has been applied for

ISBN: HB: 978-1-4729-7135-7; TPB: 978-1-4729-7134-0;
eBook: 978-1-4729-7137-1

2 4 6 8 10 9 7 5 3 1

Typeset by Deanta Global Publishing Services, Chennai, India
Printed and bound in Great Britain by CPI Group (UK) Ltd,
Croydon CR0 4YY

Bloomsbury Sigma, Book Fifty-three

Illustrations by Julian Baker

To find out more about our authors and books visit www.bloomsbury.com
and sign up for our newsletters

# SWAY

## Also available in the Bloomsbury Sigma series:

For Prishita, India, April

*Because you are the future, and*
*I owe you an unbiased world*

# Contents

# Introduction

*'The cause is hidden. The effect is visible to all.'*

Ovid

'Oh, it's all right, you're a girl,' he said with a laugh.

This was a graduate student I shared an office with during my PhD. I asked for his help with a mathematical problem, and even though I had proven myself better at maths than him on more than one occasion, he patronisingly comforted me as he sat me down to tease out that mathematical algorithm. I was taken aback and, although usually I would let such remarks go, on that occasion I was feeling less generous. I asked him what he meant. 'Girls aren't good with numbers, and you're a girl,' he said with a smile. Even though he insisted it was only a joke, I wondered then if he believed this on some level. How did his general perception that girls are not good at numbers come about? And, in turn, how might these throwaway, supposedly jokey remarks that carry such skewed beliefs contribute to a wider societal bias?

Now, as I run sexism workshops in primary schools, so many boys – and girls – as young as seven years old tell me that boys are better at maths. 'Boys are also better at football,' they tell me very seriously. These implicit gender biases are reinforced from a very young age. When someone remarks that my spirited three-year-old is 'loud for a girl' or that 'she sure is bossy', they are assigning some specific behaviours that carry the bias that girls are supposed to be quiet. Consider if a boy was doing the same thing. Might he be excused with a 'boys will be boys' or 'he sure is a little leader'? These gendered stereotypes occur in words, images and books around us without us even realising it, and rely on a gender binary that forces children into one of two boxes. Lauren Child, Waterstones Children's Laureate for 2017–19, said, 'I don't know if it's just our culture, or whether it's a boy thing, that [boys] find it very hard to pick up a book or go to a film if a girl is the central character. I don't know where that comes from, but it worries me because it makes it harder for girls to be equal.' An in-depth study of the 100 most popular children's picture books of 2017 shows that male characters are twice as likely to take leading roles and are given far more speaking parts than females. Where other, non-human creatures feature in books, the gender bias is even more marked. Whenever an author reveals a creature's sex, there is only a 27 per cent chance the character is female. Research in education shows that wrong answers provided by boys are more likely to be overlooked. In contrast, girls are more often criticised for incorrect answers, and teachers tend to provide them with less praise for correct answers. An unconscious bias therefore develops that boys' knowledge is more highly valued than girls', which can convince girls they are less competent than boys.

In recent years, the interest in unconscious or implicit bias has increased. These terms are now being used to explain everyday discriminatory behaviour, and references to research into unconscious bias as a key to understanding and tackling social discrimination are at an all-time high. As a rough indication, just in the first three months of 2019, there were more than 3 million mentions on social media.*

---

* This is from a personal analysis of social media, particularly Twitter feeds, using analytical software and tools.

Hillary Clinton mentioned it in her first presidential debate in September 2016, saying that implicit bias in policing can have 'drastic consequences'. In April 2018, a Starbucks manager in Philadelphia called the police on two black men sitting peacefully inside a coffee shop. The culprit, according to Starbucks' CEO and the city's mayor, was implicit bias, and Starbucks closed its doors for half a day to put more than 150,000 employees through a training programme. Most recently, Prince Harry talked about unconscious racism in an issue of British *Vogue* guest edited by Meghan Markle, the Duchess of Sussex, something he has possibly become increasingly aware of as he navigates married life alongside a person who is bi-racial and who continues to face discrimination from the British media due to her race. However, as the awareness, coverage and content around unconscious bias escalates, there is also plenty of misleading information out there. Not all bias is implicit. Unconscious bias does not explain all prejudice and discrimination. And there is a real danger of unconscious bias being reduced to a 'trend' or a 'fluff word' and being used to excuse all sorts of discriminatory behaviour. This is why it is now becoming more crucial, more urgent, than ever to understand what unconscious bias really means, how it is formed, and what its underpinning scientific principles and theories are. Awareness is always the first step. Only then can we begin to address it.

To understand how the notion of bias came about, I investigated the etymology of the word. It is believed to originate from the Indo-European root *sker-*, which means 'to turn or bend', and could have foundations in the 13th-century French word *biais* meaning 'at an angle or crosswise', with its parallel Greek word having the same meaning, i.e. to cut crosswise. Bias of Priene was one of the

seven Greek sages* from the sixth century BC. He is the
sage of probity, with a strong moral compass, and said, 'If
you are a judge, make a Prienian decision,' and 'choose the
course which you adopt with deliberation,' warning against
hasty decision-making. According to Diogenes Laertius, a
biographer of Greek philosophers, Bias of Priene is believed
to have been distinguished for his rational decision-making
skills as an advocate and in defence of the truth. We cannot
know for certain whether the word bias comes from Bias of
Priene, but it is possible that he inspired how we understand
bias. When the word entered common English parlance in
the 16th century, it was used to mean an oblique or slanting
line. In the 1560s and 1570s, the game of bowls adopted
bias as a technical term to refer to balls that were weighted
on one side† so they curved when bowled. Shakespeare
uses 'bias' in the literal sense, but also figuratively as in *King
John* (ii:1:575): 'Commodity, the bias of the world.' In this
quote, the word means a predisposition, inclination or
prejudice, similar to how it is most commonly used today.

In his 1897 book, *What Is Art?*, Russian novelist Leo
Tolstoy wrote:

> That most men – not only those considered clever, but even
> those who are very clever, and capable of understanding
> most difficult scientific, mathematical, or philosophic
> problems – can very seldom discern even the simplest and
> most obvious truth if it be such as to oblige them to admit
> the falsity of conclusions they have formed, perhaps with
> much difficulty – conclusions of which they are proud,
> which they have taught to others, and on which they have
> built their lives.

---

* The wise men of Greece. Not the herb.
† Actually, it isn't the weight but the shape that makes the ball curve,
but most people believe it is the weight that affects trajectory.

We are reluctant to re-evaluate our beliefs and like to believe that we are all egalitarian and carry no biases. Later, I look at how biases are linked intrinsically to our notion of self-concept and self-identity, which is why it is often so difficult to shake them off (see Chapter 2).

In this book I am looking primarily at examples where a bias is misdirected and creates prejudice and discriminatory behaviour through a negative association with a certain group or community. Yet bias is not always negative. For instance, a parent's bias that their child is the smartest, cleverest, most beautiful is an evolutionary response, designed to trigger parental love and care. This can extend to close friends and family too. In such cases, mostly there is no negative bias against any group. However, if this positive bias creates a negative discrimination against someone else, or if it gives an undue advantage to the favoured group over someone else, then it becomes problematic. Positive unconscious biases can be challenging too, such as that of a 'model minority' (see Chapter 5), which is so often ignored.

My interest in unconscious bias has been hugely shaped by my own experiences. And, while a major thrust of the book is scientific, I do bring some personal anecdotes into the book to support and supplement, as they are integral to the story here and important in understanding the personal impact that unconscious bias can have on individuals. I was born in India, into a deeply patriarchal society, where gender divisions are laid down firmly. Growing up as one of three sisters, I did not conform to the stereotype of a meek, quiet Indian woman. I had the opportunity and the freedom to denounce the roles that many women in India are expected to play: a traditional Indian wife, daughter-in-law and mother. Because I was outspoken and knew my mind, I was often called 'rebellious', even when I moved to the UK. This made me acutely aware of the stereotypes that are so deeply entrenched in society and the norms against which everyone is judged. I came to the UK to study for a PhD. Fairly often I would hear fellow PhD students talk disparagingly about other foreign students in the university, and then they would smile at me and say things like, 'Of course, I wasn't talking about you,' or 'You're not very foreign,' or 'You're almost British.' It surprises me to realise this now, but I actually took this as reassurance. It meant I was accepted, I was one of them, I fitted in. As is common in most UK universities, the postgrad population was strongly multicultural, yet even so I was one of very few women of colour. I didn't have to try hard to fit in. I could speak more or less flawless English. I went to the pub. I dressed the same. I understood their jokes and laughed with them. I could make fun of them and be sarcastic. 'You "get" the British way,' someone once told me, and 'You're not very Indian.' When I heard 'not very Indian' for the first time, it took me aback. I wasn't sure what it meant, and I didn't know whether I should feel pleased or offended. But I had this nagging feeling that a part of me was being stripped away.

As time passed, I did everything I could to avoid drawing attention to my race and my skin colour. I was already a woman in a male-dominated work environment. As the first female lecturer employed in an engineering department at one of the leading UK universities, I'd heard suggestions that my appointment was a consequence of their efforts to be diverse and inclusive, a result of positive discrimination. My reaction was to water down my ethnicity and avoid any reference to it, to avoid double-bind bias.* I shortened my

---

* A 'double-bind' is a dilemma where an individual receives two or more conflicting messages with one often negating the other. It affects gender bias, with women often seen as either 'too likeable' or 'too bitchy'. In this case, while on one hand a person's ethnicity can result in them being seen as 'less capable', it can also lead to their

name to make it easier for people to say. In hindsight, I don't think I did any of this consciously or as a deliberate act so as to appear more 'white'. Perhaps it was an unconscious act to counter the internalised bias that I myself held against my fellow Indians. I had seen enough movies to know how Indians were caricatured: geeky, awkward, bad dress sense. But, in doing so, perhaps I lost part of my own identity, my sense of belonging. In doing so, I also avoided talking about race, racial identity and politics with my eldest daughter who was born in India but grew up in Britain. We had no Indian or Asian friends and we lived in places where we were often the only people of Indian descent or women of colour. This didn't bother me – it didn't even occur to me until recently, when someone asked me how it felt to be a 'foreigner' in Britain, after living in the country for more than 20 years and thinking of it as home.

This was where my fascination with unconscious bias started, particularly why and how we carry these biases within us. As a behavioural scientist, I have always been interested in what makes us react and behave as we do. Teaching user-interface design and knowledge representation, it became more apparent to me how bias is inherent in the actions we take and every decision we make. In my own academic research, as early as my master's thesis, I started questioning the objectivity paradigm and how truly free from bias our technologies are. I examined bias from a multidisciplinary perspective to develop a more integrated framework for understanding and tackling it. This book is the culmination of my own wide research and

accomplishments being perceived as due to positive discrimination. I discuss several different examples of double-bind bias throughout the book.

a deep-dive into the work done by others in this field. It is an exploration of the brain and behaviour, and finding synergies between society and psychology to try and understand why we act the way we do, how we think, learn and connect, and process information. I look at how changing technology and the way we are interacting and working is shaping our biases, but also being shaped in return; the way our brain processes biases and why; and the moral and ethical questions surrounding unconscious bias.

I focus on implicit or unconscious bias, which is different to explicit bias (these are attitudes and beliefs on a conscious level, such as hate speech), although understandably there can be overlap in the way these are expressed in the form of discrimination, prejudice and injustice. My aim is to focus on those biases that take us away from absolute rational, logical decision-making. I use the terms 'implicit bias' and 'unconscious bias' interchangeably, referring to those biases that exist without our conscious knowledge, the ones that manifest themselves in our actions and reactions often without us realising it, rearing their heads when we least expect it and sometimes taking us by surprise.

Implicit bias was introduced in 2006 in a paper by Anthony Greenwald as 'the new science of unconscious mental processes that has substantial bearing on discrimination law'. The paper refuted the long-standing belief that humans are guided solely by explicit beliefs and by their conscious intentions. We gather millions of bits of information and our brain processes that information in a certain way, unconsciously categorising and formatting it into familiar patterns. Some studies suggest that the brain is capable of processing approximately 11 million bits of information every second, but our conscious mind can handle only 40–50 of those bits. It is clear that much of our processing happens in our subconscious minds. Within the field of implicit cognition, there are many constructs and processes that function outside the conscious attentional focus, such as implicit self-esteem, implicit memory and implicit attitudes. The label 'implicit' is being applied to a variety of procedures and processes that share a common theme – they are not direct, deliberate, controlled, intentional self-assessments. For instance, when we cannot retrieve a memory explicitly, we might still behave in a certain way that shows we have some traces of past experiences embedded as implicit – or unconscious – memory record.

For a while, implicit bias was conceptualised as a latent construct, existing within individuals independent of the situational context. It was theorised as existing from a young age, and being relatively stable, unchanged by recent events. In social psychology, there is a long-standing assumption that, although people can revise their conscious beliefs in view of recent experiences and events, traces of past experiences linger on and shape our implicit beliefs and biases. However, unconscious bias is not as latent or stable as previously believed. Developments in neuroscience have demonstrated that many biases are formed throughout our life, through societal and parental conditioning, and held at the subconscious level. Although it would be easy to blame them on our environment – as much of our inherent implicit biases are shaped by the way we were brought up, what we see around us, the images and media that we have been exposed to – we need to take some responsibility for our inherent biases, and that's when we can take control of them. Unconscious bias is also problematic to capture and accurately pinpoint because it is hidden and can often be in complete contrast to what we consider our beliefs and associations to be. There are certain psychometric tests, such as the Implicit Association Test (IAT), that have claimed to be a reliable measurement of unconscious beliefs. They are widely promoted in media and in academic research, and so we do not often hear the critiques of this test, and the problems with its reliability and robustness. So, if unconscious bias cannot be measured reliably, how can we really take control of it? This also raises the question of moral responsibility. If I don't know about it, am I really responsible for it? I look at some of these contentious discussions in unconscious bias on morality and accountability in the final chapter.

We often think that unconscious bias only covers race and gender, but it is far more pervasive than that. Disability, sexuality, body size, profession and so on all influence the assessments we make of people, and form the basis of our relationship with others and the world at large. Stand-up comedians exploit our unconscious biases to deliver effective punchlines, testing our implicit bias through the use of paraprosdokians – a figure of speech that allows a speaker to play with expectations, to introduce new meanings by tapping into our tendency to form quick judgements and biases. For instance, Groucho Marx said, 'I've had a perfectly wonderful evening; but this wasn't it.' See what he did?! We assume he is talking about this particular evening, but of course he isn't. He moves away from the cliché and delivers the punchline, testing our implicit bias. In producing meaning, the paraprosdokian goes beyond our expectations of language, with the joke resolving only when we find the right framework in which to interpret it. Then there's a 'click' and realisation of an incongruity, and we have the sudden shift in perspective. This is 'Incongruity Resolution Theory', where manipulations of our mental categories and schemas – processes of which we are not consciously aware – are given an offbeat spin. Often comedy resorts to evoking a gendered or racial stereotype when a punchline is delivered, with snappy one-liners exploiting these unseen features of our minds. Here this creates discomfort and irony, but in other circumstances it can have significant social consequences, since in normal everyday situations we rarely have the opportunity to resolve the incongruities.

When information gaps cause such incongruity and ambiguity, individual attitudes are known to influence how people perceive events and objects. But attitudes are also known to shape the information that we see, even in very familiar situations. For instance, when YouTube launched the video upload feature for their app, 5–10 per cent of videos were uploaded upside-down, and for a while Google developers were baffled. Eventually they figured out it wasn't poor design; they had only considered right-handed users. Their unconscious bias had overlooked the fact that left-handed users would turn the phone/app by 180 degrees. In fact, left-handedness has suffered from an unfavourable perception for a long time. Scissors, musical instruments and knives are all designed for people who are right-handed, disadvantaging left-handed users. In this case, the prototypical category or the societal norm is right-handedness, and society is unconsciously biased towards it.

In our society, 'man' is another prototypical default norm, as neurobiologist Daniela Pollak commented in the *New York Times* in May 2019: 'we live in a world where the assumption is that males are the standard, the reference population, and females are the ones that are odd', resulting in gender bias. Here, a clarification is essential. Some people use gender and sex interchangeably. In this book I use 'gender' and have avoided the use of the word 'sex'.* The

---

* According to the World Health Organization, 'sex' refers to the biological and physiological characteristics that define men and

term 'gender' as we use it today originated from the social sciences. It originally referred to the social constructs that we have developed to explain differences between men and women, but the definition is expanding every day. Rather than socially imposed identification of a person and categorisation as a particular gender, we are now moving towards self-identification, i.e. how a person categorises themselves within a society. Some societies are rigid and recognise only two genders. Other societies allow more space on the spectrum, such as the Hijra[*] in India, which is recognised as a third gender by the government, or the notion of genderqueer.[†] Much like gender, sex is a spectrum too. Sometimes the lines between sex and gender[‡] can get blurred as we try and understand what kind of behaviours and biases are biologically determined and which ones are culturally constructed. In this book, it has not been possible

---

women, and 'gender' refers to the socially constructed roles, behaviours, activities and attributes that a particular society considers appropriate for men and women. Gender, though rooted in biology, is influenced by one's environment and experience.

[*] Hijras do not fall into the standard traditional conceptualisation of sex and gender, with many of them being transgender.

[†] A spectrum of gender identities that are not exclusively masculine or feminine, and are outside the gender binary. Other variations are now increasingly being acknowledged such as genderfluid, amalgagender, demigender, bigender, pangender and agender.

[‡] Many sex difference researchers think of the brain as being a mosaic of male and female traits and that hormones, genes and the environment are all playing roles in shaping male and female individuals. There is no 'gender centre' that we know of, and a lot of how we see ourselves depends on cultural norms. Our environment and the choices we make can also impact our biology and development. In this way, while sex and gender are two distinct things, the variability by which these exist and how they inform each other is vast and constantly changing. I discuss this more in Chapter 7.

for me to investigate at great length the bias against trans[*]
people, since much of the research in social sciences and
psychology, currently and historically, examines gendered
differences between male and female. Nevertheless, the
idea of stigmatisation due to the fear of the unknown,
which I discuss later in this book, will also apply to
these groups.

Technology can reinforce these biases too. We are
moving into a truly transformational period of information
revolution, on the way to technological singularity – a
hypothetical future where technological growth will
become uncontrollable and irreversible, resulting in
unfathomable changes to human civilisation. Some
scientists and philosophers argue that we are already in the
midst of this major evolutionary transition where digital
technology has infiltrated the fabric of human society in a
way akin to life-sustaining dependence. We tend to believe
that technology is objective, that it can help systems and
processes be free of any biases, but this is not true. Any
hopes we now have that technology will help remove biases
and bring forth a more rational and unprejudiced era are
problematic. In Chapter 12, I discuss the way biases in the
real-world become assimilated within the technology itself,
for instance in recruitment platforms, search engines and
social media algorithms. These algorithms create biases
as well as learning from the biases that are so deeply
entrenched in our society. For instance, when looking at
traditional stock-image websites, we might note a big
diversity problem. A search for 'diverse workplaces' brings

---

[*] Used as an umbrella term to include people whose gender identity
is the opposite of their assigned sex (trans men and trans women), it
may include people who are not exclusively masculine or feminine
(people who are non-binary or genderqueer, including bigender,
pangender, genderfluid or agender), or those who are cross-dressers.

up images showing groups of people around a table, typically young and slim, including an obligatory black or brown person, though with light enough skin that they do not stand apart. This is far from a truly diverse and inclusive workplace. When I search for the term 'accountant', I find images of white men dressed in suits. To find more diverse images, it is necessary to qualify search terms with 'black accountant' or 'female accountant'. There are inherent biases built into these collections – not only pertaining to gender and race. Technology incorporates the biases from the designers and the data engineers who develop these systems. It then also reinforces existing biases and stereotypes, or creates new biases when it is applied in a societal context.

Each of us form and carry unconscious biases of some sort. It's not only the behaviour of bigoted, racist or sexist people but of everyone, including you and me. So really the answer is to go to the roots, to understand the processes that shape us, to be aware, to acknowledge that we are all biased – to a certain degree – and that we all discriminate. We judge, we exclude people, we stereotype. Sometimes that's a little tough to comprehend. Our unconscious biases can be balanced by bias control mechanisms that turn instinctive responses into more socially acceptable reactions. However, what is socially acceptable varies and our bias control mechanisms are not independent moral guides. There has been an upsurge in diversity training with the aim of freeing ourselves from our unconscious biases, but we cannot erase our biases completely. Awareness and action are possible; obliteration is not.

The consequences of stigma and of unconscious bias and prejudice are enormous – physically, mentally and socially – but to discuss all these is impossible within the scope of this book. There is no space to explore the strategies that people use to avoid or tackle stigma, although I will be touching on how implicit bias can be acknowledged and addressed in the final chapter and in the epilogue. I also discuss stereotype threat and how this affects people's well-being in Chapter 5.

Talking about discrimination and prejudice isn't easy. In some ways this has been a difficult book to write, to not only draw and reflect on my own personal experiences but to also weave disparate interdisciplinary threads into an effective narrative. Many of the case studies and examples in this book might be triggering to those who have experienced similar injustices. It might also make you more aware of your own privileges as the stark reality of your own biases become apparent or as you acknowledge the way your privileges provide you with an armour against many of the societal biases and stereotypes. The truth can be uncomfortable, but if we don't face reality these implicit biases will shape and transform our society in a way that we had never thought possible.

The world is changing at a pace that, while exciting, can also be terrifying. I will not resort to hyperbole and call this the most amazing, the strangest or the most alarming time that we have lived in, because many other periods in history must have seemed likewise. But there is something unsettling, an air of uncertainty and mistrust. The world does seem to be extraordinary at the moment. At a time when partisan political ideologies are taking centre stage, and we struggle to make sense of who we are, who we want to be and who we will become, it is crucial that we understand why we act the way we do. This book doesn't present a pessimistic view, though neither is it optimistic. Instead it attempts to view our contemporary society through a lens that enables us to reflect on and consider the forces that shape us. It is about understanding the way we put up walls between 'us' and 'them' before we even realise we are doing so, how we interpret the messages we get from the media and the politicians, and the attempts to make sense of the noise and understand how our biases shape the way we react to these messages.

It might seem like we are bound to our biases and unable to escape them. However, as Raymond Williams, a Welsh Marxist theorist, said in 1989, 'To be truly radical is to make hope possible, rather than despair convincing'. I believe that by addressing the biases at the individualistic level, we can begin to understand the societal and structural inequities and injustices. That is my hope and my aspiration, anyway.

And if you're wondering what happened with my fellow grad student, so happy to help a mere 'girl' with a complex maths problem, he tried hard but couldn't solve it. I did though.

# SECTION I
# HARDWIRED

## CHAPTER ONE

# Gut Instinct

About 18 months ago, my one-year-old wasn't well. Doctors had been telling us for a fortnight that it was just flu and it would pass. But that one particular morning I could feel something was terribly wrong. I picked her up, put her in the car and rushed her to the local emergency room. The medical staff thought I was overreacting. 'We just have to give this time,' they told me yet again. On that occasion, though, I could feel a sense of panic rising inside me, and I ignored all suggestions of overreaction. Sometimes you just know things aren't right; you can feel it in the pit of your stomach, your heart starts to race, and there is a growing sense of unease. I insisted – some would say I created quite a scene – that they admit her there and then. They finally agreed, she was taken in, and within five minutes her heart rate had spiked dangerously and she had gone into sepsis shock. I still have nightmares about what might have happened.

This is called 'maternal intuition'. If you are a parent or carer, you are probably familiar with this feeling of when something just doesn't seem right. It might seem like an instinct – and it is often called so – but it is most likely a cumulation of experience that we have of our own children, and the little signs and cues that we notice because we know them so well. Our response to it might seem like a spur-of-the-moment decision, without rational thought, but it isn't. When the doctors and nurses refused to take my concerns seriously, they were most likely acting on their implicit bias, which is that parents, especially mothers, can become hysterical when it comes to their children's health. There is research to show that health professionals are less likely to take women and girls seriously, and their pain and illnesses are often not tackled immediately. Data also shows that people from minority ethnic communities face prejudice and bias from healthcare professionals and are less likely to be diagnosed correctly or prescribed treatment. So a combination of these biases likely played a role in why it took so long for our daughter to be diagnosed, why our concerns were ignored for so long, and why I was perceived as a 'hysterical parent'. The doctors' and nurses' instincts told them that nothing was wrong, even when it was. You would think that people in such roles, where it can be a matter of life and death, would not act on instincts but make rational decisions. Yet they do. Also, when people are stressed, tired and overworked, they are more likely to fall back on their instincts.

We are often told to trust our own instincts. 'Listen to that feeling in the pit of your stomach,' we are reminded. First impressions count. And we all rely so much on our first impressions of others. We might think that our gut instinct is just an inner feeling – a secret interior voice – but in fact it is shaped by a perception of something visible around us, such as a facial expression, a tone of voice or a visual inconsistency so fleeting that often we're not even aware we've noticed it. Psychologists now think of this moment as a 'visual matching game'. So a stressed, rushed or tired person is more likely to resort to this visual matching. When they see a situation in front of them, they quickly match it to a sea of past experiences stored in a mental knowledge bank and then, based on a match, they assign meaning to the information in front of them. The brain then sends a signal to the gut, which has many hundreds of nerve cells. So the visceral feeling we get in the pit of our stomach and the butterflies we feel are a result of our cognitive processing system. Gut instinct can be very useful when making quick decisions in everyday life, but often it can lead to errors that have far-reaching consequences, such as in healthcare, during recruitment and in legal contexts.

Psychologist Antoine Bechara at the University of Southern California studied brain-damaged patients who could not formulate intuitions while making decisions. They had to decide purely via rational, logical reasoning. 'They ended up doing such a complicated analysis, factoring everything in, that it could take them hours to decide between two kinds of cereal,' Bechara says. Our gut instinct allows us to expedite this process. When our brains make a match between the current state and our cognitive models based on our previous experiences, we think of it as our intuition, but it is merely a predictive process where the results of this matching have not yet reached our conscious awareness.

When we use our gut instinct, we are allowing our brain to make quick judgements and we are valuing speed over accuracy. This gut feeling – where we use emotions to make snap decisions – is also called System 1 in dual process theory* though we often can't tell exactly which rule our intuition is using. System 1 is the unconscious reasoning – mostly involuntary and often independent of working memory – which means that we don't have time

---

* In psychology, this explains how our thoughts can arise in two different ways as a result of two different processes: usually, there is the implicit or unconscious process (System 1), and the explicit or more controlled conscious process (System 2).

to exercise our cognitive rational thinking. It is rapid, more subjective, and value-, context- and domain-specific. System 2 is the more rational and logical system. It is mostly voluntary processing of information, detached from emotions and more controlled. When we are rushed, stressed and relying on gut instinct (which is automatic and subconscious), there is no time to deploy the slower and more deliberate System 2. Even though System 1 processing might be rushed, it isn't always inaccurate, and once we have collected a lot of data from past experiences, we can often rely on this more. The problem is that our recollection of past memories and contexts might not always be accurate and is often dependent on our current emotional state. We can also make ourselves believe things to confirm our biases. For instance, we might have an incorrect memory of a situation or an event, and we can make decisions based on this erroneous past memory – a decision based not entirely on rationality or logic but on wishful thinking. In a simple event such as predicting whether it is going to rain today or whether there will be a storm, we might draw on our memories and conclude that the weather looks bad enough for there to be a storm. We make such decisions almost every day, but they are not always reliable.

Humans are not naturally rational. Information overload is exhausting and confusing, so we filter out the noise. We only see parts of the world. We tend to notice things that are repeating, whether there are any patterns or outliers, and we tend to preserve memory by generalising and resorting to type. We bullet-point our memories, draw conclusions from sparse data and use cognitive shortcuts to create a version of reality that we implicitly want to believe in. Once this reduced stream of information comes in, we connect the dots, fill in the gaps with stuff we already think we know, and update our mental models of the world. But when this happens, we can sometimes filter out information that would help us make rational, logical and unbiased decisions, and we are more likely to imagine connections and information that reinforce the biases we carry. We often ignore details that contradict our existing beliefs, and we are more inclined to believe and notice flaws in others.

We pick out bits of information that help us make quick decisions. When rationality is constrained due to the time limit on making these decisions, people 'satisfice' – aim for a satisfactory solution – based on cognitive shortcuts. Nobel prize-winning economist Herbert Simon called this the notion of 'bounded rationality'. Satisficing* is a decision-making strategy or cognitive heuristic, a sort of mathematical optimisation process employed to reach an optimal goal when some information is missing or a problem is too complicated to compute. But when we use shortcuts and satisfice, we are more likely to deploy our implicit biases. Simon created an analogy using scissors to define this theory in his 1990 paper for the *Annual Review of Psychology*: 'Human rational behaviour is shaped by scissors whose blades are the structure of task environments and the computational capabilities of the actor.' Simply speaking, the two blades of the scissors represent context and cognition, and they have to work together, so in order to understand human behaviour we have to look at both the context or the environment, and the cognition or the

---

* Herbert Simon observed in his Nobel Prize in Economics speech that 'decision makers can satisfice either by finding optimum solutions for a simplified world, or by finding satisfactory solutions for a more realistic world. Neither approach, in general, dominates the other, and both have continued to co-exist in the world.'

mind. Kurt Lewin, a Gestalt[*] psychologist, proposed this equation[†]:

$$B = f(P, E)$$

Here, $B$ is behaviour, $P$ is person, $E$ is environment, and $f$ denotes that behaviour is a function of both a person and their environment. The Gestalt psychology framework theorises that a person's behaviour may be different in different contexts, even with physically identical environments. Similarly, two different individuals placed in exactly the same situation will not necessarily adopt the same behaviour, or have the same gut instinct, because their psychological situations and frames of references are fundamentally different. So, although we talk about standard norms and common forms of bias, we have to be aware that two people could – and often will – choose to behave completely differently in the same situation.

In their book *The Invisible Gorilla*, Christopher Chabris and Daniel Simons highlight how our everyday intuitions about the world can be unintentionally flawed. They describe an experiment in which subjects were asked to watch a short film of two teams passing a basketball. The participants were asked to count the number of passes made by one of the teams. Participants were so absorbed in the

---

[*] Gestalt theory is based in the philosophy that the whole is something else than the sum of its parts.

[†] This equation was first presented in Lewin's book, *Principles of Topological Psychology*, published in 1936. It was proposed as an attempt to unify the different branches of psychology with a flexible theory. This equation is directly related to Lewin's field theory. Field theory is centred around the idea that a person's life space determines their behaviour.

task that they did not notice a woman wearing a gorilla suit crossing the basketball court and thumping her chest before moving on. She does this relatively slowly and is on screen for nine seconds. Roughly half the subjects did not see the gorilla. These kind of cognitive* errors emerge as a result of inattentional blindness,[†] where there is a lack of attention to an unexpected object. When our attention is focused on one thing – or one task – we fail to notice other unexpected things. Rather than focusing on every tiny detail around us, we only notice things that we believe to be most important, and how we categorise the objects in this hierarchy depends on our existing cognitive models and biases. In this case, people miss the gorilla because they do not expect a gorilla to appear in the middle of a basketball game in a real-world setting and so it lacks ecological validity.[‡] A cognitive illusion arises from the interaction of perceived reality with assumptions about the world and leads to 'unconscious inferences'.[§] We form a partial

---

* Cognitive processes are psychological processes involved in acquisition and understanding of knowledge, formation of beliefs and attitudes, and decision-making and problem-solving. They are distinct from emotional and volitional processes. The word cognition comes from the Latin verb cognosco (con-, 'with', and -gnōscō, 'know'), itself a cognate of the Greek verb γι(γ)νώσκω (gi(g)nósko), meaning 'I know, perceive' meaning 'to conceptualise' or 'to recognise'. In psychology, the term 'cognition' is normally used within an information-processing view of an individual's psychological functions; in a branch of social psychology called social cognition, the term is used to explain attitudes, attribution and group dynamics.
† First coined by psychologists Arien Mack and Irvin Rock.
‡ Something that can be replicated in a real-world scenario.
§ 'Unconscious conclusion' is the term used by James P. C. Southall in his 1925 English translation of Helmholtz's Handbuch der physiologischen Optik (Treatise on Physiological Optics). Today, the concept is more widely referred to as unconscious inference. This is

snapshot of the entire world depending on our context and goals – and the missing pieces in our mental schemas lead to unconscious errors in memory recall while making a decision based on our gut instinct.

Conformity affects what we choose to remember, and this in turn shapes our world-view and our biases. Biases that affect our gut instinct are also shaped by the people around us. We are influenced by their actions and their decisions. Psychologists have categorised three main types of conformity. Compliance is the first level, where conformity is merely public while our underlying attitudes and beliefs might be completely different and remain unchanged. This is informational conformity bias, when we believe unconsciously that an individual or group has more knowledge about a specific situation. Identification is the middle level of conformity, which is a short-term change whereby we modify or alter our beliefs when in the presence of a particular group. The normative conformity bias is that we believe unconsciously that by conforming to others' views, we will be liked and accepted by them. On the other hand, sometimes an internalisation of these social and cultural norms can take place, which will lead to a shift in internal attitudes and beliefs. This is internalised conformity, the third and the deepest form of conformity.

In an experiment by Solomon Asch in 1955, a group of people were asked to compare the size of two lines. Everyone got it right when they answered privately, but when the answers were public, 36.8 per cent of people gave the wrong

---

a term in perceptual psychology coined in 1867 by the German physicist Hermann von Helmholtz to describe an involuntary, pre-rational and reflex-like mechanism that is part of the formation of visual impressions.

answer if someone gave the wrong answer before them. People gave the wrong answer because they assumed the person before them knew more than they did, or even when they knew the right answer they would rather be wrong and be part of the crowd. This is called 'herd mentality' or confirmation bias. We all have a perception – a mental representation – of what is socially acceptable and what is not.

As early as the fifth century AD, we have an anecdotal story of the Greek philosopher Diagoras of Melos proposing confirmation bias. When shown the votive gifts of people who had supposedly escaped death by praying to the gods to save them from a shipwreck, he pointed out that plenty of people had died at sea in spite of their prayers, yet these cases were not likewise commemorated. This meant that people only wanted to see and believe what confirmed their theories about the existence of God and the power of prayer, even though there might be evidence for the contrary. The philosopher Karl Popper proposed in 1959 that there is a tendency to confirm a hypothesis rather than falsify it, and in the 1960s the cognitive psychologist Peter Wason also demonstrated that people tend to seek information that confirms their existing beliefs. If – because of a prior experience or because of what you have read in books and research – you already believe that men are better at reading maps than women, then you might place greater importance on any 'evidence' that supports what you already believe, and rate it more relevant, rather than focus on facts and evidence that help you disprove this bias. In an election, people will seek out information that confirms their favoured candidate as the best. They have a bias towards a particular candidate because they might have similar beliefs as theirs, or because of their race or gender. They might even seek 'proof' that further backs up this belief while discounting examples that don't support the idea. Unfortunately, this stops them from making an informed and rational decision. We are motivated to protect our own existing views, also called my-side bias. Often, people refer to this as 'trusting their gut'.

★★★

Our instincts help us to assess people and situations quickly, determine whether or not we can trust them, and make timely decisions. In this way, as we will see in the next chapter, they are essential for our survival. The bad news is that in this process, we also form biases that cloud our instincts. Our unconscious biases change how our instincts react to certain situations, and the way we perceive others, and can compel us to choose one object or person favourably over another. We might impose personality traits on people that make it easier for us to process information about them in the future, or mistakenly compare them to someone else because of our confirmation biases and erroneous memories. A prejudice is a negative attitude towards a group and its individual members, such as an active dislike of foreigners, or homophobia. For instance, if I am biased towards a particular flavour of ice cream, I will tend to choose that over other flavours every time I walk into an ice cream shop. However, my bias for this particular flavour can be overcome if I receive some new information such as, say, popularity of a new flavour. Prejudice, on the other hand, would be an active dislike of a certain flavour of ice cream so I am unlikely ever to choose the flavour I am prejudiced against even when there is strong evidence to show me that other flavours are not better.* According to

---

* I am writing this book while sitting in my office in sweltering heat, and so ice creams are really on my mind. It might sound inane but it makes an effective example.

Susan Fiske, Professor of Psychology at Princeton University, prejudices are emotional biases that can lead to discrimination, and can alter our instincts about people and situations.

Social norms underlie our gut instinct about people. Our default bias is associated with these social norms. Often bias is created when a particular object or person does not meet the normative standards in society, and our instinct is to view them with suspicion and to alienate or stigmatise them.

Do you remember watching that viral video where Robert Kelly, an associate professor of international relations at Pusan National University, is being interviewed live on the BBC when his two children wander in, and a woman of East Asian racial heritage frantically tries to remove them? An anonymous[*] survey I conducted via social media forums revealed that over 70 per cent of people – most of whom claimed to be liberal, open-minded and non-prejudiced – immediately assumed that she was a nanny. This prompts concerns regarding the racial biases inherent in our society about people of certain ethnic origins being assumed to be in subservient roles as helpers or assistants. It also raises questions about the perception of mixed-race couples, with people naturally assuming we mate with people who are the same as us.

You might also remember the contentious comments made by Professor Tim Hunt that sparked a fierce response across social media. In a speech delivered at a lunch for female journalists and scientists, entitled 'Creative Science – Only a Game', he said: 'Let me tell you about my trouble with girls ... three things happen when they are in the

---

[*] It was anonymous because people are reluctant to openly admit and confront such biases.

lab … You fall in love with them, they fall in love with you and when you criticise them, they cry.' Since then the media furore around these comments has reignited the debate about unconscious bias towards women. More recently, in August 2019, the chef Marco Pierre White told the *Irish Independent* that 'The real positive with men [in the kitchen] is that men can absorb pressure better, because they are not as emotional.' In both cases, these people's biases and preconceptions are highly likely to affect their instincts about certain candidates in the lab or in the kitchen, and influence the hiring decisions they make.

John Nash was a Nobel-winning mathematician, and the film *A Beautiful Mind* was based on his life. He proposed a model for how actions and reactions around a norm operate in a micro–macro feedback loop. In this case, a norm gives a person a rule of thumb for how they should behave. A norm gives an expectation of how other people act in a given situation (macro). A person acts in the best way possible given the expectation (micro). For a stable norm, people's actions and behaviours remain the same without change, which is termed the micro–macro feedback loop. Our instinct is to resort to the normative default.

Our instincts about and against people are also formed due to association and affiliation. Skin colour is often one of the first cues for assigning group memberships and we all do this, no matter how much we deny it. In 1968, the day after the assassination of Martin Luther King, Jane Elliot, an educator and anti-racist activist, decided to address the problems of racial prejudice by dividing her third-grade class into groups on the basis of eye colour. All her students were white, and none of them could relate to the feeling of being a black person in America, so she wanted them to understand what discrimination feels like.

As seen in the PBS Frontline Documentary *A Class Divided*, Elliot showed how easy it was to turn her seven-year-old pupils into hatemongers by making the blue-eyed children the targets of discrimination by the 'better' brown-eyed children. After dividing the children, she told them that people with brown eyes were smarter, faster and better than those with blue eyes, as intelligence was a factor of how much melanin we have. She also gave the brown-eyed children longer lunch breaks and other privileges. Soon, the brown-eyed children became more confident and condescending towards their classmates, calling them 'stupid' and shunning them in the playground. The blue-eyed children became meek and withdrawn. Her blue eyes/brown eyes exercise, although also controversial, is considered a landmark in showing how environmental cues can shape our biases and reinforce our in-group memberships. It confirmed that prejudice against members of the out-group is learned in children. However, if it is not addressed and unlearned, we can carry these biases throughout our lives.

During Hurricane Katrina in the US, two photographs in particular made news amid the wide-spread havoc and destruction. In one photo, a dark-skinned young man is shown in New Orleans flood-waters, a 12-pack of Pepsi under his right arm, holding a garbage bag with his left hand. A caption read: 'A young man walks through chest-deep flood-water after looting a grocery store in New Orleans.' In the second photo, a light-skinned woman, packages floating in tow, also navigates through New Orleans waters, a man trailing her. The caption: 'Two residents wade through chest-deep water after finding bread and soda at a local grocery store.' Do you see how images and words can shape our biases but also show the underlying biases against certain groups of people? Here two images created a racial divide. It showed the underlying bias of 'them' against 'us'. So much of what we encounter in the form of unconscious bias is grounded in this notion of category membership, of how we form the notion of in-group and out-group. When people carry out such tests where they rely on quick decisions about people they do not yet know, they fall back on their instincts and their deep-rooted prejudices and judgements.*

In high-pressured situations, there is more likelihood of an instinctive action. In his book *Complications*, Atul Gawande, an American surgeon, writes about how his decision to pick the correct diagnosis for a condition whose initial symptoms did not differ hugely from another was not for any logical reasons. He relied on his instincts. In an article in the *Journal of the Royal Society of Medicine*, a nurse argues that the role of instinct is integral to medical care, especially when deciding whether to wake up a patient to do regular tests or let them rest and recover after a surgical procedure. In the case Mueller v. Auker in 2008, the court ruled that clinical instinct is a 'well-recognised and accepted feature of medical emergency practice'. Much of medical decision-making relies on a priori diagnosis based on past experiences and instinctive feelings, which is largely accurate. However, it has been shown that clinical instinct can fail when the medical professional does not identify with the patients. In a study, eight clinicians were asked to categorise 400 spinal patients into the four categories associated with a Distress Risk Assessment Method

---

* Racial bias and inequality is a monumental topic in itself, so it is not possible to cover everything pertaining to it in this one book, where the focus is on broader scientific theories underpinning unconscious bias. However, it is a topic very close to my heart, with my own personal experience as a woman of colour, so I touch on this in Chapter 8.

(DRAM). The study found that the clinicians were only 44 per cent accurate when using instinct alone. If we go back to my own experience of my daughter being unwell, where I talk about clinical instincts, we can see how easy it is for these to be shaped by underlying racial biases. This is why race impacts the experience of patients, and research by the American College of Obstetricians and Gynecologists (ACOG) shows that black women are three times more likely than white women to die during childbirth.

★★★

Our instinct or what we sometimes call intuition isn't some magical or mysterious thing. It is an innate universal animalistic behaviour. Our instincts help us navigate the world. Socrates wrote, 'I decided that it was not wisdom that enabled poets to write their poetry, but a kind of instinct.' For artists, instinct is considered an asset. But when it comes to making important decisions about people or situations, we cannot always rely on instinct. Darwin defined instinct as independent of experience, but more recent research in psychology and neuroscience has shown that it is continually being honed; it is fluid and malleable. When new memories are formed in our brains, the millions of neurons in our cerebral cortex fuse. But this fusion is not permanent and depends to a great extent on subsequent use and reinforcement. So our instinct is not based on some sort of innate behavioural patterns, but on our past experiences, interactions, our situations and our contexts. Our instinct is a result of an accumulated knowledge and so its value cannot be discounted, especially when making quick decisions. But it is also shaped by our biases and prejudices, and so cannot be comparable to acting with complete rationality in accordance with evidence. The key is to not fall back on it for decision-making but rather to use it as a trigger for sparking analytical and logical thought. It is vital to filter possibilities quickly at a subconscious level and direct our decision-making to a point where our rational, conscious mind can take over, one where we can acknowledge and evaluate our biases openly.

Friedrich Nietzsche, in his book *The Birth of Tragedy*, saw an enduring Apollonian and Dionysian dichotomy[*] in human behaviour. One god, Apollo, stands for logic and reason while the other, Dionysus, stands for chaos.[†] The Apollonian rational thinking is balanced by Dionysian instinct. There is a place for both.

---

[*] Although Nietzsche is credited with first bringing this to light in 1872, it was used before him in German culture. Since then, this dichotomy has been applied in various contexts from sex and cultures to urban form.

[†] In Greek mythology, Apollo and Dionysus are both sons of Zeus. Apollo is the god of the sun, of rational thinking and order, appealing to logic, prudence and purity. Dionysus is the god of wine and dance, of irrationality and chaos, and appeals to emotions and instincts. The ancient Greeks did not consider the two gods to be opposites or rivals, but often entwined by nature.

CHAPTER TWO
# The Dawn of Time

Since the dawn of human history, our very survival has depended on our skill at sidestepping danger. The brain has developed systems that make it unavoidable for us to not notice danger and respond to it. The aversion towards any sort of threat or negativity, whether from objects, ideas or people, is likely to be grounded in the need to stay safe and to survive. Humans are tribal creatures with carefully designed dominance hierarchies. They have competed over limited resources and mates (and still do) and have done everything they can to ensure reproductive success and the survival of their progeny. Much of human physiology has therefore been adapted to serve a specific purpose and a specific function.[*]

However, cognitive biases – those that are formed due to the interaction of our cognitive processes with the environment around us – pose a certain challenge because evolutionarily such errors do not make sense. We adapt to survive and flourish, so why are we programmed to resort to errors and biases? Why would we have errors as part of our engineering? It appears to be a design flaw. Yet, from an evolutionary perspective, a behavioural response is a design

---

[*] Darwin's evolution theory of natural selection states: more individuals are produced each generation than can survive; phenotypic variation exists among individuals and the variation is heritable; those individuals with heritable traits better suited to the environment will survive; our adaptations are designed in order for us to survive.

feature rather than a flaw if it contributes to fitness* in some way. When it is designed for solving a problem in a domain-specific way then it is not a fault but an asset. For instance, the features of an eye only make sense if we view them in terms of what value they offer to its function. Similarly, the menopause is something that has puzzled biologists for decades, but the reason why humans outlive their fertility, unlike most other mammals, can also be explained from an evolutionary perspective.† Our unconscious biases could therefore be seen as adaptive mechanisms.

Our brains have evolved to reason adaptively rather than rationally or truthfully. How and why do we see the world as we do? There are many theories that have attempted to explain this, often from behaviourist and cognitivist perspectives. In simple terms, a behaviourist philosophy suggests that the environment plays a major role in ascertaining an individual's behaviour and response, along with their history and current motivation, thereby ignoring the significance of internal cognitive processes and biology. A cognitivist approach, on the other hand, assigns significance to conscious thought as a critical part of the process of assimilating information from the environment.

---

* Darwin uses the phrase 'survival of the fittest' in *On the Origin of Species* (1859) to describe the process of natural selection. But he did not coin the phrase. It was borrowed from English philosopher Herbert Spencer, who first talked about survival of the fittest in his *Principles of Sociology*, first published in 1855. Evolutionary fitness is how well a species is able to adapt to and reproduce in its environment.
† No other mammal (except perhaps pilot whales) exhibit reproductive cessation in nature. As per evolutionary biologists, menopause is either: 1) adaptive, suggesting it is biologically more advantageous to rechannel reproductive energy into helping existing descendants later in life, or 2) non-adaptive, indicating menopause is an artefact of the relatively recent dramatic increase in human longevity.

In the 11th century, Avicenna, an Islamic philosopher and theologian, proposed the 'floating man' or the 'flying man theory' while he was imprisoned in the castle of Fardajan, near Hamadhan. He argued that when a person is – hypothetically – floating or flying in air, they know that they are doing so even without any awareness of the environment around them or even if they have no sensory experience. The basic premise of floating man is that the brain is where reason and sensation interact, and so 'I am' is at the core of all thinking, much like the Descartian *Cogito, ergo sum* or 'I think, therefore I am'. Descartes said that the mind exists without the body. There is an inherent debate centred in mind–body dualism in much of the philosophy of thought and perception. According to the ecological psychologist James Gibson, we perceive our environment in terms of affordances* and these are context-dependent. We respond to others around us, and the environment, in order to take advantage of opportunities or respond to fear or threat from another individual. And our costs and errors are minimised in a way that is most beneficial for us in terms of reproductive and social fitness.

Being prejudiced against our perceived out-group or being able to identify 'others' gave us evolutionary advantage and increased the chances of safety and survival. This is also a response to our natural tendencies to build tribes. Humans appear to have a bias that members of out-groups or competitive tribes are less magnanimous and more dangerous than those who belong to our in-groups. To give us the most competitive advantage and to adapt to any changing threats, this out-group bias is stronger and more

---

* Affordance is what the environment offers the individual. James J. Gibson coined the term in his 1966 book, *The Senses Considered as Perceptual Systems*, in relation to animals.

salient than in-group favouritism. It was initially suggested that this notion of fear or threat was to prevent disease transmission and to give humans the best chance of survival, but it seems to be much more than that. For ancestral humans, the costs of falsely assuming peacefulness on the part of an aggressor were likely to outweigh the comparatively low costs of elevated vigilance, particularly towards out-group members who were not part of their regular social circle. For instance, Emma Cohen from the University of Oxford proposes that accents evolved to furnish the 'honest signal'* of group membership, which is needed to drive the growth of non-kin cooperation – interactions between unrelated individuals or those perceived as out-group members – in human evolutionary history.

A fearful reaction to dangerous things is one of the most fundamental reasons for identifying someone as 'out-group' and for developing stereotypes and prejudices. For instance, to most people, darkness denotes fear and danger, and psychologists have shown that darkness can trigger the latent tendency for ethnic stereotypes. In an interesting study carried out by researchers at the University of British Columbia, 92 undergraduates (67 women, 25 men; 53 east-Asian heritage, none black) watched slide shows of African-American men variously smiling and scowling. Different groups were shown these slides in either dim lighting or near-blackness. Participants also completed a word-matching questionnaire about

---

* In biology, signals are traits and behaviours that evolve because they change the behaviour of the recipient to benefit the signaller. They are shaped by mutual interests between receiver and signaller; within species, such as humans, this increases with kinship. Signals are considered honest if they convey useful information to the receiver, so that its behaviour in response is advantageous and increases its 'fitness'.

beliefs in a dangerous world. The results showed that when the photos were encountered under some ambient darkness, there was a tendency to associate more derogatory stereotypes with the images. These participants were seen to support racial and ethnic stereotypes representing violence more so than those completing the task in a brightly lit room. The trend was more pronounced in men than in women.* When we make decisions under uncertainty, such as in a dark room, we rely on cognitive biases. These are designed to reduce the cost of errors – especially in terms of how much we are likely to lose or suffer in terms of our chance of survival – rather than being fixated on the number. The overall cost of these errors overrides the number of errors.

The 'smoke alarm analogy' explains why we develop cognitive shortcuts against threat and fear, even when they seem like extreme responses. Smoke detectors are designed to be extremely sensitive to the presence of smoke so that they don't fail to respond in case of an actual fire. But this means they often cause false alarms. We tend to get annoyed when a minuscule amount of smoke sets off an alarm, but the cost of the alarm not sounding when there is a real threat of fire has huge, often irreversible implications. The same principle explains how over-responsiveness of many of our snap judgements is a survival mechanism. Just as our smoke detectors can be over-responsive, so can our snap judgements. These responses appear overcautious, but the inconvenience is minor compared to the harms they protect against. When there is uncertainty and ambiguity then these biases will be

---

* Other research has indicated that men might be more sensitive than women to variables that trigger activation of racial stereotypes, especially that pertaining to physical harm. The debate continues regarding whether there are indeed any gender differences.

expressed even when there is no real threat or danger. Adaptations should function similarly, swaying on the side of caution. This does not justify a discriminatory behaviour based on our learned biases. Neither can it justify prejudice against a group or an individual based on the justification that false alarms happen and will happen. Our cognitive errors in judgement and shortcuts might be explained through evolutionary adaptations for survival but they are not universal, and neither are they hardwired into all of us. Our environmental cues might be the same, but the way we perceive these and what the environment offers us – our affordances – are relative.

## Three theories

Evolutionary psychologists have discussed three main ways in which our implicit biases are formed.

The first theory is heuristics or shortcuts, proposed by Daniel Kahneman and Amos Tversky. The brain looks for strategies and fixed rules or templates to ease the burden of carrying out trillions of mental processes at any given instant. Human judgements do not follow the mathematical rules of probability. For instance, if you have ever been to Las Vegas, you might have experienced the 'gambler's fallacy': the mistaken belief that if something happens less frequently in the present then it is more likely to happen in the future, meaning a gambler on a losing streak is more likely to keep playing in the belief that a win is highly probable any time soon. You might have also seen or experienced the 'hot-hand' fallacy that a streak of good luck will continue: the mistaken belief that someone is on a 'winning streak' on the roulette table, for instance, ignoring the rules of probability and logic that state they have an equal chance of winning or losing again. It seems

THE DAWN OF TIME

logical to use simpler strategies, as this cuts down the cognitive processing needed for problem-solving. It is a primitive tendency to perceive positive correlations in the same repeating event happening over a period of time. Monkeys do it too. They show a win-stay/lose-shift strategy in uncertain environments similar to the hot-hand bias. In research published in the *Journal of Experimental Psychology: Animal Learning and Cognition* in 2014, Tommy Blanchard and colleagues from the University of Rochester New York suggest that this is an evolutionary strategy to navigate difficult and uncertain foraging environments.

Such strategies are evolutionarily more efficient, as here speed is more important than accuracy. Yes, of course there are benefits to using more accurate strategies, but the cost of using more complex problem-solving pathways is higher. So in terms of a cost–benefit analysis, it makes sense to use shortcuts even if they are less accurate and result in cognitive errors or biases. There is clear evidence from a number of studies that demonstrates we make decisions differently when under time pressure or when we have limited resources. The use of recognition heuristics, such as selecting the option that is instantly – or more – recognisable is another example of such a heuristic.[*]

Kahneman and Tversky were not the first to propose the theory of cognitive shortcuts. The mathematician Laplace[†] had already discussed the phenomenon in terms of visual illusions in 1825, which he explained as such:

> When an observer placed in utter darkness sees, at different distances, two luminous balls of one and the same diameter, they seem to him to be of unequal size. Their internal images

---

[*] As are others that are discussed in Section II of this book.
[†] Joshua Miller and Andrew Gelman provide an excellent summary of Laplace's *Essai philosophique sur les probabilités* from the 1800s.

will be proportional to the corresponding images depicted on his retina. But if, when the darkness lifts, he catches sight at the same time of the balls and all the space between them, this view enlarges the internal image of the further ball and makes it almost equal to that of the other ball. Thus, it is that a man, seen at distances of two and four metres, seems to us of the same size: his internal image does not change, although one of the images depicted on the retina is twice the size of the other.

Use of cognitive shortcuts is not arbitrary. In fact, the specific strategy of employing limited computational power* to problem-solving is designed so that it protects the survival interests of humans over a period of time (evolutionary time, of course). As we know from Darwin's theory of evolution, the fittest survive. In biology, fitness is not just physical strength but how well an organism is adapted to its environment, which increases its chances of survival and reproduction. In most cases, the errors we make in categorising based on our visual and aural cues, and the judgements we make on this basis, are not problematic. However, sometimes they can have drastic consequences, for instance if a harmless object such as a phone in someone's hand is assumed to be a gun, or in fact vice versa. The process of categorisation also determines what people pay attention to, what demands and captures their attention, how they organise these categories and what they assign salience to, and what they consider significant enough to recall later. A bias may occur in some situations but not others (context effects), or with certain classes of information and not others (content effects), and so the social, cultural and environmental context plays a

---

* Used here in terms of our brainpower. Currently, we do not know the full extent of the computational power of our brains.

role in the evolution of biases. We saw an example of this in the ambient darkness experiment described above. Deployment of these shortcuts also depends on our motivations and position in social hierarchies. Use of stereotypes* is an example of this kind of shortcut.

The second of the three evolutionary theories – termed the error management theory – proposes that biases are not merely a result of shortcuts but also an adaptation that serves an important function. Martie Haselton from the University of California and David Buss from the University of Texas at Austin suggest that judgements about opportunities and threats, particularly in cases of uncertainty, consistently deviate towards the extreme response. It is better to be careful than to be sorry. When we process information, our cognitive frameworks can produce two kinds of errors: one, where it would have been better not to take any action at all; and two, where we fail to select the best action out of the different options. Of course, ideally, we would always make the optimal choice and make no errors. But in the real world, much of the decision-making is a game of probability, there is uncertainty, and errors are very likely. We constantly weigh up options in terms of what is more likely, assigning weight and value to attributes. So there will always be a certain amount of error in any judgement. In terms of biases that affect us, the biases resulting from the notion of threat are especially pertinent. Our assessment of threat is biased and influences how we view an oncoming threat. In a study published in *Acta Psychologica* in 2013, it was shown that people perceived an oncoming spider to be moving much faster than it actually was, and faster than other less

---

* Stereotypes, and associated mechanisms, are discussed in detail in Section II.

threatening objects such as balls. During this experiment, lights were turned off and 16 participants were assigned to a ball or spider scenario in alternating order. In each trial, a similarly sized orange ball or orange spider appeared in front of the participant. The paddle – a white rectangle of a fixed depth but set to one of three varying widths – appeared at a distance away. Participants clicked the mouse to initiate each trial, and then moved the mouse left and right to move the paddle left and right. The object to be blocked zigzagged towards the participant at one of six speeds. After each blocking attempt, participants estimated the speed of the object by pressing the corresponding button on the mouse. The threat of the spider and its speed was assessed to be much greater when they had a smaller paddle to avert it than when they had a larger paddle. The implication is that threatening objects (spiders) look faster than non-threatening objects (balls), and objects that were more difficult to block also looked to be moving faster than objects that were easier to block, even when they are the same speed. This experiment shows that when there is no way of avoiding a threat, the perception of its impact is much higher. In case of a threat, overcautiousness is better because the false negative (failing to avoid threat) is highly costly, whereas the false positive (avoiding contact with threat) may have small social or interpersonal costs but is unlikely to have significant consequences on survival.

Robert Kurzban and Mark Leary in *Psychological Bulletin* propose that the same propensity to false positives may lie at the root of many forms of stigmatisation and prejudice, including racism, ageism and homophobia. Contact with unfamiliar out-groups might have historically increased the risk of contracting dangerous pathogens unknown to locally adapted immune systems. In-group favouritism is, therefore, seen as an evolved mechanism selected for the advantages it offered for the strengthening and coalition of the affiliated social circle. People who feel more vulnerable, stressed and anxious will have more implicit associations between any out-group members and the threat of contracting infectious or contagious disease. Similarly, people who are more prone to illnesses are likely to have more prejudice against older people, who are perceived to carry more diseases. This error management and cost–benefit perspective offers a framework to understand why the benefit of exaggerated ostracization – the act of ignoring or excluding individuals – possibly outweighed the costs. Ostracization usually occurs to strengthen the group by eliminating weaker or non-conforming members. Ostracism among humans was first known to occur in Athens more than 2,000 years ago, when citizens voted to expel individuals by writing the nominated individual on ostraca (shards of pottery). Interpersonal ostracism – sometimes known as the silent treatment – still happens even in the digital age: what is now referred to as ghosting.

The third, and final theory – the artefact theory – is that biases are a product of applying the wrong strategies in the wrong context. This could be when a person is placed in an inappropriate situation or when the incorrect normative standards are applied, such as assessing the cognitive performance of humans in a laboratory setting. There are researchers who debate that the flaws or errors we term as biases are in fact a result of our incorrect definition and understanding of rational behaviour. They recommend that a reconsideration of the standards used to judge performance can radically change conclusions about human rationality. What this theory and its proponents are saying is that in human evolutionary history, the information that was available to our ancestors was used for finding the best strategies for survival and reproduction. What was a good solution for that particular context is not necessarily suited to modern needs. So it isn't that our minds are woefully scrambled or that we are lacking in cognitive processing capacity; instead we are trying to find a fit between the solutions that were optimal in a more primitive world in our evolutionary past with the modern world, where they do not perform as well.

## Selfish self-absorption

Much of our implicit biases arise because of our tendency to notice something vivid – either something that has been primed in our memory and looks familiar or something that is unusual and extraordinary and stands out. Our perception of entities in the real world changes depending on our position and the environmental content, which also depends on the interaction of sensation and experience in the brain. So, besides heuristics, there are also biases that can arise because of the process itself – because of social influences, processing errors, emotional motivations or moral compulsions, or because of the distortions arising from storage and retrieval of memory. Many of these can be explained with social cognition theories. Social cognition is the branch of psychology that studies how people process the information around them to make sense of themselves and other people: how they interpret this information, how they analyse it, and how they use it to choose the best course of action. Whereas many of the evolutionary explanations refer to causation* in historic

---

\* Causation indicates that one event is the result of the occurrence of the other event, i.e. there is a causal relationship between the two events. One frequently used causation vs correlation example is that smoking is correlated with alcoholism but doesn't cause alcoholism.

(evolutionary) time having shaped the mechanisms of our mind, social-cognitive explanations usually refer to causation occurring in our current time and involving contemporary motives and goals.

Social psychologists widely accept that one main reason for biases is to form a sense of self and identity, and because we are all basically selfish. William Graham Sumner first mentioned ethnocentrism in 1906. In his seminal book *Folkways* he uses this as a term to define a range of discriminatory behaviours associated with in-group bias (the technical name for this view of things in which one's own group is the centre of everything, and all others are scaled and rated with reference to it). There is a tendency in the individual to be rigid in their acceptance of the 'culturally alike' and rejection of the 'unlike'. This kind of in-group favouritism can be quite explicit (prejudice) or subtle and implicit (bias), where the attitudes of in-groups are always considered virtuous and superior, and their standards as universal. Any deviation from this self-assigned social norm is considered contemptible and inferior. These kinds of behaviours are based on group boundaries that are typically defined by one or more observable characteristics, such as language, accent, skin colour, physical features or religion. Identification with a social group forces an individual to maintain a sense that their group is positively distinct from other social groups. This is done primarily to create a sense of self-worth. To establish this distinct identity, individuals are compelled to create distance from the out-group. This is why there is a tendency to organise the various groups and individuals in hierarchies, since it is easier to process hierarchical relationships more fluently than egalitarian relationships. This in turn also creates a justification for the isolation and marginalisation of certain communities. Often, one person is the main leader, and this person is granted more influence, status, control, money and additional benefits than other individuals. These social stratifications become well established in society, so most people are familiar with these relationships. And as they are more familiar, they are then processed more fluently, thus becoming self-perpetuating. Therefore, although people claim they reject inequality, they do exhibit a natural affiliation towards some social statuses.

People's sense of self is partly informed by differences in status between groups, and so they try to sustain a positive in-group identity. When we favour our in-group automatically, we are more inclined to disfavour the out-group, and people who dislike or hold these automatic implicit biases against one out-group are more likely to hold the same for many other out-groups. When you meet someone new and they are, for instance, wearing a T-shirt with your favourite football team's crest on it, in most cases, you are bound to feel a certain affinity with them and decide subconsciously that you already like them. Your attitudes will be shaped by this initial judgement and perception. These are explicit biases, ones that you can recognise and explain to someone else. On the other hand, if you meet someone and feel uncomfortable around them but are not able to articulate why that might be, it could be that this person reminds you of someone from your past who you did not get along with or is part of a community that you are uncomfortable with. This is an implicit bias.

★★★

A collaborative international study, including academics from Princeton and Sorbonne Universities published in the *Journal of the Royal Society Interface* shows that when people are trying to conform to the views of their neighbours, they lose their natural abilities to observe and evaluate their environment closely. We are evolved to observe our in-group members and people around us. But when our own beliefs contradict those around us, this becomes a challenge because humans generally detest the notion of 'standing alone', and people can spend too much time copying each other and lose the ability to make their own decisions. The team from the University of Exeter's mathematics department that were part of this research group developed these social interactions as a mathematical model to observe how the use of social information has evolved within animal groups. By using a simple model of decision-making in a dynamic environment, they showed that individuals overly rely on social information and evolve to be too readily influenced by their neighbours, termed a 'classic evolutionary conflict' between individual and collective interest. Dr Colin Torney says: 'Our results suggest we shouldn't expect social groups in nature to respond effectively to changing environments. Individuals that spend too much time copying their neighbours are likely to be the norm.' Individualism is not prioritised and can lead to 'groupthink', which is a classic herd mentality behaviour that also underlies the formation of echo chambers and filter bubbles, gangs, and other more extreme groups such as the Ku Klux Klan. Critical thinking becomes impaired and there is a rise of intense emotion within the group, which leads to impassioned behaviour based on biased beliefs and emotions. This is when tribalism comes into play. We belong to a tribe. We want to belong to a tribe. An extreme example – but nevertheless a very valid one – could be understanding how people justified the atrocities against the Jews during the Holocaust as part of their moral compass. They believed that it was OK because the group they identified with believed so too.

Social development theory – an extension of social identity theory – makes the distinction between bias as a preference for the in-group and prejudice as active denigration of the out-group. Even children as young as four or five years old start moving from an undifferentiated understanding of racial categories to active awareness and thereafter a bias in favour of their own ethnic and racial category. They also start forming a sense of the hierarchies in their environment that determine the communities and characteristics they prefer. Later in Chapter 9, we will see examples of this, where young children choose dolls with a certain skin colour or body shape based on what is the idealised norm around them. Daniel Bar-Tal, Professor of Research in Child Development and Education at Tel Aviv University, showed in 1996 that, even when as young as three years old, Jewish Israeli children held explicitly negative stereotypes of Arabs. In the case of children growing up in conflict and war, racial biases and prejudices can emerge very early on. It can develop into prejudice as early as six or seven years old if these children identify very closely with their social group or if they belong to groups where blatant bias and expression of prejudice against others is the norm, or if there is a perceived threat from these outside groups. But in the current political climate, the language and the fractured discourse around race and ethnicity in the media can also lead to children feeling conflicted and biased towards any groups that are not their own.

★★★

People have a basic need to feel good about themselves, and most neurotypical people do like themselves. Unconscious self-enhancement or 'implicit egotism theory' suggests that people tend to unconsciously favour those objects that they associate with their own self. The fact that implicit egotism stems from a positive evaluation of the self has been demonstrated by laboratory experiments where people with low self-esteem were shown to gravitate away from (rather than towards) choices associated with the self. For example, the 'mere ownership effect' shows that even when people own pens or keychains, they evaluate these objects more favourably than they would otherwise. Similarly, people like the letters that appear in their own names more than other letters in the alphabet, and this effect is particularly pronounced for people's first and last initials. This is because a person has an automatic tendency to evaluate themselves positively, and this is then transferred to other attributes associated with their self, such as their name. Jozef Nuttin was a Belgian psychologist who discovered the name-letter effect* when he noticed he liked car licence plates that contained letters in his name. Initially disputed, this unconscious self-enhancing bias has been documented by researchers in more than 14 countries around the world, thereby showing that it is largely independent of social and cultural contexts. I have seen first-hand how this effect develops in children. The first letters that my three-year-old twins started to recognise from a very young age were the first letters of their names, and they would jump up and down every time they noticed that letter anywhere, calling it 'my letter'. An analysis of a large database of charity donations revealed that a disproportionately large number of people donate to disaster relief following hurricanes with names that share their initial letter.

---

* Nuttin called this the 'Narcissism beyond Gestalt and awareness' where – independent of visual, acoustical, aesthetic, semantic and frequency characteristics – letters belonging to an individual's own first and/or family name are preferred above not-own name letters.

Another expression of implicit egotism, or an unconscious bias towards things associated with self, is seen in normative determinism,* which is the hypothesis that people would gravitate towards work that fits their names (also called aptronym or 'name-is-fitting' bias). Psychologist Carl Jung cites Sigmund Freud as an example because he studied pleasure and his surname means 'joy'. The self-concept and associated unconscious bias have been shown to play a major role in some important life decisions. Psychologists Brett Pelham and colleagues from the State University of New York (SUNY) write in the *Journal of Personality and Social Psychology* that students are likely to evaluate their teachers more favourably when they give lenient grades, because they satisfy the students' desire for good feedback. So students' unconscious self-enhancement will bias their evaluations of the teaching skills. They also discovered that people are attracted to other people whose names resemble their own, and that their choice of presidential candidates was influenced by the name – or the initial – of the candidates. People even prefer partners with names that sound similar to their own. A 2004 study published in the same journal looked at marital records analysing data from two databases of marriages in the US states Georgia and Florida, and found a correlation between spouses' surnames, either matching whole surnames or starting with the same letter. It could be debated that the results were skewed due to ethnicity,

---

* Nominative determinism, literally 'name-driven outcome', is the hypothesis that people tend to gravitate towards areas of work that reflect their names, and that their name plays a significant role in determining key aspects of their job, profession or even character. The name fits because people, possibly subconsciously, made themselves fit. The term has its origin in the 'Feedback' column of the British magazine *New Scientist* from 1994.

but the study tried to avoid this by limiting to common Caucasian* surnames. So there might be some truth in that our enduring romantic bonds are influenced by our implicit egotism. I should know; I married someone whose initials are the same as mine!

***

Evolutionarily speaking, many of our cognitive adaptations are designed to stop us from interacting with those who are likely to be poor exchange partners and instead to join groups that allow for cooperation and give us an advantage in between-group competition. However, in doing so, we activate stereotypes and prejudices. Most people face stigmatisation† of some sort during the course of their lives, and it affects so much of our everyday micro-interactions. Many of the theories in stigmatisation are based on Erving Goffman's seminal work from 1963 in which he proposed that individuals are stigmatised when they have a deviant attribute that does not meet societal expectations and norms. Goffman – perhaps the most famous sociologist of the last 60 years – classically defined stigma as an 'attribute that is deeply discrediting' where this attribute could be something that is physically discernible such as skin colour,

---

* I have a problem with the use of this word, although this is what the researchers have used in their study and published paper. Caucasian is actually a 19th-century anthropological idea that was based around a false conception that the human species originated in the Caucasus Mountains. The use of this word is based in a Eurocentric racial ideology, in which the idea of race is associated with skin colour. I would prefer to use 'European-American' here.
† In ancient Greece, a stigma was a brand burned into a slave or a criminal's skin to symbolise disgrace. In the 1500s, the word stigmatise meant literally 'to brand or tattoo'.

body size or a physical disability, or it could be something that is hidden such as mental illness. Due to such a negative or socially undesirable attribute, the person's whole social identity is discredited. This then leads to other people assuming that this specific individual is incapable of partaking in normal social interactions: the idea of 'not fitting in'. For instance, in certain male-dominated domains, being a woman is likely to be seen as a disadvantage, which might be linked to the idea that the woman wouldn't be able to fit into the workplace culture, office and locker-room banter as she is not the normative gender in that domain. When an individual's actual social identity (one that can be proven, such as their race) does not align with their virtual social identity (one that forms the societal expectations of a norm for such a property, such as a 'white person' is for race), this clash results in a bias against them, followed by stigmatisation and prejudice, and consequently their marginalisation in society.

Three other theories have been proposed to explain how negative evaluations of an individual are formed. First, the presence of a trait that is a deviation from the norm and discredits the bearer. This is also known as the 'horn effect', where one negative attribute can impact on the perception of the individual as a whole. The second states that the individuals might be ostracised and not considered fit or legitimate to partake in social interactions because of the unpredictable nature of their actions. These would include individuals who are drug addicts, alcoholics, etc. Once they have been labelled, they are beyond the protection of social norms. Consequently, this creates a bias towards the larger social group, which leads to the stigmatised individual becoming invisible. The third theory is where a single defining feature of stigma is difficult to define. Intersectional biases and compound biases fall into this category, such as

those assigned to a 'black woman' or a 'gay black woman'.*
There is an inherent notion of power and discrimination in
any act of stigmatisation, and in the process relating to
social creation and reproduction of structural inequalities.
By excluding some in favour of others, the stereotypes
associated with these individuals and their affiliate groups
are devalued and validated. In doing so, discriminatory
practices are maintained. Those who are stigmatised do not
wish to interact with those who do not share the same
labels, and those who do not have these devalued labels try
to ignore or disparage the individuals who do, thereby
treating them differently in the process. This really is the
foundation of discrimination.

Although we can now understand that this cognitive
bias would give us an evolutionary advantage, and we
understand from evolutionary and social cognition theories
how some individuals might be negatively evaluated, it is
not that easy to see the links between negative evaluation
and stigmatisation. Stigmatisation is based in exclusion of
an individual or group, not just because of a negative
evaluation or because of a maligned identity, but also
because they possess certain characteristics and behaviours
that are not considered worthy of normal social interactions.
The notion of stigmatisation is based in shared values of a
social group, and exclusion or rejection due to personal
idiosyncrasies is not considered part of this framework.
While there are various theories providing a reasoning
behind this leap from the social to the individual, three are
particularly strong. The most popular one is the suggestion
that stigmatising a group or an individual belonging to a
particular group boosts one's own self-esteem and gives a
psychological and social advantage. The other suggestions

---

* Intersectionality is discussed in more detail in Section II.

are that people also negatively evaluate others to boost perception of oneself by others in own and other social groups, or to justify some of the existing social, political and economic structures. Although this assumption remains in place – that a threat to self-esteem can lead people to be biased against others – there has actually been no evidence to prove that self-esteem or social identity has anything to do with being prejudiced against some groups while not towards others. Self-esteem and social identity theories intersect and provide some justification, but these cannot fully explain why certain groups are excluded while others are not.

Evolutionary theories tell us that many of our unconscious biases have evolved as cognitive adaptations to help us distinguish friend from foe and as a way of keeping ourselves safe from danger. They explain why we form a sense of 'otherness' for some, why we might create stereotypes, and why we tend to take cognitive shortcuts. Even though some of these implicit biases may have developed as evolutionary mechanisms to help us survive, it would be incorrect to suggest that they are necessarily hardwired, that we inherit and acquire them just because we are humans and because that is the way we are supposed to be. These biases are often learned. This means they can also be unlearned. If our biases are meant to be shortcuts, then they are meant to make us more productive and efficient by preserving our cognitive resources for those tasks that matter most. But, as we all know from experience, not all shortcuts are good for us. Sometimes shortcuts can lead us down a blind alley, and sometimes we can get lost. In the same vein, some of our implicit biases are mental shortcuts that lead us to make snap judgements about situations and people. We parse the useful information from what we perceive as redundant and false in order to make the best – or quickest and most efficient – behavioural choices and those requiring minimum cognitive effort.

As I write this, I am wary of being misconstrued as suggesting that our biases are not really our fault or that we are evolutionarily and biologically predetermined to be biased. This is not my intention. We are not designed to be racist or sexist. Race is an artificial construct. Gender is a social construct. We can address these biases and rectify their effect on our actions and decisions. We can stop ourselves from being prejudiced. Discussion of the evolutionary basis of cognitive biases does not give us permission to act in a discriminatory way. Implicit social cognition is often disrupted by conscious information processing. For ancestral humans, the cost of disease and aggression from individuals that were not part of their immediate social circle was significant. This means they could have developed a bias to assume they were less kind and generous, more dangerous and ill-tempered because the benefit of assuming so outweighed the cost. This is, however, not the case anymore, so we cannot justify xenophobia, racism and prejudicial actions as an evolutionary mechanism or as something that is inherently in-built within us. As humans, we are more self-aware than some other primates (or at least we are supposed to be). Social psychologists have also suggested that bias effects can change, recede and reverse depending on the context and so the biases are less fixed and more adaptive than originally supposed. So merely saying that we are suspicious of any 'foreign' groups because we were ancestrally influenced to do so is an excuse – and a feeble excuse at that. Many of our ancestral and historical biases are conspicuously absent now as the nature of threat changes in modern times. In-group bias is common but it is entirely dependent on the person whether these biases are implemented and exercised. As we examine unconscious bias closely and look at research studies throughout the book, it is easy to see that some of these very primal instincts and biases can be evoked by politicians; for instance, consider President Donald Trump's call to send the immigrants back home. As we become more attuned to how our prejudice and stigma of out-groups is illegal and morally wrong, and that we do not necessarily face the same kind of threats from those who do not look or sound similar to us, we can re-evaluate our historic biases and adapt our responses to our modern norms of morality.

Our adaptations developed because our human ancestors needed to find mates and reproduce, avoid getting killed, protect their families, sidestep diseases and compete for the best (and limited) resources. We evolved some psychological mechanisms that helped us achieve these goals. However, today, as we consider the biases as a limitation in our rational thinking, we have to consider whether these adaptations are secure and robust enough to perform well against modern standards and lifestyles. We do not operate on the same social models; our economic and social challenges are not the same. Humans are also evolving much faster than ever before through adaptations and mutations. It seems that we have evolved at a rate that our cognitive processes haven't been able to keep up with. The demands on our processing capacities are different and so are our canons of morality. Today we live – and wish to live – very differently, seeking satisfaction, happiness, fairness and pursuing the quest for an egalitarian society. Our knowledge of how our evolutionary psychology motivated us to behave does not align with our wishes and desires today.

Only when we can understand both our psychological adaptations and our modern frameworks can we begin to acknowledge and address our unconscious biases.

## CHAPTER THREE

# All in Your Head

❛The capacity to discern "us" from "them" is fundamental in the human brain,' writes David Amodio, Associate Professor of Psychology and Neural Science at New York University.

'Chris' is an eight-year-old child with Williams Syndrome (WS), which is a rare neurodevelopmental disorder caused by deletions of about 26 genes from the long arm of chromosome seven. Children with WS are known to have unusually friendly natures because they lack the sense of fear that other people feel in various social situations. Helen Tager-Flusberg, based at Boston University, studies the social behaviour of children with WS and says that 'When they're four or five … whether they know you or not, within about five minutes you're their new best friend.' These children are overly friendly because they do not fear strangers.

We know from research in social development that children as young as six or seven start stereotyping people according to race and gender, and children as young as nine months old can show preference for race/colour of the people they are most exposed to in the first year of their life. A study carried out by a team of researchers from Germany and France in 2010 revealed that Chris and 19 other children like him show no racial bias and did not develop negative attitudes about other ethnic groups. They did show patterns of gender stereotyping found in other children, but their responses were significantly less stereotype-consistent for racial attitudes. The children were recruited from the same ethnicity so it was unlikely that their different exposure to the racial groups had an impact on these results. This was the first indication of an absence of racial stereotyping in a human group. The research has significant indications for how stereotypes are formed and maintained in our brains, and it shows that the neural pathway that is responsible for racial bias is somehow lacking in children with WS. It also shows that there must be different neurobehavioural mechanisms for the development of gender and racial bias. Hence the mechanisms underlying the formation of different stereotypes are not uniform. Since WS is characterised by an absence of social fear, this area of the brain must in some way contribute to the development of racial bias. On the other hand, it does not seem to have any connection to the development of gender bias.

Empirical evidence has shown that the neural zones that respond to stereotypes include the amygdala, the prefrontal cortex, the posterior cingulate and the anterior temporal cortex, and that they are described as all 'lighting up like a Christmas tree[*] when stereotypes are activated. Recent neuroscience studies have used functional magnetic resonance imaging (fMRI)[†] to demonstrate that people use different areas of the brain when reasoning about familiar and unfamiliar situations over a range of reasoning problems. Familiar situations are processed in a system involving the

---

[*] The term 'lit up' is often used during brain imaging studies and implies that certain parts of the brain become more activated than others during certain tasks. But fMRI scanning does not show a lightbulb view of the brain or detect electrical changes in the brain, as 'lights up' would suggest.

[†] A modern neuroscientific method that provides a non-invasive measure of neural activity by assessing regional changes in blood oxygenation, i.e. blood oxygen level dependent (BOLD) response.

frontal and temporal lobes whereas unfamiliar situations are processed in the frontal and parietal lobes. These two similar but dissociated processes provide a biological explanation for the differences between heuristic reasoning (more likely to lead to implicit bias) and formal logic.

## Structure

Human brains balance two primordial systems.[*] One includes the amygdala,[†] a brain region that can generate fear and distrust of things that pose a danger, such as unfamiliar situations and places. The amygdala is our emotional learning centre, important for acquiring, storing and expressing cues related to fear and threat, and associated with strong emotions, including happiness, fear, anxiety and sadness. It is the centre of our threat response, receiving information straight from our senses, and helps us figure out if someone is safe to approach or not. Through the amygdala, the brain processes billions of stimuli per day and must quickly choose what to focus on. Investigations into post-mortem brains have shown that the amygdala can be subdivided into three major sets of nuclei: the basolateral group (basal, lateral and accessory basal nuclei), the corticomedial group (cortical and medial nuclei), and the central nucleus. Each has different afferent and efferent[‡] connectivity and functional profiles. In general, the

---

[*] Please see the Appendix for diagrams of the structure of the human brain.

[†] The amygdala is an almond-shaped structure in the brain (its name comes from the Greek word for 'almond') close to the hippocampus, in the frontal portion of the temporal lobe.

[‡] Afferent neurons are sensory neurons that carry nerve impulses from sensory stimuli towards the central nervous system and brain, while efferent neurons are motor neurons that carry neural impulses away from the central nervous system and towards muscles to cause movement.

amygdala has been associated with lower-level emotional processing, particularly of negative stimuli. Studies with amygdala lesion patients, i.e. a damaged amygdala, show that they are less likely to stop and do a risk assessment, and they are more likely to trust and approach unfamiliar faces. A detailed study, by Laura Harrison and colleagues from the California Institute of Technology, of a 14-year-old girl suffering from Urbach–Wiethe disease, which causes progressive amygdala damage, has shown that the amygdala has a role in the assessment of fear and threat, even when specific sensory stimuli are absent. In this experiment, three patients with rare bilateral amygdala lesions, along with control subjects (who had the amygdala intact), made approach-related judgements about photos of intact faces and of the same faces with all internal facial features obscured. Direct comparisons of the judgements of these stimuli showed that the patients had a greater tendency than the control subjects to rate the blurred faces as more approachable than whole faces. The results showed that the amygdala plays a significant role in determining the approachability of individuals and the level of threat posed.

The amygdala has fascinated scientists for more than 50 years. In 1956, a study showed that bilateral amygdalectomy[*] in rhesus monkeys resulted in a reduction in fear responses and overall tameness. If you have read or watched the documentary *Free Solo*, you will be familiar with Alex Honnold, believed to be the greatest free solo climber. He ascends without a rope or protective equipment of any kind in treacherous landscapes where, above about 15 metres, any fall would likely be lethal. Even just watching him pressed against dangerously narrow precipices with barely

---

[*] Surgical removal of the amygdala.

any space to hold on to the rock above him makes me feel nauseous with vertigo. Neurobiologist Jane Joseph has performed fMRIs on high-sensation seekers. In an fMRI test with Honnold, using a range of extreme images as stimuli as reported in the *Medical Journal of Southern California*, Joseph found that there was almost zero activation in his amygdala. This is a really unusual brain reaction and could explain why Alex feels no threat in free solo climbs that others wouldn't dare attempt. But this also shows how our amygdala activates in that split-second to warn us, and why it plays an important role in our implicit biases. The amygdala likely activates as we walk down an unfamiliar dark alleyway and hear unexpected sounds or see a stranger appear and walk towards us. It causes us to make assumptions about the threat level of the situation. We are likely to feel a flood of emotions as our heart starts beating faster and our palms become sweaty. This all happens without any conscious reasoning or effort. It then takes explicit engagement on our part to involve the prefrontal cortex, which gives out the message to our amygdala that all is under control and there's nothing to worry about, that perhaps that stranger is not a stranger at all but a neighbour, and that the sound we heard is possibly only an owl. Evolutionarily, humans are primed to respond to any notion of threat to ensure fitness and survival, so this kind of response is crucial. Our conscious brain does not have the opportunity to interpret all the information that we see, so our initial instincts are less likely to be based on interpretations that are fully processed and will often include biases of some kind. As time passes, our socialisation and personal memories and experiences produce unconscious biases and apply them while the amygdala labels and categorises incoming stimuli efficiently and unconsciously, leading to people rapidly categorising others as 'like me' and 'not like me', and consequently 'in-group' or 'out-group'.

The amygdala – as the super-fast, rash and emotional part of the brain – needs a balance, so it is also well connected to other brain regions, including the medial prefrontal cortex (mPFC), which acts as the 'sensible' part of the brain by putting an inhibitory control over emotion. The prefrontal cortex (PFC) lies right at the front of the brain and occupies almost 10 per cent of its volume with dense interconnections to other parts of the brain. It is involved in high-level executive functions such as controlling our snap judgements, instead focusing on long-term planning. The ventromedial prefrontal cortex (vmPFC) is involved in ascribing feelings, desires and motivations to specific people, while the dorsomedial prefrontal cortex (dmPFC) is used to assign beliefs and knowledge (in addition to some emotional states). Some scientists believe that the vmPFC is influential in behaviours that make people 'more human' and the dmPFC in those that define them as 'less human'. This is linked to infrahumanisation theory, discussed later in this chapter.

The story of Phineas Gage has been passed down as urban legend. Gage was a railroad construction foreman who survived when a large iron rod was accidentally driven into his head at his brain's left frontal lobe. The accident occurred in 1848 and was first written up by Dr John Martyn Harlow 20 years later. His account was held as the reliable version for more than 150 years, although it is now under debate. According to Harlow's report, Gage went from being 'strong and active' with 'an iron will' and of 'temperate habits' to 'fitful', 'irreverent', 'grossly profane' and 'impatient of restraint or advice'. This story has been used to demonstrate the transformational impact of damage to the prefrontal cortex on an individual's capacity to carry out executive functions* that consequently affects their personality. Although there could have been other factors influencing the huge variation between Gage's pre- and post-accident personalities, there have been numerous other research studies to show that prefrontal cortex damage leads to poor performance on tasks that require the use of long-term strategies and inhibition of impulses. Patients with prefrontal cortex damage can experience blunted emotional responses, which negatively affects their ability to make rational decisions. Patients with prefrontal damage, especially in medial and orbital regions, often lack awareness of social norms and the consequences of their own actions.

Implicit processes unfold rapidly, require little cognitive effort and involve posterior cortical and subcortical regions of the brain. They are explained by the heuristics theory that our brain takes shortcuts rather than relying on rational logic. Explicit processes are deliberate, cognitively taxing, consciously accessible and largely rely on the prefrontal cortex. When we are tired, distracted, anxious or stressed, the information cannot be sent to the PFC fast enough for it to be managed and so the regulatory filter fails. It is then more likely that we process the incoming stimuli at the level of the amygdala, which is why our implicit bias becomes more evident.

## In-group/out-group

As we've seen, the amygdala is the control centre for social decision-making, and it is the brain area that has been

---

* Executive functions are a set of cognitive processes that all have to do with managing oneself and one's resources in order to achieve a goal. It is an umbrella term for the neurologically based skills involving mental control and self-regulation.

reported most frequently in studies of black–white race attitudes. When our amygdala is activated, the cognitive tendency is to generalise more. This is where the information is processed; however, other parts of the brain are involved in the pervasion of implicit racial bias. Such information goes through the hippocampus as well, which is the part of the brain that forms links between memories and quickly deciphers the meaning of data received. Because the hippocampus matches new, incoming information with subjective memories, data can be matched to make someone believe their understanding of the data is 'accurate' when it is simply being related to their own subjective memory or experience.

People use different areas of the brain when reasoning about familiar and unfamiliar situations. When we meet someone new, we are not merely focusing on our verbal interaction. Within a matter of seconds, we encode (turn behaviours into neural signals) identifiable information about the person and form an impression of them, while our prefrontal cortex simultaneously monitors and evaluates neural information from our five modalities* and keeps us focused on sticking to social norms or to those that are personally important to us. So while we are evaluating a person we are also assigning them certain labels. However, we are not aware of this since the prefrontal cortex can engage in this outside our conscious awareness. These decisions are taken on a subconscious level in the first instance, before we go into the more conscious, slow and controlled processing. When we see an in-group member in pain, our brain reacts differently to how it does when we see an out-group member in pain, and the difference in

---

* The five modalities correspond to the five senses: visual, auditory, kinesthetic, olfactory and gustatory.

this empathetic response indicates the in-group favouritism, which in turn affects behaviour. We are more likely to help an in-group member. This is called 'parochial altruism'. Some people might even take delight in the suffering of out-group members. But it all depends on the context. We are not hardwired to be cruel or less empathetic towards anyone who is not a member of our in-group. Our level of empathy towards an out-group member is shaped by cultural factors that determine our evaluation of them. In such a case, parochial altruism can be undermined. It is pretty obvious that if we feel more positively towards an out-group member, we would be more inclined to help them.

A study published in the journal *Neuron*, carried out by researchers from the Max Planck Institute for Human Cognitive and Brain Sciences in Germany and psychologists from Kansas and Zurich, concluded that two neurobiological processes work together to determine our level of empathy and consequent desire to help another. Football fans witnessed a fan of their favourite team (in-group member) or of a rival team (out-group member) experience pain. They were able to choose to help the other by enduring physical pain themselves to reduce the other's pain. Helping the in-group member was best predicted by anterior insula[*] activation when seeing them suffer and by a questionnaire based on self-reports of concern. As a cortical centre of visceral information processing, the anterior insula is considered to play a crucial role in emotional experience and subjective feelings.

---

[*] The insular cortex, or 'Island of Reil', is hidden deep within the lateral sulcus of the brain. Depending on the technique employed, the insula can be divided into anywhere between two and 13 distinct subdivisions. The insula serves a wide variety of functions in humans, ranging from sensory and affective processing to high-level cognition.

Studies have highlighted the important role of the left anterior insula in cognition and empathy, to distinguish emotions like disgust, fear and happiness. In contrast, not helping the out-group member was best predicted by nucleus accumbens activation and the degree of negative evaluation of the other. The nucleus accumbens is thought to play a major role in the 'reward circuit' of the brain and in forming memories from vivid environmental stimuli, both positive and negative. This study showed that empathy-related insula activation can motivate, whereas an antagonistic signal in nucleus accumbens reduces the propensity to help. The study also shows that increasing empathy in people by, for example, providing them with more information about out-group members can reduce their bias towards them and override their callousness toward the suffering of the out-group member. Sometimes the more we know, the less we fear and the more we care.

Stereotyping is different, as here we deliberately – albeit only conceptually – link social groups to a particular set of perceived inherent and immutable qualities. This is a process known as 'essentialising'* and involves the encoding and storage of stereotypical concepts and their application in judgements and behaviours. As such, it employs a different neural network from that of the snap judgements of prejudice and incorporates structures in the cerebral cortex that support conscious thought and long-term memory that is not based on personal experience.† Besides affecting performance and sense of belonging, the threat and fear of being stereotyped leads to elevated blood

---

* Stereotypes and associated processes are discussed in detail in Chapter 4.
† Such cases include things that are common knowledge, e.g. the names of colours, the sounds of letters, capital cities and other basic facts acquired over a lifetime.

pressure and increased cardiovascular activity. Cortisol is like a natural alarm system, released by the adrenal gland in response to stress. Use of non-invasive brain stimulation techniques* – like those pioneered by Alvaro Pascual-Leone (Professor of Neurology and Associate Dean for Clinical and Translational Research at Harvard Medical School) and colleagues – have shown that the anterior temporal lobe is involved in the formation of stereotype representations.

Once these stereotypes have been developed, it is easier to maintain them than to break them. As discussed previously, it is simpler and more comfortable to stick with a familiar situation and group membership, rather than question the status quo, which feels risky. In a 2005 study mapping the brains of participants in a simulated gambling activity that looked at attitudes towards risk, it was seen that switching from our inherent default beliefs evokes activation of the anterior insula – the part of the brain associated with unpleasant emotions like disgust and fear. So questioning our in-group associations and out-group stereotypes is akin to moving away from a safe position and can be accompanied by danger warnings from a relatively primitive part of the human brain. Research in behavioural economics shows that individuals exhibit more regret when negative outcomes result from non-default actions as opposed to routine actions. So individuals are more willing to stick with their original beliefs to avoid this surge of negative emotion associated with deviating from the typical

---

* An electric current applied to the outside of the brain affects brain cell activity. The researchers decipher which brain region is being used to perform which mental task as the participants complete a series of tasks. The non-invasive technique allows researchers to map the brain regions associated with specific socio-cognitive behaviours with participants in their primitive settings.

status quo, such as a stereotype or a bias. In this study, the notion of regret was evoked by telling the participants that the unchosen option was the best option. Increasing regret correlated with increased activity in the medial orbitofrontal cortex, the anterior cingulate cortex and the anterior hippocampus. The more regret a person reported feeling, the higher the activation in the medial orbitofrontal cortex. The researchers also noted that as the trials went on, the participants' behaviour became increasingly risk-averse, correlating strongly with the activation of the medial orbitofrontal cortex and the amygdala. In another gambling study, published in the *Journal of Neuroscience* in 2010, sticking with the default option was associated with activation of the ventral striatum, which has a prominent role in emotional rewards' processing, and ensures that we feel 'rewarded' when we stay with what we already know rather than shifting our perspective. Default bias therefore occurs because we are avoiding any intense emotions associated with losing* or any such aversive event happening due to us switching from the default. People are more likely to stick with what they know, and they are more reluctant to take a stand because switching doesn't activate the reward pathway. They subconsciously believe and understand that there is more emotional cost involved with switching, such as loss of status and social acceptability, and they feel more responsible for the outcome. Our tendency to react more strongly and remember any negative information– known as negativity bias – is also linked to our aversion to risk. Negative information is parsed more quickly in the human brain and this is why we tend to remember negative evaluations of a person more easily than their positive traits. We choose the safe option – the

---

* I look at loss-aversion and status-quo bias in Chapter 6.

one we are most familiar and comfortable with – because
we are actively trying to eliminate regrets.

Benjamin Franklin observed that 'Singularity in the right
hath ruined many; happy those who are convinced of the
general opinion.' We are highly susceptible to be influenced
by choices of others. A wide range of deception-detection
literature shows that the percentage of statements judged as
truthful is significantly higher than the percentage of
statements correctly classified as truthful. This is called
truth bias.* We are more likely to believe that what the
other person is telling us is the truth, rather than to question
its credibility. We all know the effects of peer pressure and
the impact it can have on autonomous choice. This is how
political parties create momentum and harness the power of
the herd mentality to influence behaviours and choices.
This is how social media influencers become influential. If
a person sees someone with millions of followers, they are
more likely to follow them and buy into the choices that
they promote. This does not always have to be a negative
thing. Positive lifestyle choices such as the eco-movement
have become mainstream, and confirmation bias can be
used to create social momentum for change. For instance, a
study on conservation behaviour in 2008 found that hotel
guests were more likely to reuse towels when informed that
guests who had stayed in that same room had reused towels
than if they were informed about the behaviour of guests in
general. An fMRI study at the Donders Institute for Brain,
Cognition and Behaviour in the Netherlands revealed that
social conformity is reflected in the activity of the ventral
striatum and the dorsal aspect of the posterior medial frontal
cortex (pMFC), brain areas that are often implicated in

---

* There is more on the different kinds of cognitive heuristics and
biases that affect our actions and decisions in Chapters 5 and 6.

reward processing and behavioural adjustments. When we
are influenced by others' opinions and views, the reward
centre of the pMFC is activated, and this is especially likely
to happen when someone is deemed an expert.

A study carried out in 2009 asked participants to rate
female faces in terms of attractiveness, after which they
were shown the projected aggregate judgements of all the
participants. When they saw the faces a second time,
participants' ratings were shown to shift in the direction of
the group judgements. This study was set up to imitate
social psychological studies that investigate persuasion.
Neuroimaging results showed that when individual ratings
differed from those of the group, activity in the rostral
cingulate zone (an area in the medial prefrontal cortex
believed to be involved in the processing of conflict)
increased, while activity in the nucleus accumbens (an area
associated with the expectation of reward) decreased. The
strength of these activation signals indicated the strength of
the conformity too, so that when the difference between
the opinions was over a certain threshold, people adjusted
their behaviour and aligned their opinion with that of the
group. Social conformity is therefore underlined by a
reward and punishment duality process in the brain. We
feel rewarded when we conform to the views of the larger
group, and the strength of our association with our in-group
as well as the distance between the in-group and out-group
membership determines the strength of the signals in the
brain activating the reward pathways. There is also the fear
of being excluded and rejected by others, which manifests
as an error signal that screams 'you are too different' – the
ultimate fear. The reward for aligning views with the
group, and the aversion to being out of line with the group
view, act as reinforcers. Group opinion affects our
judgements of facial attractiveness, which in turn play a

critical role in human social interaction, and also shapes how we decide what is beautiful and what is not. As we know from the previous chapter, normative conformity is established when a person wants to be liked and accepted by a group. So a deviation from group opinion is detected by neural activity in the paracingulate region[*] and ventral striatum (associated with reward-related behaviour), which then produce a signal that denotes a need for social conformity.

A study published in the *Proceedings of the National Academy of Sciences*, led by Adrianna Jenkins and Jason Mitchell from the department of psychology at Harvard University, along with C. Neil Macrae of the University of Aberdeen, found that when we make decisions about people we perceive to be similar to us, the areas in our brain associated with introspection 'light up'. People use the vmPFC to make judgements about others like them and the dmPFC to make judgements about people who are not like them socially, religiously or politically. The scientists presented a group of subjects with pictures of two people, each with a description. Both pictures were of white people, so race was not a factor in the study. After the subjects viewed the pictures and descriptions, they were asked to decide which person was most like them and which person was least like them. The scientists used fMRI to scan the subjects' brains while asking them 66 questions about each person's preferences and potential behaviour. When the subjects answered the questions about the similar person, the vmPFC activated.

---

[*] The cingular cortex is an integral part of the limbic system, which is involved with emotion formation and processing, learning and memory. The combination of these three functions makes the cingulate gyrus highly influential in linking motivational outcomes to behaviour, e.g. a certain action induces a positive emotional response, which results in learning.

However, when the subjects answered the same questions about the dissimilar person, the dmPFC activated. Finally, when the subjects were asked to answer the same 66 questions about themselves (to predict their own behaviour and preferences, and to assess their own habits), the vmPFC activated – the same part of their brain that they used to judge the person who was most similar to them. This indicates that when we make decisions about people like us (or in-group members) we use a different process than the one we use to judge out-group members.

A link between the amygdala and ventral striatum is important in the translation of emotion. Thanks to face-recognition experiments, it is now a proven fact (and part of expert scientific testimony) that people are better at recognising own-race faces. It has also been shown that we are better at recognising and recalling own-gender faces. Furthermore, when we see familiar photos of people we love and care about, this region is activated. Studies from the Erasmus Institute of Neuroeconomics in Rotterdam using fMRI found that a neuronal response similar to a 'prediction error' (when the actual outcome differs from the predicted outcome) was triggered in 'dopaminergic areas' (the primary areas that synthesise and release the neurotransmitter dopamine), the rostral cingulate zone (associated with the processing of conflict), the pMFC and the ventral striatum. These areas – together, one of six major dopaminergic pathways in our brains – are associated with reward-related cognition, such as that of pleasure from certain stimuli, incentive and positive reinforcement. The researchers found that the amplitude of this neural error signal is a good prediction of the individual's tendency to conform to the opinion of the group, i.e. the strength of their social conformity bias. In a related experiment, the researchers investigated the underlying hormonal mechanisms for this, and showed that a neuropeptide, oxytocin (commonly known as the hormone of love), stimulated in-group conformity. In this experiment, participants were explicitly divided into two groups so that they had a sense of their membership of a specific group. They were then asked to rate the attractiveness of unfamiliar symbols and were shown ratings of their group members in advance. Those who were given oxytocin showed more conformity with others in their own group as compared to those who were given a placebo. The researchers concluded that oxytocin (also termed the herding hormone) may stimulate individuals to conform to the behaviour and beliefs of others in their group rather than those perceived to be in the out-group.

★★★

Detection of trustworthiness has been crucial for human survival. Of course, facial expressions matter but research shows that humans also decide whether they can trust another person even when they have a neutral face. This underlying process of social cognition – the ability to understand actions, behaviour and disposition of others – underlines our social interactions. When we are threatened or we are encountering negative reactions such as fearful faces and averted eye gaze, the amygdala is activated. Faces play a key role in determining memberships and in signalling social cues such as trustworthiness. We are biased to find some faces more trustworthy than others. We can make these decisions milliseconds after we meet someone new, even when the target person is not doing any activity that is related to trust. This is too short a time for any rational decision-making to kick in. Judgements of trustworthiness can often summarise other relevant trait inferences such as attractiveness.

fMRI investigation suggested that facial trustworthiness is related to the activation of areas such as the amygdala, the insula and the fusiform gyrus (FG). A meta-analysis[*] of 316 research articles in neuroscience by Sara Santos and collaborators from the Visual Neuroscience Laboratory at the University of Coimbra in Portugal in 2016 supported the theory that the amygdala plays a major role in processing negative emotions such as untrustworthiness. The amygdala response increases as the faces are perceived to be less trustworthy, showing that untrustworthiness signifies fear or threat, even when subjects are performing tasks that do not require explicit evaluation of faces. They also showed the role of other structural regions, namely the insula, posterior cingulate and medial frontal gyrus. Lesion studies show that patients with amygdala lesions, dysfunction or damage in the amygdala were not able to judge others' trustworthiness. In fact, patients with bilateral amygdala damage judged untrustworthy-looking faces as if they were more approachable and trustworthy. In clinical conditions such as autism and schizophrenia, social cognition is affected and the response of the right amygdala is diminished, which is thought to play a role in the detection of changing emotional stimulus.

There is a tendency to categorise people as 'socially desirable' and 'socially acceptable', which can evoke feelings of fear, mistrust and threat for some faces. When we create a perception that someone is trustworthy, we can assign a 'halo effect'[†] to them. When we implicitly assign positive qualities to someone, we also assume that

---

[*] A systematic method of statistical analysis that combines data and results from a number of independent studies on the same topic.

[†] The people who are deemed to be attractive within the social and cultural norms have a quality that is deemed 'worthy' and this effect spills over to how the rest of their personality is perceived.

they would have other positive qualities too. So, for instance, someone who is trustworthy is assumed to be a nicer, kinder, cleverer person too. Or we might be more inclined to hire someone as soon as our cognitive heuristics implore our brains to assign them the 'trustworthy' category. The reverse is also true: when untrustworthiness is assigned, a 'horn effect' could assign someone other negative qualities. Pictures of 'socially undesirable'* people result in reduced mPFC response compared to pictures of 'socially desirable' people. Such negative evaluations lead to stigmatisation of the socially undesirable individuals or groups. Infrahumanisation theory[†] states that people see some groups as less human than others; they judge out-groups as not experiencing complex emotions to the same extent that the in-group does. It is a tacitly held belief that the in-group is more human than the out-group, or the out-group is 'subhuman' (less than a human or not human at all). According to Lasana Harris and Susan Fiske from Princeton University, social groups that elicit disgust are processed differently in the mPFC. In this study, participants first described a day in the life of a pictured

---

* As used to define homeless people in this experiment carried out at the Department of Psychology and Center for the Study of Brain, Mind, and Behaviour at Princeton University published in *Social Cognitive and Affective Neuroscience* in 2008. These are labelled as 'socially undesirable' because they are considered outliers, which then explains why they are likely to be stigmatised, ignored and marginalised as they do not fit the social norms.

[†] The term was coined by Jacques-Philippe Leyens and colleagues in the early 2000s to distinguish infrahumanisation from dehumanisation (denial of humanness) associated with extreme inter-group violence such as genocide. According to Leyens and colleagues, infrahumanisation arises when people view their in-group and out-group as essentially different and accordingly reserve the 'human essence' for the in-group and deny it to the out-group.

social group member before rating the person on a variety of dimensions. Results showed that social group members who elicit disgust are perceived as less warm, competent, intelligent, articulate, similar and familiar. The mPFC activates less to members of extreme out-groups that elicit disgust, although it all depends on the context as to what we perceive as 'disgusting'.

## Gender

When we look at an image of an object, our brain either sees it as a sum of parts or as one global whole, similar to how we might make sense of a large image made up of a mosaic of smaller images. Our brains undergo two disparate processes to see the image from both perspectives: one to view the collective whole, and at the same time one to perceive the individual smaller images in the mosaic. There is extensive literature in cognitive psychology showing that different processes underlie people and object recognition: global processing in the former, local in the latter. Objectification theory suggests that the bodies of women are sometimes reduced to their sexual body parts, a view that represents a powerful and potentially damaging way of seeing and treating women. A study published in the *European Journal of Social Psychology* shows for the first time that there might be two different processes underlying our perception of men and women. This difference in how our brain perceives male and female bodies gives a clue as to why women are more often the target of sexual objectification. The first study to link such global vs local cognitive processes to gender bias, and objectification theory, it shows that images of men are seen as a whole, while those of women are more often perceived as an assemblage of various parts. In this study conducted by Sarah Gervais and colleagues from the University of Nebraska-Lincoln, participants were randomly presented with dozens of images of fully clothed, average-looking men and women. Each person was shown from head to knee, standing, with eyes focused on the camera. After a brief pause, participants were then shown two new images on their screen: one was unmodified and contained the original image, while the other was a slightly modified version of the original image and showed a sexual body part. Participants then quickly indicated which of the two images they had previously seen. Women's sexual body parts were more easily recognised when presented in isolation than when they were presented in the context of their entire bodies. But men's sexual body parts were recognised better when presented in the context of their entire bodies than they were in isolation. A follow-up study conducted at the University of Trento, and published in *Scientific Reports* in April 2019, measured brain activity with an electroencephalogram (EEG) while both male and female participants were exposed to images of scarcely or fully dressed male and female models, together with doll-like avatars that were created on the basis of the same models. The results showed that an object is noticed less when it appears among a group of scarcely dressed women, as compared to the larger positive brain activity when it is placed among men. Female doll-like avatars are less clearly differentiated from real women, implying that the recurrent sexualisation of women in media or video games might have stronger effects in real life on how women are treated, compared to hyper-masculine representations.

There is a widespread myth that women are inherently not as good at mental rotation tasks (the ability to match different 2D and 3D objects by rotating them in the mind)[*] as men[†] or at maths in general. There is evidence that this is the underlying reason for the lack of women in architecture and construction industries, and it could explain why there are fewer women in the game-design industry. This is also cited as one of the reasons for male candidates performing better on the maths section of analytical reasoning tests such as SAT and GRE.[‡] We will see in Chapter 5 that the fear of being stereotyped – stereotype threat – impairs performance. Brain imaging shows this too. Women experiencing stereotype threat while taking a maths test showed heightened activation in the ventral stream of the anterior cingulate cortex (ACC), a neural region thought to be associated with social and emotional processing, thereby indicating the additional cognitive load that the threat of a stereotype imposes. Women who are reminded of gender differences in mathematical abilities perform worse on subsequent maths tests compared to men.

Maryjane Wraga and colleagues from the departments of psychology and neuroscience at Smith College and the University of California, Berkeley tested 54 right-handed women between the ages of 18 and 34 years old, dividing them into three groups: one was given positive stereotype information, the second negative stereotype information, and the third neutral cues before the start of the

---

[*] *Why Men Don't Listen, and Women Can't Read Maps*, a book by Barbara and Alan Pease, was influential in perpetuating this gender difference in spatial abilities.

[†] Having studied architecture, I am personally offended by this suggestion, of course. But research has also shown that this kind of neuro-sexism is unfounded.

[‡] SAT and GRE are standardised tests for college admissions in the US, to undergraduate and postgraduate respectively.

experiment. The fMRI results found that under negative stereotype control, the participants showed an activation in the right medial frontal gyrus extending into the left rostral–ventral anterior cingulate, a region associated with the processing of negative emotions such as anger and sadness. The negative stereotype–control contrast also resulted in activation in the right orbital gyrus, believed to be the general site in the brain for social knowledge of norms such as gender stereotypes. Women under stereotype threat showed increased activation in the ventral ACC and the amount of this activation had a direct consequence on their performance in the mental rotation task. This established that when individuals were made aware of the stereotype, they were more likely to experience stereotype threat. The participants' performance on the test underwent a degradation because of the increased mental load, seen here as increasing neural activity. This tells us that stereotype messages alter the efficiency with which our brain processes and performs on a particular task, especially when the threat of stereotype is high.

## Race

There is a growing interest in uncovering the neural basis of racial evaluations, as the explicit admission and acknowledgement of racial bias is becoming socially unacceptable and illegal, and people like to believe that they are egalitarian. Many of the techniques used to study prejudice, especially racial bias, work well on explicit bias but are not as effective for studying implicit attitudes. The effect of race on neural activity is not that substantial, but the behavioural impact is huge, with repercussions across a range of decision-making domains. Even in hypothetical employment-discrimination cases, a study at the Cognitive Science Programme at Yale University in 2012 found differential brain activities for black and white faces that could predict the difference in the compensation awards offered. As we've already seen, social perceptual processes in our brain are linked to making sense of faces, categorising people according to gender and ethnicity, or interpreting other social cues such as trustworthiness. Using EEG methodology, research has documented that faces can be consciously distinguished from other kinds of stimuli within 170 milliseconds, and ethnic in-group and out-group faces are differentiated within 250 milliseconds. Distinctions between ethnicity (mainly between black and white faces) and facial recognition can occur as quickly as within 30–50 milliseconds.

One of the most influential studies in understanding the neurological underpinnings of race was carried out by Mary Wheeler and Susan Fiske in 2005, where they had European-American participants view photographs of unfamiliar African-American and European-American faces and perform a social categorisation task, indicating whether the person in each photo was over 21 years old. They reported significantly greater amygdala activity (indicative of a perception of threat, as we have seen) in response to African-American faces compared to European-American faces. Other fMRI studies measuring amygdala response to out-group faces have taken different forms, but all show a strong correlation between measurable amygdala activity and implicit racial bias. In 2000, researchers from the Nuclear Magnetic Resonance Center, Massachusetts General Hospital and Harvard Medical School in Boston offered the first fMRI study directly investigating race-related amygdala activity. The authors admitted that their research was not aimed at uncovering any racial differences in amygdala activity; rather it was 'explicitly designed to assess fMRI responses to out-group vs in-group faces across subjects of both races.' The results show that amygdala responses to human face stimuli are affected by the relationship between the perceived race of the stimulus face and that of the subject. When individuals see facial images of people from an ethnic background different to their own, it often activates the amygdala more than seeing people of the same ethnicity. The amygdala, prefrontal cortex and fusiform face area (FFA) in the brain are believed to be the neural substrates underlying race information processing. The FFA is a part of the human visual system that is widely thought to have an evolutionary purpose to perceive and identify faces, developed specifically for facial recognition, but more broadly it is instrumental in identifying objects that are visually similar. Increased FFA activation is seen in both Caucasian and non-Caucasian faces when viewing their own-race faces. On the other hand, an fMRI investigation with African-American and Caucasian-American individuals showed increased amygdala activation for non-Caucasian individuals in both groups, signalling an implicit racial bias and perception of social threat. The authors also suggest that these findings indicate cultural learning rather than innate bias, so African-Americans are taught by the dominant group to fear members of their own in-group. The stereotype threat creates a fear of belonging to the in-group.

Circling back to the Williams Syndrome (WS) patients discussed at the start of this chapter, studies show that reduced social fear and hyper-sociability in WS individuals is linked to diminished amygdala reactivity to social threats, and to decreased interactions between the FFA and amygdala. This is consistent with other studies to indicate that decreased amygdala and FFA activity and interactions reduce implicit race bias in those with WS, because of the diminished signalling of the social threat associated with a racial out-group. Social fear and mistrust contribute to racial stereotyping. The authors conclude that social fear is not necessary to create gender stereotypes but important for forming racial stereotypes.

Usually there are executor areas in the brain that are able to self-regulate and suppress amygdala activation and related biases. Psychologist Elizabeth Phelps of New York University and her colleagues found that there is a network of brain regions that is consistently activated in neuroimaging studies of race processing. This network overlaps with the circuits involved in decision-making and emotion regulation, and includes – besides the amygdala and the FFA – the anterior cingulate cortex (ACC) and the dorsolateral prefrontal cortex (DLPFC). According to their study, the ACC is involved in detecting these conflicts between our explicit and implicit intentions while assessing race. People can also have an implicit bias and choose not to act on it, and the DLPFC is the one most likely to be trying to regulate the emotional responses that conflict with our egalitarian goals and beliefs.

The *Daily Mail* created a clickbait headline from this research, sensationalising and suggesting that racism was 'hardwired into our brain' and therefore innate. But Professor Phelps asserts that the cultural context is very important: 'race attitudes are largely culturally determined and shift over time.'[*]

Eva Telzer and colleagues from the University of Illinois showed in their research published in the *Journal of Cognitive Neuroscience* in 2013 that this differential perception of race

---

[*] The *Guardian*, 2 July 2012.

associated with amygdala activity was not innate, and not seen in children, but developed over a period of time, especially in adolescence. This significant study quashes any suggestions that we are born 'racists' and that we have racial prejudice in our nature. Instead, it shows that differential amygdala response to African-American faces does not emerge until adolescence, reflecting the increasing salience of race across development, and how the implicit – and explicit – cues around us affect the way we start forming stereotypes and prejudices. The researchers examined the neurodevelopmental trajectory of the amygdala in response to race across childhood and adolescence ranging from four to 16 years. Thirty-two youths viewed African-American and European-American faces during a functional brain scan. Results also suggest that greater peer diversity was associated with attenuated amygdala response to African-American faces, suggesting once again that frequent contact with out-group members may reduce the importance of race in how we differentiate and identify people (discussed further in Chapter 8). The more positive contact we have with people from different ethnic groups, the less likely we are to form the notion of threat associated with unfamiliar faces, and the less likely we are to imbibe the stereotypical messages that we receive from words and images in the media around us. Diversity therefore becomes critical, especially for our children, to normalise the multicultural world that we live in.

## Accents

The way we respond to different accents can also be explained by amygdala response to in-group and out-group memberships. While repetition of our own accent elicits an enhanced neural response, repetition of another group's accent results in reduced neural responses. Patricia Bestelmeyer at the School of Psychology, Bangor University is studying neural markers of accent bias, and she spoke to me from her home in Wales. She moved to the UK from Germany to study as an undergraduate at Aberdeen in the early 1990s. I asked her if she faced any prejudice due to her German accent (which is very mellow now, much like my own Indian accent, hinting at our history but mixed in with our experiences of living in different places over time). 'There were many 18-year-olds who told me how Germans killed their grandparents every time they heard me speak. There was a lot of negativity from the Second World War,' she told me. 'Germans also have a reputation of being incredibly organised, and so people assumed from my accent that I would be too.' Our accents are a reminder of our national identity and can be a reminder of any negative historical events.[*] Clearly, accents are a huge part of our social identity.

The neuropsychology of accents received interest after media reports of people who woke up after a stroke speaking with a 'foreign accent'. A foreign accent is characterised by some phonetic errors on consonants and vowels, as well as non-traditional stresses and rhythms. The patients may start lengthening their syllables. In 2003, an American woman started speaking with a British accent, and she felt that she was left with no 'sense of her own self'. The 'foreign accent syndrome' was first coined by the French neurologist Pierre Marie in 1907. There is a reported case of a Norwegian woman who suffered shrapnel wounds in 1941 and started speaking with a German accent. She was completely ostracised by her community, due to the negative perception of German people at that time. Another of these patients, Mrs Walker, said in a report on the BBC: 'I've lost my identity, because I

---

[*] Accents and associated biases are discussed in detail in Chapter 10.

never talked like this before. I'm a very different person and it's strange and I don't like it. It's very hard and I get very upset in my head, but I'm getting better.' Kath Lockett, speaking on *Good Morning Britain* in 2014, said that she felt bereft of a homeland; she just wanted to go home.

Accents are increasingly being seen much like a fingerprint – a unique identifier for an individual. As our tone and style changes depending on who we are speaking to, we regulate our voices and accents to express who we are. Carolyn McGettigan, a researcher at the Royal Holloway University, identified the brain regions and interactions involved in impersonations and accents. The team asked participants (all non-professional impressionists) to repeatedly recite the opening lines of a familiar nursery rhyme with their normal voice, by impersonating individuals, or by impersonating regional and foreign accents of English. The study showed that when a voice is deliberately changed, it brings the left anterior insula and inferior frontal gyrus (IFG) of the brain into play. We know that the role of the anterior insula in empathy has been supported by numerous neuroimaging studies reporting activation in response to others in pain, and to expressions of disgust, fear, anxiety and happiness. The IFG is a part of the prefrontal cortex and is linked to processing of speech and language, showing that a change in voice and accent is linked to a strong emotional response. When comparing impersonations against accents, areas in the posterior superior temporal/inferior parietal cortex and in the right middle/anterior superior temporal sulcus (which are associated with empathy and social perception) showed greater responses. Patti Adank, one of the first academics to investigate the neural substrates of accent processing, studied the variation between standard Dutch and an artificial, novel variation of Dutch. Her study revealed that bilateral mid and superior temporal gyri (STG), planum temporale, as well as left IFG are involved in processing accents, and a considerable delay in the comprehension of words spoken in isolation in an unfamiliar regional accent was seen.

Bestelmeyer and her colleagues at Bangor published in 2015 in the journal *Cerebral Cortex* the results of their neuroimaging experiment – the first to show that increased social relevance of, or greater emotional sensitivity to, in-group accents is likely to underlie the own-accent bias. This bias is seen as a significant interaction between the accent of the participant and the accent of the speakers. The imaging data showed that repetitions of the participant's own accent were associated with increased activation in bilateral amygdalae, right rolandic operculum, and anterior cingulum. By contrast, repetitions of another group's accent showed decreased activations in these regions, indicating that there is an increasing perception of the importance or relevance of those accents that are similar to ours. There was no evidence of strong activation to out-group or 'foreign' accents. This study is similar to the neural activation seen in response to in-group and out-group faces, where greater activation is seen in the left amygdala and the left orbitofrontal cortex for in-group faces. These results for accent bias are also similar to the areas typically seen in neuroimaging studies of face perception (i.e. fusiform gyri). What is interesting about the experiment carried out by Bestelmeyer and her colleagues is that they used typical Scottish and English accents, and it may be that the cultural narratives around the long-standing rivalry between Scotland and England could have prompted the bias against the accented speakers. Although this was not tested in the experiment, it would be an interesting factor to explore. It is known that cultural and social norms can affect neural processing, and so it is conceivable that the strength of the activation to out-group may be less prominent in the case of a different pair of accents with less historical rivalry.

In studying the neural basis of accent discrimination and bias, it is tricky to dissociate the other interferences as it is highly likely that more deliberate attention is paid to unfamiliar accents. Also, what scientists like Bestelmeyer are aiming to discover is whether these neural markers of accent bias are due to the emotional response to own-type accents, or whether it is because similar-sounding accents capture our attention more easily. The 'affective processing theory' proposes that there is a positive bias exhibited for others who speak with an own-accent. This is produced by an unconscious emotional reaction just because we like it. Simple as that. This theory has developed, and draws support, from neuroscientific research investigating affective prosody (a key component underlying accent) and vocal emotion, which activates the important brain regions associated with the processing of emotion, predominantly the right hemisphere. The amygdala once again plays a role in detecting the social relevance and importance of the specific contexts. It is also possible that own-accent bias is due to the fact that own-accents are similar to the prototype of an accent stored in our brains as a social norm, and so they are easier to process and categorise than out-group accents, which are more dissimilar than the prototype. The further away a voice is from the average stored in our brain, the more distinctive and less attractive it is rated.

***

We have seen that people are more likely to pay attention to and remember the negative messages about a rival political party than even the positive messages of their own party. Brain imaging has also shown that people judge the news of corruption within their own party less harshly than the same news from a rival political party. Researchers from Madrid Open University studied this partisan bias with supporters of local rival parties PSOE and PP (socialist and conservative political parties respectively). The supporters ranked their parties 9 or 10 on a scale of 1 to 10 as to the strength of their support, hence indicating a very strong membership and sense of belonging to their in-group. The supporters underwent brain scans while they were exposed to written negative messages about party corruption and some other, more positive messages. The participants had to judge how much they penalised or supported the practices described in response to these messages. The messages about corruption showed the most activation in concerned sections of the brain, reaffirming the theory that we tend to remember and pay more attention to negative news and facts than to positive information. Statements about political corruption were associated with stronger activation of the anterior insula, dorsomedial prefrontal cortex, amygdala, orbitofrontal cortex, thalamus, precuneus, middle frontal gyrus, and inferior parietal gyrus, all regions associated with the processing of punishment, risk, disappointment and rejection. When exposed to messages about the rival party, the brains of PP (conservative) voters showed stronger activation than the left-wing voters in the orbitofrontal cortex and the thalamus (both areas linked to risk and ambiguity) regardless of whether the information was about corruption or positive actions. Positive political messages were associated with activation of the anterior cingulate cortex. The results reveal that negative political messages exerted the greatest impact on the brains of the voters. These results also indicate that the partisan bias against the rival parties was relatively more significant to people than any positive bias towards their own party.

It can also be reliably shown through brain imaging that people are not just favourably inclined towards people who are the same as them (in-group favouritism or familiarity and confirmation bias) but also often actively biased against those who are outside their group (out-group derogation). Mamdooh Afdile – a filmmaker studying for a PhD in neuroscience at Aalto University – decided to use cinema to explore this. Afdile created a 20-minute stimulus film exploring biases in two social groups: 14 self-identifying heterosexual and homosexual men. He wanted to see if watching the movie biased the viewers subconsciously towards the test subject, whose face he flashed for the audience for 40 milliseconds before and after the movie. The bias around sexual orientation is different from race or gender, as it cannot be formed just by looking at someone's face. The subconscious response to the face of the test subject after seeing the movie compared to before seeing it was significantly different between the two groups, and this result was not symmetrical. The results from the heterosexual group showed a very mild negative bias response; interestingly, those from the homosexual group showed a very strong response in brain regions associated with in-group empathy, such as the medial prefrontal cortex, frontal pole, anterior cingulate cortex, right temporal parietal junction, and bilateral superior frontal gyrus. In previous research, these brain areas have been connected to social perception, self-referential thinking and favouritism. This study shows that the brain can respond in a biased way to traits that we don't detect using our basic senses, and that are based on learned knowledge and not only external factors.

The various studies in neuroimaging have therefore shown that our brain has two facets. The first facet is the reflective system, where the key function is for controlled processing of conscious, explicit processes and the brain requires time to reflect. Here, motivation and effort are required to engage this part of the brain. The second facet is the reflexive system, where the automatic processing takes place. It is possible for the reflexive system to interpret a stimulus differently to the reflective one, so while the intention and motivation might be to be fair and just and treat everyone equally, the implicit and the quick response might be for self-enhancement and to protect oneself from any threat.

Research using fMRI has given us an insight into how we respond to biases at a neural level, and how inter-group prejudices activate the areas of our brain associated with threat and fear. It has also given us more insight into the way we form in-group favouritism and associations, and how negative out-group biases are even more prominent than in-group empathy. We respond more strongly to negative news and information than to positive stimuli. Much of the neural research has been based in research using face perception, as that is the first stimulus we usually have that shapes trust and bias. However, these results are not foolproof. Investigating why we favour one person over another poses many challenges, since critical neurocognitive mechanisms involved in this behaviour are to a large extent automatic and implicit. There are also parallel implicit and explicit processes that can lead to inconsistent findings, especially when different stimuli and activation methods are used across different experiments. Often, even when people show tolerance at a conscious level, this is not necessarily an indication that they do not carry implicit biases and that they can be suppressed by these explicit expressions. This makes it difficult to measure and report response to implicit biases.

Knowing about our brain and its inner workings tends to fascinate us, and fMRI investigation gives us crucial insight into how our brain holds the key to the formation of our automated and unconscious biases. This research also shows that – based on the neuroscience principles of brain plasticity, which means the brain can change with experience and environmental influences – we can perhaps change our automated responses if we change our environmental influences and cues. The research here also has potential to show that our cognitive responses are a factor of our social context, based on the range of neuroscience experiments conducted using different settings and priming information. We can also better understand the interaction of biology and interpersonal behaviour. However, much like any other scientific technique, the limitations of fMRI should be understood and acknowledged. There are ethical considerations in the use of neuroimaging as well, which are beyond the scope of this book. To understand the underlying neural landscape of cognitive biases better, we need to ensure that the absence of activity in a brain region does not necessarily imply that it is not being involved in the creation or reinforcement of a particular bias.

Hereinafter, what would be really useful is to understand if – and how – we can translate knowledge about the neurobiology of our underlying behaviour into designing interventions for addressing bias, especially that which creates stigma and discrimination.

# SECTION II
# SMOKE AND MIRRORS

## CHAPTER FOUR

# Back in Your Box

On 1 March 2019, John Smyly, a police officer in Boulder, Colorado was patrolling the area when he came across Zayd Atkinson on a patio behind a 'private property' sign. He challenged and confronted Mr Atkinson, who was carrying a trash grabber and a bucket, about his presence, and Mr Atkinson showed him a student ID. As the short video first posted on YouTube shows, Zayd continued to collect trash when Mr Smyly radioed for help and became threatened by the student. 'You're probably going to get tasered in a second, because you have a weapon,' Smyly told Atkinson before brandishing his taser. Zayd Atkinson is African-American. The officer hastily socially categorised him as black, which activated his underlying stereotype 'black = threat' and 'black = crime'. He judged and interacted with this individual based on these generalised assumptions without consideration of him as a harmless individual who was not breaking any laws.

We all tend to generalise, but sometimes this has more drastic consequences than on other occasions. Social categorisation occurs spontaneously, and quite quickly when we encounter people around us. Often we don't even realise that we are constantly assigning people membership of different groups, such as race, academic status, social class and gender. Once we assign a social category, we are then more inclined to interact with that individual as per their social category membership rather than as an individual. These judgements are based on a very limited sample dataset, where the conclusions from the limited evidence are then extrapolated to ascribe a certain property to the whole group. Research by Louise Pendry and C. Neil Macrae in 1994 showed that there is a dynamic interaction of cognitive and motivational factors in the formation of stereotypes. Stereotypes are acquired effortlessly, and we're more likely to rely on them when cognitive load is high (such as when we're distracted, tired or in a hurry). For instance, in an experiment they found that when college students were distracted for 25 seconds with a request to remember an eight-digit number, they were more likely to remember stereotypic attributes about another person. Stereotypes are also activated more quickly when the target individual matches one or more of the attributes more closely. It is then easy to hypothesise that if the target matches some of the characteristics, they should match all the characteristics of a stereotype.* Once a stereotype has been established, the target person is viewed from the assumptive lens of the perceiver rather than the actual information of the target itself. In this way, stereotypes become a self-fulfilling prophecy.

The first time the word 'stereotype' was recorded was in 1922 by the journalist Walter Lippmann. He used it to describe the cognitive and behavioural patterns of humans to depict pictures in our minds that represent the 'strange connection' between facts and reality and our subjective interpretation of them. The word had been used prior to this but in a completely different context: it had been coined in 1798 by the French printer Didot, and had originally referred to a printing process where fixed and similar cast reproductions are produced. In their landmark paper in the *Annual Review of Psychology* in 1996, James Hilton and William von Hippel, psychologists from the

---

* This is termed a fallacious generalisation.

University of Michigan and Ohio State University respectively, stressed that stereotypes are 'mental representations of real differences between groups [...] allowing easier and more efficient processing of information.' Stereotypes are selective. They are localised around features of a group that are the most distinctive and distinguishable, and that allow us to maintain the least differentiation between different members of the same group, and the most differentiation between members of different groups. Charles Judd and Bernadette Park from the University of Colorado call this a related 'kernel-of-truth hypothesis', implying that stereotypes are almost always based on some empirical reality but that they will always entail overestimation and exaggeration.

The formation of a stereotype can be linked to Tversky and Kahneman's cognitive heuristics and shortcuts (discussed in Chapter 1). When people overestimate the likelihood of a characteristic in a particular social group, then stereotypes are activated, such as the idea that all Asian people are good at maths because, on average, they might be better at maths than any other group. But that does not mean that each Asian person is better at maths than every non-Asian person. However, it is often easier to arrive at that conclusion rather than taking the time to judge each person on their own individual merit. In doing so, the differences between the groups are not only highlighted but also exaggerated. As a result, when people think of this group, they tend to focus on what is most distinctive about the group and will neglect any other characteristics. Clearly this has implications for the accuracy and fairness of our decisions.

From stereotype knowledge, we go through a process of stereotype endorsement, activation, categorisation and then application. Stereotype activation is an increased access to knowledge about social groups, while stereotype application is the use of this knowledge in the perception and judgement of others. Stereotype application depends on the stereotype being activated, whereas stereotype activation is independent of stereotype application, as activation does not have to necessarily lead to application. Often our stereotypes are activated because of the information we have seen or received around us, which is then easily available in our episodic memory.[*] In an experiment in 2012, Regina Krieglmeyer and Jeffrey W. Sherman from the University of California, Davis showed pictures of 24 black faces and 24 white faces to student participants, following which blurred black-and-white drawings of faces were used as target stimuli.[†] Based on this, participants were asked to rate the drawings on how threatening or how athletic they appeared. The students were more likely to judge the drawings as threatening or athletic when they had been primed[‡] with black faces rather than neutral or white faces.[§] Facial cues are the primary

---

[*] Our personal unique memory of a specific event, which is different from the memory of the same event by another individual.

[†] A stimulus in a visual display that a person has to respond to in some way during an experiment or a procedure.

[‡] In psychology, priming is an implicit-memory technique in which the introduction of one stimulus influences how people respond to a subsequent stimulus without conscious guidance or intention. It is used in a lot of implicit-memory tasks. For example, a person who sees the word yellow will be slightly faster to recognise the word banana. This happens because the concepts of yellow and banana are closely associated in memory. The word butter is more likely to be better recognised if it follows the word 'bread' rather than 'dog'.

[§] This has been termed the Stereotype Misperception Test (SMT). The SMT is modelled after the Affect Misattribution Procedure (AMP), which is an indirect measure of attitudes. While in the AMP evaluative judgements are made for Chinese characters, here in the SMT trait judgements were made based on faces.

motivators for a stereotype in most cases, as they are often the first thing we notice about other people.* The most prominent dimensions of a person's appearance are usually age, gender and race, unless there is another aspect that is strikingly different and makes a person stand apart (such as a distinct birthmark or a tattoo, for instance). Gender is often the first category we assign, and this is perhaps why it is tricky for some people to understand the notion of non-binary† individuals.

Stereotypes activation and application is often motivated from an 'out-group homogeneity effect', where the tendency is to see out-group members as more alike than in-group members. As a result, out-group members are more likely to be perceived as interchangeable or superfluous and more likely to be stereotyped. People believe that they are likely to have more contact with members of the in-group, and so they take the time and make the effort to collect and organise information about them more carefully than out-group members. For out-group members, they are much happier to resort to quick judgements and rely on abstract information and stereotypes. In some cases, the stereotyping and homogenising of out-group members happens irrespective of how many members of the out-group a person knows. This is specifically pertinent in male/female gender biases, as these gender stereotypes persist even though there is no foreignness between the two groups. Stereotypes are also formed and reinforced by 'in-group favouritism'. Rather than a negative emotion being the motivation for prejudice and bias against the

---

* Voice is another, in which case the accent can act as a cue for stereotypes.
† Non-binary is a spectrum of gender identities that are not exclusively male or female – identities that are outside the gender binary.

out-group members, it is possible that this arises because positive emotions such as kindness, admiration, sympathy and trust are reserved for the in-group members. People can make choices that confirm their self-identity, and self-esteem (as discussed in Chapter 2) and that make them feel good about themselves. This leads to an in-group favouritism and consequently a bias against those who do not contribute to the enhancement of self-worth.

People also tend to resort to stereotypes when they suffer a setback to their self-esteem, and unfortunately prejudice is a way for them to regain their self-worth, to fulfil a need for self-enhancement or to adjust socially. People want to 'fit in' socially and culturally,* and they often have a desire to not appear prejudiced, which can shape the activation, maintenance and application of stereotypes. A research study was conducted with students in 1997 that first showed how self-esteem could be inherently linked with bias and prejudice. In this study, half a group of students were told they scored in the top 10 per cent for their university, and half were told they scored below average. They were then asked to evaluate a Jewish or Italian candidate for a job, in a seemingly unrelated study. The results showed that students who suffered a blow to their self-esteem by being told that they were below average evaluated the candidate more negatively when they seemed Jewish than when they seemed Italian. On the other hand, no difference was found among the students who were given positive feedback about their intelligence. Also, surprisingly, the same students were shown to increase their self-esteem on a self-reported questionnaire after they had devalued the Jewish candidate. The anti-Semitic prejudice was stronger in

---

* This desire to conform to social stereotypes is termed as endorsement.

candidates who suffered a blow to their self-esteem, and in doing so they gained a sense of self-worth. The students who were 'below average' were then asked to address the source of their insecurity and write down a few paragraphs about something they valued. By priming and activating the implicit egotism, the degree of anti-Semitism reduced.

Status hierarchies affect the strength of stereotype activation and application. People higher up in a social hierarchy[*] are more likely to make inaccurate judgements about others and stereotype them, compared to those lower down in the social hierarchy. In fact, those who are perceived to be on the lower rungs of social power (or self-report to be so) naturally have a more precarious social position, and so they allocate more time and energy for social judgements. They are more careful about such judgements and about using stereotypical information. On the other hand, those who have social privilege of any form can allocate their cognitive resources elsewhere and are more likely to use shortcuts that use stereotype-consistent information. There is less of an attempt to disconfirm any stereotypes. These social and status hierarchies are, of course, determined by our social and cultural norms. While being activated by social hierarchies, stereotypes also force people and groups to be identified as higher or lower status. 'Status characteristics theory' states that socially significant and observable characteristics – such as gender and race – form status hierarchies based on relative value, competence and prestige, which are determined according to shared social and cultural beliefs. These

---

[*] Social hierarchies are seen in a broad range of organisms, in ants, bees, primates and fish. One of the most common employed in humans is socio-economic status, but social hierarchies can vary across many different social dimensions, such as wealth, race, education, class, etc.

cultural beliefs then manifest in the form of stereotypes that create the basis for determining the rules for social interaction, evaluation and judgement. For instance, research shows that within the workplace, a white male is assigned higher-status characteristics and so is afforded more prestige and increased influence. Women often lack perceived legitimacy as leaders.

In a research study at the US Naval War Academy, a large-scale military dataset[*] (over 4,000 participants and 81,000 evaluations) was analysed to examine objective and subjective performance measures including a list of 89 positive and negative leadership attributes that were used to assess leadership performance. No differences were found in objective measures such as 'grades', but in the subjective measures women were assigned significantly more negative attributes. Men were described using a range of positive terms such as competent, logical, analytical; women were described as compassionate and enthusiastic. On the negative spectrum, the only two terms that were used for men were arrogant and irresponsible, while for women there were around 10, including temperamental, excitable, vain and indecisive. In the way these 28 attributes were assigned, it is clear that women leaders are judged considerably more harshly, with fewer positive attributes, even when their performance on an objective scale is no different to that of men. If this is indeed the case, then it is easier for men to excel as leaders, and more difficult for women to overcome these beliefs about their leadership abilities, so it becomes a vicious cycle and the stereotype

---

[*] Military datasets were used as the military is an interesting and significant setting to evaluate gender bias given it is a long-standing and traditionally male profession that has, over several decades, according to the researchers, worked to eliminate formal gender segregation and discrimination.

that men make better leaders is perpetuated and reinforced. This would explain why female lawyers with masculine names are more likely to become judges, and there is research to show that 'masculine-looking'* applicants are more likely to be hired than 'feminine-looking' applicants for leadership positions.

Much like any other cognitive representations, these stereotypes are maintained and persist because we tend to believe what we already know about members of the stereotyped categories. Yaacov Trope and Eric Thompson in 1997 found that individuals addressed fewer questions to members of categories about which they had strong stereotypes and that the questions they did ask were likely to confirm the stereotypes they already had. Patricia Devine, Professor of Psychology at the University of Wisconsin-Madison, conducted a series of experiments that laid out the psychological case for implicit racial bias – the idea that it is possible to act in prejudicial ways while sincerely rejecting prejudiced ideas. Even if people don't believe racist stereotypes are true, those stereotypes, once absorbed, can influence their behaviour without their intent or even awareness. We tend to remember the information that confirms our stereotypes better than that which challenges it.

★★★

Traditionally, stereotyping literature has focused on discrete categories of sexual identity, race, gender and so on. The

---

* Here masculine-looking and feminine-looking are being used as per existing social norms and definitions of what masculine and feminine is, and how researchers used it in the study. It does not mean that I agree with these labels or definitions!

'intersectionality* of stereotype' effect is a relatively new framework that is being used to explain how some people can face unique challenges at the intersection of multiple identity groups. The prototypical example of a category often comes to mind more easily. When assessing whether someone is a member of a particular category, the extent to which the person is similar to the category prototype is considered. White women are seen as prototypical of 'women'. Black men are seen as prototypical of 'black people'. 'But black women are seen as neither prototypical of black people nor women,' Rebecca Mohr proposes in her dissertation at Columbia University. In such cases of non-prototypical identities, rather than weighing up racial and gender stereotypes and considering which ones should take priority, there is a conjoined effect to create mutually active compound categories. Although social psychologists Valerie Purdie-Vaughns and Richard Eibach argued that the politics on intersectionality can 'resemble a score-keeping contest between battle-weary warriors,' I believe that it is a very useful framework to understand how some people can fall between the cracks. For instance, when we consider the gender pay gap in the workplace, women of colour can be left out of this discussion, as they are metaphorically invisible due to the additional penalty of their ethnicity.

Stereotype activation for multiple identity groups depends on which specific aspect of a person is perceived

---

* Intersectionality is an analytic framework for investigating categorical inequality. It maintains that looking at inequality linked to any one social division in isolation is misleading because multiple categories of social division (i.e. race, gender, sexuality, class, (dis)ability) intersect in ways that are co-constitutive and mutually reinforcing. Research on intersectionality is an understanding of power that is relational and contingent rather than fixed and binary.

to be more predictive of a person's qualities. When a person is seen to be very feminine and caring, it is likely that this could evoke the stereotypes associated with gender, rather than race, as here it would be understood that these characteristics occur because of the target person being a woman. When an antisocial act is being talked about concerning a white male, then the category 'male' and associated stereotypes are more likely to be activated, while in a similar situation with a black male, the stereotypes associated with race are likely to become more significant.

There is a story narrated by Brent Staples, an African-American reporter. Staples noticed that white passers-by were often uneasy when he went on his night-time strolls. They clutched their purses, avoided making eye contact, and carefully altered their paths to eliminate potential contact with a black man wandering alone at night. Staples then began whistling Vivaldi, to convey a signal that he was educated and nonviolent. Within moments, there was a drastic change in the expressions and body language of others. They did not feel threatened any longer. They did not perceive Staples as just a black man. He was now an upper-class black man, and this altered their perception of him and any stereotypes that they attributed to him because of his race. The intersectionality effect creates a new set of stereotypes that are unique to such a compound category of 'educated or upper-class black man'. While in this case, the intersectionality resulted in a positive stereotype because one category (upper-class) superseded the other (black man), often a multiple identity can create further discrimination according to the 'Intersectionality Invisibility Model'. Intersectional invisibility is the general failure of people to fully recognise individuals with intersecting identities as members of their constituent groups. People with multiple subordinate group identities, such as a 'gay Indian woman', are not perceived to be a prototypical member of any of the single identity groups that they belong to, and consequently they may experience an acute form of bias, which is invisibility discrimination. This leads to subversive oppression of those who are non-prototype since information about them is processed less efficiently and remembered more slowly and less accurately, causing the narratives and experiences of these non-prototypical groups to be ignored and omitted in social history. This invisibility makes them unfamiliar to others, which can lead to neophobia (fear of novelty). Also, since they are unfamiliar, they are less likely to be remembered, influence others or have their voices heard. While prototypical members of oppressed groups might face explicit biases and blatant discrimination, the non-prototypical members of such groups face more subversive and implicit forms of bias. Research by Jessica Remedios and Samantha Snyder that appeared in the *Journal of Social Issues*[*] shows that those individuals who are stigmatised in more than one way (for instance, a 'black woman engineer') felt more invisible and reported greater stereotype concerns than those who had one or zero stigmatised identities. By looking at the intersection of categories, the multiplicity of diverse experiences can be considered, which is essential as we talk about addressing unconscious bias and creating more inclusive communities. When many social identities are stigmatised, they might not be visible immediately, as such individuals can conceal their real self in a public

---

[*] In the Special Issue 'Tell It Like It Is', commemorating the 50th anniversary of Martin Luther King, Jr.

setting for fear of stigma (such as a homosexual footballer, or a religious individual in a secular setting). This is one of the reasons why there is a lack of adequate empirical data concerning LGBTQI+ individuals, especially those in leadership positions and politics. Many people still do not reveal their sexual identity openly because of a fear of discrimination.

Ursula Hess and her team at the University of Quebec showed in 2000 an intersectional effect between gender and emotion. Men are stereotyped as more aggressive and women as more docile. In an experiment conducted by their team, male faces were perceived to be angrier and female faces were perceived to be happier. Stereotypical beliefs regarding emotions are culture-specific, can influence our recall of memories and events, and can also affect gendered socialisation of children. Since women are perceived (at least in Western societies) to be more emotionally expressive than men, they are also expected to smile more. Women may be criticised for not smiling enough* because they are seen as stepping outside a stereotypical cultural and social norm. Since childhood, there is also evidence that emotions are mentioned more when talking to girls than when talking to boys, especially emotions relating to sadness. This can then lead to men being more cautious about expressing emotions, which has been linked to 'toxic masculinity' and the trope that 'boys don't cry'. The American Association of Psychology has suggested strong links between these stereotypical beliefs

---

* This is the basis for the term 'resting bitch face', which is a facial expression that unintentionally appears as if a person is angry, annoyed, irritated or contemptuous, particularly when the individual is relaxed, resting or not expressing any particular emotion. It is applied more negatively to women than to men, while also using the gendered term 'bitch'.

around 'masculinity' and the rise in mental health disorders in men.[*]

The intersectional effect of gender and emotion is also seen in the myth of the 'angry black woman'. Such stereotypes characterise black women as aggressive, ill-tempered, illogical, overbearing, hostile and ignorant without provocation. Although empirical evidence is non-existent that there is any difference between black and non-black women in how they experience and express anger, this stereotype persists in mainstream media and culture. This stereotype was recently highlighted by the media in a furore over a cartoon of Serena Williams. During the US Open final, Williams received a code violation for coaching, a penalty point for breaking her racquet and a game penalty for calling the umpire a 'thief'. She was then depicted in a cartoon in the Australian newspaper *Herald Sun* as a childish figure having a tantrum and spitting the dummy. Similar words have been levelled at former First Lady Michelle Obama in recent years. Michelle has talked about being called an 'angry black woman' on the campaign trail[†] and of how she was perceived to be emasculating her husband. Author Britney Cooper said on an NPR podcast[‡] that 'whenever someone weaponises anger against black women, it is designed to silence them. It is designed to discredit them and to say that they are overreacting, that they are being hypersensitive, that their reaction is outsized.' Blair Kelley, Associate Professor of History at North Carolina State University, says that this has its roots in 19th-century America, when

---

[*] I covered this in my TEDx talk in March 2019, and there is more information in an episode of the podcast 'Outside the Boxes', available on most common platforms.

[†] *New York Post*, 6 July 2019.

[‡] Episode 24, February 2019.

minstrel shows (with comic skits and variety acts mocking African-Americans) became popular. Professor Kelley says in an article on the BBC website that 'black women were often played by overweight white men who painted their faces black and donned fat suits to make them look less than human, unfeminine, ugly. Their main way of interacting with the men around them was to scream and fight and come off angry, irrationally so, in response to the circumstances around them.' This was then perpetuated and reinforced via the 1930s programme *Amos 'n' Andy* through the character of Mrs Sapphire Stevens. Michelle Obama talked about this on *The Oprah Winfrey Show*: 'You think, that is so not me! But then you sort of think, well, this isn't about me,' she said of the 'angry black woman' label. 'This is about the person or the people who write it… We are so afraid of each other, you know?'

★★★

Stereotypes often have their basis in fear and threat, fear of difference and of being confronted with something that is unfamiliar and uncomfortable. If you have watched the Netflix show *GLOW: Gorgeous Ladies of Wrestling* you would have been confronted with a number of stereotypes. When I first watched it, I was really uncomfortable with the way it seemed to reinforce some of these tropes such as 'welfare queen', 'fortune cookie', 'white saviour', and 'Muslim terrorist'. World Wrestling Entertainment (WWE) has had a persistent problem with these stereotypes and the wrestlers built on the audience's biases in order to create conflict and emotion. But, on deeper reflection, it is quickly clear what this television show does. It plays with these stereotypes in an ironic way, challenging and subverting them to toy with the audience's expectations and make them confront their biases in the process. What this show also highlights is how we consume messages about stereotypes and how we internalise and accept them. When the wrestling character 'Beirut', playing a mad terrorist, steps into the ring, the audience starts to respond to her like she's an actual terrorist. They quickly become more and more reactionary, shouting out to her opponent to 'end' her.

Stereotypes are often created out of distorted singular realities, and when these are spread in words and images they become reinforced as biases in the wider subconscious. For instance, the stereotype 'welfare queen' has been used to demonise those on public assistance or state benefits for decades, especially in the US. It's a politically potent image, depicting an undeserving aid recipient getting rich off the backs of taxpayers, a stereotype that is now also prevalent in the UK as 'benefit cheats' and frauds. From Ronald Reagan to Bill Clinton, presidential candidates used welfare reform, and the moniker of 'welfare queen', as political cards. The term is believed to be based on a real person, Linda Taylor, who was identified by the *Chicago Tribune* in 1974 as a person who had committed welfare fraud while driving fancy cars. In 1976, Reagan referred to this case for the first time, to show the way welfare was affecting the economy. He said in one of his presidential speeches, 'In Chicago, they found a woman who holds the record. She used 80 names, 30 addresses, 15 telephone numbers to collect food stamps, Social Security, veterans' benefits for four non-existent deceased veteran husbands. Her tax-free cash income alone has been running $150,000 a year.' And this stereotype stuck. Josh Levin, the author of a new book *Queen,* said in a PBS News hour that, 'I think this idea of the welfare queen was something that was so powerful. I mean, such a strong message politically. And you can see that in how she was arrested for kidnapping in Chicago. She was accused of murder. But all of that information got left out and sanded away. That's not something that Reagan ever mentioned, certainly.' The notion that her welfare scheming and fraud was part of her wider personality disorders and criminal inclinations was left out. The message that she was on welfare, black and defrauded the system remained.

When stereotypes are played out and reinforced in the media, this quickly dehumanises individuals, makes whole groups homogenous, gives us permission to exercise our biases, and normalises such labels. Thessaly La Force, a features editor for the *New York Times*, writes about how films have enabled a stereotypical representation of Asian-American men as helpless and needy, lecherous and creepy, with feminine demeanour.* La Force shows how these jokes echo two of the most pernicious stereotypes of Asian men ever to appear onscreen in Western culture: the detective Charlie Chan, who appeared in a series of films from the 1920s to 1980s, who was neutered and servile; and Fu Manchu, an archetypal evil mastermind whose sinister and predatory behaviour was depicted in novels and media for much of the last century. For instance, a 2013 study by Glenn Tsunokai and colleagues at Western Washington University reported on online heterosexual dating patterns in the 20 largest American cities using 1,270 internet dating profiles. They employed logistic regression to examine the odds of one's willingness to date someone of a specific ethnicity. In this study, it is seen that when Asian people initiated contact, white men replied to Asian women whereas white women rarely replied to Asian men. And, when white men reached out to Asian women,

---

* *New York Times*, 28 August 2019.

Asian women tended to respond to white men over men of their own race. Media depictions shape identity formation, and the way that Asian men are represented – emasculated with a lack of perceived sexuality – has huge cultural and mental health consequences.

★★★

We also often unconsciously employ stereotypes without thinking about the words we are using to describe people. The 'Proud not Primitive'* movement, for instance, was started in India to address how media uses language to talk about tribal communities. Sophie Grig, coordinator of the Proud Not Primitive movement, said, 'We need to stamp out all use of this derogatory and dangerous language with reference to India's tribal peoples. No media should be using these terms.' Often when tribal communities are stereotyped as 'primitive' it creates the perception that they are backward and that they need to be developed and brought into the mainstream rather than be proud of the sustainable ways of life they have developed over generations.† Such attitudes and stereotypes may then be used to justify the takeover of their land in the name of development. Dr Richard King makes a very insightful observation in his 2016 book *Redskins: Insult, Team, Brand*: 'A common belief in the contemporary United States, often

---

* Proud Not Primitive is part of Survival International's worldwide 'Stamp It Out' campaign, which challenges negative stereotypes of tribal peoples. Stamp It Out has been endorsed by UK newspapers and renowned journalists.
† The BBC guidelines on Reporting and Portrayal of Tribal Peoples state: 'We should take care over the use of terms that have the potential to be misleading or discriminatory, such as "primitive", "backward", "savage" or "stone-age".'

unspoken and unconscious, implies that everyone has a right to use Indians as they see fit; everyone owns them. Indian-ness is a national heritage; it is a fount for commercial enterprise; it is a costume one can put on for a party, a youth activity, or a sporting event.' This sense of entitlement, this expression of white privilege, has a long history, manifesting itself in national narratives, popular entertainment, marketing schemes, sporting worlds and self-improvement regimes. Besides this sense of entitlement based on status hierarchy, such descriptions also serve to reduce the experiences of a diverse group into a microcosm of something much larger. The National Congress of American Indians states that, 'There are 567 federally recognized Indian Nations (variously called tribes, nations, bands, pueblos, communities and native villages) in the United States. Approximately 229 of these ethnically, culturally and linguistically diverse nations are located in Alaska; the other federally recognized tribes are located in 35 other states.' Despite this cultural and linguistic diversity, American Indians are largely depicted as violent and aggressive barbarians, perhaps carrying a tomahawk or scalping knife in hand.* Stereotypical language such as savage, pagan, injun, brave, buck, chief, redskin, squaw, papoose and other terms become commonplace. Many of these originally benign words have been removed from their cultural origins and contexts and weaponised, turning them into racial and pejorative labels. Such cultural caricatures are a common form of homogenisation of an entire group – one way that such groups are kept oppressed and marginalised.

---

* You can find more information on this and harmful stereotypes of other marginalised groups too at www.ferris.edu/HTMLS/news/jimcrow/ (accessed 18 June 2019).

In September 2019, images of the Canadian Prime Minister Justin Trudeau dressed as Aladdin and wearing a 'brownface' for a fancy-dress party were revealed in the media. This has reminded us how Orientalism – or stereotypical, colonialist representations of Asia, especially the Middle East – has been pernicious and persistent. In the 20th century, in books and in media, the Middle East has been portrayed in popular culture as a barbaric world where lecherous sheikhs lived in gaudy palaces among large harems. Even as recent as 1992, the opening song in Disney's version of *Aladdin* contained the lyrics: 'Where they cut off your ear if they don't like your face' and 'it's barbaric, but hey, it's home!' The word 'barbaric' was replaced by 'chaotic' in the 2019 version. The story of Aladdin was not even in the original Arabic-language version of *One Thousand and One Nights* and only first appeared in French in the early 18th century, reflecting a European reimagining of the Arab world and its people. This is one of many examples of fairy tales creating damaging myths and stereotypes. When such stereotypes become widely acknowledged in Western society, people might feel a sense of ownership over these representations and are comfortable adopting these caricatures for their own purposes. Such incidents are reminders of why we need diverse stories.

★★★

Stereotypes and prejudice are evidently interlinked. They can fuel anti-group movement, mass hysteria and support for discriminatory policies, as we have seen with Islamophobia since the events of 9/11 in the United States. Muniba Saleem, an assistant professor at the Institute of Social Research, University of Michigan, gives numerous examples of how media representations of Muslims fuel anti–Muslim hostility and policies in America, and reinforce the bias that 'all Muslims are terrorists'. Such stereotypes have led to political candidates calling for increased surveillance of the Muslim American community, potentially closing down mosques, and requiring Muslim Americans to register to a database. Jack Shaheen, an award-winning screenwriter, showed in his 2014 book *Reel Bad Arabs* how more than 900 Hollywood films stereotype Muslims as 'brutal', 'cruel' and 'uncivilised', and with ongoing egregious smearing of Arabs this creates a distorted singular view of the community.

Often, implicit stereotypes emerge in casual offhand remarks that seem inconsequential. I've been doing an informal study on the very first thing strangers often say to me. Here are my favourite four so far:

'How long are you in the UK for?'
'Your English is *really* good.'
'When did you last go back home?'
'I love a good curry.'

All pretty benign and mostly well meaning, I would say. In most of these cases, there is a genuine desire to learn and to form a human connection, even if only on a superficial level. However, if I dig deep, each of these provides clear evidence of implicit bias based on the social, cultural and religious stereotypes that people carry of others who look like I do: a brown person, a woman. I carry the burden of being stereotyped as the 'perpetual foreigner'*, one who is never truly perceived as British.

---

* This term was originally used to define the alienation that Asian-Americans have felt in the USA, but is now being applied to other ethnic minority groups too.

I will tell you a story of a warm, sunny summer's day in 2009. This was in a small, friendly town somewhere in the middle of England, home to me and to my daughter. One day while out shopping for my daughter's new school uniform and shoes, we were laughing and giggling as we wandered through the narrow streets. It had been one of those idyllic afternoons where I had loved every moment I had spent with her. As we went back to the car park, a police officer approached and stopped us. He was armed. He wanted to see my ID, and to find out who I was and where I lived. My then nine-year-old looked confused and I could see the fear on her face. It transpired that while we were out harmlessly shoe-shopping, another customer had called the police because we 'looked suspicious', because we 'looked like shoplifters', because we 'looked like we were up to no good'. Their words, not mine. We were the only non-white people in that town and community, so I suppose it was no surprise that we had been racially profiled. This person had seen us (or me) and had made a snap judgement based on my skin colour. If asked, I doubt strongly they would admit to being racist or prejudiced. They were merely doing their duty as an 'active and conscientious citizen'. But stereotypes are harmful. It affected me and more so my young daughter. It changed her perception of who she was and of how she fitted into this place she called home.

It is never the explicit biases and prejudiced attitudes that hurt the most; it is the more insidious, subversive and implicit attitudes that do the greatest harm. Research published in the journal *Developmental Psychology* has shown that a 'perpetual foreigner' stereotype is related to discriminatory victimisation experiences, which increase the risk of depressive symptoms. A survey in 2012 conducted by the National Hispanic Media Coalition (NHMC) and Latino Decisions demonstrated how the stereotypes about

Latinos in the United States, especially those perpetuated by the media and the political agenda, centre on narratives around illegal immigrants. The report shows that a high percentage of non-Latinos considered Latinos and 'illegal immigrants' to be the same. Over 30 per cent of respondents believed that more than 50 per cent of all Latinos were undocumented. The immigration debate has altered the perception of Latinos (who comprise more than 18 per cent of the country's total population), and the normalisation of the word 'illegal' has dehumanised a whole group of people. The problem with recognising and countering some of these stereotypes is that often the implicit bias is already deeply ingrained and difficult to address, more so because of the hidden nature of the bias. But, additionally, countering these socially entrenched biases often requires going to the other extreme to swing the weight of the collective cognitive representation far enough. This can then be problematic as it could result in a reinvented set of stereotypes.

Stereotypes can vary in content and in salience as per context, but also they can be contradictory, with an inherent duality. In literary studies, critics such as Homi Bhabha and Rey Chow have theorised that cultural stereotypes prevail because they work through repetition and ambivalence, easily shifting between contradictory meanings: Indian parents are overbearing and pushy; Indian mothers are too controlling; Indian mothers are very nurturing and loving. How many of these stereotypes do we regularly see on television and in films? Shows such as *The Simpsons* and *The Kumars at No. 42* depict characters such as Apu as corner-shop owners – often deeply religious and with large, close-knit families – or such as Rajesh Koothrappali from the sitcom *The Big Bang Theory* as educated and aspirational but still socially awkward and rebelling against a strict upbringing. This skewed representation and narrative contributes to the lack of understanding and the irrational constructions of their perceived identity. Jennifer Hernandez in her analysis of the autobiographies of Richard Rodriguez and V.S. Naipaul arrives at a dual stereotype that South East Asian people are either too eager or too awkward to assimilate. In much of the colonial culture, the 'native' or 'ethnic' is stereotyped as both indolent and lascivious. However large the country might be, such identities end up becoming a 'combined construct', too visible and invisible at the same time.* So much popular media creates a narrative around trains overcrowded with people, cows roaming the streets, bodies floating in the Ganges, the pervasive smell of curry, that the implicit descriptors associated with all these representations are 'disgusting' and 'parochial'. Stereotypes lead to prejudice and discrimination, and dehumanising of the individual experience and stories. In 2010, President Barack Obama commented on how these prevailing stereotypes of Indians were adversely affecting India–United States relations, and that such stereotypes have 'outlived their usefulness'.

'Immigrant' as a stereotype and the immigrant achievement gap is on the political agenda across the world currently and has become an important talking point. As per an Organisation for Economic Co-operation and Development (OECD) report in 2010, immigrant students score lower in achievement tests than non-immigrant students, and they leave school earlier. In most places, immigrant groups are faced with negative stereotypes, although not all immigrant stereotypes are negative and not in all contexts. For instance, Hispanic students have a

---

* 'In Beijing, Indians are seen as stereotypes or not seen at all', Krish Raghav, *Quartz*, 31 December 2012.

negative stereotype in academic situations, whereas Asian students are seen as diligent and high achievers. The burden of being the 'token' representative of a community or a group against which such stereotypes are held can be huge. It can cause self-consciousness and an impairment of the cognitive functioning and memory, due to the supra-awareness of the environment and attempts to suppress any stereotypes. The sense of threat to self-identity is activated, also causing affective responses such as stress and anxiety. Just being in the minority among others who would be stereotyped as more successful or the 'norm' can create this threat. This is the notion of a benevolent stereotype or a model minority.

Richard Jones[*] said in an interview in the investigative news magazine *Mother Jones*, 'There is something about the Asian girls. They are cute. They are smart. They have a kind of thing going on.'

When Laura Kim, an editor for digital storytelling at *The Times*, expressed a desire to be promoted, her ex-boss said: 'You're so good at what you do. [...] Normally, Asian women keep their heads down and stay very quiet.' Laura has spoken about how these words have been branded on her brain since then.

One might argue that these are positive stereotypes. We might think that positive stereotypes serve to address the injustice and go towards balancing the inequalities. With the recent emphasis on diversity, and a drive to demonstrate multiculturalism within personal and institutional spaces, there is a strong motivation to make positive statements about members of traditionally marginalised social groups. People, of course, find it easier to express positive

---

[*] The self-proclaimed prophet of the racist alt-right movement.

stereotypes more explicitly too. Positive stereotypes might be flattering and innocuous, but they also demonstrate insidious bias and – in the case of different ethnic communities – they perpetuate the idea of 'model minorities': the trope that if all minorities worked as hard and were as diligent, they would be as successful as the model minority. This then creates competition and division between the different minority communities themselves. The notion of model minority also promotes the idea that the only way to gain respect and acknowledgement is to work hard, not be any trouble and accumulate an impressive list of accomplishments.

A study by John Oliver Siy and Sapna Cheryan published in 2013 in the *Journal of Personality and Social Psychology* shows that positive stereotypes such as 'Asians are good at maths' and 'women are nurturing' evoke negative reactions because they interfere with the desire to be seen as individuals separate from their groups. So, when someone tells me that 'you are really good at science (for a woman)', despite it being complimentary, it is establishing a depersonalised form of bias. When individual achievement is diminished because of the group membership and an associated stereotype, it can create anger and annoyance, as has been demonstrated in several research studies with Asian-American students. 'Of course, they are good at maths. They are Asian' becomes a call to reduce the individual to a racial group membership and devalue their achievement as something inevitable.

Aaron Kay and colleagues from Duke University claim in the *Journal of Experimental Social Psychology* that positive stereotypes are an insidious means of promoting antiquated beliefs about different social groups. They even go as far as to suggest that positive stereotypes are more detrimental than negative ones for an egalitarian social perception of these target social groups. Saying that 'African-Americans are superior athletes' creates a misconception that any negative stereotypes for these groups have been neutralised. Such notions can reinforce the idea that differences between black people and white people are biological, and perpetuate the dangerous notion of race being a biologically determinant category rather than a spectrum. Interestingly, in their study, positive stereotypes tend to lead to stronger negative beliefs about black people than negative stereotypes. The researchers suggest that positive stereotypes 'may be uniquely capable at reinforcing cultural stereotypes and beliefs that people explicitly eschew as racist and harmful.' A positive stereotype and a negative stereotype, therefore, go hand in hand without us realising it. A strong athletic and physical ability can equate to the incorrect assumption of lower cognitive ability, or a nurturing side can be the flip side to not being authoritative enough and perceived as a leader. It is yet another form of double-bind bias.

Positive stereotypes serve to justify the existing inter-group inequalities. They are such untypical forms of bias that they tend to fly under the radar of any attempts to address injustice and inequalities. Bias and stereotypes have been associated with negative categorisation and hostility for so long that anything less threatening than that can be considered a positive shift. Positive stereotypes create a duality: they reek of favouritism while also applying depersonalisation. The American psychologist Gordon Allport said, 'People may be prejudiced in favour of others; they may think well of them without sufficient warrant.'

In a *New York Magazine* piece in 2017, Andrew Sullivan repeated an oft-quoted trope that Asian-Americans, with their 'solid two-parent family structures', are the perfect example of how to overcome discrimination, as they had turned negative stereotypes into positive ones through sheer hard work. Besides dismissing the systemic inequities facing other marginalised communities such as African-Americans, this also projected a monolithic image of the Asian-American community, ignoring the vast disparities within the group (such as research showing that Bhutanese-Americans are much poorer than Japanese-Americans). By using a section of the community as a 'model', such a statement also trivialises the other barriers and challenges individuals might still be encountering, and it alienates those members of the community who do not conform to these stereotypes. Such sweeping generalisations also create prescriptive expectations that can impose pressure on the person, and lead them to perform poorly on that measure, as well as distracting from the task in hand. This also means that often the members of the stereotyped communities would internalise these persistent and pervasive messages and limit themselves to particular domains where they feel they would be seen more favourably. For instance, young women when told that they are 'more creative' or 'more nurturing' might pick up the message that they would be more suited to a particular career that aligns with their inherent abilities and forgo aspirations to enter domains such as science and technology, where they might not be seen as favourably. This might be a way for women to protect themselves from the hostile sexism that they could otherwise encounter. Asian students might consider themselves more suited to science and maths and less to creative subjects, and they might feel pressure to not only conform to these positive stereotypes but also selectively self-stereotype themselves to avert the possibility of a negative stereotype. This becomes a way of self-preservation that, although in the short term creates a sense of safety and well-being, in the long run means the community becomes a materialisation of the stereotypes and social norms that the individuals were trying to avoid in the first place.

Since positive stereotypes tend to be prescriptive rather than descriptive (which is often the case for negative stereotypes), they can lead to more rigid and deterministic views of the stereotyped communities, thereby making them even more marginalised. In this way, the stereotypes work to isolate them, not allowing them the freedom to move away from stereotypical associations, and always be viewed as the 'other'. Women are more likely to face this benevolent sexism. When someone talks about chivalry, or that 'women are more deserving of respect', in some cases this can create a feeling of well-being for women; however, in other cases it reinforces the idea that women are defined by their biological sex, that they need to be taken care of and looked after by men because they are somehow weaker than men. According to L'Heureux Lewis-McCoy, a professor of sociology and black studies at the City University of New York, what is most problematic about positive stereotypes is that they become so mainstream that it is easily forgotten how they emerged in the first place. In an NPR podcast, he explains that 'we tend to miss the things that shape their opportunity.' For instance, the notion of 'strong black women' or 'angry black women' stems from the fact that they had to be stronger and more resilient to overcome obstacles because the world was an unfair place for them, with racial injustice, sexism and slavery. When such tropes are maintained, it can lead to the conclusion that these women do not need support or a fair world because they are already strong.

Positive stereotypes such as 'Asian people are good at maths' can be activated when the participants were primed with race-related questions, so there is a stronger sense of self-identity and group membership when undertaking a test. This has been shown to improve the performance of the target group, which is termed the stereotype lift[*] or boost.[†] For instance, in small group tutorials at Cambridge University, men often outperform their female counterparts, tending to be more outspoken and at ease expressing their opinions because they are aware of the positive stereotype identities associated with being 'male'. At the same time, they are aware at some level of the negative stereotypes of women, and this can give them extra motivation and further enhance their performance. However, positive stereotypes create stress and anxiety too, and people can 'choke under pressure'. The promise of being viewed through a positive stereotype ultimately sets up the individual (and the community) to fail, according to Jennifer Lee, Professor of Sociology at the University of California, Irvine. She has noted how this pressure to conform to the image of a high achiever, and the pressure to excel, may lead to depression and suicide among the Asian-American community. Furthermore, as it creates a bias that their achievements are due to their group membership and their biology rather than their own individual achievement, they are judged by a harsher yardstick. Thomas Espenshade and Alexandria Radford from Princeton University found that Asian-Americans need a nearly perfect Standardised Admissions Test (SAT) score of 1,550 to have the same chance of being accepted into one of the top universities as white students

---

[*] Stereotype lift means that the individuals who are aware of negative stereotyping of out-groups can elevate self-efficacy and motivation after comparison with the denigrated out-groups, resulting in improved performance.

[†] Stereotype boost is the positive result of activation of positive stereotyping, which refers to the performance improvement of individuals in situations when their positive stereotype identities are activated.

who scored 1,410 and African-Americans who scored 1,100. This has also been referred to as the 'Asian Tax', arising out of the implicit bias bolstered by positive stereotypes. Not all Asian-Americans are the same; not all have the same academic ability. Certain students, who are not as academically able, are disadvantaged by the positive stereotypes of their group.

In a research study published in 2018 in the *Asian American Journal of Psychology*, Shruti Mukkamala and Karen Suyemoto from the University of California, Irvine and the University of Massachusetts Boston respectively examined the intersectional benevolent stereotypes of an 'Asian woman'. In popular media – television, films and books – Asian women have long been stereotyped as either a 'geisha' – docile, passive, submissive, subservient – or a 'dragon lady' – manipulative and untrustworthy, brittle and shrill. Their representations veer from quiet and invisible to being seen as sexual objects. The lazy and discriminatory hyper-sexualisation and fetishization of Asian women (primarily by white men) solely based on race is termed 'Yellow fever' and is not uncommon. These stereotypes are usually first disseminated through popular media and then transcend the confines of the media and manifest themselves in everyday society. Louis Theroux created a documentary on the splurge of matrimonial agencies in Bangkok aimed at helping middle-aged white men find young Thai wives because they believed them to be soft-spoken and nonconfrontational. In the *Australian Sydney Morning Herald*, Jessica Tu writes of her own personal experience of how these stereotypes are enforced on her just because of her Asian racial heritage as someone who would be 'sweet in the kitchen' and a 'tiger in the bedroom'. Diversity has been a huge issue in Hollywood, and Asian women are so often cast for their exoticism.

The South Korean actress Claudia Kim was recently cast as Nagini – the snake – in J.K. Rowling's *Fantastic Beasts* series, a move that was criticised for perpetuating the hyper-sexualisation and exotification of East Asian women. While all women might face sexualisation because of their gender, hyper-sexualisation is the objectification of a person because of their race or ethnicity. R.O. Kwon, author of *The Incendiaries*, recounts[*] her personal experience of being complimented by strangers as 'adorable, cute, silky, shiny'. The pervasiveness of benevolent bias and prejudice is evident in the words people have used to describe Marie Kondo, the Japanese-American tidying-up consultant, a case in point being the three white feminists who called Kondo 'pretty little pixie' with 'fairylike delicacy' on Twitter.

Vanessa Ntinu, a 21-year-old writer, also recounts her own personal experience of being hyper-sexualised in Madrid because of her identity as a black woman. She was called a whore, assumed to be a sex worker and sexually harassed in broad daylight. The intersectional effect of bias here is mediated via a stereotype of 'black woman = promiscuous and unchaste' underlined by their representations in popular media as 'raunchy woman', 'angry black woman', 'baby momma', 'black Barbie', 'gold-digger' or 'welfare queen'. These are stereotypes that a research firm partnered with *Essence Magazine* uncovered in a survey of 901 black women. Thirty of the women surveyed kept visual diaries for one and a half weeks, logging the media images they saw. Stereotypes were pervasive, with their images going from one extreme to another. The harmful effects of stereotype are indisputable.

---

[*] In an article in the *New York Times* (23 March 2019).

It is not just Asian and black women who are stereotyped. In the 2019 Champions League match between Tottenham Hotspur and Liverpool, Son Heung-min became the second Korean footballer to play in a Champions League Final and the first one to score. He is one of the most expensive players signed by the club. Dr Hyun-Joo Lim, a senior lecturer in sociology at Bournemouth University, says* that Europe views Asian players as first and foremost 'good workers'. The coverage of Son tends to focus a lot on his 'hard work, his discipline, his filial piety'. She argues that it is difficult to afford him the status of a superstar, as superstars are understood to be prodigious and bestowed with natural talent, rather than industrious and diligent. The football journalist Rory Smith says that such stereotypes have been a barrier to recruiting more Asian players because other players, scouts and coaches expect them to be a certain kind of person, an obedient citizen but not a superstar. Asian people are seen as formulaic, cold, inexpressive and unemotional. The 'robotic and automaton' stereotype abounds – the model minority who memorises by rote, the non-spontaneous technicians raised by Tiger Moms on Suzuki music† training from a young age but falling short on emotive expression. Despite some of the leading classical musicians being of East Asian heritage, such as Sarah Chang, Yo-Yo Ma and Lang Lang – who have excelled not only technically but also in their

---

* In an article in the *New York Times* (30 May 2019).
† The Suzuki method is an internationally known music curriculum and teaching philosophy dating from the mid-20th century, created by Japanese violinist and pedagogue Shinichi Suzuki. The method aims to create an environment for learning music which parallels the linguistic environment of acquiring a native language. Children often start this very young as they don't need to learn how to read music, but instead learn to play by ear.

interpretation and expression of the music they perform –
these stereotypes persist.

The UK-based charity Stonewall, in their 2004 report
'Understanding Prejudice: Attitudes towards minorities',
states that benevolent prejudices serve to justify and mask
hostile attitudes and biases. For instance, gay men are
stereotyped as 'fun' and 'caring', 'more feminine than
straight men' and 'into fashion, have tidy apartments, and
love Madonna'. Movies and television often show them as
a sidekick, the 'gay best friend'. They can't just be dull and
boring, staid and regular; they always have to be funny,
with an uncanny understanding of women. Not only does
this create a bias that a gay person looks and acts a certain
way, it also immediately isolates any young person growing
up and identifying as gay who does not conform to these
stereotypes. It can cause a huge crisis of confidence and
identity, and affect their mental health and well-being.
Ashley Brooks, a psychology researcher at Anglia Ruskin
University who is conducting a study into 'ambivalent
homoprejudice', says that 'these stereotypes can be
exhausting' – a sentiment echoed by the stand-up comedian
Hannah Gadsby in her groundbreaking show *Nanette*. She
bemoans the exuberant, party-going stereotype of the gay
community, when she wants to sit at home and have a quiet
cup of tea, asking, 'Where are my people?'

In essence, stereotypes of any sort are bad – even if they
are positive – because they lead to group-based biases, and
they give out the message that people can purport to know
everything about an individual based on their group.

★★★

Our stereotypes do not just affect our behaviour towards
others but also our beliefs about ourselves. The threat of

these stereotypes can create social and educational inequalities. The stereotype threat is the fear that our performance may be viewed through a biased lens. The fear of being judged and stereotyped can affect performance on important tasks. When stereotypic representations of behaviour are activated, related behaviours are also activated. These activations can be induced in laboratory conditions through 'priming', where the participants are introduced to stereotypic words and images before their behaviour or actions are recorded in response to a set of instructions.

According to an integrative model of stereotype threat, this state is characterised by a sense of physical discomfort, as the interplay of a physiological stress response, increased monitoring of the performance situation, and the regulation of negative thoughts and emotions. It happens both on the cognitive and affective side, where an impairment in cognitive processing and thought is observed and more attention is paid to try and overcome any stereotypes. When an individual is acutely aware of a negative stereotype relevant to the task at hand and fearful of the discrimination that could result from the bias, they are more stressed and anxious, more self-conscious about their performance and consciously try to suppress any negative thoughts. This is more likely to happen in situations where our self-concept and identity is very important, and when we are performing those important tasks that are crucial for self-enhancement, such as sitting an exam. This has an impact on our working memory,* increasing heart rate, blood pressure, and level of cortisol as a response to the perceived threat, and reduces cognitive resources available to focus on the task, thereby

---

* The part of short-term memory concerned with immediate conscious perceptual and linguistic processing.

affecting performance. These physiological reactions are often subconscious, such as increased cardiovascular activation when women in a science and technology conference setting were shown videos of how men are better at maths and science than women. People facing stereotype threat are more likely to be extra vigilant around others. When people are worried that they might confirm a stereotype by performing poorly, their fear can unconsciously make the stereotype become self-fulfilling. The repeated exposure to stereotypes also leads to internalising of these biases.

Stereotype threat can undermine academic learning. In 1995, psychologists Joshua Aronson and Claude Steele carried out a word-completion experiment with groups of African-American and European-American students. The results showed that when the African-American students were aware of the significance of the test as a diagnostic test, they performed more poorly. Their self-evaluation of the stereotypes associated with the African-Americans activated the stereotype and affected their performance. Steele calls this 'racial vulnerability', leading to a self-actualisation of others' views of one's racial identity and associated bias and taking on a 'victim's mentality'. This view is outdated now, since it puts the onus back on the one being discriminated against and facing bias, but the principle that one can internalise an inferiority anxiety remains true and has been shown by numerous other studies. The individual does not even have to believe in the stereotype themselves, as this can happen subconsciously. Instead, the mere awareness and suspicion that such a stereotype exists and is perceived to be true is enough to activate the stereotype threat and cause individuals to perform poorly. It is a reason why girls might underperform in science and maths at school, even as early as primary school, as stereotype threat is heightened in such traditionally male domains. While observing how girls and boys learn in a maths classroom, even though textbooks and teachers are the same and the students are being treated the same, Steele wondered: 'Is it possible, that they could still experience the classroom differently, so differently in fact as to significantly affect their performance and achievement there?' The messages they get from the people around them might make them aware of the stereotype and it can even affect how quickly they learn novel concepts, and their performance on tasks of perceptual learning.* In engineering or science departments, the stereotypes can be activated in classes with very few female students, and where the instructor is male too.

In 2017, less than 30 per cent of applications in UK universities to economics, computer science, mathematics and natural sciences – subjects typically seen as male-dominated – were from women. The opposite effect was seen for subjects such as history of art and education – typically seen as soft subjects attracting more women than men. One male student, 'Ben', told me that he wanted to study history of art but was concerned that it was a feminine subject and that he would be perceived as taking the 'easy way out'.† Undergraduate examination results show how stereotype threat can influence learning and performance. For computer science alone, the proportion of students

---

* Examples of perceptual learning tasks include differentiating two musical tones from one another or categorisations of spatial and temporal patterns as in reading and playing chess, etc. Perceptual learning is employed in everyday life to make distinctions between two closely related and overlapping categories. These effects are described as the result of categorical perception.

† Besides the masculine–feminine binary trope, this is also inherently sexist to associate a female-dominated subject as being 'easy'.

gaining a good honours degree is significantly higher for
male students than female students over the last 10 years,[*]
giving the perception that men are better at such technical
subjects. These statistics can deter women from applying to
this course, giving them the perception that they do not
belong there. Valerie Jones Taylor and Gregory Walton
report in the *Personality and Social Psychology Bulletin* that
this a 'double jeopardy', where the women (being the
'underdogs') are under subconscious threat of proving this
stereotype to be true, which makes it difficult for them to
learn new concepts, and feel the pressure to demonstrate
that their learning is on a par with the men.

Matthias Mehl along with Toni Schmader from the
University of British Columbia and their doctoral students
examined how the stereotype that women talk more than
men could affect women's disengagement with academia,
especially in traditionally male-dominated STEM
disciplines. They collected data from 396 participants who
wore a voice recorder that sampled ambient sounds for
several days. Participants' daily word use was extrapolated
from the number of recorded words. The results showed
that both male and female participants spoke around 16,000
words every day and the stereotype of female talkativeness
was unfounded. However, this stereotype persists (and is
discussed in more detail in Chapter 7). In a follow-up
experiment, workplace conversations of 45 female and
male STEM faculty were sampled using the Electronically
Activated Recorder.[†] Again, there was no evidence that

---

[*] From Cambridge University examination results for 2009–19.
[†] This is a more naturalistic and unobtrusive method of data
collection, where the device automatically turns itself on and off as
per the programming. It can, for instance, be set to record for 30
seconds every 12 minutes and so gives soundbites from people's
daily lives, and picks up on things that people don't often notice.

women were more talkative than men. However, there was another interesting observation: when male scientists talked to other scientists about their research, it energised them; when female scientists talked to other female scientists they sounded perfectly competent, but when they talked to male colleagues they sounded less competent. The more time the women faculty members spent talking to their male colleagues, the less competent they felt and the more disengaged they became from their work. Here, the threat of being monitored and considered less competent by their male colleagues can force the female academics to worry about it and wonder if they are sounding incompetent. This does not mean in any way that the problem is in the 'women's heads'. On the contrary, the problem lies with the stereotypes prevalent in these fields, as well as with the lack of adequate representation and role models, which makes any female academics feel more aware of the stereotypes and the threat of being stereotyped. This can then drive them to quit science. It is a vicious cycle.

Recently, while researching and writing an article about women in football, I realised that there has been no British Asian female footballer in the England team and hardly any at the development level and club level. This seems extraordinary considering that British Asian people form around 7.5 per cent of the overall population in the UK as per 2018 census figures. The under-representation of British Asian individuals in football can be seen as a sign of natural hierarchies, in a similar vein as the women who disidentify with maths and engineering at university because of a perception of gender bias in these disciplines. This can make them avoid or withdraw from a domain because of the fear of stereotypes. The general consensus from the British Asian women I spoke to during the course of this study was that 'football wasn't for people like us'. 'Bala' told me that she loved football as a young girl, but then very quickly was the only Asian girl in the football team. She had heard stories of racism and bias towards black and minority players in men's football and she did not feel that she belonged in this world. She told me that she could fight against her parents and the wider community, but it was too stressful to try and fit in. She always felt like an outsider. Even the coaches and other players alluded to the fact that she wasn't as physically fit or as good a player, and every time she stepped onto the pitch she felt that she had to prove herself. This started causing her severe anxiety and ultimately she stopped playing. The lack of any role models creates a self-fulfilling cycle where the absence of similar others in a domain is itself a signal that one does not belong or would not be welcome. In this instance, girls from the British Asian community never become identified with football in the first place, thinking it is not for them or that they are likely to face bias and discrimination if they enter this domain.

Humans have an inherent need to belong. Beyond the signals that one could face stereotypes, humans are also sensitive to cues signalling that an individual is not valued or does not belong in a particular context or group. When an individual does not feel valued, they feel a heightened physiological response in the form of stress, which places additional load on their cognitive resources and working memory and can cause them to disidentify. The notion of belonging goes beyond just the threat of stereotype. As opposed to stereotype threat, which is primarily a measure of one's competence, the notion of belonging impinges on a person's sense of social connectedness and value.

The more one is aware of the fear of being stereotyped and facing biases, the more one is keen to avoid any confirmation of these, and the more one is responsive to any cues that hint towards rejection or performance errors. One way that individuals often deal with stereotype threat is by reaffirming their own individual self-identity and disengaging from the larger stereotyped group. This could be one of the reasons why people are reluctant to discuss their identity as a mother in a professional domain, because mothers are continually stereotyped and judged. Only 2 per cent of working women plan to leave the workforce for family reasons, yet 43 per cent of highly qualified women either completely opt out* or step off their career trajectory on their way back to work post-baby. According to research by Gretchen Livingston, a senior researcher at the Pew Research Center, 29 per cent of mothers and 10 per cent of women with a master's degree leave the workforce to care for their families. It is assumed that women are making this decision because they prioritise their families over their work. However, this is not always the case. In a study published by the American Psychological Association, Eden King shows that this discrimination starts the moment a woman announces she is pregnant. Women encountered more subtle discrimination in the form of rudeness, hostility, decreased eye contact and attempts to cut off the interaction when they appeared to be pregnant (wearing a pregnancy prosthesis) while applying for jobs in retail stores than when the same women did not appear to be pregnant. These acts of subtle sexism and microaggressions starting when a woman announces her pregnancy put her firmly on the 'mommy track' and can have a huge impact on her decision to leave the workforce. Experimental social

---

* Lisa Belkin first coined the term 'opting out' in 2003, to describe highly educated, high-achieving women who seemingly chose to 'opt out, ratchet back, and redefine work' after becoming mothers.

psychological data also suggests that the résumé of a mother is rated as showing less competence than the identical résumé when identified as that of a father or person without a child. In this study in 2004, it was shown that simply being labelled as a 'mom' seems to convey that a person is lacking in professional ability. A 2007 study comparing undergraduates and actual employers found that mothers were often more likely than non-mothers to be regarded as poorly motivated to succeed, and as a result working mothers often received a lower starting salary than non-mothers regardless of any difference in qualifications. On the other hand, fathers often receive preferential treatment and higher salaries as they are considered the 'breadwinners' of their family.

In the book *What Works for Women at Work* it has been shown that working mothers are repeatedly forced to prove their worth and competency to their colleagues and employers, and that managers are more demanding that women prove they are as committed and capable as they were pre-baby. Where men (especially fathers) are valued based on their potential, women (especially mothers) are judged on their performance. In several sociological studies, it has also been shown that mothers face more pressure from their managers to prove themselves capable of time management and deadlines. As anyone who has faced severe sleep deprivation in the early months and years of motherhood will understand, this can create a huge amount of additional stress, affecting the mental health and thereby the performance of a working mother. These subtle microinvalidations and stereotypes of mothers as lacking flexibility and commitment means that motherhood is not normalised.

Specific to gender stereotype threat is also the self-objectification theory, where girls and women living in a sexually objectifying culture internalise their objectification as a psychological response to being perceived as sexual objects. This can lead to anxieties related to physical appearance and eating disorders, as well as increased anxiety about safety and shame of self. Men, for instance, when reminded that they are not as good at 'social sensitivity' – typically considered a more 'feminine' trait – can become stressed and fail at decoding nonverbal cues and other affective information. The negative stereotypes, therefore, become a psychological burden and deplete the working memory* resources. Baby-faced men are more likely to go into nurturing professions. Leslie Zebrowitz from Brandeis University in Massachusetts found that baby-faced boys and men stimulate the amygdala, the emotional centre of the brain (as discussed in Chapter 3). Because they face the fear of being stereotyped as such, they are more likely to work hard to overturn these expectations and break the stereotypes by being quarrelsome, hostile, aggressive, academic high-fliers and winners of military honours. The fear of stereotype threat makes them strive for a more aggressive image and can lead to anxiety.

★★★

Both prejudiced and unprejudiced people are aware of stereotypes. One group chooses not to exercise their stereotypical beliefs, while others do. Some people are

---

* As discussed on p. 139, this is a cognitive system with limited capacity, which holds information temporarily, such as the ability to remember and use relevant information while in the middle of an activity (e.g. remembering the steps of a recipe while cooking). The four kinds of memory are: sensory, short-term, working and long-term.

more reluctant to let go of their idea of fixed categories. Else Frenkel-Brunswik* studied young children, some of whom had previously been documented as prejudiced and ethnocentric. She showed the children a sequence of cards[†] that transitioned from an image of a cat to a dog. On the first card, the animal is clearly and distinctly a cat. On the last card, it is just as clearly and distinctly a dog. But in between, the cat slowly transforms into the dog. The children were asked to identify the animal on the card at each stage. It was seen that among those children who had previously shown prejudicial tendencies, there was a greater reluctance to give up the idea of the original object and category. They were more rigid about category boundaries, and they did not do so well with ambiguous transitional categories. For them, the idea of letting go of their original beliefs was more difficult. That is not to say that it was impossible, though. If we evaluate a new person or an out-group member in a slower and more controlled manner, we can have a more non-biased response. We need to consciously take the time to counteract these stereotypes and the environmental messages that we absorb. We need time, intention and adequate cognitive capacity and resources to be aware of the activation of stereotypes and then to significantly reduce the application of any stereotypical beliefs on others around us. We might not be

---

* A post-World War II psychologist who sought to understand why some people seem to find prejudiced and fascist ideas so appealing. Born in 1908 to a Jewish family in what is now Ukraine, Frenkel-Brunswik twice escaped the forces of prejudice herself. When she was young, a 1914 pogrom forced her family to flee to Vienna. When Germany annexed Austria in 1938, she sought refuge in the US.
[†] This was before sophisticated eye-tracking and digital devices, which are often now used to record reaction time.

able to negate all the stereotypical effects, but having the motivation and desire to do so is a good start.

We might all think we have egalitarian views, but good intentions are not enough. We have to watch how our associations could be influencing our behaviour and perception and consequently affecting social justice. In a satirical video 'Racist Glasses' by Rudy Mancuso and Anwar Jibawi, which went viral in 2016, a person picks up a pair of glasses and sees the world through the eyes of a Trump voter. The video cleverly shows how we impose our stereotypes on people when we encounter them: for instance, when two young black men – chatting casually and wearing ordinary clothing for their age – are seen through these glasses, a startling transformation takes place. These men shape-shift into 'thugs' wearing gold chains and holding guns with masks over their faces. This is a visual metaphor of how our implicit associations and stereotypes shape and distort perceptions of other people. Our implicit stereotypes act as a lens through which we see the world.

Yes, we should stand up against egregious stereotypes and question them, I hear you say. You might also assert that you don't always know and realise when you are stereotyping individuals and communities. We might say this happens automatically, but what is crucial to disentangle here is that there are two different processes: stereotype activation and stereotype application. The activation of stereotypes is often an automatic process and is very much dependent on social and cultural norms and the media perpetuation. Stereotypes are maintained because it is easier to do so in most cases than to disprove them, and it is easy to hold on to them because they become such an integral part of our lives, of our social groups and beliefs, of our media messages, and of our social-media echo chambers and tribes. There is empirical evidence that shows stereotypes are developed and maintained by exposure to clichéd media representations*, and these messages influence our thinking and behaviours. The tweets and public rallies vilifying 'foreigners' and 'immigrants' to the cries of 'go home' are not just dangerous in that specific instance, but they would also increase the strength of the automatic association between a group concept ('immigrant' or 'brown person') and a stereotypical attribute ('foreigner', 'ISIS supporter' or 'outsider'), leading to an increase in implicit stereotyping. This stereotype activation might be implicit, but the application and consequences are likely to be explicit, such as a police officer openly positing on Facebook that the American politician and activist Alexandria Ocasio-Cortez should be shot. The media and political representations can sow the seeds of discrimination and prejudice by perpetuating negative stereotypes for a specific social group.

What stereotypes do is create prejudiced attitudes while in turn reinforcing and promulgating implicit biases. What they also do is create a relentless drumbeat that influences

---

* In a study in 2013, 185 participants read a total of 12 newspaper texts in a controlled lab experiment. Within the text, the foreign nationality of the offender was mentioned only once in the headline and once in the body of text in each of the 12 articles. It was found that reading tabloid articles in which a specific social group is presented as criminal influenced readers' explicit stereotypes in which they expressed judgement about the prevalence of criminal foreigners in the real world. The findings also showed that participants' memories were linked to implicit stereotypes in which there was an automatic association between categories of foreign country and criminal. The results support the hypothesis that the mass media's influence is directly linked to forming implicit stereotypes that then may increase the likelihood of applying explicit stereotypes.

social policies and assimilation of stereotyped communities. As the author and activist Chimamanda Ngozi Adichie cautions in her TED talk from 2009: 'The problem with stereotypes is not that they are untrue, but that they are incomplete.' Stereotypes, therefore, pave the way for a broad-brush approach to social and cultural identity, creating a monolithic identification, where individuals are dehumanised as a homogenous mass. A single story is dangerous because when we show a single story, we tell people that this is all they are and all that they can be and, as Ngozi Adichie says, 'And that is what they become.'

CHAPTER FIVE
# Bobbsey Twins

People want to be with people like themselves. They subconsciously choose to engage and interact with people who look like them or have the same beliefs. This is why romantic partners and close friends can sometimes look like each other, a phenomenon called homophily. Homophily – from Ancient Greek ὁμοῦ (*homou*, 'together') and Greek φιλία (*philia*, 'friendship') – is the tendency of individuals to associate and bond with similar others, as in the proverb 'birds of a feather flock together'. Much like regular Bobbsey twins,* who look alike and think alike. Evolutionarily we wanted to stay closer to genetically similar kin and avoided those who looked different, as they might bring contagious diseases or turn out to be aggressive. People tend to cherry-pick people and information that confirms pre-existing beliefs. In *The History of the Peloponnesian War,*† Thucydides described this tendency: 'It

---

* The Bobbsey twins featured in a children's series of books published from 1904 through 1992, written under the pen name Laura Lee Hope. The books chronicled the lives of the Bobbsey family, including two sets of fraternal twins, aged 12 and six. The term 'Bobbsey twins' took on a figurative sense soon after the publication of the first book, and the wholesome stories were easily parodied. Even though the stories are seldom read anymore, the figurative term 'Bobbsey twins' is still occasionally seen.

† A historical account of the Peloponnesian War (431–404 BC), which was fought between the Peloponnesian League (led by Sparta) and the Delian League (led by Athens). It was written by Thucydides, an Athenian historian who also happened to serve as an Athenian

is a habit of humanity to entrust to careless hope what they long for, and to use sovereign reason to thrust aside what they do not fancy.'

You can easily test your confirmation bias. Think of your three closest friends and the people that you usually date. We tend to date the same kind of people as us and are more likely to be close friends with people who are the same ethnicity as us. When people like living with those who are similar, or date those who look and have the same background as them, these preferences can be an indication of an unconscious bias towards people different from them. In an experiment, 174 student participants looked at photos of eight individuals and rated how much they liked them, whether they perceived them to have similar attitudes to them, and how close they would choose to sit near each person given the choice. Participants said they would sit nearer those individuals who resembled them physically, and also thought they would share their attitudes and therefore like them more, and expected to be accepted by them, more so than those who were physically dissimilar to themselves. This effect is much more than just people of the same race or gender aggregating together.

Wolfgang Munchau in the *Financial Times* likens confirmation bias to a drug: 'It is very easy to get hooked on to it and lose all sight of any rational and moral thinking, and it feels very pleasurable to be riding the wave.' As we saw in Chapter 2, if we consider the limited cognitive resources that we have, confirmation bias makes sense. It takes a lot more energy to collect and evaluate new evidence – especially when this information is unclear or

---

general during the war. His account of the conflict is widely considered to be a classic and regarded as one of the earliest scholarly works of history.

we are rushed – than to rely on beliefs and information that we already have. It would be too tiring and time-consuming to evaluate our world-view constantly, so we prefer to strengthen it. As Neil deGrasse Tyson says, 'people prefer reassurance to research', and so we avoid validating what we hear and see. We also prefer to avoid confrontation* and so we select people who agree with us and surround ourselves with them, so the world can become what we believe it to be. Confirmation bias can give us a skewed view of information because we tend to interpret it to reinforce our current views rather than assessing what it actually says. In a Stanford University study, half of a group of students were in favour of capital punishment, and the other half were opposed. Both groups were given details of two of the same fictional case studies to read, and half of the participants were told that one study supported the negative views of capital punishment and the other study opposed it. The other participants were given the inverse information. The results showed that the majority of student participants remained fixed to their original views and, in doing so, pointed to the data that supported it and discarded the evidence that did not.

★★★

Although the world around us is becoming increasingly multicultural, structural issues are often difficult to overcome. If everyone around you is the same as you, it is difficult to try consciously to find friends who do not

---

* This is why people are more likely to hide behind their online personas or anonymous social media accounts to 'pick a fight' because it is easier to do so rather than contradict and debate with someone face-to-face.

belong to the same class, colour and background as you. Even our slight preferences can have a huge impact on larger-scale macro behaviour such as racial segregation of neighbourhoods and cities. Thomas Schelling, a professor emeritus of economics at Harvard and a Nobel laureate, was intrigued by the lack of stable integrated communities in Detroit. He noticed that there was a 'tipping point' in the suburban communities at which large numbers of the white population began to leave a specific residential area as African-Americans or other minorities moved in. He developed a mathematical theory in 1971 to explain the patterns of racial segregation. This theory, published in an article titled 'Dynamic Models of Segregation' in the *Journal of Mathematical Sociology,* asserted that even very slight and moderate preferences for racial uniformity can lead to racial segregation and divide at the macro level. According to this theory, there is a point of discomfort beyond which people's unconscious biases start affecting their decisions, such as moving out of a neighbourhood because too many people from a minority community have moved in.

Schelling demonstrated this hypothesis using a simple agent-based model[*] in a chessboard design with two kinds of entities labelled pennies and dimes[†] that represented any two groups in the society such as smokers and non-smokers or different racial identities. These entities or 'agents' occupy cells in a grid, and a cell can be occupied by one agent only. The rule in this model is that the coins

---

[*] An agent-based model is a computational model in which individual objects or phenomena can be designed as agents with specifically assigned behaviours and rules in order to study their interaction over space and time. An agent or an entity in this model can represent individuals, organisations or groups.

[†] Also called Schelling Segregation Model (SSM) or Schelling Tipping Model.

preferred to be next to coins of a similar type. Rules* could
be specified that determined whether a particular agent was
happy in its current location. If it was unhappy, it would try
to move to another location on the board or possibly just
exit the board entirely. Schelling moved the coins according
to the preference rule and found there was a general tendency
to move towards complete segregation among different
types of coins even if the initial preferences were very slight.
The basic premise of his theory is that racial segregation
could arise even when no single individual, family or group
had any racist tendencies but rather many had slight racial
preferences. Junfu Zhang, an economist at Clark University
writes, 'if every agent requires at least half of her neighbours
to be of the same colour – a preference far from extreme –
the final outcome, after a series of moves, is almost always
complete segregation.' Tiny actions can cause ripples, and
even waves.

Besides the tendency to only see and unconsciously seek
out new evidence that is consistent with our prior views
(i.e. a confirmation bias), we also spend considerable energy
in denigrating arguments that run counter to our existing
beliefs (disconfirmation bias). Many studies have shown
that such partisan influence results in dramatic differences
in individual perceptions and interpretations of key political
events, such as the effect of immigration on the economy.

Often when we are picking up our phones or tablets and
browsing, we are doing so while waiting in a queue or

---

* The basic assumption is as follows: an agent, located in the
centre of a neighbourhood where the fraction of friends $f$ is less
than a predefined tolerance threshold $F$ (i.e. $f < F$), will try to
relocate to a neighbourhood for which the fraction of friends is at
least $f$ (i.e. $f \geq F$). Note that a high threshold value of $F$ corresponds to a low agent's tolerance to the presence of strangers
within the neighbourhood.

having our coffee or pretending to be working, and so we skim, share and retweet quickly. These processes happen in an instant without much consideration of the reliability of the information we are seeing. We tend to believe people who share our beliefs without taking the time to fact-check all the information. With the emergence of 'identity politics', this has given rise to the recent phenomenon of fake news. Anything that doesn't conform to your tribe's views is shunned and labelled as fake news. It is not always falsified information, but it is often opinions that differ hugely from our own that are labelled fake news by politicians and the media alike. Jonathan Freedland in the *Guardian* terms it a new kind of cognitive bias called Tribal Epistemology,* which is when the truth no longer corresponds to facts or evidence but rather when a specific assertion agrees with the viewpoint of the tribe or social group one belongs to. The boundaries between 'works for us' or 'good for us' and 'true' have blurred. Of course, this isn't a new phenomenon; we have been sorting ourselves into tribes since the beginning of human evolution, as we saw in Chapter 2. It has just been ignited by the recent political climate, media and technology, and by our tendency to believe in stories and narratives rather than facts. Everyone loves a good story.

Ideas, effects and beliefs can spread between individuals in a population as if they are infectious. This is the social contagion theory. The *Macmillan Dictionary of Psychology* defines contagion as 'the spread of ideas, feelings and, some think, neuroses through a community or group by suggestion, gossip, imitation etc.' The exposure to popular beliefs is enough for them to spread. Ethnic hostility is particularly prone to social influence. Social bias is also

---

* Epistemology, simply speaking, is the creation of knowledge.

contagious. The out-group bias is contagious and is much more likely to be imitated than favouritism towards members of the same group. It is also likely to be imitated more than hostility towards people of the same race and ethnic group. The social environment plays a significant role in whether a bias and the consequent hostile action is considered acceptable or not. Jana Cahlíková, a scientist from the Max Planck Institute, led a study with adolescents from schools in eastern Slovakia to show that students were more likely to act on their negative biases towards the out-group members and consider such prejudiced – and often destructive and aggressive – behaviour more acceptable when their compatriots showed the same biases against them. Dr Cahlíková says, 'Our results suggest that fragile social norms can lead to a sudden change in individual behaviour towards other ethnic groups – from good coexistence to aggression.' This provides a clue to the kind of social contagion behaviour associated with negative biases and racial hostility that can spread very quickly, even in communities and groups that seem peaceful. The susceptibility to follow destructive behaviour increases when this hatred is targeted towards an out-group member. This could be a clue to why we are seeing a rapid rise in racial hatred and the emergence of the far right around the world.

Nonverbal cues during social interactions can enable leaking and spreading of social bias too, and this can start from early childhood. Even preschoolers pick up on such nonverbal cues from adults around them. If someone is already carrying these negative biases, brief exposure to negative nonverbal signals can activate and enhance the bias. It is also easy to pass them on to children who do not already have any such negative beliefs, even when there is no explicit intention to do so. Such cues can include avoiding eye contact, increased physical space and avoiding body contact, and these can create the impression of an 'infected' environment, which can further spread these social biases. A seemingly innocent gesture or an inflection in a tone, such as crossing over to the other side of the road, clutching a wallet more carefully, or using a patronising tone can be caught by children. When children notice these nonverbal cues, they can not only activate existing biases, but can form new negative biases towards the target and towards any other member of that group. When four- and five-year-old preschoolers were shown a video with positive attitudes, they generalised these positive beliefs too. This research has important implications in understanding how social biases catch on and spread. This is especially potent when children live in fairly homogenous communities and do not have much out-group contact and interaction.

## Echo chambers

Bill Gates has said that technology such as social media 'lets you go off with like-minded people, so you're not mixing and sharing and understanding other points of view ... It's super important. It's turned out to be more of a problem than I, or many others, would have expected.' Social networking websites like Facebook are fostering homophilic environments and communities, where people of similar ideologies only interact with each other. When a Facebook user likes or interacts with an article or post of a certain ideology, an algorithm is designed to show that user other posts of the same ideology, resulting in homogeneous personal networks. These kind of limited social worlds and echo chambers have huge implications for the information people receive, the attitudes they form and the interactions they experience. This kind of behaviour is termed 'group-think'. We talk about 'finding our tribe' on

Instagram – those people who share the same world-view, the ones who will like and comment on our posts. It can be a very positive and uplifting experience, but it can also lead to serious problems in extreme cases, where anyone not agreeing with your viewpoint is trolled and harassed, where we only trust certain sources and people and believe what they say is true. It raises the question of whether these sources are perpetuating these biases by only telling us what we believe in, hence creating an information 'filter bubble' and strengthening our confirmation bias. The term 'filter bubble', coined by Eli Pariser, is used to describe how someone using social media or online search platforms develops a one-sided perspective or political view because they only interact with accounts that have similar backgrounds or sentiments. It then creates a unique information landscape for each of us based on our own pre-existing beliefs. This means that users exist in their own cultural and ideological bubbles, do not encounter conflicting views, and start believing that their view is universal.

The two terms – echo chambers and filter bubbles – seem synonymous and are often used as such, but some suggest that 'echo chamber' is used much more frequently as an epithet, to refer condescendingly to someone else's failings, while 'filter bubble' is much more often used to refer to one's own blind spots or to discuss the phenomenon in a neutral or academic way. Filter bubble is also now increasingly being used to describe only online mechanisms of information polarisation, such as the algorithms you find on social media and search engines. On the other hand, echo chamber refers to both online and offline mechanisms, which complement each other and act simultaneously. In this way, echo chamber is appropriate to refer to human information behaviour; filter bubble is for algorithmic information filtering and the way the results are presented.

In his book *Filter Bubble,* Pariser says, 'Your identity shapes your media. This portrays how we are allowing the media to formulate our thoughts because of the repeated messages we encounter daily.' We must remember that algorithms by themselves do not produce filter bubbles or subsequently echo chambers; they only consolidate and amplify the existing information behaviour patterns (we will see more of this in Chapter 11). It is up to the individuals themselves to accept or to deny fake news uncritically, to verify or falsify reports or to ignore them. If filter bubbles are made by algorithms and echo chambers by users, the echo chambers influence the filter bubbles; however, filter bubbles strengthen existing echo chambers as well. Our beliefs are reinforced by being amplified inside this metaphorical echo chamber. Networks amplify the flow of information, but highly connected people can also suppress the spread of information online. This inhibits our ability to think logically about the broader pictures and diverse viewpoints, and this means that when we meet resistance or challenging views, we are more likely to react more radically and with prejudice. This kind of bubble also leads to a false notion of social homogeneity, where users form very strong in-group identities and create more distance from any groups that are different to their own, and hence a more fractured society. It is also impossible to see how biased this bubble can be once we are inside it, which all of us are most of the time. The *Guardian* in 2017 showed that more than 60 per cent of Facebook users were entirely unaware of any algorithmic curation on Facebook at all, though this is likely to be different now as there is more discussion and awareness around fake news. Nevertheless, even if we are aware of this curation and algorithmic manipulation, our instinct is to trust the information that matches our own world-view, and we are likely to make decisions based on this information.

Our biases are created, manipulated and perpetuated by what is called the 'availability cascade'. The more we hear something around us, the more we believe it. It is worth reminding ourselves that these echo chambers are merely amplifying normal human behaviour. As the writer Mark Twain allegedly noted: 'A lie can travel halfway around the world while the truth is putting on its shoes.'* Social contagion underlies such viral phenomena. We pay selective attention to things that interest us, and then we start seeing and noticing the information that backs our beliefs everywhere. This kind of collective bias creates trends and viral phenomena on social media, when suddenly some non-obvious event triggers multiple people to talk about the same subject. Viral memes are very likely working through a similar channel. So is FOMO or 'Fear of Missing Out', as when we begin to see something around us frequently, it might seem to us that we are the only ones missing out if we don't subscribe to it. As we tend to pay more attention to items at the top of a list due to position bias, our social influence bias – or what is commonly called 'frequency bias' – kicks in. Linguist Arnold Zwicky proposed in 2006 that frequency bias is a combination of attention bias and confirmation bias: seeing and then believing. This bias is the seeming appearance of a newly learned (or newly paid-attention to) concept in unexpected places. This frequency bias, or the Baader-Meinhof phenomenon, also works for other situations and affects our social behaviours and interactions. It is one of the primary bases of popularity and social influence culture. If

---

* This quote is widely attributed to Mark Twain but is not actually by him, which is delightfully ironic!

we see something more frequently, even in a different context, we are likely to believe its status and position in society is higher. We might also start noticing similar situations and words more regularly – much like, after watching the movie *Jaws*, many people reported seeing the word 'shark' just about everywhere.

★★★

The notion of nationality is intricately linked to identity and belonging and to race. Social psychologists theorise that adults implicitly associate nationality with a specific social category membership, such as a particular race, even when they explicitly state – and insist they believe – that people across all social categories should be treated equally. These associations between nationality and social category membership emerge early in life and are shaped by cultural context. Britain's decision to leave the European Union in July 2016 came as a surprise to many people. But this was a result of the increasing threat that some UK nationals were feeling towards their national identity. It was an interplay of several complex factors but primarily a consequence of unconscious bias and ethnocentrism. While any sort of blatant display of prejudice is stigmatised and abhorred, the covert, subtle forms of prejudice arising from a perception of cultural differences and the hardening of lines between in-groups and out-groups have become more prominent. Most people would be shocked to discover they carry implicit biases against any groups and would react with outrage at any suggestion that they organise racial groups into hierarchies; they do not want to be prejudiced or display any discriminatory behaviour. But these implicit aversive attitudes can be exhibited in other behaviours such as moving out from areas where there is a different ethnic

majority population. When the cognitive bias (the belief
about a certain person or group resulting in stereotypes)
and the affective bias (associated with a feeling or emotion)
are activated, this results in prejudice. This can lead to a
conative* action such as voting to leave the EU to conserve
the in-group ideology and way of life.

What has happened with the Brexit referendum is that it
is now shaping new biases and belief systems. With strong
views on either side, the membership of a certain political
party is shaping the identities and opinions of individuals
through a mechanism termed 'partisan motivated
reasoning'. Our behaviour is motivated by our partisan
beliefs and views. Paul Goren and his colleagues from the
University of Minnesota summarise this in the *American
Journal of Political Science* as: 'When someone hears a
recognizable partisan source advocating some position, her
partisan leanings are activated, which in turn lead her to
evaluate the message through a partisan lens'. So, if the
source and recipient share a party label, the latter will trust
the former and accept the message without reflecting much
on message content. But if the source of the message and
recipient lie across the partisan divide, the recipient will
mistrust the source and reject the message, again without
much reflection. Pariser quotes the American commentator
Jonathan Chait as saying: 'Partisans are more likely to
consume news sources that confirm their ideological
beliefs. People with more education are more likely to
follow political news. Therefore, people with more
education can actually become mis-educated.'

Brexit has brought into sharp focus how the explicit
biases of people, their emotive implicit biases and their

---

* As opposed to cognitive and affective, conative is a more purposeful
and striving action, but not necessarily a rational one.

inherent desire to trust others who have the same beliefs as their own can be used to manipulate information and hence an individual's behaviour. For instance, Arron Banks, the wealthy donor partly responsible for the Brexit campaign, explained that the leave campaign's media strategy was to connect with people emotionally rather than 'the remain campaign [that] featured fact, fact, fact, fact. It just doesn't work.' It was seen that the more socially isolated people were, the more likely they were to vote for leaving the EU. Those who had spent time with foreigners were 15 per cent less likely to vote leave.[*] The world-view shaped by their wider social networks – both online and offline – and their propensity to travel beyond their home town had a strong influence on their support for the EU.

A similar scenario has played out on the other side of the pond. We tend to pay more attention to threat. History has shown, from Hitler to Trump, that leaders who like to appeal to the authoritarian bias can appeal to the public by enhancing the perception of threat – both real and imagined – and offering simple solutions. The social psychologist Thomas Pettigrew proposed in 2017 that one of the reasons Trump won the presidential election was because of the lack of inter-group contact. Trump's white supporters have experienced far less contact with minority ethnic communities than other Americans. A 2016 study showed that 'the racial and ethnic isolation of Whites at the zip-code level is one of the strongest predictors of Trump support.' Trump support increased as distance from the Mexican border increased. Small Midwestern towns in the US that have faced rapid increases in Latino immigration, where diversity index rose by 150 per cent over a short time before the presidential elections, saw a 67 per cent

---

[*] The *Guardian*, 17 December 2016.

vote for Trump.* This perceived threat of loss of familiarity, the threat of losing the in-group identity and the fear of invasion of the migrants meant that individuals paid more attention to Trump's anti-immigration rhetoric. This was also seen as a factor in the EU-Brexit vote, where the speed of the growing migrant population also created fear and anxiety, and voters paid much more attention to this threat than to other factors. This was evident in the areas that had witnessed more than a 200 per cent rise in immigrants by 2015, and who voted an astounding 94 per cent to leave the EU.† Cities such as London had witnessed the growth in a diverse population slowly over the years, so the positive inter-group contact had countered the threat bias in these areas. On the other hand, rural communities and smaller towns had witnessed a sudden increase in immigration and so had not had a chance to achieve optimal inter-group contact, and their attention bias to threat was at a peak. This affected their inter-group bias, threat to familiarity, and evoked neophobia. It offers a likely explanation for the rise of 'nationalistic ideology' and the right-wing movement in Europe and elsewhere.

Partisan bias affects our perception of facts and news. University of Minnesota professor Howard Lavine, who specialises in political psychology, says that 'People are increasingly shuttering themselves within partisan echo chambers. They're told over and over again that everything the other party does is bad. This tendency has been getting stronger.' Trump's election and the rise of far-right ideology in several parts of Europe can also be attributed to the rise of authoritarianism and social dominance ideology. The social dominance ideology is a belief in a 'dog-eat-dog

---

* *Wall Street Journal*, November 2016.
† *The Economist*, 16 July 2016.

world' and a need to dominate those lower in the hierarchy. This is a well-studied phenomenon in psychology, triggered by threat and fear and characterised by deference to authority, aggression toward out-groups, a rigidly hierarchical view of the world, and resistance to new experience. Individuals believe that the authorities should be obeyed because they are in the best position to know what is good for the country. This is again linked to inter-group bias, where certain groups are believed to have a higher status than others. According to Thomas Pettigrew, Trump's speeches – studded with such absolutist terms as 'losers' and 'complete disasters' – are classic authoritarian statements. His clear distinction between groups on the top of society (whites) and 'bad hombres' on the bottom (immigrants, black people and Latinos) are classic social dominance statements.

***

Today the political and ideological divides are deeper than ever. In the US, a study of recent campaigns has shown that candidates routinely spend more time attacking their opponents than promoting themselves. The same study showed that the 2004 Swift Boat ad impugning Senator Kerry's Vietnam record generated more news stories than the war in Iraq. This sort of campaigning is built on the theory of partisan bias where we tend to believe more strongly in the negative messages about rival parties. This growing partisan bias and divide can be seen in the results of a longitudinal study where Republicans and Democrats were asked whether they would be happy for their son or daughter to marry a member of the opposing party. In the 1960s most responded with a shrug and only 5 per cent of Republicans and 4 per cent of Democrats said they would be upset by the cross-party union. In 2008, 27 per cent of Republicans and 20 per cent of Democrats said they would be upset if their son or daughter married a member of the opposite party. In 2010, 49 per cent of Republicans and 33 per cent of Democrats professed concern at interparty marriage. One of the main reasons for this jump is that the polarisation based on political affiliation and membership is becoming an ideological phenomenon. Negative campaigning is to be blamed to a large extent. This is also seen in the 'thermometer' rating, where people are asked to rate their feelings towards the two political parties on a scale of 1 to 100, where 1 is cold and negative, and 100 is warm and positive. In 1980, voters gave their own party a 72 and the opposite party a 45. After 1980, though, the numbers began dropping. By 1992, the opposing party was down to 40; by 1998, it had fallen to 38; in 2012, it fell to 30. Meanwhile, people's views towards their own parties remained largely unchanged and fell only slightly from 72 to 70 between 1980 and 2012. The numbers here tell a story even though most people deny the strength of their feelings against the opposing party members.

Although opportunities for partisan discrimination are less common than race or gender, and it isn't something that we can form instant first impressions of when we meet a person, it is fast becoming a form of social identity. This has become particularly apparent in the UK since the Brexit vote, with lines being drawn between leavers and remainers. The affiliation with a political party is now being seen as a life choice, an ideology, and families are being divided over membership of different political parties. Old friendships are questioned as people are displaying their political ideologies and partisan memberships as Facebook profile pictures, showing how it is shaping their sense of self and identity. This is why it is becoming more common for political parties to activate identity rather than policy, and to gain votes by attacking the opposing party rather than focusing on their own party's policies. The political agenda is becoming focused on delegitimization rather than persuasion.

Shanto Iyengar, director of Stanford's political communications lab, suggests that party affiliation is becoming a personal identity and even more deeply rooted than racial identity. Iyengar wanted to test whether people would be more open about their racial biases, or whether partisan bias would trump racial bias or academic excellence. In the first study, they asked about a thousand people to decide between the résumés of two high school seniors who were competing for a scholarship. The point of the project was to see whether partisan bias would affect non-political tasks as well. The résumés had three different kinds of cues: one based on academic excellence, with 3.5 or 4.0 GPA; the second a political cue, with the candidate being the president of the Young Democrats or Young Republicans club; and the third as race, with the candidate having a stereotypically African-American or European-American name. About 80 per cent of Democrats and Republicans awarded the scholarship to their co-partisan – one belonging to their own party – even if they did not have the highest GPA. The partisan identity trumped race: when the candidates were equally qualified, about 78 per cent of African-Americans chose the candidate of the same race, and 42 per cent of European-Americans did the same. When the candidate of the other race had a higher GPA, 45 per cent of African-Americans and 71 per cent of European-Americans chose them. The results showed that partisan bias is extending beyond the political domain and can lead to discrimination in apolitical contexts. However, I wonder if these results were because the respondents were more open to showing partisan bias rather than racial bias and were more eager to hide any suggestion of an implicit racial bias because racial discrimination is less socially acceptable.

Discriminating based on race or gender is socially unacceptable, while political partisan bias is built on the notion of morality. It is simpler – and more socially acceptable – to discriminate against someone who believes in guns or is against gay marriage because political beliefs are formed rather than inherited, unlike racial identity. Someone has chosen to believe in a certain ideology and so it is acceptable to blame them for it. However, extensive research in psychology of partisan belief and bias in the United States, which can also be applied to the UK and elsewhere, is that most of these partisans are not aware of the ideological and policy-level differences between the different political parties. This is also true in Indian politics, where political campaigns have drawn battle-lines to create a sense of social or economic insecurity among their followers. Such disruptive strategies have caused communal, lingual or ethnic riots in the past. One such example is Shiv Sena with their ideology of 'Maharashtra for Maharashtrians', another is the Telangana Rashtra Samithi, which is fighting for the formation of Telangana state in Andhra Pradesh. In their new book *Ideology & Identity*, Rahul Verma and Pradeep Chhibber, political scientists for the Centre for Policy Research, use data to show that the rise of the Bharatiya Janata Party (BJP) is based in the notion of the 'idea of India', 'Hindudatva' or a 'Hindu nation'.[*] The Indian Prime Minister, Narendra Modi – a controversial figure – and his party, the BJP, have used partisan politics and emotive religious ideology to activate his supporters and build a momentum for support. In India,

---

[*] *New York Times*, 17 May 2019.

partisan bias is now a major force underlying interpersonal relationships; I see this myself across my friends on Facebook. Their support for different political parties is shaping not only their own identity but also their circle of friends and is creating bias and discrimination against those who do not share their partisan beliefs. In a secular state, where Muslims and Hindus lived side by side, this has driven a huge rift between different religious associations, and made religious bias and discrimination acceptable.

Greater levels of negativity in advertising campaigns and general exposure to political campaigns both contribute to higher levels of affective polarisation. Campaigns reinforce voters' sense of partisan identity and confirm stereotypical beliefs about supporters and opponents. As we live in such turbulent times, with genuine terrorist threats and general economic stagnation, society is facing anxiety and uncertainty. In such times, attention to any cues that signify threat is increased, even when they are imaginary and seem implausible. Those who are anxious tend to overestimate the risk of a feared outcome. Modi and the BJP have used this in India to create a feeling of insecurity, with the threat coming not just from external enemies such as Pakistan and China attacking Indian borders and territories and inciting terrorism, but also from within, such as the Congress Party, which is seen as an anti-nationalistic threat. The BJP depicts its rivals the Congress Party and other opposing parties as pandering to Muslims and minorities and alleges them of policies that will directly benefit the neighbouring Muslim nation, Pakistan.[*] Anthropologists Angana P. Chatterji and Thomas Blom Hansen, along with political scientist Christophe Jaffrelot, in their recent book *Majoritarian State*, talk about how groups and regions are

---

[*] The *Independent*, 1 May 2019.

being portrayed as 'internal and external enemies' of the Indian state, and these political partisan ideologies are extending far beyond the political domain into the judiciary, academic and cultural institutions. Chatterji and Hansen succinctly sum up the nationalistic ideologies being touted in the US, the UK, India and elsewhere, in an interview in May 2019: 'It is dividing populations into "us" and "them" and provide a simple explanation for the pervasive state of anxiety and fear: "they" are getting ahead and blocking our future, "they" are stealing a future that is rightfully ours. Depending on the situation and country, "they" are social and religious minorities, people of colour, immigrants, refugees, etc. – easily portrayed as enemies of the "true" nation and of the majority.'[*]

In this new era of racialisation, where racial attitudes are being leveraged for political purposes, we are seeing a rise in racial bias across the UK, with race-related incidents becoming more common. The EU referendum/Brexit has legitimised people to make their implicit biases more explicit and openly show prejudice. In India, rather than race, religion is drawing the lines with the rise of Hindutva. The Obama era in the US led to more racially charged and polarised partisan politics, with people now divided on race more so than party policies because of the way media and political messages have reinforced implicit racial biases. For instance, some people displayed more positive feelings toward Obama's dog, Bo, when they were told he belonged to Ted Kennedy. The effect of these racial cues works both ways. People who have different implicit bias – for and against – respond differently to the same racial cues. Michael Tesler in 2016 proposed the 'two-sided' racialisation in evaluations of President Obama. Racially sympathetic

---

[*] *Indian Express*, 7 May 2019.

white people held more favourable evaluations of Obama
than previous Democratic candidates, and racially resentful
white people held more negative evaluations of Obama
than previous Democrats. Obama's election also
demonstrated that when larger issues are at play, such as the
economic crisis, race can become a secondary issue and
inter-group politics can become less pronounced.

People do not readily admit that they would discriminate
against someone based on their political ideologies or
membership of a specific political group. However, people
happily – and very readily – fall into tribes with just the
gentlest nudge. As political beliefs become part of our
personal and social identity, this activates a sense of
'belonging' and 'non-belonging', and partisan bias is
leading to more and more out-group discrimination even
in domains that have nothing to do with political beliefs.

## Seeing is believing

The political theorist Hanna Pitkin in her seminal work
*The Concept of Representation* in 1967 – and several researchers
since then – have shown that descriptive representation has
both substantive and symbolic effects, especially with
regards to race and gender. Role models matter. Role
models in those domains where stereotypes are common
matter the most. When people see someone from their
representative in-group, it can encourage them to be more
motivated and ambitious. This is especially true for
members of stigmatised and marginalised groups. When
we see someone we do not expect to see in a role that they
are not deemed to be a good fit for as per social and cultural
norms (such as women in leadership roles), it can suppress
and even modify our internal implicit biases. For this to
happen, role models must be perceived as competent, must

be the same race or gender (i.e. the same in-group membership), and must be perceived to be successful.

In a white paper published in May 2019 in the Open Archive of Social Sciences, a team investigated the effect of celebrity role models on reducing out-group biases and prejudices. Mohamed Salah is a visibly Muslim football player who talks openly about his faith (unlike many other players), even lying prostrate to pay homage to god as part of his goal celebration. He is also a vocal advocate of women's rights and gender equality, stating, 'We need to change the way we treat women in our culture.' In 2019, Salah was named by *Time* magazine as one of the 100 most influential people in the world. Liverpool fans created a chant saying that if Salah continued to score goals, they would convert to Islam, with the lyrics along the lines of 'If he's good enough for you, he's good enough for me; if he scores another few, then I'll be Muslim too.' The local area is not very ethnically diverse and in fact has much lower ethnic diversity than the UK average (approximately 4.8 per cent compared with 10 per cent). In this study, the researchers have attempted to estimate the effect of Salah joining Liverpool FC on Islamophobic attitudes and behaviours using 936 hate crime observations, 15 million tweets from UK football fans, and an original survey experiment of 8,060 Liverpool FC fans. They found that the local area experienced an 18.9 per cent drop in hate crimes and that Liverpool FC fans halved their rates of posting anti-Muslim tweets (a drop from 7.3 per cent to 3.8 per cent of tweets about Muslims) relative to fans of other top-flight English football clubs. The survey suggests that these results may be driven by increased familiarity with Islam. I am personally sceptical about the results and wonder about the reliability of the data. We cannot – and should not – draw conclusions about the reduction in racist attitudes and incidents from these statistics alone because, as we've seen, racial bias and prejudice manifest themselves in the form of implicit actions and microaggressions too, besides explicit hate crimes. Additionally, it has not been proven reliably that these effects extend beyond 'hero-worship' to the 'normal' population too. However, what this study really shows is that positive exposure to out-group role models can overturn some of the negative prejudices and out-group biases and reveal new information that humanises the out-group at large.

There must be an optimal inter-group contact to reduce inter-group prejudice because there must be a delicate balance between threat and contact. Of course, exposure to racial out-group members can also make the negative stereotypes about them immediately accessible in our consciousness, termed 'automatic stereotype activation'. Once activated, stereotypes can be cognitively taxing to suppress. These stereotypes can then create implicit negative bias without our knowledge. But it has also been shown that such implicit biases can be overturned quickly, and mutual trust can be developed between diverse pairs. This was seen during Barack Obama's election in 2008, when racial prejudice was expected to play a huge role but, due to the 'extended contact' effect, the highly polarised views were countered. According to the extended contact hypothesis, knowing that in-group members have cross-group friends improves attitudes toward this out-group. Inter-group bias, prejudice and fear have been shown to reduce, and inter-group empathy to increase, as a result of more inter-group contact.

Representation and role models especially matter in political elections, where voters often make quick decisions to avoid cognitive load and they only have the information they garner from media outlets on which to base their decisions and perceptions of candidates. Obama's presidential candidacy and election had some effect on the racial attitudes in America: the 'Obama effect'. People claimed that a post-racial society had been achieved, and research has shown some change in wider attitudes and biases towards black people and minorities, such as deeming them to be more intellectual. Although these were localised and more significant in the younger population, it is significant because his success in the political domain, as the first black-American president of the United States, sent a powerful message to fellow black-Americans that they can also make significant achievements despite the systemic and deep-rooted racial bias and stereotypical beliefs. Even though some scholars argue that Obama avoided depicting himself as black during his political campaign (to escape any racial prejudices among the white voters), his meteoric rise and positive media exposure created a salient positive exemplar that increased activation of positive qualities associated with 'black' in general, and 'black leaders' more specifically. This helped overturn some of the racial prejudices by creating more positive nonverbal behaviours and inter-group interactions that are essential for reversing implicit racial biases. The Obama effect therefore extended to other domains and reduced stereotype threat among the black-American community. Besides racial bias, Obama also represented a different kind of black masculinity, more in touch with his emotions and comfortable in showing them. Obama successfully countered the 'angry black man' trope and navigated the aggressiveness and empathetic qualities needed from a leader, bridging the gap between the usual polarised masculine and feminine stereotypes.

In a series of studies, Dr Arthur Aron found that merely being in the same class where other interracial pairs were interacting can reduce levels of prejudice. It was also found that this significantly reduces anxiety during encounters with other members of that second group, as gauged by stress-hormone levels in the saliva. This links back to social identity theory, in Chapter 2. Individuals have an urge to expand their identities (termed 'self-expansion'), and this need to expand the identity group can be manipulated. In the late 1960s, when the black politician Richard G. Hatcher was vying to become mayor of Gary, Indiana, one neighbourhood near the steel mills was running nearly 90 per cent against him. After he was elected, Mayor Hatcher closed the dump, which was a big concern for local citizens because of its bad smell. In the next election Hatcher got nearly 40 per cent of the vote from the neighbourhood. Thomas Pettigrew, who helped do the polling, said that 'A lot of people living there cared a lot more about the dump than the colour of their mayor.'*

Diverse representation allows us to access counter-stereotypic views that help us question and examine our own beliefs and biases. However, it is not enough to have salience; a demonstrable success is very important for any role models to overturn stereotypes and implicit biases. In one influential study, David E. Campbell and Christina Wolbrecht found strong evidence that Geraldine Ferraro running for the US vice-presidency in 1984 had a strong role-model effect on young women. In years that featured women candidates with a high, national-level profile, young women were significantly more likely than young men to see themselves becoming politically involved. The opposite was true in years without national female role models. It was predicted that the election of a first woman president – that is, a Hillary Clinton victory – would increase perceptions of gender equality in the United

---

* *New York Times*, 6 November 2008.

States. In 2018, pre- and post-election data analysis revealed that perceived gender equality indeed decreased immediately after election day, but only for those who preferred Clinton over Trump – thus increasing polarisation between Trump and Clinton supporters on gender-related issues.

According to a UK House of Commons briefing paper from March 2019, there were 209 women Members of the House of Commons. At 32 per cent of the membership, this is an all-time high, but still not enough. In May 2019, five Cabinet members (22 per cent) were women, and the prime minister was also a woman (until 7 June 2019). The highest proportion of women in the Cabinet was 36 per cent (between 2006 and 2007), so it isn't a level playing field just yet. It can be argued that Margaret Thatcher and Theresa May as female prime ministers did not affect gender bias or overturn gender stereotypes because of the widespread criticism of their policies. Their premiership did not inspire young women to go into politics. Media sexism (discussed in Chapter 7) gave out negative messages – albeit implicit – that women do not make good leaders. Furthermore, the way these two leaders isolated themselves from women's rights and gender issues created a divide between them and the general female population, and they were not seen as part of the in-group to which this stereotype threat applies.

★★★

We all seek, in subtle ways, to confirm our pre-existing beliefs. And in hindsight we tend to overestimate how predictable an event was. When we watch news and scroll on social media, we unconsciously filter what we are seeing or reading depending on our implicit biases, which dictate what we find irrelevant and what is worthy of our attention.

Here, we have looked at how so many of our decisions in the real world and in the digital domain are shaped by our confirmation bias. Confirmation bias can work hand in hand with availability bias and recall bias to create errors in judgement.

A recent incident was seen in early 2019. While the media went into a frenzy over an image of Diane Abbott, shadow home secretary, drinking a mojito on a train journey, there was considerably less uproar over Michael Gove's* admission that he had taken the class-A drug cocaine 'on several occasions at social events more than 20 years ago.' Abbott had to apologise for drinking on Transport for London public transport, and there were calls from public, politicians and the media for her to resign. Fast-forward, and not just Gove but three other Conservative Party leadership candidates admitted to taking drugs. Rory Stewart said he took opium when it was passed round at a wedding in Iran; Andrea Leadsom admitted she had tried cannabis at university; and foreign secretary Jeremy Hunt told *The Times*: 'I think I had a cannabis lassi [drink] when I went backpacking through India.' Diane is a black woman. The other four are all white. Clearly, race and gender intersect here to demonstrate the inherent bias and the double standards in how we decide who is guilty and who is exonerated as we hear the news – and reactions to it – unfolding in the digital domain. This also demonstrates the power of confirmation bias, the implicit belief that black people are more likely to abuse drugs and alcohol. People will seek out information that confirm this belief, and then impose these judgements on anything they see and hear. They will also seek out information that will portray

---

* Gove was vying for the Conservative Party leadership as this book was being written in June 2019. He since lost.

certain groups in a negative light. By not seeking out objective facts, by interpreting information in a way that only supports their existing beliefs, and by only remembering details that uphold these beliefs, they often miss important information. Neuropsychologist Daniel Siegel asserts that once a belief pattern has been established, our neurons want to fire in line with that pattern, which makes it difficult to change a belief system.

People believe what they want to believe. People accept things on the grapevine that align with their world-view. Often, we don't even wait to assess the validity of what we see and hear. If it aligns with what we believe in, then it must be true. If someone believes that climate change is 'fake news' it is highly likely they would only seek out information that would support their view. As we've seen, this bias is especially enhanced where political associations and beliefs are concerned. People reply to survey questions in a way that favours their preferred political party and beliefs, even when they do not completely believe in their responses' veracity and legitimacy. Professor Howard Lavine calls this 'gratifying their partisan identity', an expressive act that gives us a psychological benefit when our group is doing well, and we crave this sense of well-being.

So we shut ourselves in our partisan echo chambers. And, we all – consciously or unconsciously – seek out our Bobbsey Twins. Don't you?

## CHAPTER SIX

# Hindsight is 20/20

Along with confirmation bias, discussed in the previous chapter, there are many other cognitive biases and heuristics that explain what might seem like irrational behaviour. These can also explain some of the choices we make and decisions we take every day.

Tim Urban's 'Inside the Mind of a Master Procrastinator' is one of the best TED talks I have watched – and have since watched several times.* It is funny and enlightening, and Tim talks about how procrastination might be much more insidious than we consider it to be. Ted O'Donoghue and Matthew Rabin in the *Quarterly Journal of Economics* define procrastination as the 'present bias in preferences, on account of which agents delay doing unpleasant tasks that they themselves wish they would do sooner.' I was intrigued to find out that a cognitive heuristic termed 'present bias' is the reason we all procrastinate. Present bias or 'hyperbolic discounting' is the tendency people have, when considering a trade-off between two future moments, to give more importance to the sooner one. This kind of bias follows a hyperbolic curve rather than an exponential curve. We will delay a reward only if we perceive it as offering us a much higher return. This is also the bias that comes into play when I give in to temptation and eat yet another chocolate biscuit even though I know I need to cut down

---

* Of course, this gave me a valid excuse for procrastinating. If you are watching a TED talk, you are not procrastinating, right?

on sugar for long-term health benefits. My willpower does not hold up to this inherent bias where I focus on instant pleasure, and I believe that the next time I am offered a biscuit I will be able to turn it down.

Research shows that people under-save for retirement, focusing more on the present moment than the distant future. In an experiment by Hal Hershfield, a marketing professor at the University of California, Los Angeles, the students observed virtual-reality avatars showing for a minute or so what they would look like at the age of 70. The students were then asked what they would do if they unexpectedly gained $1,000. The students who had been shown their older self said they would put an average of $172 into a retirement account. That's more than double the amount that would have been invested by members of the control group (those who hadn't seen their older self), who were willing to save an average of only $80. Similarly, if we are given two similar rewards, we are unconsciously biased to choose the one that arrives sooner. The options that delay the reward make it less attractive and it is discounted.* When a group of students were offered two choices – $150 now or $200 in six months – a significant majority chose the $150 being offered to them in the present. Then, when offered the choice between $50 now and $100 a year from now, many chose the immediate $50. However, given the choice between $50 in five years or $100 in six years almost everyone chose $100 in six years, even though it was the same choice seen at five years'

---

* The amount that people discount future rewards has been mathematically represented too. The classical economic view is that the future reward is reduced by a factor of $1 / (1 + k) t$ where $k$ is the constant discount rate per time unit and $t$ is the length of the delay. The amount a future reward is discounted depends therefore only on the length of the delay, given a constant discount rate.

greater distance. Our preference for things and our choices can be distorted by our relative distance to these options, as the hyperbole distorts the value of these choices for us due to our present bias. We are hardwired to choose a smaller gain today than a larger gain tomorrow.*

## Grass is not always greener

Would you prefer to lose £5 or gain £5? Most of us prefer making rather than losing money. However, we carry a status quo bias – what Daniel Kahneman and Amos Tversky termed 'loss aversion bias' – that compels us to focus on 'not losing money' rather than 'actively gaining money'. The status quo bias can be shaped by a number of complex and interacting factors, such as the economic – and cognitive – costs involved in making the transition, aversion to taking risk and threat of losing what one presently owns, plus the potential for regretting a change. Status quo bias is a powerful unconscious bias and equates to 'When in doubt, do nothing.'

Losses have been shown to be almost twice as psychologically harmful as gains are beneficial. In other words, individuals feel twice as much psychological pain from losing $100 as pleasure from gaining $100. This bias means that individuals are reluctant to give away what they possess in favour of something that 'might' be more profitable to them in the future. In an experiment by Jack Knetsch and colleagues in 1984, the participants had in their possession either a lottery ticket or $2. Sometime later, each subject was offered an opportunity to trade the

---

* Neuroscientists have shown that our preference for smaller immediate rewards and the power of 'now' activates several regions across our brains including the medial prefrontal cortex, anterior insular cortex, middle temporal gyrus, middle frontal gyrus, and cingulate gyrus.

lottery ticket for the money or vice versa. Very few subjects chose to switch. We prefer to largely stay where we are and hold on to the status quo because we are naturally averse to losing our current reality, especially if it relates to a clear loss or gain of privilege or status. This is what stops us from finding an alternative career path. We resist change, we cannot clearly evaluate what we have not experienced yet, and we are inherently programmed to stay on our current path unless there is strong evidence that the alternative is far better. This can cause inertia and reluctance to do anything to change our status quo, even when we might be unhappy in a current job or relationship. People just seem to prefer their current state of affairs because they deem that the pain of giving it up would be greater. Such loss aversion can also be seen in gameshows such as *Deal or No Deal*.* A study in the *International Review of Finance* examined the data from 102 episodes of the Australian version of the programme and showed that risk aversion increased with the stakes, where people were more likely to take a lower-value deal rather than gambling for a higher prize.

Status quo bias interacts with other non-rational processes such as endowment effect,† an idea linked to prospect theory in cognitive psychology. The prospect theory states that individuals make the choice based on a cognitive heuristic where they model the value of the losses and gains rather than considering the final outcome. We weigh up all

---

* The game begins with 26 suitcases of prizes ranging from 50 pence to £250,000, with most of the prize money amounting to £10,000 or less. The contestants are asked to select one suitcase to be set aside and are then asked to continue eliminating the rest of the suitcases by choosing between the offers made by the bank or staking their chances on an unknown amount in any particular suitcase.
† Where we value what we have more than what we do not. This has also been shown to be a trend in market-driven societies.

our choices as per a reference point of 'now' (i.e. the status quo), and losing $x$ hurts more than gaining $x$. Staying with the current or choosing what has worked in the past also requires less mental effort to maintain and, as we have established, our brains are looking for the path that requires the fewest cognitive resources. One factor driving this status quo bias is the difficulty of the decision process. Faced with many choices, people might suffer inaction because of this implicit bias. In supermarkets, for example, there is vast choice of different brands of the same product, and consumers may actually leave the store empty-handed because of a difficulty-induced bias. Choice can be demotivating. A study showed that people are more likely to purchase luxury chocolates or gourmet jams if the choices were limited to around six rather than 24 or 30. This seems counter-intuitive to the idea of 'the more choice, the better' that we are usually led to believe.

Our status quo bias is also linked to a perception that 'anything that has existed and survived is good'. People treat existence as a prima facie case for goodness – both aesthetic and ethical – and longevity increases this preference, a theory that correlates with the notion of 'survival of the fittest'. In most cases, we also tend to like something more when we are familiar with it. This familiarity bias (also called 'mere exposure' effect) is the psychological phenomenon that the more we are exposed to something, the more likeable that person, object or situation is likely to be. We are biased towards anything that is more familiar to us, as the repeated exposure is a sort of conditioning signalling about the lack of negative consequences and protecting against the fear of novelty.

Familiarity with election candidates has also been shown to affect the assessment of their competence. It is the feeling of seeing ourselves in someone or identifying with them.

Familiarity in relation to political choice was manipulated in an experiment where participants were shown a composite of the candidates' faces with their own faces. Recognising their own face in a candidate's face led to more positive judgement of the candidate. We know that familiarity bias happens very quickly without conscious and rational thought, and that it is a cognitive shortcut we employ to assess people around us, deciding whether we trust them or not. Assessing trustworthiness has been shown to precede any judgement of competence, and an assessment of competence can be seen as a rationalisation of the unconscious familiarity bias. The competency assessment happens implicitly too. We don't realise and are often unaware how and why we have judged someone to be more competent than another.

In a study conducted by psychologists at Ohio State University in 2013, 148 undergraduate students were asked about their views of US presidential candidates Mitt Romney and Barack Obama, how likely they were to vote in the election (or if they had already voted), and to rate themselves as a Democrat or a Republican and as liberal or conservative. These students then compared 450 pairs of slightly different images of Romney's face and were asked to select the one in each pair that they thought looked most like him. The participants were very familiar with Romney as the study was conducted over the course of several weeks in November 2012, both in the days just before the US presidential election and immediately afterwards. After this first stage, the photos were then used to create two composite photos of Mitt Romney's face: one based on the choices of Republican-leaning participants, and another based on Democratic-leaning participants. In the second stage of the study, a different group of more than 200 adults were asked to select the image from these two that looked most like Romney and the one that looked most trustworthy. Overall they chose the ones generated by the Republicans as being a better likeness as well as more trustworthy and positive. The results showed how the same face appeared different to Republicans and Democrats, with their political attitudes shaping their biases towards presidential candidates. 'That our attitudes could bias something that we're exposed to so frequently is an amazing biasing effect,' said Russell Fazio, Professor of Psychology at Ohio State University and senior author of the study.* The findings suggest that people may not just interpret political information about a candidate to fit their opinion, but that they may also construct a political world in which they literally see candidates differently.

The English psychologist Edward Titchener also documented the effect almost 100 years ago, and described the 'warm glow' felt in the presence of something familiar just merely through exposure and repetition. Familiarity signals safety, especially when we are feeling vulnerable and unhappy. Happiness, on the other hand, makes novelty attractive and can make the familiar feel very boring. This is perhaps why we seek out our childhood favourite sweets and home-cooked meals when we are lonely or sad. University of California, San Diego psychology professor Piotr Winkielman and colleagues examined the idea by presenting participants with constellation-like random dot patterns made familiar through repeated exposure. Some of the participants were put in a good mood and others in a bad mood by asking them to recall joyous or sad events in their lives. This mood was maintained by appropriate background music for the rest of the test. Finally, the researchers measured the participants' emotional and memory responses to the dot patterns that they had previously been familiarised with. This was done with questionnaires, but also with skin

---

* Ohio State University website (accessed April 2019).

conductors to assess sweat and facial electrodes to detect frowns and smiles. The sad participants preferred the familiar patterns, while this trend was not seen in those who were happy. However, this was not due to happiness reducing familiarity itself, which was still robust and rated highly even when the participants were happy. But happiness cools the warm glow of familiarity.

There is an old adage that 'familiarity breeds contempt', but in fact studies have shown that fear of novelty is heightened in unfamiliar and stressful situations. There is a high cognitive load associated with neophobia. So, when we are in an unfamiliar environment, a familiar face can bring a 'glow of warmth', while the same face in our everyday environment may evoke only a yawn. But our mood can also affect how we react to unfamiliar situations. Impressions are more positive when we are in a good mood and negative when we are in a grump. An environment's safety or danger has also been linked to a person's mood. If they are in a bad mood the environment feels more threatening, whereas it seems more benign when the person is in a good mood. Familiarity bias depends on context. In some cases, it is even possible that happiness encourages the exploration of novelty and inspires a 'warm glow of the unfamiliar'. But when people are feeling threatened and insecure, in situations such as environmental, economic or political upheaval, they are more likely to fall back on their implicit familiarity and status quo biases and be prejudiced against those different from them, seeking comfort with those who are familiar and similar to them.

## All the way to the top

Harriet Zuckerman's PhD research from Columbia University consisted of hour-long interviews with Nobel laureates in the early 1960s. These interviewees repeatedly suggested that eminent scientists receive disproportionately positive credit for their contributions to science, while lesser-known scientists get little credit for their often very significant, if not comparable, contributions. As a laureate in physics put it: 'The world is peculiar in this matter of how it gives credit. It tends to give the credit to already famous people,' and as a chemistry laureate says, 'If my name was on a paper, people would remember it and not remember who else was involved.' This theory of accumulated advantage, or misallocation of recognition, is linked to the bias that people who are already high-status will be evaluated more positively than those who are not, irrespective of quality, and this leads to even further inequality.

We saw in Chapter 4 that we tend to organise people in hierarchies. Humans rank others hierarchically to make sense of the world. Evolutionarily, this is how allocation of resources worked. Status hierarchies were organised either through prestige or through coercion, and in some ways this hasn't changed much. Social scientists have done extensive work in how status is linked to prestige and access to opportunities and resources. Status is associated with characteristics such as race and gender and is linked to not only economic and social benefits but also psychological rewards. The 'Matthew effect', coined by social scientist Robert Merton in 1968, upholds the adage that 'the rich get richer, and the poor get poorer'. Merton derives the term from the first book of the New Testament, the Gospel According to Matthew, where in the text of the King James version, it reads, 'For unto everyone that hath shall be given, and he shall have abundance; but from him that hath not shall be taken away even that which he hath.' This status-based screening is driven by unconscious biases that are 'non-functional', which means that these biases are not intentionally designed to select for better outcomes but are discriminatory nevertheless. People evaluate others based on the recognition they have achieved, and this will lead to different outcomes for two people with identical qualities but different status. For instance, a scientific researcher will have their latest work cited, they will get more funding and even more recognition if they have already received an award, because the academic community carries a bias that expects them to perform at a higher level than their colleagues. This underlying bias makes their research seem more cogent to others. Simine Vazire, Associate Professor of Psychology at University of California, Davis, says in a paper in *Nature* that 'recognition is awarded partly on the basis of past recognition', especially in academia. For instance, reviewers are more likely to accept papers by famous authors when they know the authors' identity than when they are anonymous.

Books by famous authors sell more than those who are relatively unknown, even when they are of relatively equivalent quality. This can make concessions for well-known academics and authors to be inconsistent with the quality of their work, something that would impact a lesser-known individual more. Physicist and information scientist Derek J. de Solla Price observed this phenomenon when studying the network of citations between scientific papers. The network analysis shows visual evidence of interconnections with influential people or most cited academics appearing as 'hubs' – nodes or vertices in this scale-free* network – that have much higher connection

---

* A network is called scale-free if the characteristics of the network are independent of the size of the network, i.e. the number of nodes. That means that when the network grows, the underlying structure remains the same.

than average. This can be explained much more easily by the concept of 'six degrees of separation'. The 'six degrees of Kevin Bacon' in the Hollywood film industry is similar, where anyone involved in the Hollywood film industry can be linked through their film roles to Bacon within six steps,* thereby demonstrating the power of connections and its role in assigning status.

The bias underlying the Matthew effect also underlies the 'halo effect', where there is a tendency to see higher-status individuals as more competent and powerful. A study by Jerry Kim of Columbia University and Brayden King, an associate professor of management and organisations at the Kellogg School, examines the cognitive biases that affect umpires in Major League Baseball. They analysed pitches thrown during the 2008 and 2009 seasons and made a startling discovery that higher-status pitchers – those most valued and recognised by public and fellow players – receive more favourable calls from umpires on similar pitches than lower-status pitchers. The lower-status pitchers are more likely to be penalised than their more well-known compatriots. This unconscious bias and favouritism can accumulate and affect the outcome of a game.

Social status hierarchies have the effect of biasing attention, not only in terms of social attention but also eye gaze. Experiments with eye-tracking systems have shown that both reflexive and voluntary gaze is most often focused on high-dominance faces in group situations. People who already have higher status will be noticed more easily and be more prominent. A status bias has been seen to affect

---

* Also called the 'Bacon number'. Similarly, the Erdős number describes the 'collaborative distance' between mathematician Paul Erdős and another person, as measured by authorship of mathematical papers.

patterns of scientific collaboration, growth of sociotechnical and biological networks, propagation of citations, scientific progress and impact, career longevity, evolution of common words and phrases, and education, as well as many other aspects of human culture and decision-making. Social status is perceived through achievement and 'valued dimensions', which change as per social and cultural norms. In a certain cultural context, academic achievement might be seen as a sign of social status, while in others significance might be assigned based on how rich someone is or even how many followers they have on social media. This kind of hierarchy exists because individuals from both higher and lower status benefit from it – the former achieving respect and regard and maybe financial rewards, with the latter learning from those who are of higher status than themselves.

## I knew it would happen!

On 31 March 2009, six Italian scientists and a former government official met in the ancient city of L'Aquila to discuss the possibility of a major earthquake in the region. Despite recent tremors recorded nearby, the group concluded that it was impossible to predict a major earthquake. Six days later, a 6.3 magnitude earthquake hit, killing more than 300 people. Three years later, an Italian court sentenced the group to six years in jail for manslaughter for their failure to warn the public of the pending earthquake. Of course, it isn't easy to debate whether the court was justified in making this decision or not without knowing the intricate details of this case. But, to me, it appears that the court had overestimated the likelihood of the outcome in hindsight. The scientists did not know the outcome, so they analysed the data and evidence and made an educated guess. It is easier in hindsight to predict the outcome.

Often when I am watching Hercule Poirot on television or reading a mystery thriller, I find myself saying 'Oh, I knew it' or 'I could see it coming' – after the fact! – much to the annoyance of people around me. This is hindsight bias, sometimes referred to as the 'I-knew-it-all-along phenomenon'. It involves the tendency people have to assume that they knew the outcome of an event after the outcome has already been determined. Even as a speaker or a writer, hindsight bias can compel us to overestimate how much the listeners or readers know and understand.

Being asked to recollect an event that has happened in the past places a high cognitive load on us, and we are more likely to fall back on our implicit bias and use heuristics for any sort of decision-making. We may distort our earlier predictions after we know the outcome, or we may view events as inevitable, assuming that the outcome was always going to happen. We also assume that we knew this all along. This can be caused by false memory or recall bias because how we tend to recall past events depends on our current context and emotional state, as well as on how pleasurable past events were.

With hindsight bias there is a tendency to view things as more predictable and inevitable than was actually the case. For instance, in 1991, researchers Martin Bolt and John Brink asked college students to predict how the US Senate would vote on the confirmation of Supreme Court nominee Clarence Thomas. Prior to the vote, 58 per cent of the participants predicted that he would be confirmed, but when they polled again after Thomas had already been confirmed, 78 per cent of the participants said they had thought Thomas would be approved.

Baruch Fischhoff, an American academic, is credited with first coining the phrase: 'In hindsight, people consistently exaggerate what could have been anticipated

with foresight.' Fischhoff gave undergraduate subjects a
description of an unfamiliar 19th-century war between
Britain and the Nepalese Gurkhas in the form of a 150-word
description of the conflict, including the strengths and
weaknesses of each army. This description listed four
possible outcomes of the conflict (British victory, Gurkha
victory, stalemate with no peace settlement, and stalemate
with a peace settlement). Subjects were told that one of the
four possible outcomes had occurred but provided no
information about the actual outcome. Subjects read the
materials and then answered the following question: 'In
light of the information appearing in the passage, what was
the probability of occurrence of each of the four possible
outcomes?' Subjects who were told that one of the outcomes
had occurred made inflated estimates of the likelihood of
that outcome, as compared to the subjects who were given
no information about the outcome. In this study, and in the
replications that Fischhoff ran with other scenarios,[*] it was
seen that when the participants were provided with an
outcome, their assessment of the likelihood of that outcome
increased by between 6.3 and 44.0 percentage points.[†]
People not only tend to view what has happened as having
been inevitable, but also to view it as having appeared
'relatively inevitable' before it happened. They believe that

---

[*] Fischhoff was keen to emphasise the replicability of the psychological
experiments, and that 'priming' and the specific context affected the
outcome, which is why it was important to test these in various
scenarios to remove any inherent bias.
[†] In the experiment, the participants were not asked to estimate
probabilities of the possible outcomes of a future conflict between
the British and the Gurkhas, so they were not learning from past
events. Instead, they were asked to predict a past event without any
knowledge of the outcome, although they were given some options
for the outcome.

others should have been able to anticipate events much better than was actually possible. The experiment that launched the concept of hindsight bias was carried out in 1975, in which the participants were asked to rate the likelihood of various outcomes to the then US President Nixon's pending trip to China and the Soviet Union. For example, participants rated the likelihood that Nixon would meet Chairman Mao and that Nixon would declare the trip a success. After Nixon completed the trip, the participants were asked to recall their initial predictions. The results were clear; the participants gravitated towards the actual event outcomes. For instance, participants who initially thought it unlikely that Nixon would meet Mao later recalled that they had thought this meeting likely, because it had actually happened in real life.

Hindsight bias affects our ability to learn from our experiences. When we believe that we already knew what was going to happen, we are likely to overestimate our abilities. We all tend to selectively recall information consistent with what we now know to be true as we try and impose meaning on our own knowledge. 'If you feel like you knew it all along, it means you won't stop to examine why something really happened,' says Neal Roese, who along with Kathleen Vohs* also proposed the three-tier misinformation bias structure for hindsight bias. In this structure, the first level of hindsight bias is memory distortion, which involves misremembering an earlier opinion or judgement ('I said it would happen'). The second level, inevitability, centres on our belief that the event was inevitable ('It had to happen').

---

* Roese and Vohs sum up hindsight bias as 'myopic attention to a single causal understanding of the past (to the neglect of other reasonable explanations) as well as general overconfidence in the certainty of one's judgements'.

And the third level is foreseeability, which involves the belief that we personally could have foreseen the event ('I knew it would happen'). This is also linked to confirmation bias, discussed in the previous chapter, where we choose to selectively view information that confirms what we already know to be true. People also have a need to see the world as orderly and predictable and to avoid being blamed for problems. Hindsight bias has been found to be greater when the outcome is negative rather than positive, which aligns with outcome bias where people pay more attention to negative events, and the more severe the negative outcome, the more pronounced is the hindsight bias.

After Donald Trump won the presidential election, I remember speaking to many of my friends who said the same thing: 'I knew he was going to win,' 'Oh, it was always going to happen,' or 'The signs were always there.' During the election process, and through all the debates, and even through all the exit polls, many people had believed firmly that there was no chance Trump would ever become president. The thing with hindsight bias is that it influences our memory of the past in a way that makes us overconfident of being able to predict the future accurately. Or we tend to edit our memories to make it seem that we couldn't have predicted the outcome and feel less foolish that we didn't see the inevitable signs.

Hindsight bias is not learning from experience or foresight. It is a complex cognitive bias, embodying any combination of three aspects: memory distortion, beliefs about events' objective likelihoods, and subjective beliefs about one's own prediction abilities. Three theories have been proposed for hindsight bias, from motivational and cognitive perspectives. The first is that people have a natural inclination to believe in a just and fair world, with the 'just deserts' bias that 'people get what they deserve'. However, research studies have only managed to find a weak correlation between a just world belief and hindsight bias. The second theory – also part of the motivational framework explaining hindsight bias – maintains that this bias stems from a natural tendency for individuals to want to avoid appearing foolish. Thus the individuals assert that they could have predicted the outcome even if (perhaps especially if) no one else around them could. Termed 'impression management', this has explained hindsight bias to some extent but, much like the first motivational theory, cannot provide a full explanation. The third theory states that hindsight bias is a more deeply ingrained cognitive process termed 'creeping determinism', a sense that what happened to us was in fact inevitable. Fischhoff described creeping determinism as 'when we apply a filter to the past to produce a series of events that seems obvious in hindsight, tossing out everything else that kept those events from being obvious as they happened. It's connecting the dots on an otherwise blank piece of paper, having erased the previous scatter of dots from which no discernible pattern could emerge.' Hindsight bias hampers our ability to connect the dots.

Hindsight bias happens at sporting events, in court rooms, in medical decisions and in business, and is one of the most common 'decision-traps'. In 2018, President Trump tweeted: 'Watching the Dodgers/Red Sox final innings. It is amazing how a manager takes out a pitcher who is loose & dominating through almost 7 innings, Rich Hill of Dodgers, and brings in nervous reliever(s) who get shellacked. 4 run lead gone. Managers do it all the time, big mistake!' Richard Thaler, Nobel Prize winner in Behavioural Economics, responded to this tweet with: 'Hindsight Bias Illustrated'.

As hindsight bias developed as an information-processing adaptation targeted at a common world, it should not be expected to differ across different cultures. Rüdiger Pohl and Michael Bender published an article in the journal *Experimental Psychology* from the results of an experiment carried out across many different countries and cultures over the internet rather than face-to-face. The 225 respondents participated in a hypothetical scenario, from four different continents (Asia, Australia, Europe and North America). Hindsight bias was large and similar for all samples except for German and Dutch participants. If someone is highly surprised he or she will be less likely to exhibit hindsight bias, and if the element of surprise is minimised then the hindsight bias will be more prominent. Of course, cultural aspects may determine whether someone experiences surprise or not at a particular situation, and the individual motivations of people will vary even in the same context, but the worldwide stability of hindsight bias cannot be discounted. The researchers concluded that this is because hindsight bias relies on a cognitive process where the cultural conditioning does not play a huge role. Unlike racial and gender-based biases, this kind of bias is therefore less informed and shaped by our cultural and social norms. It has also been suggested that perhaps hindsight bias is a form of adaptive learning, where to preserve the load on our memory and cognitive resources, we are advised to update our cognitive model as soon as new information is available; and we also forget – or 'put aside' – any previous model that might be wrong. We do this to be able to retrieve relevant information most suited to our current circumstances and thereby lose access to out-of-date information.

The lesson we learn from understanding hindsight bias is that we cannot predict the future from the past. In discussing some of the cognitive heuristics that shape our biases, cognitive psychologists often use them to assert that these are shortcuts taken when a person is rushed or unmotivated to make the most rational or correct call. However, as we saw in Chapter 2, these biases aren't always errors. Sometimes people assign the status of bias to behaviours that they find difficult to categorise and label as appropriate as per the normative standard,* but they can also lead to functional decisions as well as rational judgements. In this way, it is important to remember that not all unconscious biases are dangerous or damaging for us, though many do lead to prejudice and discrimination. Also, we need to remind ourselves that what seems so obvious to us now might not have been so clear when it happened. To paraphrase Arthur Conan Doyle: 'Nothing is so easy as to be wise after the event.'

## What would you say?

Amos Tversky and Daniel Kahneman in their landmark work in 1983 asked participants to solve the following problem:

> Linda is 31 years old, single, outspoken, and very bright. She majored in philosophy. As a student, she was deeply concerned with issues of discrimination and social justice, and also participated in anti-nuclear demonstrations. Which is more probable?
>
> 1. Linda is a bank teller.
> 2. Linda is a bank teller and is active in the feminist movement.

More than 80 per cent of participants chose option 2, regardless of whether they were novice, intermediate or

---

* Dina Berkeley and Patrick Humphreys wrote a paper about this: 'Structuring decision problems and the bias heuristic' in 1982, if you are interested in reading more.

expert statisticians, even though the mathematical probability of Linda being both a bank teller and a feminist activist is much lower than the probability of her being a bank teller alone. This is an excellent example of how our brain makes connections where none exist. This is also an example of 'conjunction fallacy', which happens because of our representative bias. Here, most people read the description and use a representative heuristic to choose the statement that is most representative of Linda from the brief description. We also have an inherent bias that detailed statements are more likely than general ones. There has been criticism and debate on this problem, but it remains one of the earliest and most well-known examples of the way our brain interprets information, makes connections and deduces things about people.

In another example, the participants were asked:

Suppose Björn Borg reaches the Wimbledon finals in 1981. Please rank order the following outcomes from most to least likely.

- Borg will win the match
- Borg will lose the first set
- Borg will lose the first set but win the match
- Borg will win the first set but lose the match

Participants rated 'Borg will lose the first set but win the match' more likely than 'Borg will lose the first set'.

We believe that specific conditions are more probable than general ones, simply because it is more descriptive and interesting, so a conjunction of two statements – or conditions – is more believable than one. This is a 'conjunction fallacy'.

★★★

Our biases have a huge impact on how we recall certain events and situations. We tend to be swayed by what we easily recall and remember, what is most familiar to us and what is easily available to us in our memory. This can be affected by our beliefs, our contexts, how often we see something, how prominent something is and how much significance we assign to certain events and individuals. We assume that our recollections are representative and true and then we tend to discard events that are outside of our immediate memory. We tend to remember tragic accidents and incidents more than happy ones. We might believe that there are more plane crashes than car crashes because we remember reports of an air accident more vividly than those of a car crash.

This demonstrates the power of narrative – the narrative fallacy – where we avoid looking merely at facts but always attempt to weave an explanation, a logical link and a story around them. This is because stories make facts interesting. We look for stories that strike a chord in us, and so we fall victim to the narrative fallacy by believing that the better the story, the more likelihood of it having happened.

# SEX TYPE-CAST

## CHAPTER SEVEN

# Sugar and Spice

The actress Anne Hathaway admitted that the first time she worked with a woman director – Lone Scherfig, in the film *One Day* – her instinct was to doubt her. 'I really regret not trusting her more easily,' Hathaway said. 'And I am to this day scared that the reason I didn't trust her the way I trust some of the other directors I work with is because she's a woman.' Accusing herself ruefully of 'internalised misogyny', Hathaway said[*] that when she sees a film directed by a woman, she finds herself focusing on its faults; when it's by a man, she looks first at its merits. On the difference between men's and women's careers, Hathaway also says: 'That journey is way harder than it should be. It's not equal.'

A Yale University study found that male and female scientists – both trained to be objective – were more likely to hire men, consider them more competent than women, and pay them $4,000 more per year than women. A science faculty rated male applicants for a laboratory manager position as significantly more competent and hireable than female applicants. They also offered a higher starting salary and more career mentoring to the male applicant. When this was pointed out to them explicitly, the faculty members were often shocked as they hadn't realised they were being discriminatory or biased in any way.

---

[*] On ABC's *Popcorn with Peter Travers* in 2017.

Gender stereotypes are formed very early on and are pervasive and continue to create inequalities between men and women. Charles Stangor and colleagues from the University of Maryland say in the *Journal of Personality and Social Psychology* that gender categorisation is both a perceptual and a cognitive process. The perceptual bias allows us to focus on differences between individuals, exaggerating those of our in-group and out-group more than is true to reality. These gender binaries and differences persist despite research showing that gender is a spectrum rather than these two opposing values. Much of the implicit and explicit gender bias starts from the caveat that there exist two homogenous groups predetermined and defined by their biology.

Aristotle proposed the theory of 'dualism' – whereby something is one or other, true or false, logical or illogical – and in doing so created a binary bias. It is believed that in around 350 BC he borrowed from Pythagoras to expand his table of opposites and impose a dual hierarchy on everything in this world. Aristotle assigns the attributes curving, dark, secret, ever-moving and not self-contained to the 'female' side, while the terms straight, light, honest, good, stable, self-contained are attributes on the 'male' side. In this way, he can be considered the founder of sex polarity. He was the first philosopher to argue that women and men have irreconcilable philosophical differences and that women are inherently inferior to men. Philo, another Greek philosopher in the Aristotelean tradition, further reinforces this gendered divide in saying that 'female gender is material, passive, corporeal and sense-perceptible, while the male is active, rational, incorporeal and more akin to mind and thought.' Aristotle's belief that women – being endowed with irrationality, weakness, passivity – were not capable of abstract reasoning and therefore should be bound to the domestic sphere created a powerful legacy of gender discrimination that persisted and dominated in our society.

Consider this scenario: a father and his son are in a car accident. The father is killed and the son is seriously injured. The son is taken to the hospital, where the surgeon says, 'I cannot operate, because this boy is my son.' Even though this is a relatively well-known example now, almost 85 per cent of people were thrown by this riddle in an experiment performed as recently as 2014. The researchers ran the riddle by two groups: 197 Boston psychology students and 103 children, ages seven to 17. Many who did not find this confusing admitted that their first instinct was to consider this to be a homosexual couple, which also implied that they first considered the surgeon to be a man. The results were no different for an alternate version of the riddle: a mother is killed, her daughter sent to the hospital, and a nurse declines to attend to the patient, saying, 'That girl is my daughter.' Very few people guessed that the nurse might be the child's father. In January 2018, a research study showed the pervasiveness of gender stereotypes. Across four studies, students solved riddles with gender stereotype-consistent (e.g. doctor is male) or gender stereotype-inconsistent (e.g. doctor is female; barber is female) solutions. The time taken to solve them, and their perceived difficulty were measured. Results indicated that students solved the stereotype-inconsistent riddles more slowly than stereotype-consistent riddles. Also, stereotype-inconsistent riddles were rated as more difficult to solve than stereotype-consistent riddles.

Persons about whom null or ambiguous gender information is available are more often considered male than female. The default prototype for a human category is male, and neutral terms have masculine connotations. Gender schemas are formed early in life. Our life experiences can change and shape these to a certain extent, but overall these early schemas are very powerful. For instance, women are associated with reproductive functioning, and men are more likely to be associated with competence. The image that pops into our brains when we think of 'doctor', 'scientist', 'pilot', 'football coach' and 'surgeon' is often male. The order we receive the information in and how we receive information can also affect our recall of information and bias. There is inherent gender bias in much of our language. For instance, male-referring words such as bachelor, master and lord have more positive connotations than the feminine equivalents – spinster, mistress and lady – that belittle them and place them in an inferior position. Sexism in language is also seen in how female-oriented terms are often placed second to male terms, such as 'husband and wife', 'brother and sister', and 'man and woman'. This is called a 'male-firstness' bias, which can seem like a trivial point but reinforces the second-place status of women. So many terms in our vocabulary are gendered too: manhandle, manmade, manpower, mankind, and so on.* Penelope Eckert and Sally McConnell-Ginet in their book *Language and Gender* report that sometime in the 16th century, it was decided that the male pronoun would be the norm, as 'the masculine gender is more worthy than the feminine' and this was then conventionalised and went unquestioned until relatively recently.

According to a study in *The Journal of Sex Research*, Malachi Willis and Kristen Jozkowski show that when male terms are shown before female terms in scientific writing, it can influence people's interpretation of the research results

---

* In July 2019, Berkeley in California introduced a bill to remove some of these gendered words from the city code and replace them with gender-neutral words such as 'humankind'.

and also their recall of its contents. In previous research, the authors had already shown that peer research in academic journals is not free of linguistic sexism. To assess the presence of 'male first' in academic writing, Willis and Jozkowski examined 862 contemporary articles from 10 social science journals across three disciplines: sexuality, health and psychology. They tallied common gendered pairs (e.g. women and men; male and female) and calculated percentages indicating how often men were presented before women. The authors found that 'male-firstness' bias was present in each of the 10 journals. In the most recent experiment published in 2019, the effect of male-firstness on the perception of the quality of the academic writing and recall was evaluated. It is shown that male-firstness is not an overt but a more latent (unconscious) form of gender bias – a stronger and more harmful form of sexism than that which is easily recognised and explicit. Seeing male-firstness in texts also reinforces the implicit bias that men are more important and have to be given premium position.

Words and images are powerful forces that shape our reality and create implicit bias. Language matters. Language can influence cognition and there is a certain theoretical framework, called linguistic determinism, which shows that how our language is structured can determine the way we perceive the world. If no gender-based information is available, we assume a gender based on our stereotypes and social norms, and we are more likely to rely on our implicit biases.

## Women are all tongue

There is a widespread understanding that men and women talk and write in a certain way, differently from each other. These differences can be seen even in relatively short pieces of content (such as a tweet).* Males are believed to convey their thoughts in a rather concise manner with more facts and summaries, while women are much more likely to imbue their texts with a greater level of social interaction, emotion and empathy. The relative use of pronouns varies too. The data journalist Ben Blatt used statistics to analyse large sets of classic literature, modern bestsellers and contemporary literary fiction. His findings show that from 100 such books, male writers used 'chief' and 'rear' most often, while 'pillows' and 'curl' featured heavily in writings by women. The most startling difference was in the use of pronouns such as 'he' and 'she'. In books written by men, there is a tendency to write women out almost completely, with 'she' being used only once in *The Hobbit*. On the other hand, in books written by women – and even if the subject is very female-oriented, for example *The Joy Luck Club* – there is still 29 per cent occurrence of 'he'.

Although in saying that women use a different way of communication and language, linguists are reinforcing these gender stereotypes, there is nevertheless some value in understanding how these myths can shape people's perception of gender and communication. According to Deborah Cameron, Rupert Murdoch Professor of Language and Communication at Worcester College Oxford, women's (spoken) language consists of the following features:

1. Disfluency (stopping and starting)
2. Unfinished sentences
3. Speech not ordered by the norms of logic
4. Speaking less than men in mixed groups

---

* In a poll that I conducted over Twitter, 86 per cent of people (from 125 who responded) believed that there is an inherent difference in the way that men and women write and speak.

5. Cooperative strategies in conversation (seeking approval and providing support)
6. Couching statements in questions

The overall proposition is that women show subordination, emotional empathy, lack of authority and generally lack of confidence. Robin Lakoff, a prominent linguist, also suggested that women added more questions to the end of their sentences than men. Lakoff proposed that 'women's talk is more polite than men's; women use more tag questions (e.g. 'isn't it?'), use weaker directives, avoid swearing, and use more empty adjectives (e.g. 'cute') than men.' The author Naomi Wolf wrote in 2015 that 'even the most brilliant [women] tend to avoid bold declarative sentences and organise their arguments less forcefully [than men]'. However, Professor Elizabeth Stokoe in her book *Talk: The Science of Conversation* calls the whole science that is used to provide evidence for the difference between male and female ways of talking to be built on 'shaky foundations'. Such headlines asserting that women write and speak differently to men recycles the same traditional view of women as being less assertive and logical; therefore women's place in society – an inferior place – is maintained through this language. These claims that women and men write and speak in different ways do not ever get debunked or tested rigorously, and they become part of the urban myths that everyone quotes and believes in. And, as we know, the more we hear something, the more likely we are to believe in its veracity.

'Then you should say what you mean,' the March Hare went on.
    'I do,' Alice hastily replied; 'at least – at least I mean what I say – that's the same thing, you know.'

— Lewis Carroll, *Alice's Adventures in Wonderland, 1865*

This is also yet another example of pseudoscience that highlights differences between men and women by asserting that there is a distinction based in their biology and behaviour, and in doing so drawing these gender divides even more emphatically. In focusing primarily on gender, there is a higher possibility of making erroneous claims about women and men, while at the same time missing other explanations for the way people talk. Professor Stokoe says: 'Researchers do not really study gender difference. They simply create and maintain it. They make selective observations to confirm what we already know about how women and men behave.'

There is also a common assumption that women talk more than men. 'A woman's tongue wags like a lamb's tail' is an old proverb, as is the French proverb 'Foxes are all tail and women are all tongue.' In 2018, David Bonderman, the venture capitalist on the board of Uber, was at a meeting addressing sexism. Arianna Huffington, a fellow board member, was discussing the results of a gender discrimination report and mentioned that research had shown that once there had been one woman on a board, more were likely to be hired. Bonderman interrupted Huffington, saying: 'Actually, what it shows is that there's much more likely to be more talking.'[*] He resigned soon after.

The words used to describe women talking in popular literature and in common parlance perpetuate this myth: words such as chatter, gossip, prattle, natter – and the myth of men being the 'strong silent type' – persist. These stereotypes exist across different cultures. A Japanese proverb says: 'Where there are women and geese, there's noise', and a Scottish one: 'Nothing is so unnatural as a talkative man or a quiet woman.' Many self-help books

---

[*] The *Guardian*, 13 June 2017.

assert that women use an average of 20,000 words a day, compared to men's mere 7,000 words. However, in a meta-analysis across 73 studies with children, it was found that there are very minor differences in the number of words girls and boys speak (and this is only until the age of two and half years, at which point language skills start developing at almost the same rate). This analysis gives some indication that girls use more affiliative speech (pertaining to social and emotional bonds) and boys more assertive speech. However, it is worth questioning how much this is due to gendered socialisation and expectations, and the implicit cues they receive from their environment and peers. The assertion that women talk more than men is clearly a myth.

A study by researchers at Bingham State and Princeton University showed that when women are outnumbered, they speak up to a quarter less than men. Women deliberate; they do not often speak until they are 100 per cent confident. Research has also shown that more men have a propensity to 'mansplain' and as they become more powerful, they become more voluble. Women take longer to process thoughts before they feel comfortable saying them out loud compared to men. This effect has also been shown in studies carried out in the classroom, where men are seen to be more outspoken than women. In a Harvard University study, Catherine G. Krupnick researched gender influence on participation within various classroom settings. This found that male students spoke more often than female students. Yale Psychologist Victoria L. Brescoll found that male senators with more power (as measured by tenure and leadership positions) spoke more on the Senate floor than their junior colleagues. Women, on the other hand, become more concerned about backlash (see stereotype threat) as they reach leadership positions, so female leaders are likely to speak less often than men in spaces with equal representation of men and women because they are fearful of being perceived as aggressive. The final part of this study showed that powerful women are in fact correct in assuming that they will incur backlash as a result of talking more than others. Women are punished for talking, while men are rewarded.

Language studies have shown that men interrupt more than women. Julia Baird in the *New York Times* says, 'The prevalence of the manologue* is deeply rooted in the fact that men take, and are allocated, more time to talk in almost every professional setting. Women self-censor, edit, apologize for speaking. Men expound.' A study from George Washington University found that men interrupted 33 per cent more often when they spoke with women than when they spoke with other men. Forty participants (20 male) had brief conversations with trained male and female communication partners in a repeated-measures, within-subject design, and 80 three-minute conversations were transcribed and coded. According to the researchers, over the course of a three-minute conversation, men interrupted women 2.1 times. In contrast, during conversations of the same duration, men interrupted other men only 1.8 times – and women on average interrupted men only once. An analysis of 43 studies by two researchers at the University of California, Santa Cruz from 1998 found that men were more likely to interrupt women with the intent to assert dominance in the conversation, meaning men were interrupting to

---

* The manologue is similar to mansplaining and is 'characterized by the proffering of words not asked for, of views not solicited and of arguments unsought. It is underwritten by the doubtful assumption that the audience will naturally be interested, and that this interest will not flag.' (*New York Times*, 20 April 2016)

take over the conversation floor. This asymmetrical nature
of interruptions has social significance. Interruptions
affect the assessment of individuals involved, as well as
confirming social status and hierarchies. There is research
to show that interruptions are associated with dominance
and not only reflect unequal power (as in parents and
children) but also serve to legitimise it. Interruptions are
seen as assertive if they are carried out by the individual
with more power and privilege in the social hierarchy,
while the same interruption connotes insubordination if
it is performed by the one who is seen as lower in status.
They can also indicate that the interrupter regards the
partner as less worthy.

What is clear from these studies is that the context
matters, and although there is a general widespread
perception that women talk more, it is more likely to be in
informal contexts and in an exploratory manner, while
men take centre stage in more formal settings such as
media, conferences and classrooms, where any talk has a
status-enhancing potential. In a paper in 1991, Janet
Holmes from Victoria University of Wellington, undertook
an analysis of 100 public meetings and showed that in 93 of
these meetings men dominated the conversation, asking 75
per cent of the questions. Even when there was an equal
number of men and women, men asked more than 62 per
cent of the questions, hence dominating the conversation.
Mark Liberman, Professor of Phonetics at the University of
Pennsylvania, says that the idea that women talk more than
men is as pervasive as the Inuit having 17 words for snow
(they only have one), and the idea that women talk more is
just an 'urban myth'. Nevertheless, this idea persists. Dale
Spender, an Australian feminist, says in the book *Language
Myths* that this is because 'The talkativeness of women has
been gauged in comparison not with men but with silence.

Women have not been judged on the grounds of whether they talk more than men, but of whether they talk more than silent women.'

The bias has been created because women are expected to be silent – 'good women do not talk' – and girls are taught to be nice, selfless, polite, quiet. Moreover, women learn from experience that every time they express an opinion, they walk a tightrope. Either they are judged to be too aggressive and too 'mouthy' or they are interrupted and shut down while someone else takes their idea and runs forth with it. It seems that the 'strong silent type' persona for men is also a myth and a stereotype. When this idea is perpetuated, it becomes more acceptable for men to equate 'strength' and 'masculinity' with silence.

Language is a result of socialisation. It is an anchor for societal norms and has to be understood in context. If the language is conveying that women feel they are the inferior sex, then this reflects the wider societal perception and view of women. Both women and men self-stereotype and internalise the wider stereotypes. Many of these biases arise from the idea that men and women constitute two homogenous groups and that the variation between the two is significantly more than the variation within each group itself. Sexism is a unique sort of bias as the prejudice towards women from men does not fit into the traditional mould of antipathy. In fact, most men who are misogynists claim to love women. Susan Fiske and Peter Glick, who have worked on this gender duality for a long time, emphasise the idea of 'ambivalent sexism', saying that 'a man's interest in marrying a woman does not necessarily suggest he rejects sexism. That a sexist might reject women at work yet fervently embrace them at home cuts to the core of how ambivalence toward women differs from racial ambivalence.'

## Born leaders

Women and men are treated differently in the workplace. Women, in essence, face a double-bind bias. They are either too 'soft' to be good leaders or if they demonstrate qualities that are more 'masculine' they are considered too aggressive and therefore not a good leader. The masculine–feminine stereotypes count not only against women but also against men. These push people into certain boxes, and when they demonstrate qualities that are not seen as the norm they are more likely to be bullied.

In 2017, Pew Research Center asked 4,573 Americans these questions: 'What traits does society value most in men and in women? What traits does society say men and women should not have?' The respondents answered with more than 1,500 unique words describing traits that they thought society does and doesn't value for each gender.[*] Americans are much more likely to use 'powerful' in a positive way to describe men (67 per cent positive) than women (92 per cent negative). 'Honest' was used much more frequently to describe men (200 times) than women (100 times). 'Beautiful' was only used for women. 'Provider' was only used for men. The most interesting results were that certain personality traits are seen as positive for one gender but less positive or even negative for the other gender. For instance, 'strength' is one value that was seen as a really positive trait for men, but not so much for women. They also saw 'leadership' and 'ambition' as traits that society values more in men than in women, while 'compassion' and 'caring' were seen as positive traits for women but more negatively for men, thereby revealing the widespread societal culture of 'toxic masculinity'. This is a stereotypical notion of masculinity that restricts the

[*] Pew Social Report, 24 July 2018.

range of emotions available to men (they are not expected to cry, for example), which perpetuates tropes such as 'boys will be boys' to justify aggressive behaviour by men. The gender bias can be seen also in the words that were used exclusively for women in the Pew Center research: 'multitasking', 'beautiful', 'maternal'. The data showed how gender-type characterisations and biases are deeply embedded in our society. While 51 per cent of the respondents thought that women should be 'independent', 49 per cent of them still thought they shouldn't, alluding to the submissive roles that women are expected to inhabit. This is a surprising reality of subversive sexism and traditional gender norms in 2017!

The Reykjavik Index for Leadership measures the extent to which men and women are viewed equally in terms of the suitability of individuals for positions of power from a dataset of 10,000 people.[*] The Index runs from 0 to 100; a score of 100 means that across society, there is complete agreement that men and women are equally suited to leadership in all sectors. This was conducted across 20 different sectors in the G7 countries.[†] The results divided them into two groups: a group of four that have relatively high Reykjavik Indices (the cumulative score across all sectors), led by the UK (72), followed by France and Canada (both 71) and the US (70); and a group of three – Italy (57), Germany (59), and Japan (61) – that are a step change below those four.

---

[*] Report on Women Leaders Global, June 2019.
[†] This is a group of seven countries that have the largest and most advanced economies in the world with highest per capita income. When breaking down the numbers, the G7 countries represent over 46 per cent of the gross domestic product globally based on nominal values. The countries in this group have more than 62 per cent of the global net wealth – or a total of $280 trillion.

At first glance, it would seem that women and men are perceived to be equally suited to leadership by more than 70 per cent of the people surveyed for the UK and the US, and above 55 per cent for most countries in the G7 group. However, as we delve deeper into the results, it is interesting to see the variation across the different sectors, with results showing that some professional domains are still considered 'masculine' professions and some as 'feminine' thereby demonstrating the underlying gender bias and the entrenched masculine–feminine polarity. Defence and police, gaming, engineering, and intelligence services are disproportionately seen as suiting male leadership by both men and women. Healthcare and well-being, fashion and beauty, and childcare are seen as suiting female leadership by both men and women. Women in each of these countries are much more likely to believe in the equal suitability of men and women to leadership roles, as compared with men. This dissonance is especially evident in Germany, where 70 per cent of the women surveyed believe that men and women are equally suited to leadership roles, while only 61 per cent of men agree. There is no sector across all the countries where men are more likely than women to consider gender a non-issue when evaluating the suitability of individuals for positions of power. The way this bias is particularly noticeable in the political arena is very interesting. As per the Reykjavik Index for Leadership, 58 per cent of people surveyed in the UK felt comfortable with having a woman head of government. In the UK, we've had two female prime ministers now, but in both cases bias around gender norms and roles have played out in their portrayal by the media and their perception by the general public alike. In the US, 52 per cent of the people surveyed considered men and women to be equally capable of leading the country and heading the government. However, there have still been no female US presidents. In Italy the number of women who would be comfortable with a female leader is particularly low (57 per cent) – much lower than the G7 average of 67 per cent. Internalised misogyny also persists.

Experiments conducted by Laurie Rudman and Stephen E. Kilianski from Rutgers University published in the *Personality and Social Psychology Bulletin* showed that, although women's explicit attitudes were more egalitarian than men's, they had similar implicit biases against other women. Self-reported feminists showed less explicit as well as implicit prejudice against female authorities. A 1996 international Gallup Poll found that the majority of respondents favoured male as opposed to female bosses. Women expressed this preference similarly to men, if not even more often. There has been research to show that some women believe there is no gender bias anymore, and also many women often carry an implicit bias that women are inferior and less capable than men. A study conducted recently by Andrei Cimpian, an associate professor in the department of psychology at NYU, and Lin Bian, a doctoral student at the University of Illinois, showed that there is an implicit bias that women are 'intellectually inferior to men'. From two experiments with more than 1,800 participants of both genders across more than 30 disciplines, the researchers found that when a job requires someone of intellect, women had 25.3 per cent lower probability of being appointed. Genius, brilliance and innate intellectuality are seen as 'masculine' traits, and if a discipline is perceived to require this, then women are under-represented. In a large-scale and geographically diverse study of around 1,800 academics from 30 institutions across the US in 2015, it was seen that when women consider a field (or discipline) to require innate talent for success, they were less represented in this discipline. In comparison, disciplines that require hard work had more female representation, and women considered these fields to be more hospitable.

This gender bias persists from early childhood when these stereotypes start forming. The researchers enlisted 192 children aged between five and seven and taught them how to play two team games, with half of them informed that the games were specifically for clever children. When asked to select teammates to play the game with, the children who knew the game was for clever children showed bias against girls. The authors write: 'stereotypes discourage women's pursuit of many prestigious careers; women are under-represented in fields whose members cherish brilliance.' When raw talent and the requirement to have 'an aptitude that cannot be learned' is seen as a prerequisite for academic success, it creates a false belief that this domain isn't as appropriate for women, and consequently creates a gender divide. This kind of binary gender divide and the implicit gender bias manifests itself in the way children are raised and nurtured. Even mothers have different expectations for their babies when they start crawling. There is no discernible difference between the motor skills of children of different genders. On a range of crawling tasks with 11-month-old infants, mothers underestimated the abilities of female children while overestimating those of male children. It all starts the moment a child is born.

What this discussion shows is that there still exists a gender authority dichotomy where men are naturally afforded a higher status from the simple virtue of being a man, and more men are seen in more powerful social roles in various domains such as political and religious. There is an implicit 'male leader' prototype. And this creates a generalised belief that men are better at controlling resources and should have access to more authority. Women are penalised for being in power, as there is an implicit 'lack of fit' perception between women and power.

★★★

In 2012, Ellen Pao filed a gender-discrimination lawsuit against her employer, the venture-capital firm Kleiner Perkins Caufield & Byers, maintaining that she was penalised for the same behaviours for which her male counterparts were praised. Her experience wasn't unique; a 2016 survey of hundreds of women in technology, titled 'Elephant in the Valley' (such a great name!), revealed that the vast majority experienced both subtle and overt bias in their careers. They asked more than 200 women, focusing on those with at least 10 years of experience, with a broad age range and 75 per cent with children. These women hold positions of power and influence: 25 per cent are CXOs,* 11 per cent are founders, 11 per cent are in venture capital. In addition to capturing start-up companies' data, they also surveyed employees from large organisations including Apple and Google. The survey found how pervasive double-bind bias is and how, even in the top professional echelons, it is very difficult for women – especially in a male-dominated domain such as tech – to strike the right balance without being seen as too meek or too harsh. If women adhere to traditional social norms they are perceived as 'likeable' but at the same time not competent or authoritative enough to be in a leadership role. On the other hand, if they act incongruously to the socially expected gender-type behaviour, such as being ambitious and aggressive, they are judged as 'unlikeable'

---

* A CXO, a chief experience officer, is an executive responsible for the overall experience of an organisation's products and services.

and 'not-people-focused'. Of these women, 84 per cent have been told they are too aggressive (with half hearing that on multiple occasions), 47 per cent have been asked to do lower-level tasks that male colleagues are not asked to do (e.g. note-taking, ordering food), 59 per cent have felt they have not had the same opportunities as their male counterparts, and 90 per cent witnessed sexist behaviour at company offsites and/or industry conferences. The unconscious biases are especially evident in the more implicit attitudes manifesting as microaggressions and micro-incivilities. Furthermore, 88 per cent of the women experienced clients and colleagues addressing questions to male peers that should have been addressed to them. This kind of behaviour might seem inconsequential, but such microaggressions – communicated via verbal or nonverbal messages – are targeted at people based on their membership of a marginalised group, and in this way demean and devalue them, 'othering' them, highlighting their inferior status and marginalising them even further. The fourth annual 'Women in the Workplace' report from LeanIn. Org and McKinsey & Company highlighted gender-based microaggressions still faced by women in 2018 and showed that 64 per cent of women are still exposed to this form of discrimination, with non-white women experiencing it more than anyone else.

The 'gender roles theory' proposes that even though women occupy almost half of the workforce, their social roles differ, as traditional labour divisions are still emphasised, and this is the primary structural cause of gender inequities. In gender roles, there is a descriptive bias of 'what is' and a prescriptive bias of 'what should be'. According to the gender incongruency hypothesis, gender-based bias is created when the position and the perceived gender do not 'fit'. Female leaders pay a price in terms of negative evaluations and harsher measures of assessment if they 'trespass' and intrude on traditionally male domains and occupy male–dominated leadership positions, as they are seen as breaching expectancies and implicit beliefs that men should occupy powerful roles. Women are perceived to be 'unfamiliar' as they break the normative prototype of male entitlement. There are also the implicit stereotypes of men being more agentic (active and resourceful) and women being more communal (convivial and collaborative) that create the bias that men 'make things happen' while women provide support.

Some would, no doubt, argue that society is generally becoming more egalitarian, and that women are benefiting more as a result of the gender revolution. Much like racism, sexism has become more ambivalent and also more subtle because of the increasing awareness and stigmatisation of any explicitly negative prejudices. Therefore, people also insist that there is no gender bias skewed towards men as women are considered 'warmer' and 'more nurturing', and so 'women are wonderful'. The phrase 'women are wonderful'(WAW) was coined by Alice Eagly and Antonio Mladinic in 1994 after finding that both male and female participants tend to assign positive traits to women, with female participants showing a far more pronounced bias. But, as Kristin J. Anderson says in her book *Modern Misogyny: Anti-Feminism in a Post-Feminist Era*, women are wonderful – and preferred – only when they adhere to traditional gender roles. These do not consider the implicit attitudes towards gender, as they are often vastly different from the self-reported gender stereotypes. This WAW effect is akin to ambivalent sexism, a positive stereotype[*] that while disguised as a compliment harms even more

---

[*] We discussed the harmful effects of positive stereotypes in Chapter 5.

than a negative stereotype. A global group of more than 36 researchers published a cross-cultural study across 44 cultures in the *International Journal of Psychology* in 2018, showing that the more gender-egalitarian the society, the more it benefits men as compared to women. Even more significant is the conclusion that when the gender bias is measured implicitly – such as assessing personality through showing photographs of men and women – rather than directly, it reduces the WAW effect in even the most gender-egalitarian societies. Women have to work harder than men in order to prove their competency and capability as leaders, by both putting in more time and energy and by monitoring stereotypical expectations they face as women. However, this hard work can create a negative bias of women leaders being unfavourably judged as 'trying too hard'.

Both hostile sexism (such as anti-feminism) and benevolent sexism (putting women on a pedestal) hurt women, and experiments with Implicit Association Tests (IAT)* show that men demonstrate more of both, as compared with women.

## Petticoat politician

Media sexism is the term used for when media is reporting on sexism in society (media reproducing sexism and gender bias) and also when they portray a more gender-segregated picture than reality (media producing sexism). Women continue to be judged through a different lens than men. The language used around female candidates relies on trite

---

* These are described and discussed in detail in Section IV of this book. It is a test used in psychology to measure the automatic implicit associations, but it has faced controversy in terms of what it measures and how reproducible the results are.

gender stereotypes and has persisted since Victoria
Woodhull ran for US president on the Equal Rights Party
ticket in 1872 and was dubbed 'the petticoat politician' by
the *New York Herald*. Termed 'gendered mediation', the
media representation of politics reinforces rather than
merely reflects gendered and sexist stereotypes, norms and
assumptions. Gender is emphasised more for women
politicians, and they are often regarded as novelties or
trivialised while their male counterparts are portrayed as
the norm. This means that media is a good measure of
societal sexism, but at the same time, it also makes society
more sexist than it would be otherwise by perpetuating the
gender bias and stereotypes. Because of the societal reaction
against sexism and more awareness around gender prejudice,
so much of sexism can be quite subversive and implicit.
The gendered reporting creates a negative stereotype of
any woman in leadership positions, which can in turn stop
other women from putting themselves forward for
leadership roles, as well as perpetuating the myth that
women do not make good leaders. This can also include
downplaying the role and contribution of women in
leadership roles, and allocating them much less airtime so
that people do not see them as often as male candidates.
Much if not all of this is implicit bias, the underlying bias
being that what women have to say is not as important as
men; at the same time, women are penalised more strongly
for any mistakes as compared with men.\*

---

\* Why do I focus on female political candidates here? Because the
entrenched societal structures are biased towards men in general, and
against women. This trend becomes especially significant when we
talk about women in leadership roles and in the public eye. Some
may dispute this with the suggestion that there is no gender bias and
that I am being selective to prove my theory of an implicit bias
against women. I strongly disagree, of course.

The Bem Sex-Role Inventory, created by psychologist Sandra Bem in the 1970s, categorises descriptive language into masculine, feminine and neutral groupings based on how individual words are perceived by the public. Bem found that words like 'ambitious' and 'assertive' have been associated with masculinity, while words such as 'compassionate' and 'loyal' have been associated with femininity. When journalists write about women running for political office, they might – consciously or not – choose gender-coded words to describe these candidates, and these descriptors might in turn affect how the public views these candidates. Visual messages are also very powerful in reinforcing implicit gender biases. For instance, in the 2002 election in Bosnia and Herzegovina, the Organization for Security and Co-operation in Europe (OSCE) highlighted that only 3 per cent of the airtime on television and 1 per cent of print media space was allocated to women candidates, suggesting that the media downplayed the role of women as political actors. In the US presidential election, Hillary Clinton blamed the media for treating her unfairly, and analysis of the data shows the same. The media gave Trump too much unfiltered media time. A *New York Times* article in May 2016 showed that none of the three major cable news networks – CNN, Fox News or MSNBC – carried Clinton's speech to a workers' union in Las Vegas, instead choosing to broadcast a live feed of an empty podium on a stage in North Dakota where Donald Trump was about to speak. On another occasion, the cable networks aired Trump's address to the National Rifle Association live while a speech by Clinton in Detroit days later, to a labour union, did not receive the same coverage, as all networks skipped the speech. A report by the Berkman Klein Center in 2017 analysed the statements in the media related to Trump's and Clinton's scandals and found that nearly 70,000 sentences were written about Clinton's email scandal alone compared with fewer than 50,000 sentences written about all of Trump's various alleged scandals including sexual harassment, treatment of women, taxes and involvement with Russia.* While Trump's political and policy issues such as immigration, trade and jobs had almost 80,000 statements written about them, Clinton's views on trade, immigration and jobs received much less attention, with only about 35,000 statements written about them. Social media echo chambers also play a role in creating and strengthening these gender biases, and they give a clue to the emotional impact of a candidate. The social media analysts Impact Social studied posts on Twitter and other social media platforms in Florida. Even when they had stripped out the mainstream media, they found that Trump was well ahead of Clinton when it came to positive comments. When it came to 'share of voice' online, he was also winning. While this can indicate that Trump's supporters were more vociferous and active online, it also hints at the media bias created online between male and female politicians. People tend to believe more of what we see and hear. And as we believe something more, it reinforces the bias that it must indeed be true. It is then talked about even more, thereby becoming a self-fulfilling prophecy.

The more significant impact of media sexism is when media focuses on the misrepresentation of women, building on the implicit gender bias that already exists in society but also creating a more gendered representation that feeds into strengthening existing ones and creating implicit gendered attitudes. A 2008 book by Erika Falk compared the presidential campaigns of selected female

---

* *Washington Post*, 12 September 2017.

candidates in the United States, between 1872 and 2004, against comparable male candidates and found that media sexism had not changed over time. In fact, a study in 2018 by Blair Williams, a PhD student, showed that media coverage of the UK's female prime ministers has become more gendered from Thatcher to May. Blair compared newspaper coverage (the *Guardian*, the *Daily Telegraph*, the *Mirror* and *The Sun*) of Margaret Thatcher and Theresa May during their first three prime ministerial weeks in 1979 and 2016 respectively. This analysis showed that in the first three weeks of their respective terms as PM, on average, Thatcher's gender was mentioned in 44 per cent of the articles surveyed while May's gender was mentioned in 48 per cent. Interestingly, Thatcher's appearance was only mentioned in 15 per cent of articles while May's was mentioned almost twice as often. The frequency with which the *Daily Telegraph* discussed appearance markedly increased – from 19 per cent to 43 per cent – while *The Sun* also doubled from 12 per cent for Thatcher to 24 per cent for May. Furthermore, while Thatcher's femininity was emphasised on average in 33 per cent of the articles, media emphasis on May's femininity increased to 45 per cent. These results clearly show that the media is becoming more fixated on the appearance of our female leaders. This is one of several studies over the last few decades to have shown that women are scrutinised much more with regards to their ability and competence to lead, with many stories in the media focusing on their appearance and family. In 2018, Massachusetts Congressional candidate Brianna Wu called out the *Boston Globe* for using an old photo of her with bright anime hair and wearing a T-shirt at a gamers convention[*] standing next

---

[*] Photo seen in the *Observer*, August 2018.

to two male opponents wearing suits, even when she had done a photoshoot with them in more professional attire a few days beforehand. In fact, comments on women politicians' appearance is a consistent trope in media, often involving comparison to pets and other animals and pets as a means to infantilise and dehumanise them. Disagreements between women are referred to as 'catfights'. May's authority and political significance, for instance, has been mocked by continual use of the term 'kitten', specifically with reference to 'kitten heels', while Angela Merkel was mocked for her short 'unfeminine' hairstyle and Clinton for her pantsuits. Women can also be infantilised by calling them 'girls', with Merkel called 'Kohl's girl' and shown as a little girl with a purple headband on the cover of a German satirical magazine, and May called a 'head girl'.

Research in 2017 by Girlguiding, the UK's leading charity for girls and women, showed that nearly half (41 per cent) of girls aged between nine and 16 think there has been a rise in media sexism in the last six months, while more than a third (39 per cent) said this has knocked their confidence and would deter them from going into politics. Stefanie Simon and Crystal L. Hoyt showed in an experimental study in 2012 that women exposed to gender-stereotypical media advertisement images report less leadership aspiration than those exposed to counter-stereotypical images. The media have a responsibility to engage young women in voting and support the belief that their opinions matter. Renee Engeln, a professor at Northwestern University, calls this appearance-obsessed culture 'beauty sick' and argues that when a 'women's emotional energy gets so bound up with what they see in the mirror, it becomes harder for them to see other aspects of their lives.'

In 2016, the *Telegraph* suggested that Theresa May was the best candidate for the job because 'she had no children (could be a turn-off for some but it does mean she's less likely to be distracted on the job). She cooks a new recipe every week and goes to church every Sunday'.* The 'mother' stereotype often surfaces in questioning around women's suitability for a role with more responsibilities. Once they become mothers, women are seen as nurturing and caring, which can count in their favour in certain domains. But the question of whether they can juggle work and family – and be a good mother as well as a capable professional – always comes to the fore, whereas it is not an issue for men who become fathers.

From creating an overtly sexualised, feminine and helpless view of women, to dehumanising them using female terms or labelling them as masculine, language subversively cashes in on the wider implicit gender bias that women are not as capable as men. In the case of Sarah Palin, she was overtly sexualised, with much of the media coverage around her beauty pageant background and her attractiveness, such as Maureen Dowd of the *New York Times* calling her 'Caribou Barbie'. Even when there is nothing overtly sexual about female politicians, such references can be made to belittle them and, by focusing merely on their bodies and their clothes, render them trivial. All four stereotypes of professional women surfaced to some degree in media portrayals of Clinton and Palin. In Thatcher's and May's case in the UK, both have been portrayed as masculine, robotic, unemotional and unempathetic – as iron maidens – thereby creating a narrative that they are not adhering to the feminine norms and are displaying too many masculine traits. Thatcher was

---

* *Daily Telegraph*, 28 June 2016.

literally called 'The Iron Lady'; similarly, in Germany, Merkel is called 'Iron Frau'. In doing so, they are ridiculed and lose the trust of the wider public. Both also play into the 'older women' trope as being too aggressive and shrewd, thereby reducing their credibility. While anger and outrage can be seen as a positive quality – indicating passion – in men, anger is seen as an ugly attribute in women, leading to accusations of having a tantrum or a meltdown, with Thatcher accused of 'flying off the handle too quickly'. Likewise, Clinton has been described as 'overly ambitious', 'calculating', 'cold', 'scary' and 'intimidating'.

Media sexism is harmful. Women cannot get it right. But, more so than that, the gendered representations in the media affects how men – and women – perceive leaders. While affecting the women in the public eye* directly, it also signals that women considering a political career must overcome powerful informal norms, thereby dissuading other women from aspiring to top leadership positions. It can stifle leadership and political ambitions, and further widen the gender divide. Despite the fact the wider populace is not directly targeted by any of the media campaigns, the ambient sexism can affect their self-esteem and worth, and they can internalise this bias (similarity-attraction theory). This has been evident in a number of experiments. Rachel Garrett and Dominik Stecula asked 269 university students to read a newspaper article from the newspapers 'The Globe' and 'Mail' about a small-town mayoral race in 2018. In different versions of the article, the gender of the political candidate and the words used to describe them was changed, but everything else about the

---

*There is not enough data on non-binary and transgender candidates and their reporting by the media, and so I limit the discussion to men and women.

articles was exactly the same. One version used feminine-coded descriptive language; another version used masculine-coded language; a third used neutral language such as 'friendly', 'flexible' and 'adaptable'. The results showed how much language matters in creating implicit biases. A woman politician described with masculine-coded adjectives was seen as almost 10 per cent more qualified and 7 per cent more competent than a woman described with feminine adjectives. The results also indicated how much of this gendered language can be internalised as self-bias, as even female respondents rated the female candidate described with feminine adjectives lower, and the female candidate described with masculine adjectives higher, and the masculine-described female candidate as almost 15 per cent more qualified.

Tessa Ditonto from Iowa State University carried out computer simulation studies to assess how people perceive competence and how it affects their biases and perception of political candidates. The study showed that, although voters care more about competence than gender, they are much more demanding of female candidates than of men and use different parameters to assess relative competence of different genders, and that voters of all genders were more forgiving of male candidates. Once a female candidate is assessed as incompetent, the voters are less likely to vote for her even if it meant voting for a candidate from the opposing party. In contrast, male candidates were not judged as harshly, and the party affiliation and membership took precedence. Political theorists have suggested that this could have been one of the factors instrumental in Donald Trump's victory over Hillary Clinton. As we saw in Chapter 6, party membership is becoming a stronger affiliation, especially in American politics, but also here in the UK and in countries such as India. However, in this case, it is seen that gender and the assessment of gendered competence can even outweigh party identification.

## All in the genes

Harvard president Lawrence Summers reignited the debate on the biologically deterministic nature of intelligence by suggesting that women may be under-represented in the sciences because of a lack of 'intrinsic aptitude' for science compared to men. Summers' statement reflects the theoretical position that intelligence is an innate ability and that men's brains are somehow different from those of women. Google engineer James Damore famously – or infamously – circulated a memo[*] that became public knowledge in which he asserted there is inherent difference in biology that means women are less suited to STEM subjects and therefore less successful at such careers. The Pew Research Center in 2017 shed some light on the perception that there are inherent biological differences between men and women. They found that when women perceived differences in areas of work, emotions and parenting, they were more likely than men to believe that it was due to societal reasons. Men on the whole ascribed these differences to biology.

Much of this masculine–feminine polarity has been reinforced by research in neuroscience that theorises the notion of a male and a female brain. Neuro-sexism is the practice of claiming there are fixed biological differences between female and male brains, which can explain women's inferiority or unsuitability for certain roles. This isn't a recent phenomenon. In the 19th century the

_____

[*] https://gizmodo.com/exclusive-heres-the-full-10-page-anti-diversity-screed-1797564320

corpus callosum, a bundle of nerve fibres that connects the two hemispheres of the brain, was considered the centre of intellect and was said to have a greater surface area in men. Then, in the 1980s, we were told that, no, it is larger in women and this explains why the emotional right side of a woman's brain is more in touch with the analytical left side. Now, though, that theory has been discredited too.

By spotting sex-dependent activity in certain brain regions – such as those associated with empathising, learning languages or spatial processing – neuro-sexist studies have allowed an established 'go-to list' of sex differences to flourish. This includes things such as men being more logical and women being better at languages or nurturing. As historian of science Londa Schiebinger explains in *The Mind Has No Sex*, 'Women were not to be viewed merely as inferior to men but as fundamentally different from, and thus incomparable to, men.' In the Victorian era, the idea that women were inferior to men was replaced by the notion that women were hysterical, disorganised and emotional – the hormone-driven counterpoints to rational, stable men. This meant that female animals were omitted from much of biomedical and neuroscience research. However, in recent years, numerous neuroscience studies have offered clear evidence disproving the idea that males are less hormonal. In another study published in the journal *Biology of Sex Differences* in 2016 by researchers at the University of Michigan, female rats were shown to be no more variable than male ones when used in biomedical studies. In fact, they found that in some cases, male rodents living in groups were messier because their testosterone (essentially working on the brain like oestrogen) fluctuates. This fluctuation depends on the dominance hierarchies in groups.

Many popular science books* have reinforced this myth. It is assumed that male and female brains are very different because male and female behaviour differs so significantly. But over the last few decades, neuroscientists have been looking for major anatomical differences and found very few: more neurons or neuronal spines here and there in one sex or the other, with great variations from one individual to the other, but that's about it. The very concept of a male and female brain has been found to be flawed. Cortex thickness is commonly quoted as thicker in females, whereas white matter volume is often quoted as larger in males. However, even here there is considerable overlap and it is more of a trend rather than an absolute marker of sex.

Analysis of MRIs of more than 1,400 human brains from four datasets reveals extensive overlap between the distributions of females and males for all grey matter, white matter and connections assessed. Moreover, analyses of internal consistency reveal that brains with features that are consistently at one end of the maleness–femaleness continuum are rare. Rather, most brains are comprised of unique 'mosaics' of features, some more common in females compared with males, some more common in males compared with females, and some common in both females and males. These findings are robust across sample, age, type of MRI and method of analysis, and corroborated by a similar analysis of personality traits, attitudes, interests and behaviours of more than 5,500 individuals, which reveals that internal consistency is extremely rare. For example, it can be shown that a 'characteristically male' density of dendritic spines or

---

* Some of these include: John Gray's *Men Are from Mars, Women Are from Venus* in the 1990s, Louann Brizendine's *The Female Brain* and *The Male Brain* and Barbara and Allan Pease's *Why Men Don't Listen and Women Can't Read Maps*.

branches of a nerve cell can be changed to the 'female' form simply by the application of a mild external stress. Biological sex alone cannot explain brain differences; to do so requires an understanding of how, when and to what extent external events affect the structure of the brain.

In data taken from 4,860 adolescents from the National Longitudinal Study of Adolescent Health in the US, the variables in which young women and men differed the most included worry about weight, depression, gambling, involvement in housework and engagement in sports. This all seems gender normative. But not a single person had only feminine or only masculine scores on these variables. Rather, what was typical of about 70 per cent of these men and women was a mosaic of so-called feminine and masculine characteristics. Although there are sex differences in brain and behaviour, when we move away from group-level differences in single features and focus on the level of the individual person or brain, we find that the differences, regardless of their origins, usually 'mix up'. The reason for this mixing-up of characteristics is that the genetic and hormonal effects of sex on brain and behaviour depend on and interact with many other factors.

The gendered notions of intelligence start forming from as early as six years old. A recent study by Lin Bian, Sarah-Jane Leslie and Andrei Cimpian with 48 boys and 48 girls divided into groups of 32 five-, six- and seven-year-olds showed that five-year-old girls think girls can be 'really, really smart' but from six years up they think brilliance is much more likely in boys, and as they start assimilating this stereotype, they showed a more negative attitude towards a project or activity said to require 'smart' people. This study was limited to the American context, and carried out with middle-class children, 75 per cent of whom were white. I met Seth Stephens-Davidowitz when we shared a TEDx talk stage at Warwick University in 2018. Seth has done some fascinating analysis on aggregate data to show the persistent gender bias in the way we bring up our children. His work, which he also wrote up as an op-ed in the *New York Times* in 2014, shows how we bring our implicit bias to parenting. Seth analysed aggregated Google results to show that even today, American parents focus more on their boys to be brainy and their girls to be skinny. For every 10 US Google queries about girls being gifted, there were 25 about boys. On the other hand, for every 10 Google US queries about boys being overweight, there were 17 equivalent ones for girls, yet in reality boys are 9 per cent more likely to be overweight than girls.

Neuroplasticity is one of the major breakthroughs in the gendered brain debate. Different short- and long-term experiences will change the brain's structure. It has also been shown that social attitudes and expectations such as stereotypes can change how the brain processes information. Supposedly brain-based differences in behavioural characteristics and cognitive skills change across time, place and culture due to the different external factors experienced, such as access to education, financial independence, even diet. Stereotypes can affect how the brain responds to various cues. This means that as soon as we soak new-born cerebral sponges into a world of pink and blue divisions, we start shaping and forming their gendered identities and imposing differences in their brains, and we direct them into socially and culturally gendered pathways. This kind of research has huge implications for people who do not identify or conform with a particular gender or those who are transitioning. And it has a huge impact on the way we bring up and educate our children.

★★★

It is a common belief that men have much superior natural abilities in visuo-spatial tasks. Much of the bias that women are not as good as men at science and maths comes from a study that showed gender differences in 3D rotation of spatial objects, but it has consistently been shown that there is more in-group difference in spatial abilities than between groups, and there is no consistent variation between men's and women's abilities to navigate or discern spatial rotation and objects. In Chapter 5 we saw how this can lead to stereotype threat and the lack of women in STEM-related subjects. Differences in mathematical aptitude can also be explained by a notion of 'belonging' and of identifying with the in-group by choosing subjects and disciplinary domains where individuals feel they belong, are more similar to others and are likely to perform well. When teachers and parents give the message that 'girls are as good at maths as boys' then it is still setting boys as the standard, and so language matters. In another randomised double-blind study, science faculty from research-intensive universities rated the application materials of a student – who was randomly assigned either a male or female name – for a laboratory manager position. The male applicant was rated as significantly more competent and hireable than the (identical) female applicant, offered a higher starting salary and more career mentoring by the faculty members. The gender of the faculty participants did not affect responses, such that female and male faculty were equally likely to exhibit bias against the female student. These biases, of course, are not explicit as there is no desire to inhibit advancement of women or recruitment of more women, especially in the STEM fields, but instead indicative of the implicit gender bias that means we assess women to be less competent and capable. The gender bias and gap is not seen just in STEM domains but also in other 'softer' disciplines such as philosophy and music theory (from demographic reports of various professional societies). This gap does not just lead to a lack of diversity in design of technologies (discussed in detail in Chapter 11), but it has also been estimated that closing the gender gap in the STEM field would increase the EU GDP per capita by 0.7–0.9 per cent in 2030 and by 2.2–3.0 per cent in 2050.

When I was studying for my PhD, most women were assumed to be doing social sciences or human geography – or 'soft' sciences, as some people used to call them – while men were assumed more likely to do the hardcore 'macho' sciences, such as geology or computational geography. I was then (in 2006) the first female lecturer ever appointed to a geomatic engineering department in a leading UK university, and when I moved away from there in 2008 there was only one other female academic in that department, where research areas intersected technology, mathematics and spatial abilities. It is not clear whether this was because not many women entered this discipline due to stereotype threat or because there was gender bias at the hiring and recruitment stage. Or both.

Even within medicine, these gendered boundaries are often laid out very clearly. We might consider that we have achieved gender equity with more women doctors, but a recent study has shown that there are gender stereotypes within the field of medicine too. Women are under-represented in leadership positions in academic medicine. Women and men begin their medical careers at similar rates but they do not advance at the same rate. Studies indicate a systematic bias that has resulted in relatively fewer appointments to academic chairs. In 2015, 32 per cent of associate professors at medical schools in the US were women, while only 20 per cent of full professors, 14 per cent of department chairs, and 11 per cent of deans of medical schools were women. A review[*] in 2019 in the NHS, by Professor Dame Jane Dacre, also found that male consultants (senior doctors) outnumber female ones by almost two to one, that two-thirds of the senior medics were men, and that men in the NHS earn about 17 per cent more than their female peers. The gender stereotypes were also exhibited in the niches that women were forced into. Women are over-represented in medical specialities that involve lower pay, such as public health and occupational health, but under-represented in better-paid areas of expertise, including surgery.

There are plenty of cases of gender bias from patients too, with many assuming a woman to be a nurse rather than a doctor (with the opposite holding true for men). Medicare reimbursements in the US are lower to female physicians than to male physicians. A study published in the *Journal of Medical Education* reported an extensive analysis of almost a million IAT[†] records and a cross-sectional study of 131 surgeons. In an IAT, people sort words that appear on the screen into categories as quickly as they can. Concepts that are closely associated should be easier to sort together quickly. For example, in the Gender-Career IAT, participants sort gender (male or female) and career (career or family). In the first part of the Gender-Career IAT, participants sort words related to *male* or *career* to one side of the screen and words related to *female* or *family* to the opposite side. In the next part, they do the reverse: instead of *male/career* and *female/family* being sorted to the same side, *male/family* are sorted together, as are *female/career*. The

---

[*] Involved analysis of anonymised pay data, interviews with medics of different levels of seniority and an online survey of 40,000 doctors.

[†] In this case, a novel gender-based IAT was designed.

test uses reaction times for these tasks as a measure of the strength of associations between concepts. Here they also did a career-speciality test, where the order of the blocks was randomly assigned so that some participants were first asked to associate *male* with *surgery* and *female* with *family medicine*, whereas others were first asked to associate *male* with *family medicine* and *female* with *surgery*. The results give an interesting insight into gendered norms and stereotypes, but also into how implicit and explicit bias can differ and be expressed. In this case, it didn't come as a huge surprise to see that men were associated more with 'career' while women were associated more with 'family'. What was more surprising was that men were more likely to express this bias openly and explicitly, while implicitly there was parity between men's and women's biases.

## Feel the pain

In healthcare settings, men and women are perceived and treated differently. Women in emergency departments are less likely to be taken seriously than men. One study showed women in the emergency department who reported having acute pain were less likely than men to be given the strongest painkillers, and then waited longer to receive them. There is also a misconception that women are more likely to go to the doctor and overreact to their symptoms, meaning their reports of pain and illness are not taken as seriously.

This 'pain bias' is a manifestation of the underlying implicit bias that men are more stoic and women more likely to overreact and be hysterical and emotive. In two different studies with different dataset size and demographics, it was shown that even in children, boys were rated as experiencing more pain than girls despite identical clinical circumstances and identical pain behaviour across conditions. The sensitivity to pain can be different across different sexes, and some initial studies showed that women feel pain more intensely. It is also possible that women report the pain scores and threshold differently. This could be again due to their own ingrained biases where women do not wish to create a fuss or draw attention to themselves, or because of the random pain scale that is deployed by medical professionals. For instance, I have never been able to figure out how to give a score to my pain. I had a gall bladder problem for more than a year before it was diagnosed and scheduled for surgery. I had gone to the doctor regularly with severe debilitating pain, but I could never score it more than 6 because how do you compare different kinds of pain? Surely this wasn't the worst pain that I had ever faced or could possibly face? Surely not more than childbirth, so how could I give it a higher number? It was dismissed as gastric problems or indigestion. Studies have also shown that women who reported an abdominal problem were often misdiagnosed as having a gynaecological disorder. On one occasion, I even peeped at the notes to see what the doctor had written: 'looks all right'. It wasn't until one night when I was ambulanced into emergency that my condition was taken seriously. The added complication in perception of pain is that when people are stressed and anxious, their perception of pain can be affected. Furthermore, oestrogen alters the perception of pain and response to painkillers. This 'pain perception bias' can cloud judgement and this in turn can lead to life-endangering situations.

The errors in physicians' diagnoses and the treatments offered also have an implicit gender bias. It has been shown that doctors are less likely to take women's concerns seriously, with their pain often abruptly dismissed as psychological – a physical manifestation of stress, anxiety or depression. Doctors are more likely to diagnose women's symptoms to be non-specific. The understanding of most diseases is also based on male physiology, with most trials carried out on mice or human males, and so women's symptoms are not as well understood because of this data bias. A 2000 study published in the *New England Journal of Medicine* found that women are seven times more likely than men to be misdiagnosed and discharged in the middle of having a heart attack. Women aged 50 years or older are less likely than older men with similar severity of illness to be admitted to intensive care units or receive life-saving interventions.

A visual analysis of anatomical textbooks was conducted in 2016 by Rhiannon Parker and colleagues at the University of Wollongong on 6,044 images in which sex/gender could be identified, sourced from 17 major anatomy textbooks published from 2008 to 2013. Results indicated that the representation of gender in images from anatomy textbooks remains predominantly male except within sex-specific sections. The researchers also highlighted other forms of bias such as the visualisation of stereotypical gendered emotions, roles and settings, the lack of ethnic, age and body-type diversity. The textbooks also adhere very closely to a sex/gender binary. This study showed that the visual representation of gender in medical curricula continues to be biased, and this is likely to provide future healthcare providers with inadequate and unrealistic information about patients. The training that healthcare professionals are receiving is still biased, which can affect their views on 'sex' and 'gender' but also on what constitutes femininity and masculinity.

I spoke with Jo Norton, who was diagnosed with Upper Airways Respiratory Syndrome (a type of sleep apnoea) about four years ago at the age of 24, having suffered from extreme fatigue and tiredness for more than a decade. When she first went to her doctor ten years ago suffering from low mood, she was diagnosed with depression. Her poor sleep was not even considered as she 'didn't fall into any of the usual groups for sleep disorders'. Jo tells me that there is still an 'overweight, middle-aged men' stereotype when it comes to diagnosis of sleep apnoea. Jo had been snoring since university but, besides being acutely embarrassed about it, it wasn't even considered relevant; her doctor never asked her about it. There is a 'selection bias' in referral to sleep studies and specialists: studies have found that men are twice as likely to be referred for a sleep study than women. Many GPs rely on self-reported snoring and sleep apnoea,[*] and because men are more likely to seek help about snoring from their GP, they are more likely to receive an early referral for a sleep study. Nearly half of women snorers do not report their symptoms to their GP, often due to embarrassment or shame.

A recent study in the American Academy of Sleep Medicine found that virtually all male snorers will admit the problem, while many female snorers deny it. We don't often hear or read about women snoring. Snoring is still seen as 'unfeminine' and 'unsexy'. As well as under-reporting self-snoring, women also tend to underestimate the loudness of their snoring. In an informal study I carried out in social media groups, 72 per cent of women (from a

---

[*] Loud and frequent snoring is one symptom of this common sleep disorder, which occurs when the muscles relax during sleep. This causes soft tissue in the back of the throat to collapse and block the upper airway. As a result there are pauses in breathing, which can cause drastic changes in oxygen levels and fragmented sleep. This puts an enormous strain on the heart and can lead to an increase in heart rate.

sample of 58 respondents aged 25–45) said they would be embarrassed to be known as 'snorers' and wouldn't admit it to their doctor. Studies at Johns Hopkins Hospital Sleep Disorders Center in Baltimore show that symptoms in women can be different, often just seen as 'everyday tiredness' or misdiagnosed as depression. Women tend to have more complaints of chronic fatigue and insomnia. Women also report trouble concentrating and forgetting details and everyday tasks. Often these symptoms can be confused with hypothyroidism or perimenopausal symptoms. When women do not report snoring to be an issue, it is less likely that the doctor would consider sleep apnoea as one of the reasons for this atypical behaviour and more likely for it to be attributed to depression or hormonal imbalance. A study of 289 women published in *Gender and Genome* in 2018 reported that women with sleep apnoea have a higher risk of cardiovascular disease than men, despite milder disease severity.

There are a number of implicit biases at play in sleep-apnoea diagnosis. First, there is the patient herself. Women might not report snoring to their physicians or they might not know if they snore because their romantic partner might not reveal this information for fear of offending them. Rather than an intention to hide information, it is the socially constrained idea of gender-appropriate behaviour that can cause under-diagnosis. Second, the physicians might not consider sleep apnoea as the cause for diagnosis as women's symptoms can differ from men, and much of our medical understanding is based on male case studies. Obstructive sleep apnoea has historically been regarded as a male disease. Women have been notoriously under-represented in clinical studies (with about only 20 per cent female representation), and premenopausal and postmenopausal women are not generally studied separately.

So doctors do not have the necessary information to be able to understand and diagnose symptoms presented differently in a female patient.

Speaking to several physicians, it is clear that the dichotomy between sex and gender might cause some problems. Biological and social aspects are related, and doctors cannot just use one to diagnose a condition. But often they have to. Lifestyle choices and societal expectations of what is feminine and masculine can affect the way gender intersects with healthcare. Gender bias in healthcare settings is systemic. Katarina Hamberg, a researcher from Sweden, argues against labelling certain physiological functions and components as male or female, loaded with gendered perceptions. For instance, oestrogens and testosterone are still often called 'sex hormones' in medical literature and in clinics, even though all humans have these hormones irrespective of their sex. This can distort and produce inaccurate results and diagnoses. Gender bias can work the other way around too, as thyroid imbalances and migraines are often perceived as 'women's illnesses', and much of the advertising related to these has traditionally depicted female patients, meaning these ailments can often be misinterpreted or ignored in men.

Although suggesting that there should be an equal number of men and women in all studies and trials reeks of biological determinism, emphasising that there is an inherent gender divide based on biology, it is nevertheless advisable to have sufficient numbers of both sexes to allow for analysis of whether sex or gender is important for the results. While a gender perspective is important in medical settings, it is also important that doctors and nurses are not imposing their own gender stereotypes on patients, and in this way interpreting the similar narrative in different ways.

## Tip of the iceberg

Gender bias can be so insidious and deeply entrenched in the normative structures of a culture that no one dares even question it. I had just given birth to my first daughter and I was living in one of the biggest metropolises in the world, New Delhi. I spent a lot of my time reflecting on the pressures of being a woman in India, especially in a very traditional family set-up where women didn't go outside to work, and I was reflecting on the challenges of growing up as a young girl in this patriarchal country and what the future held for my daughter. I felt trapped and undervalued and invisible. We had several women who came every morning and help with washing and cleaning, and give my little girl a massage, and they had many stories of their own. One of these stood out for me. You could see every bit of her life's struggles in her wrinkles, but she was strong and determined. She told me stories of how she had brought up her only daughter on her own as her husband left her when she was very young. I admired her hugely for her strength and her compassion. I knew that her daughter was now married and expecting a child herself, so it made me feel even closer to her. I asked her almost every day if she'd had her grandchild and then one day she told me that the child was dead. As if this wasn't horrific enough, she then confided in me that she had killed the child with her own hands after it was born because it was a girl. She knew that her son-in-law would have left her daughter if he knew she had given birth to yet another girl. It is impossible for us to even comprehend what can motivate someone to act in this manner or to understand how deeply entrenched gender bias is in their society. This is the reality in many parts of the world where girls are not just marginalised but are considered the 'second sex', irrelevant and an affliction. Of course, female infanticide is illegal but it carries on. A recent media report confirms this. The desire among parents in India to have sons instead of daughters has created 21 million unwanted girls. A finance ministry report found many couples kept on having children until they had a boy. This is a subtler form of son preference and I have seen it occur in many families myself. This creates discrimination and prejudice against girls from a very young age.* This creates the social and cultural norms where boys are better than girls. Boys internalise this, and girls do too. And it has a bearing not only on the opportunities and resources available to them, but also it can become a matter of life and death.

Female infanticide, female genital mutilation, domestic violence against women, rape and sexual harassment continue. Many of these are first-generation gender bias† that is deliberate and involves intentional exclusion or stigmatisation. Besides these very explicit forms of gender discrimination, second-generation gender bias and everyday sexism continues to impact on women's lives, often appearing non-sexist but still discriminating against women because they reflect the values of men who developed the setting and who set the standards of practice. It is the second-generation bias that is the invisible barrier.

Gender and race are interlinked. Both are formed due to similar cognitive processes, both are affected by in-group

---

* I talked more about this in my TEDx talk in Jaipur, India in March 2019: 'Feminism is good for men: Shattering Gender Stereotypes', and it can be found on the main TED website.

† The main difference between first-generation gender bias and second-generation gender bias is whether or not it is intentional. In first-generation gender bias, one intentionally discriminates against another, whereas in second-generation gender bias, the discrimination is not intentional.

and out-group membership, both are pervasive and persistent in society, both lead to dehumanising a certain group of people due to their perceived race or gender, and both are based on prejudice and discrimination of a certain group of people to assign them an inferior status. There is also now research to show that people assume that sexists are also racists and vice versa. According to findings published in *Psychological Science*, the stigma associated with prejudice against women and people of colour seems to transfer from one group to another, with experiments showing that women tended to believe that a person who espoused racist beliefs would also show sexist beliefs and behaviour, while men of colour believed that someone who expressed sexist attitudes was likely to show racist tendencies. Experiments demonstrate a social-dominance hierarchy in the formation of these biases and the transfer of prejudice from race to sex, and vice versa, and so participants perceived the man with the racist profile as likely to hold hierarchical and therefore sexist beliefs, which led them to expect the man to show more gender stigma and unfair treatment. These results give us an insight into how stigmatised groups experience threat.

Gender bias is a huge topic, with far-reaching impact on social inequalities. Even though this chapter is one of the longest in the book, it has only touched the tip of the iceberg, focusing on science – experiments and data – that leave no doubt about gender inequalities. I have attempted to highlight the way that the invisible second-generation biases emerge and how they become so pervasive and pernicious. There is so much more to say about how gender stereotypes are formed from early childhood and how gendered socialisation takes place. There is now much research to show that this world is not designed for women, and as the #MeToo movement and the gender pay gap enter our everyday parlance, we are increasingly aware of gender disparities. But as we talk about gender bias, let us not forget about intersectionality and how certain multiple-identities can further stigmatise women and render them even more invisible. Yes, there is change, but it is glacial.

And to all the sceptics, I would just say: 'Am I not believed because I am a woman?'

CHAPTER EIGHT

# It's Not Black and White

In early 2019, the well-known rapper Stormzy pulled out of his headline slot at Snowbombing festival in Austria just hours before he was due to perform, accusing its staff of racially profiling* his friends by looking for someone carrying a weapon, 'despite no one [in their party] fitting the description.'

A recent investigation by the *Bristol Cable* and Bureau of Investigative Journalism shows that, in the UK, nearly a fifth of all people stopped and asked to prove their immigration status are British, and this figure has remained unchanged for almost seven years. Immigration officials are supposed to conduct their checks based on intelligence or behaviour that gives them 'reasonable suspicion' someone has committed an immigration offence. Yet people are being targeted as per their race and ethnicity, and since the start of 2012 British citizens have been subject to immigration spot checks more than 25,000 times. Labour MP David Lammy and other politicians have spoken about their own experiences and have insisted that racial bias is increasingly playing a role in this. The Equalities Act 2010 makes it illegal to stop someone on the basis of their race or ethnicity, but the Home Office does not routinely record the ethnicity of those encountered and so it is difficult to say with 100 per cent certainty how many of these stops were of people who

---

* In Chapter 4, I have talked about racial profiling and the specific targeting of people based on their skin colour and ethnicity, and my own experience with 'stop and search'.

were non-white. People's experiences, however, seem to echo my own and are evidence of the way race and ethnicity play a huge role in who is stopped and searched.

In December 2018, a survey for the *Guardian* of 1,000 people from minority ethnic* backgrounds found they were consistently more likely to have faced negative everyday experiences – all frequently associated with racism – than white people. This survey laid bare what minority ethnic communities had been feeling and expressing for a while. The survey found that 43 per cent of those from a minority ethnic background had been overlooked for a work promotion in a way that felt unfair in the last five years – more than twice the proportion of white people (18 per cent) who reported the same experience. The results also showed that minority ethnic individuals are three times as likely to have been thrown out of or denied entrance to a restaurant, bar or club, and 38 per cent of respondents from minority ethnic backgrounds said they had been wrongly suspected of shoplifting, compared with 14 per cent of white people. I can vouch for how this kind of racial profiling and prejudice can cause feelings of confusion, shame and terror.

Racial discrimination emerges from stereotypes. This leads to prejudice, discrimination and structural racism that is fostered in society through criminal justice, employment, media, education, healthcare and other systems. Such discrimination can also lead to interpersonal racism, where negative feelings and interactions result between individuals. This is a manifestation of structural racism, and while this is more obvious and explicit, interpersonal racism can be often unacknowledged.

---

* 'Minority ethnic' is preferred to 'ethnic minority' because it stresses that everyone belongs to an ethnic group. 'Minority ethnic' places the emphasis on the minority status rather than the ethnicity, whereas 'ethnic minority' places the emphasis on the ethnicity of the group.

Research has shown that black individuals (particularly men) have been associated with aggressiveness and criminality, and when researchers led by Iowa State University's Stephanie Madon asked psychology students to write down attributes characterising African-Americans, 'aggressive' was one of the top 10 attributes. There has not been reliable or official data openly available from the federal government as to how many police shootings have affected minority individuals, but an analysis of the available FBI data based on voluntary reports in 2012 around the country was carried out by Dara Lind for Vox. It found that US police kill black people at disproportionate rates: black people accounted for 31 per cent of police killing victims in 2012, even though they made up just 13 per cent of the US population. The *Guardian* also conducted an analysis in 2015 and found that 102 people of 464 killed by police in the US were unarmed. They also found that agencies are killing people at twice the rate calculated by the US government, and that black Americans are more than twice as likely to be unarmed when killed during encounters with police than white people. In the US, black people are more likely to be arrested for drug crimes, although they are not more likely to use or sell drugs. In 2013, according to the National Survey of Drug Use and Health, illicit drug use recorded over one month was on average 9.5 per cent among white communities, and 10.5 per cent in black communities. Irrespective of this, FBI crime reports show that drug-related arrests per 100,000 of each race were 332 and 879 in white and black individuals respectively. Of course, this is rather a broad-sweeping analysis with no indication of intersectionality within these categories of 'white' and 'black', but even just the headline data are an indication of the racial bias existing within the policing system.

In a 'weapon-identification experiment' carried out by Keith Payne of the University of North Carolina at Chapel

Hill and Yujiro Shimizu and Larry L. Jacoby of Washington University in St. Louis, participants were handed pictures of guns or other innocuous tools, and given a split-second to decide what each object was. In some cases, researchers primed participants by showing them pictures of black faces before they undertook the experiment. When primed, people more frequently incorrectly identified tools as guns. The researchers asserted that time pressure also causes errors. Without the time pressure, people make fewer mistakes. In this experiment, the researchers showed that when people were asked to perform the weapon-identification task a second time, with no time pressure, the race bias they had displayed disappears. However, it isn't just time pressure; expectations and stereotypes can play tricks on the brain as well, especially when race is involved.

Joshua Correll at the University of Colorado, Boulder, and Bernd Wittenbrink, Professor of behavioural science at Chicago Booth, led research teams analysing the role of stereotypes in shootings to show that police officials are quicker to shoot black suspects in video-game simulations. Since 2000, the researchers had been working on a platform mimicking a shooting scenario. The participants were asked to look at a series of photos of outdoor scenes in public places such as city streets and shopping malls, with photos of a man suddenly appearing holding an object. In some cases he held a gun, and in others he held an innocuous object such as a phone or wallet. If participants perceived the man to be armed, they pressed a button corresponding to a 'shoot' decision. If they thought he was unarmed, they pressed a 'don't shoot' button. Participants had to decide quickly – within a few hundred milliseconds – which button to press. Although race wasn't explicitly set as a determining factor, the results published in 2007 showed that participants were more likely to shoot a black person in error and more likely to press 'don't shoot' for white simulated scenarios. In some experiments, the participants were given a primacy cue such as a news report about a black person committing a crime. This led them to set more lenient criteria for shooting black individuals. On the other hand, when they read similar reports about white individuals being aggressive or committing crimes, it did not affect their decisions about whether or not to shoot them in the simulated task. Because the experiment was set up in a way that meant the participants did not have time to deliberate on their actions, they were relying on their subconscious biases and stereotypes about individuals based on their racial category. Use of eye-gaze capture devices during the experiment showed that participants' eyes searched for the critical object in the hand. When the scene involved an armed black man, participants' eye gaze didn't reach the object nearly as quickly (or closely) as when the scene showed an armed white man, thereby showing that participants made their decision with less detailed visual information about the object. The race of the person was used to fill in the gaps and create assumptions. The stereotypes are therefore shaping their biases and decisions in an implicit way, and African-Americans are appearing more violent and aggressive because of ingrained cultural stereotypes. In this way, stereotypes shape the perceptions of police authorities as well, which leads to racial profiling, more arrests and more convictions of black individuals both in the US and the UK.* It can also affect officers'

---

* As per the report by gov.uk on March 2019, black people were more than three times as likely to be arrested as white people: there were 35 arrests for every 1,000 black people, and 11 arrests for every 1,000 white people. Black women were more than twice as likely to be arrested as white women: there were seven arrests for every 1,000 black women, and three arrests for every 1,000 white women.

judgement when they are trying to make a decision about shooting an individual.

We assume that the legal profession is free of biases and prejudices. We believe in the law, we trust the neutrality of it and the objectivity of the people involved in decision-making. But the role of social inequalities and implicit biases in legal settings is now being understood.* Besides biases in racial profiling and stop and search, studies have also shown racial bias in criminal sentencing and the application of police force. These racial inequalities are indicative of both conscious expressions of prejudice (explicit bias) and implicit subconscious prejudices so subtle that people who hold them might not even be aware of them. Firstly, the presence of implicit racial bias raises questions about the fairness of the legal case outcomes. Secondly, each case sets a precedent for any future cases to follow, and so they can also structure the outcome of any future enquiries. Professor Douglas Rice and colleagues from the University of Massachusetts' Department of Political Science have recently published research that looks at how implicit bias is deeply entrenched in the language used in the judicial process. They analysed an original dataset of more than one million court opinions from US state and federal courts, and estimated word embeddings for more than 400,000 of the most common words found in legal opinions. In a series of analyses, they found strong and consistent evidence of implicit racial bias, as African-American names (such as DeShawn and Jamal) were associated with larger, more violent people who are prone

---

* The recent Netflix series *When They See Us* revisits the Central Park Five case, 30 years on from the gross misconduct of injustice. The case shed light on ugly truths about racism, the justice system and the deeply fraught relations between police and communities of colour both in New York City and throughout the United States.

to aggression, whereas European-American names (such as Connor and Garrett) were more frequently associated with pleasant or positive concepts and considered higher in status than 'black-sounding' names.

According to a report put together in 2017 by the Labour MP David Lammy, young black people are nine times more likely to be locked up in England and Wales than their white peers. In the year ending March 2017, 24 per cent of first-time entrants to the youth justice system were BAME* and 54 per cent of the remand population was BAME. Analysis of custodial sentences received by children and young people that built on that of the Lammy Review showed that, in 2016, young BAME people were more likely to be sentenced to custody than their white counterparts. In the year ending 2017, 45 per cent of children sentenced to custody were BAME. According to an investigation conducted by the *Independent*, which analysed figures from 2009 to 2017, one in four black teenage boys convicted of homicide was handed a maximum jail sentence. In comparison, not one white teenager was sentenced to more than 10 years. The Met Police are four times more likely to use force† with black people than with white people. These figures and studies give us a glaring insight into the extent of racial prejudice and the assumed 'neutrality' of law-making professionals, and reveal yet another huge barrier to achieving racial justice.

---

* BAME stands for Black, Asian and Minority Ethnic, an acronym used to sum up and homogenise the diverse experiences of the various cultural and social groups in Britain.
† The use of force, in the context of law enforcement, may be defined as the 'amount of effort required by police to compel compliance by an unwilling subject'. The levels, or continuum, of force that police use include basic verbal and physical restraint, less-lethal force, and lethal force.

Racialization creates a hierarchy in which those racialized as black or minority ethnic are at the bottom. One cannot invoke race without the associated hierarchy. In our society those designated as white have the authority to racialize 'others'; at the same time white is often made invisible or seen as normative. One of the key foundations of race as a social construct is intellectual ability. Racialization can, thus, lead to bias and discrimination. That bias may be unconscious or implicit, yet unconscious assumptions and beliefs of which we may be unaware or unwilling to acknowledge can affect one's behaviour.

Implicit bias is also seen in how skin colour can be used as an assessment of both physical abilities and mental abilities. In a 2006 study with around 150 white college students, New York neuroscientists David Amodio and Patricia Devine asked the participants to categorise words as either pleasant (such as 'peace', 'heaven' and 'honour') or unpleasant ('cancer', 'vomit', 'poverty') and as either mental ('math', 'brainy', 'scientist') or physical ('basketball', 'agile', 'dance'). Before each categorisation task, the subjects were shown black or white faces as a priming cue. The results were startling because these largely liberal college students who considered themselves fair and non-prejudiced were faster at categorising unpleasant and physical words when shown a black face, and faster at categorising pleasant and mental words when shown a white face. In another related experiment, it was seen that the study participants who had shown higher implicit bias were more likely to assign their (presumably black) partner to answer the questions about sports and popular culture, rather than academics. Black men, in particular, are stereotyped as powerful and strong[*]

---

[*] These stereotypes are of course not true. Researchers from Montclair State University say that: 'The 2012 Center for Disease

but not as intellectual.* A series of seven studies published
in the *Journal of Personality and Social Psychology* in 2017
showed that when participants believed the man in the
images is black, they were more likely to perceive the man
as larger, more threatening and potentially more harmful
in an altercation than a white person. And they were more
likely to say that the use of force was justified against the
black men. Another study in 2016 also showed that black
boys can be perceived as older and less innocent than
similarly aged white boys.

Many of these studies were carried out in simulated
environments, and the participant group may not be fully
representative of the rest of the country as they were
college-educated, younger and less wealthy than the
general population. Nevertheless, these cultural stereotypes

---

Control report on summarizing the 2007–2010 National Health
and Nutrition Examination Survey data places the average height of
non-Hispanic White men (20 years or older) at 177.4 cm and 90.4
kgs, and of non-Hispanic Black men at 176.4 cm and 90.4 kgs',
showing that black men on average are shorter and of similar build
to the white men.

* This myth is being reinforced and perpetuated by waves of race
science, built on incorrect beliefs that there is a 'black brain' and a
'white brain'. In 1969 the American psychologist Arthur Jenson
published a paper in the *Harvard Educational Review* claiming that
black Americans had lower genetic intelligence than white
Americans and Asian-Americans. Since then several scientific papers
and books have repeated this claim, but have been debunked by the
wider academic community. The idea that there is a correlation
between intelligence and race persists. The 2012 American National
Election Study included interviews with nearly 5,500 Americans.
Among the questions included were requests asking people to rate
white people and black people on their intelligence and work ethic.
Nearly six in 10 white people view themselves as superior to black
people, with almost 45 per cent believing that black people are not
as intelligent as them.

undoubtedly have life-or-death implications in 'shoot/ don't shoot' situations where police offices have to make quick decisions. Without appropriate training, the law enforcement personnel are more likely to resort to their racial bias.[*]

## Thicker skin

Even medical professionals are not immune to falling back on their racial bias and can often miss the correct diagnoses. Jerome Groopman says in an article in the *New Yorker* (from 29 January 2007) that most doctors typically begin to diagnose patients the moment they meet them. Research also shows that most physicians already have in mind two or three possible diagnoses within minutes of meeting a patient, and that they tend to develop these hunches from very incomplete information. The doctors are relying on shortcuts and rules of thumb – heuristics – to make their diagnosis. They can fall back on representative bias, where they are influenced by what is 'typically' true. In doing so, they can fail to consider other possibilities that contradict their mental templates of an illness. Groopman says that 'when people are confronted with uncertainty – the situation of every doctor attempting to diagnose a patient – they are susceptible to unconscious emotions and personal biases and are more likely to make cognitive errors.'

In a study involving 215 doctors (all normally involved in trauma care at Johns Hopkins Hospital in Baltimore) it was found that most of them – irrespective of their race, age or medical training – had a moderate amount of racial

---

[*] Such as the 2014 Cleveland police shooting of 12-year-old Tamir Rice: after he was killed, the officers involved reported that they thought Rice was 20.

bias and a strong preference for higher social class. In this particular experiment it was found that women, however, generally had lower levels of race and class bias relative to men. There is evidence to show that race and ethnicity can affect the treatment a patient is given. Black patients receive less pain relief than white patients. In another study, Hispanic patients were seven times less likely to receive opioids in the emergency room than non-Hispanic patients with similar injuries, and similar results were shown in black patients compared to white patients. When the physicians were assessed for their ability to quantify the pain that the patients were in, it was found they could accurately judge patients' pain severity regardless of ethnicity yet still provided less pain relief to Hispanic patients with severe injuries. Here an assessment of implicit bias was not performed but these studies confirmed the previous evidence that physicians carry moderate racial bias and that care can differ according to ethnicity. In another example, a 2012 study in the US used identical case samples to examine how paediatricians' implicit attitudes affect treatment recommendations. Results indicated that as paediatricians' pro-white implicit biases increased over the course of the study, they were more likely to prescribe painkillers for their young patients who were white as opposed to black. Similarly, white physicians who implicitly associated black patients with being 'less cooperative' were less likely to refer black patients with acute coronary symptoms for thrombolysis-specific medical care.

Race and sex have been shown to play a role in the treatment of patients with cardiovascular diseases. Research from Nina Martin and Renee Montagne in 2017 showed that a black woman is 22 per cent more likely to die of a heart disease than a white woman. National datasets were used to calculate prevalence and case-fatality rates among black and white women for pre-eclampsia, eclampsia, abruptio placentae, placenta previa, and postpartum haemorrhage between 1988 and 1999. Results showed that, although black women did not have significantly greater prevalence rates than white women, they were two to three times more likely to die from these conditions than white women. The most recent stats indicate that black women are 71 per cent more likely to suffer from cervical cancer-related death, and 243 per cent more likely to die of complications in pregnancy and childbirth. In sub-Saharan Africa maternal mortality rates are dropping, while in the US they have steadily risen for minority ethnic women between 2000 and 2014.

According to the American Cancer Society, the incidence of breast cancer in African-American women is slightly lower than in white women but their mortality rates are higher. Between 2009 and 2012, the incidence of cancer in black women was around 124 for every 100,000 women, compared to 128 for European-American women. However, the five-year survival rate between 2008 and 2011 was 80 per cent for black women and 91 per cent for white women. Several black women who had survived breast cancer reported having experienced poor treatment, such as physicians not taking the time to explain their diagnosis and options, front-desk staff treating them with disrespect, and lack of support in dealing with complications. The disparity in survival rate is largely attributed to later-stage detection among black women. This could be an indication of healthcare inequalities but also systemic racial inequalities where black women do not feel as confident in seeking medical care (possibly because of the fear of being stereotyped and discriminated) or they do not focus on themselves because they believe that they are not worth it – a materialisation of ingrained racial marginalisation.

Disparities in access to healthcare, location of healthcare services, and support to follow-up with appointments are all part of broader structural racial inequality.

Black people and women, in general, are less likely than white people and men, respectively, to undergo cardiac catheterisation or coronary-artery bypass graft surgery when they are admitted to the hospital for treatment of chest pain or myocardial infarction. Kevin Schulman and a number of collaborators in a study published in the *New England Journal of Medicine* developed 144 descriptions using all possible combinations of different experimental factors, such as race (black or white), sex, age (55 or 70 years), level of coronary risk (low or high) and type of chest pain (definite angina, possible angina or non-anginal pain). Video recordings of actors playing patients were shown to more than 700 specialists who had to assess whether to refer patients with chest pain for cardiac catheterisation. The lowest rate of cardiovascular procedures was among non-white women, and so although it was not explicitly examined whether the physicians' perception of the patient affected their judgement, it seems very likely. Implicit bias is difficult to measure, and this study in particular was unable to test whether these biases were due to explicit blatant biases or unconscious ones. Nevertheless, what the study showed very successfully was that stereotypes play a role in creating bias, and therefore prejudice and discrimination. Race and sex – and the intersection of it – creates bias even when life-changing decisions are being made.

This bias in perception of pain, and errors in treatment recommendation of pain, are also associated with a racial bias.* A study from 2016 shows that there also exists a false

---

* Chapter 7 looked at how sex/gender plays a role in perception of pain and in diagnosis.

belief about biological differences between black people and white people, such as that black people's skin is thicker than white people's skin or that black people are biologically stronger than white people or that black people's blood coagulates more quickly than white people's blood. A study examining pain management among patients with metastatic cancer found that only 35 per cent of minority ethnic patients received the appropriate prescriptions – in accordance with the World Health Organization guidelines – compared with 50 per cent of non-minority patients. There is not enough evidence to show that these biases stem from underlying racist beliefs, as racial disparity in pain perception has not shown direct correlation with racist attitudes. However, these unconscious biases could be a result of previous studies or writings that have promoted these ideas, such as the ones used to justify slavery. In the 19th century, prominent physicians sought to establish the 'physical peculiarities' of black people (such as thicker skulls and less sensitive nervous systems) that could 'distinguish him from the white man'. Other physicians believed that black individuals could tolerate surgical operations with little if any pain at all. There is also bias inherent in the self-reported pain scales, with no consideration of context. Cultural background can prevent people from interpreting the scale properly or even reporting the pain appropriately. Some cultures are more stoic than others (or are believed to be so); we've all heard of the 'British stiff upper lip', for instance. In addition, there is an inherent design bias since, as Mary Narayan reports in the *Journal of Nursing*, the assessment of pain scales can be culture-dependent. For instance, a horizontal numeric pain scale may be confusing for someone of Chinese background because Chinese language is traditionally written and read vertically. This can stop them from understanding and interpreting the scale and therefore responding inaccurately, which in turn can affect the physician's diagnosis of the seriousness of their condition and hence the treatment.[*]

Extensive research has now been conducted in the US into racial bias in healthcare, but this is an issue that is still being brushed under the carpet in the UK. Much of the research pertaining to the NHS has been focused on the treatment of black and minority ethnic (BME) doctors (which is equally crucial to understand) rather than patient experience. Minority staff have been shown to get a worse deal on pay, bonuses and grievances. Chaand Nagpaul, the first non-white doctor to lead the British Medical Association (BMA) has said that the NHS is 'subconsciously racist' and routinely overlooks minority ethnic doctors for senior posts, and that 'patients were being deprived of the most skilled clinicians because of an entrenched bias in the system'.[†] Only 7 per cent of senior clinician posts in the NHS are filled by BME doctors, although more than a third (over 200,000 staff) of the total workforce is from black and minority ethnic backgrounds. One in five nurses, more than one in three doctors and one in six of all NHS staff are from BME backgrounds, and the NHS is the largest employer of BME

---

[*] In this scenario, an error in diagnosis and treatment is not a direct consequence of a doctor's unconscious bias but instead due to the construct validity and the inherent design bias in the tool. Sometimes patients are also asked to recall how the pain has changed over a period of time. Recall bias is caused by the differences in the accuracy and completeness of the recollections. We can sometimes recall happier times and successes better than hardships and losses. Our ability to recall is also influenced by our current emotional state and by the time passed since the event itself. Other factors that can affect recall bias in self-reporting have been shown to be age, education, socio-economic status and how important the disease is to the patient.

[†] *Daily Telegraph*, 18 September 2018.

staff in the UK. Dr Nagpaul believes that minority candidates are often overlooked for promotion in favour of their less qualified white compatriots. The Discrimination by Appointment report by Public World carried out in 2013, for example, showed that shortlisted white applicants were nearly twice as likely to be appointed as shortlisted BME staff.[*] Research found that minority ethnic nurses took five years longer to be promoted than white nurses. The 2012 NHS staff survey showed that 8 per cent of staff reported they had experienced discrimination at work from other colleagues in the last 12 months, half of whom reported race discrimination. Bullying and harassment was reported by 24 per cent of staff, a much higher level than that reported outside the NHS. The large-scale NHS staff survey in 2015 showed that BME staff were more likely (14 per cent) to experience physical violence from patients, relatives or the public in the last 12 months than white staff (12 per cent), and more likely (3 per cent) to report experiencing physical violence from staff in the last 12 months than white staff (1 per cent). This is, however, not just a recent issue. As far back as 2003, the then chairman of the Commission for Racial Equality, Trevor Phillips, said that the NHS was a prime example of 'snow capping', where the organisational pyramid is white at the top and black at the bottom. The unconscious bias that is rife in the NHS affects not only the staff but also the healthcare that is provided to patients, yet it is a topic that we still tiptoe around.

## Beyond the duality

Racism is, of course, not limited to black individuals. Racial discrimination against other minority people is less

---

[*] Data was collected from 30 NHS trusts across the country.

likely to be reported or to receive as much media attention.
It is crucial to consider the racial dynamics involving other
visible as well as 'invisible' minorities. There can be an
assumption that Chinese and other East and South East
Asian communities don't experience racism or suffer racial
disadvantages, which means that they can often be ignored
in the wider race discourse. But they face what is now
being widely understood as 'invisible discrimination', as
they are considered model minorities who fit in well and
are 'almost white'. It has been reported that up to 15 per
cent of the Chinese community in Britain have experienced
racial discrimination, which is the highest percentage for
any ethnic group in this country. In a study carried out in
2012 at the Mount Sinai Medical School, New York, it was
seen that Latina and Chinese women are less likely to
receive hormone therapy, which decreases the risk of
recurrence of breast cancer, than white women. Political
scientist Claire Jean Kim argues in her 'racial triangulation
theory' that Asian-Americans 'have been racialized relative
to and through interaction with whites and blacks. As such,
the respective racialization trajectories of these groups are
profoundly interrelated' and so we need to see 'beyond
black and white.' It is grounded in the notion of 'model
minorities' discussed earlier in the book, which was first
propagated in the US in the 1960s. The mainstream media
cites Asian people's hard work ethic and material successes
as an exemplar while at the same time implying deficiencies
in the black community, thereby creating this implicit
divide of the 'good minority' vs the 'deficient minority'.
Yet, unlike black people, Asian people continue to be
inherently unassimilable to mainstream culture (although
positioned somewhere in the middle) and therefore never
really perceived as truly British or American. Although the
initial theory by Claire Jean Kim was used to define the

status of Asian-Americans outside the white–black racial duality, the same theory could be applied to other model minorities such as South Asian people – Indians, Pakistanis, Bangladeshis – who, despite the association of the positive values of hard work, are never able to shake off the questions of 'origin' and are therefore always outsiders (the stereotype of 'perceptual foreigner' discussed in Chapter 4). The South Asian community has been subject to racial discrimination for decades. Even the acronym 'BAME' diminishes the unique experiences of the different ethnic groups that constitute this contrived homogenous entity. Colonialism and subsequent independence meant that individuals felt inclined to uphold cultural values to retain their new-found identity. First-generation British Asian people adapted these attitudes after immigrating to the UK, while at the same time suffering from the colonial hangover and centuries of oppression, identifying as the oppressed, and internalising the view of the white British population being superior. Growing up with a complex sense of identity can cause a fractured sense of belonging and lead to mental health problems.

With the rise in Islamophobia, 'brown' skin colour carries the additional stigma of being labelled as a 'terrorist'. The term 'Islamophobia' entered media and political discourse in Britain in the late 1980s and early 1990s as a way of signalling a rejection of the growing Muslim population and the immigrant population from South Asian countries. A report by the Runnymede Trust in 1997 placed this right in the centre of the mainstream discourse on racial bias in the UK. The report by the Commission on British Muslims and Islamophobia, titled 'Islamophobia: A Challenge For Us All', broadly defined Islamophobia as 'unfounded hostility towards Islam' resulting in discriminatory attitudes and behaviours towards Muslims. Much like other forms of stereotype and prejudice that dehumanise individual experiences and beliefs, the notion of Islamophobia can manifest in a view of Islam as a static and monolithic world-view that encourages hostility towards the West and its values. There has been wide discussion around the term, but what is emerging is that the definition of Islamophobia is evolving and constitutes a bias towards anyone who appears to be Muslim. As the eminent sociologist Tariq Modood suggested, Islamophobia can be considered as involving both racial and religious discrimination and is thus a form of cultural racism. However, the British government recently rejected this definition of Islamophobia as constituting racism. After a six-month inquiry, the All-Party Parliamentary Group (APPG) on British Muslims had proposed a definition as 'Islamophobia is rooted in racism and is a type of racism that targets expressions of Muslimness or perceived Muslimness'. Yet, according to the government's equality advisers, the Equality Act 2010 'defines "race" as comprising colour, nationality and national or ethnic origins, none of which would encompass a Muslim or Islamic practice.' The debate continues, though it is clear that the bias extends towards not only people who practise Islam as a religion, or towards Islamic ideology, but also towards Muslim people or anyone who is perceived to be Muslim.

## Fair and lovely

Race has always been a contentious issue in how attractiveness is defined. Colourism remains a major issue in media – in print, television and films. In Western societies, 'white' remains the norm. In societies such as Asia, colourism alludes to an imperial hangover, where 'fair skin' equates to beautiful. According to an analytical study by the *Guardian* of 214 covers published by the 19 bestselling glossies in 2017 in the UK, only 20 featured a person of colour, although around 14 per cent of the UK popluation is BAME, according to the Office for National Statistics' latest estimate, published in June 2016. Clearly this is not an accurate representation of the society at large. The covers of four magazines – *Marie Claire*, *HomeStyle*, *Your Home* and *Prima* – did not feature a single person of colour throughout 2017. The study also found that this was not confined to women's magazines. While the men's magazine *GQ* featured two black cover models in 2017, the other men's magazine included in this study, *Men's Health*, had just one, and neither publication featured men from any other minority background.

The data analysis company The Pudding looked at 19 years of *Vogue* magazine covers, spanning 228 issues with a total of 262 female cover models, using a combination of facial recognition and clustering techniques to blur the background, pixelate the faces, and then identify which of the pixels were showing 'skin'. They used a scale of 'lightness' as a standard measure to compare all the models across the 228 issues. The results were startling but hardly surprising: until 2015 no solo black model had featured on the cover of *Vogue*, over a span of 146 issues, since Naomi Campbell in 2002. At the beginning of the research in 2000, even the models on the darker shade of the spectrum had very light skin, such as Halle Berry. In some cases, the photographs of black models were digitally manipulated to make them looker lighter, a phenomenon called 'whitewashing'.

As briefly mentioned in the introduction, traditional stock photography websites almost always only feature faces that are white and young. In today's age of mass digital content-creation, platforms such as Unsplash allow photographers around the world to upload their own images in an attempt to create a free resource for everyone to use, and so you would expect it to be quite diverse. It is a surprise then to find a white bias even on such websites. The way that people have tagged these images and classified them also demonstrates the inherent stereotypes. On searching 'people of colour' there are supposedly 67,000 free photographs with this tag. However, most of these are just colourful photographs of products and food. No photographs were found using the search terms 'BAME' or 'BME'. According to a recent campaign by the beauty brand Dove, 72 per cent of women in the UK still don't feel represented in media and advertising. To address this lack of diversity, they collaborated with Getty Images and GirlGaze, the global network of more than 200,000 female-identifying and non-binary creatives to launch the initiative #ShowUs, a collection of over 5,000 images designed to subvert beauty stereotypes.[*] The gender and identity website Broadly, launched by *VICE* in 2015, released their own stock-photography platform, the Gender Spectrum Collection, billed as the first gender-inclusive photo collection. These are much-needed initiatives but not free,[†] and so still not being used regularly in mainstream media. While more websites than before now have an obligatory person of colour, they are still rare, mostly use models with lighter skin, and most depict

---

[*] The images are created by a global community of 116 photographers from 39 countries. I am not a fan of their clunky search interface, and they haven't been able to escape the labelling with their categories.

[†] A single image from Getty Images costs up to £375, which makes it pretty exclusionary, meaning these images are not changing people's perceptions as much as they ought to.

a skewed version of what true diversity and inclusivity should look like.

There is an inherent bias in the wider domain of photography against darker skin too. 'Skin-colour balance' in still photography printing refers historically to a process in which a reference card showing a 'Caucasian' woman wearing a colourful, high-contrast dress is used as a basis for measuring and calibrating the skin tones on the photograph being printed. This is called a 'Shirley card', which until recently has been used as a standard colour-test card and has been the recognised skin ideal standard for most North American analogue photo labs since the early part of the 20th century. It continues to function as the dominant norm. Professor Lorna Roth reports a personal communication with Toru Hasegawa, a video engineer at the NHK (Japan Broadcasting Corporation), who told her that 'American television is discriminatory because it is biased against Japanese skin tones.' In her research on Shirley cards, Roth looked at the notion of 'technological unconscious' and 'cognitive inequity' where there has been little focus on the way these skin-colour biases have been built into the apparatus of visual reproduction. The multiracial Shirley card by Kodak was then developed to address the inclusivity concerns, and this included three women with different skin colours, dressed fashionably in brightly contrasted clothing. Nevertheless, the skin colour for all three women is still on the lighter end of the spectrum and, although it was developed in 1995, it took several years for it to become publicly available. The industry then gradually moved on to digital cards, but this colour bias continued. An example is DuPont's Digital WaterProof image of a black female with a very light complexion that paralleled the 'Caucasian' Shirley prototypes. Film emulsions – the coating on the film base that reacts with chemicals and light to produce an image – could have been designed initially with more sensitivity to the continuum of yellow, brown and reddish skin tones. However, there was little motivation to acknowledge and recognise the need for an extended range as the market was focused on catering for white consumers. These examples show how deeply embedded the normalisation of 'whiteness' is within our social and cultural discourses. What is most visible becomes the norm and the standard for beauty. It also contributes to the 'othering' of certain communities, as they are given the message that they are not part of society, that they do not belong. Many of these technological issues have since been corrected and improved, but we still see images of women of colour[*] that have clearly been lightened.

The higher status and apparent desirability for light-skinned women of colour are well known in hip-hop lyrics and videos. Additionally, negative stereotypes rooted in colourism are common in media representations of people of colour, with dark-skinned actors disproportionately cast as criminals compared with lighter-skinned actors. The lack of diversity on screen is startling, and even in Bollywood – India's primary film industry – only fair-skinned women get the leading roles. This creates a deep-rooted desire for lighter skin.

Colourism, a term coined by the activist Alice Walker in 1982, is the bias that 'white is beautiful', creating the aspiration for white skin. It is not restricted to Western

---

[*] Lupita Nyong'o on the cover of *Vanity Fair*, Beyoncé in a L'Oreal ad, Halle Barry for *Bazaar* are just a few cases where images have been photoshopped to create the impression of a 'white-passing' woman of colour.

societies. Indian and African societies still believe that the colour of a person's skin determines their worth and their attractiveness. This practice can be traced to India's centuries-old caste system, which is based on rigid hierarchies of social and hereditary occupations. The term for caste ('varna') in India's ancient epic *Mahabharata* refers to 'skin colour'.* Here, the Brahmins – the upper caste – were designated as white, while the lowest caste – the untouchables or the Dravidians – are described as dark or black; the darker your skin tone, the lower your place in the social hierarchy.

Colour prejudice is widespread, and advertisements of products such as 'Fair and Lovely' face cream, the most popular skin-whitening cream – which I used obsessively, but reluctantly, during my teenage years[†] – show dark skin as a barrier, and fair skin as a way to overcome the stigma of being born a girl and to achieve confidence and conquer 'womanly hesitation and fears'. Just looking at the matrimonial column in any Indian newspaper makes it evident how skin colour is the constant and most important factor when finding a prospective partner, irrespective of gender. Prominent Indian brands such as Lakme and Tanishq feature only fair-skinned models, and the recent

---

* There is some debate among cultural historians on this since the literal meaning in Sanskrit is 'colour'. In ancient Vedic texts, 'varna' was used alternatively for a 'category'. Either way, it was used as a moniker for classification.

† I fervently hoped to become 'lovely' and for all the aunties to finally stop telling my mother that 'she would get such a good husband, if she was just a little *gori* [fair].' Yes, fair = lovely! My female friends and I were regularly told to not go out in the sun as we would become *kali* (dark and tanned), which would be terrible for our prospects. The Fair and Lovely cream marketed by the consumer goods behemoth Hindustan Unilever has more than a 50 per cent share of the market.

line-up of Miss India contestants in 2018 came under criticism as they all looked alike: fair-skinned with straight, long hair. Hindustan Pencils, the manufacturers of the popular brands such as Nataraj and Apsara, started a Colorama crayon series with a peach-coloured crayon labelled as 'skin' – nowhere close to the most prevalent skin colour of Indians. As a child, I remember drawing faces and colouring them with pink or peach-coloured crayons, confused because they looked nothing like me.

The idea that fair skin is beautiful is deeply rooted in the colonial hangover and the shame that Indians carried for looking the way they did. Historians have discussed how the British perpetuated and reinforced skin-colour discrimination, as they claimed themselves to be a 'superior' and 'intelligent' race and justified why they were born to rule the 'inferior' and 'black-coloured' Indians. They gave menial tasks to those Indians or 'natives' who were dark-skinned and kept the ones who were fairer as allies in better administrative roles, thereby creating a divide based on skin colour.[*] This shaped the common people's association of white-coloured skin with the ruling class, with power, with desirability, and with beauty. Unknowingly, it became a practice of attaching greater societal superiority and power to the fairer-skin individuals, which in turn dictates and shapes the desire for a Westernised concept of beauty with lighter skin – even after so many years of independence. Indian society internalised this shame and projected the stigma upon all Indian women, who are, of course, the

---

[*] The East India Company in the 1600s named its Fort St George settlement in India 'White Town' and its Indian Settlement 'Black Town'. Churchill infamously remarked, 'I hate Indians, they are a beastly people with a beastly religion,' and Kipling quotes in *The Undertakers*: 'English men were uniquely fitted to rule lesser breeds without the law.'

lowest denominator in the social hierarchy. Colourism continues to be more prominent at the intersection of race and gender, with light-skinned women being fetishized and eroticised even within their own communities.

So when we talk about colourism, we have to consider the social hierarchies within minority ethnic groups. This dominance hierarchy is often designated on the basis of who can appear more 'white' and who is more 'white-passing'. A research study by Texas Southern University found that over a 15-year period it was lighter-skinned black women – the likes of Alicia Keys, Rihanna, Nicki Minaj, Mariah Carey and, of course, Beyoncé – who dominated Top 40 airplay in the pop charts. When Matthew Knowles, Beyoncé's father, was asked how different Beyoncé's career would have been had she been darker-skinned, he was unequivocal: 'I think it would've affected her success.'* Beyoncé descends, via her mother's side, from Louisiana's 'Creoles of color' or *gens de couleur libres*, a distinct ethnic group that developed from unions between Europeans and Africans. They held a privileged position in society, as compared to enslaved Africans; they were lighter than African-Americans and hence at the apex of the shade-based caste system, which still persists to this day. In South Africa, there is even the word 'yellow bone': a flattering term for people with lighter skin tones. This intra-community discrimination happens in other Asian communities too. In China, pale skin is seen as a mark of status as it signified historically that such women were rich enough to stay indoors in the shade during the day rather than go out and work, which would darken their skin. This is no longer the case, but these ingrained implicit beliefs and biases persist, so in East Asian culture women

---

* The *Guardian*, 13 July 2019.

prefer lighter skin tones because they believe '*yī bái zhē bǎi chǒu*', which means 'a white complexion is powerful enough to hide seven faults.'

Whitening products are a billion-dollar business. In Indian beauty salons, bleaching used to be a very common procedure that was offered to any woman visiting for a facial treatment. In fact, often enough women were cajoled or persuaded into having their skin bleached. Bleaching is a harmful skin-lightening procedure, and the Nelson R Mandela School of Medicine head of dermatology Professor Ncoza Dlova warns that such procedures can cause irreparable damage to the skin and that 'patients do not even know the active ingredients of the creams they use, nor the complications of such use.' A survey by the Zero Mercury Working Group (ZMWG) shows an estimated – and staggering – 735 million users in India of fairness cream, most of whom are women and girls, and a report from the European Environmental Bureau (EEB) in November 2018 shows that demand is skyrocketing, especially in Asia, the Middle East and Africa, with sales of $17.9 billion in 2017, projected to reach $31.2 billion by 2024. This statistic is followed by Nigeria at an estimated 99.5 million users in 2002. Nigerian pop musician Dencia launched a product called 'Whitenicious' in 2014, which sold out immediately. She stated that getting a few shades lighter was a personal choice, an argument that is parroted by most skin-lightening brands. In 2014, India's skin-whitening industry launched a product called 'Clean & Dry' intended to whiten a woman's intimate parts. The shocking advertisement, which has since been pulled off-air due to a huge media furore, suggested that a woman would have a more fulfilling personal life if she chose to lighten more than just her face.

In a recent study, more than half of 1,992 men and women surveyed about product use in India had tried skin whiteners, and close to half (44.6 per cent) felt the need to try such products due to media such as TV and advertisements. 'Perfect skin, perfect life' is a slogan I read on a huge billboard with an ad for a skin-fairness cream while in New Delhi earlier this year. Routine use of skin whitener ranges from 25 per cent in Mali to 77 per cent in Nigeria, and stands at 40 per cent in China, Malaysia, the Philippines and South Korea, according to the World Health Organization. A 2017 report by research group Frontiers in Public Health found that whitening products tested in India contained 'highly active and potentially dangerous agents' such as hydroquinone, mercury, and bleaching chemicals including hydrogen peroxide. A frightening picture indeed.

Lighter skin colour is also implicitly associated with power and higher social status, and an informal experiment that I conducted online and with people across the cities of Lucknow and Jaipur in March 2019 demonstrated this. People selected those who had fairer skin – both men and women – to be the CEOs of companies and in prominent public roles. In an ethnographic study in Chennai, India, it was found that young Indian women used lightening filters in every photo of themselves before they uploaded them to social media, as they perceived this would make the images more 'likeable'. Most editing tools offer a skin-lightening option. This especially affects teenagers and adolescents, as they are particularly susceptible to societal beauty standards and ideals. Research has shown that use of skin-lightening products is also directly correlated with negative mental health: a large cross-sectional study of female university students from 26 countries found that depression was significantly correlated with the use of such products.

The bias against darker skin in India is a complex issue intersecting with gender, class, caste and geography in many ways, and there isn't really scope in this book to give it all the attention it deserves. According to a recent NGO study by the Sustainable Development Policy Institute (SDPI) in Pakistan, the social pressures for acquiring a lighter complexion are often reinforced and amplified by advertisements. In 2014, the Advertising Standards Council of India banned adverts depicting people with darker skin as inferior, but the products are still being marketed. In India, attitudes are slowly changing, with new campaigns such as 'Dark is Beautiful', endorsed by a number of Bollywood actresses, trying to break the mould. The movement is still not widespread, due to the challenges of taking on these multibillion global corporations that sell skin-whitening products, but change is happening slowly. The campaign is pushing for brands to make their advertising more inclusive, and companies are showing willingness to respond to these customer demands. But it is not yet clear how genuine this change is as many of these brands are merely repackaging and rebranding their products as brightness and glow creams. Recent activism has not been able to change the deeply entrenched ideas of 'white is better' beauty. The desire for whiter skin is a continuing legacy of imperialism and a sign of deep-seated internalised racism and social hierarchies, which cannot be addressed by merely banning any cosmetic products. Yet it is critical that we talk about colourism, as it can often be ignored while the debates around race and body positivity take place.

## Am I overreacting?

There has been much written about racial bias, explicit hate crimes, Islamophobia, the bias against minorities and the rise of the right. Much less has been said or written about aversive racism, the one that sneakily threatens and diminishes some people, but its subversive nature often makes it difficult to prove its intent or justify its impact. It can be taken as a joke, as humour that the stigmatised is expected to partake in and be an accomplice to because, in not doing so, the divide and the inferior status become even more amplified.

Often you might feel irritated and 'othered' by such comments and questions. But then you have to question your own judgement and your reaction, and wonder if you were indeed overreacting. Often such microinvalidations and aggressions are disguised as humour. But making fun of someone's accent, height or ethnicity is not a joke. The intent might not be malicious, and is frequently borne out of ignorance, but such comments tend to reinforce the differences and the non-conformity of any minority community from the majority demographic.

John Powell, the director of the Haas Institute for a Fair and Inclusive Society at the University of California, Berkeley, is credited with coining the term 'othering'. According to Powell, when 'societies experience big and rapid change, a frequent response is for people to narrowly define who qualifies as a full member of society,' and this dehumanises and separates the 'othered' from those who are not. Although in his article in the *Guardian* in 2017 he says that this process is 'largely driven by politicians and media, rather than via personal contact,' this might not be entirely true. Racial discrimination might have been an implicit act in the recent past, where people would not necessarily name the groups that were being 'othered' and instead alluded to them obliquely, but it has become much more explicit in the current political climate. Politicians, the media and social networks are all driving this climate of anxiety and fear, and we are witnessing a rise in microaggressions and micro-incivilities as people become threatened by behaviours that they deem to be different – the same behaviours and communities they had been living alongside for many years. When a suggestion is made, often as a joke, that a person has been given a job to increase the diversity of an organisation, it can create imposter syndrome, making the targeted person believe they are not there on merit but only because of their difference. Using a person's preferred pronoun (they/him/her) is not just an exercise in meaningless identity politics but a sign of respect to an individual's innermost identity and their dignity. Anything else is a sign of prejudice.

Dr Roberto Montenegro at the Department of Psychiatry, Equity Research and Innovation Center (ERIC), Yale School of Medicine, recounts an incident when he was repeatedly mistaken for a valet when waiting outside a fancy upmarket restaurant after celebrating the completion of his PhD. Montenegro tells NPR that in one swift action, he was dismissed and 'made to feel invisible'. Montenegro says, 'Individually these incidents seem benign. But cumulatively I believe that they act like sort of low-grade microtraumas that can end up hurting you and your biology.' That is the dangerous truth of these microaggressions, these seemingly non-threatening and benign incidents. They make the stigmatised target individual or group doubt themselves, doubt their instinct and their understanding of the situation, feel confused, and at the same time feel completely dismissed and shocked. They serve as a constant reminder of being perceived as different and 'not fitting in'.

Psychologist Dorainne J. Levy says that often in such cases 'there's uncertainty about whether or not your experience was due to your race, for example, or due to something unrelated, such as the other person being in a bad mood or having a bad day. That uncertainty is distressing.' Trying to figure out what happened can consume cognitive resources, can lead to an increase in stress hormones, and is akin to being bullied. It is easy to ignore such seemingly minor comments, and some have even questioned whether chastising and banning these interactions between colleagues is detrimental to positive and convivial workplace culture. But these microaggressions never exist in isolation. They are indicative of the insidious unconscious biases existing in our society and they have to be called out.

Racial anxiety is a subset of the broader kind of anxiety associated with 'stereotype threat', as discussed earlier in the book. Race has increasingly become a salient membership identifier in the current turbulent political climate, and so racial anxiety has also increased manifold. Studies are showing that people of all races and ethnicities experience physiological threat and cognitive depletion in anticipation of and following an interracial interaction. Besides physiological responses to the anticipation of discrimination and uncertainty around interacting with out-group members, it also affects verbal and nonverbal responses. Research with different ethnic groups has shown that people experiencing anxiety often physically distance themselves from each other in public spaces, avoid eye contact, and their verbal tone is less friendly and engaging. These actions can come across as microaggressions and micro-incivilities. When both sides in an interracial interaction are experiencing anxiety, both members are then bound to feel that the interaction was negative. This then creates even further implicit bias against the out-group members as the cause of anxiety, which gives rise to aversive racism, the subtler form of discrimination where people deliberately avoid someone of a different race.* In this way, stereotypes are maintained and reinforced, and rather than seeing the person as an individual, they are only seen as a

---

* Here race is again being used according to the socially constructed definition.

member of a racial category. Prejudice and discrimination is the natural next step when these racial stereotypes are maintained. In the aversive form of bias, people can often discriminate against someone and judge them because of their race but can justify it as something else. This can include making fun of someone's accent or name. People want to behave in an egalitarian way – they might be convinced they are acting in the most equitable manner – but it leaves the person being discriminated against wondering about their intentions.

This kind of racial discrimination has been shown to trigger an inflammatory response in African-Americans at the cellular level. Steve Cole at the University of California, Los Angeles had also found that such responses occur in other socially marginalised groups, such as those suffering from homelessness, PTSD and poverty, but this is the first time that such strong evidence was seen for the severe long-term impact of discrimination. The study led by April Thames, Associate Professor of Psychology and Psychiatry at the University of Southern California, focused on a group of 71 subjects. Two-thirds of the participants were African-Americans, the others were white, and 38 of the case group tested for HIV. Even though the sample size is small, this study digs deep at the physiological level to show how facing regular discrimination can alter the gene expression, and promote heart attacks, neurodegenerative diseases and metastatic cancer. The scientists extracted RNA* from the participants' cells and measured molecules that trigger inflammation, as well as those involved in antiviral responses. The research team found higher levels

---

* RNA stands for ribonucleic acid, which is essential in various biological roles, such as sensing and communicating responses to cellular signals.

of the inflammatory molecules in African-American participants, and asserted that this was a direct result of anxiety and trauma associated with long-term racial discrimination. The results also indicated that racism may account for as much as 50 per cent of the heightened inflammation among African-Americans, including those who were positive for HIV. All participants had a similar socio-economic background to eliminate the possibility of poverty as a stressor. Discrimination and bias are something they had no control over, unlike other socio-economic factors, as one cannot change their skin colour, which is the most significant cue for racial bias.

Paradoxically, people who value their objectivity and fairness are particularly likely to fall prey to biases, mostly because they are not on guard against subtle bias. This is why people who believe they can never be racist or sexist are more likely to show implicit racial bias. We used to think of racism in simple terms as a negative reaction to a person of different ethnic origin or explicit hatred towards them such as demonstrated by Nazis and the Ku Klux Klan, but it has become much more aversive and subtle since racially motivated hate crimes have been made illegal and people are aware that it is immoral to think like this.

## One drop of blood

'Race is real, race matters, and race is the foundation of identity,' said Richard Spencer, the leader of an alt-right organisation, decrying as 'total hokum nonsense' the idea that America's Founding Fathers thought all races were created equal.

Race and racial identity is a socially created construct, and we impose our ideas of which racial category one belongs to according to societal context. So someone who is considered as black or brown in the United States could be considered white in India. How someone perceives race and racial identity can shift through time and space and change with our experience, but the meanings – and social and economic status associated with certain racial categories – have not changed. The notion of racial fluidity is especially relevant to those with mixed heritage (or 'multiracial' as is the more common term), although that brings into question the rigid determinants of race. How does one determine who is black? Can a person with one-tenth black racial heritage be considered black? How do we decide who belongs to which racial category? It has been seen that people are often designated the status of the subordinate group that anthropologists call the 'hypodescent rule'. For instance, in the US, especially in the south, it became known as the 'one-drop rule', meaning that a single drop of 'black blood' makes a person black. It is also known as the 'one black ancestor rule' and some courts have called it the 'traceable amount rule'. In America, if one had black or African ancestry over three generations, it took precedence over any other heritage and made you 'not white'. Theoretically it could (and should) have worked in reverse: one drop of white blood or ancestry could have trumped everything else and made you white. But the inherent racism of this rule is evident in the fact that, in 400 years, America has never practised white hypodescent.

Cultural and social identity could also be the result of self-identification. For instance, if a person is born in England and has English parents but has been brought up since infancy in Scotland and has a Scottish accent, he can easily 'pass off' as Scottish. This is due to a couple of reasons: first, he is still British, and second, he belongs to technically the same racial group, i.e. white (even though some might consider Scots to have a distinct cultural identity and therefore to be a different ethnic group). However, a person born in India and then having lived in the UK since infancy is not able to pass off as English because they are seen to belong to a different racial category due to their skin colour, facial features and being physically distinguishable from those who are considered 'native English'. Race is therefore a complex thing and we make it too simplistic by putting people into race boxes based entirely on our perceived view of racial identity, the societal definition of race and conformity to our own group membership. There is no specific genetic configuration to a black or white racial identity. Here, race is meant to imply a perceived social construct. Yet race is primarily an emotional construction.

Faces are also strong social cues for shaping social categories and memberships. What does an American or a Brit look like? There is an inherent implicit bias that these equate to white skin. People start implicitly associating various other characteristics in determining national identity, which they would not admit openly and explicitly. Race is one of them. Thierry Devos, a professor at San Diego State University, found that this implicit perception existed even when explicit attitudes and responses said something entirely opposite. A study conducted with college students at San Diego State University in 2012 measured whether race had anything to do with seeming 'American'. The participants in one group were asked to focus on personal identity (Barack Obama vs Tony Blair) and another group to focus on race (black vs white). The group that focused on personal identity found Obama to be more American. But the group that focused on race found Tony Blair to be more American. The effect was more heightened when the students had been primed beforehand about Obama being black (or mixed-race). This effect was not as prominent when voters were primed with the age or gender of the candidate. But an awareness of the candidate's race affected how people perceive their national identity. And research has shown that the nationality of the candidate plays a huge part in ascertaining voters' preference, so people are less likely to vote for a candidate who they perceive to be not part of their nationalistic in-group. Even many African-Americans and Asian-Americans showed this pro-white bias, indicating the power of these cultural messages to shape people's implicit attitudes towards their own ethnic group. Another study found that, although people realise that Lucy Liu is American and that Kate Winslet is British, their minds automatically process an Asian face as foreign and a white face as American.

The complexities of racial identity and perceived race was seen in Rachel Dolezal's case. Born to white parents, Rachel was seen as 'black' for many years as this is how she represented herself. This is what she had to say: 'Well, I definitely am not white. Nothing about being white describes who I am so, you know, what's the word for it? The closest thing I can come to is, if you're black or white, I'm black. I'm more black than I am white. So, on a level of values, lived experience, currently, in this moment, that's the answer. That's the accurate answer from my truth. But I hope the dialogue continues to push against what is race, what is ethnicity.'* And when asked: 'Have you ever lied about your race?' she replied, 'No, because I've never been asked, "Are you human or not human?" Race as a construct is a fluid understanding.' On one hand, her passing off as a black person and creating a false narrative is an insult to those who have been historically marginalised and oppressed, and trivialises the struggles of the black community. On the other hand, it highlights the contentious issues around racial identity and our race-obsessed culture. There is no easy answer.

---

* *NBC Nightly News*, 16 June 2015.

Structural racism is so pervasive that it is impossible to explore every facet in this one chapter. But one just has to look at the history of marginalisation and oppression to understand the systemic ubiquity of racial bias. To avoid being called racist, it is easy to say that we don't notice colour. This is a lie as we notice colour in everything we do, and we notice race and skin colour of every person we meet and interact with.

## Colour blindness

Children are not colour-blind. They start developing a sense of race from the age of six months or so. Phyllis Katz and Jennifer Kofkin found in 1997 that an infant is able to nonverbally categorise people by race and gender at six months of age, as they look for longer at an unfamiliar face from a different race than when they look at someone from their own race. Children start categorising and using power-based hierarchies in play based on the social cues they pick up from all the people around them, not just their parents. They also pick up the normative accent from the region, not always the accent of their parents or carers. Children at such a young age are unable to process all the multiple dimensions associated with a person, and so they use 'transductive reasoning'.* It is easier for them to look at someone's skin colour and use that to make generalisations about their other characteristics. Children start using social cues about race and gender and observing things around them in their environment to make sense of their 'cognitive

---

* According to Jean Piaget, a developmental psychologist, children between the ages of two and four are unable to understand all the properties of classes. Transductive reasoning is a faulty type of logic during this stage that involves making inferences from one specific to another.

puzzle', assigning positive and negative salience to people and things, and making associations such as 'boys play with trucks' and 'girls play with dolls'. They might start making connections such as a person of a particular ethnicity takes the bus while someone from a different ethnicity drives their own car. They start formalising theories about how to behave because of their gender, and which people to like and dislike. They make inferences from what they observe, and conclude that these are the social norms. Middle-class white culture is normalised in Western society, and it becomes the norm as children see this in movies, books, pictures and songs. There is also plenty of research to show how linguistic categories, symbolism and labels give out implicit messages that 'whiteness' is good and positive (such as Snow White being 'white and pure'), and negative things are associated with black, such as 'evil', 'dirty', 'wicked witch' and so on. Diversity in children's books is a significant issue, with very few characters featuring from non-white ethnic backgrounds.* This kind of 'smog'† that exists all around us creates an environment where children begin to apply these linguistic connotations to people.

---

* In 2018 only 4 per cent of children's books published in the UK had a minority ethnic hero. The survey included all new books for children aged between three and 11. The proportion is an increase on 2017, when just 1 per cent of main characters were BAME. In 2018, 42 per cent of children's books published in the UK had animals or inanimate objects as main characters, meaning that a reader from a BAME background is much more likely to encounter a book where an animal is the main character than they are to encounter a book that contains a character who shares their ethnicity or cultural heritage.

† Tatum in 1997 argues that this message is so prevalent in our society it is like smog in the air. He says, 'Sometimes it is so thick it is visible, other times it is less apparent, but always, day in and day out, we are breathing it in.'

While 30-month-olds show a preference for children of the same race when shown photographs of unfamiliar white and black children, demonstrating in-group bias, the majority of children start choosing white playmates by the time they are 36 months old. This study was done in the US where there are relatively homogenous white communities. Context definitely matters, and so this pattern could be different in different cultural and social contexts. A similar study in Korea and India indicated similar preferences, where white was considered better by the majority of children. This is highly likely to be a result of the implicit, as well as explicit, cues and messages these children receive from the people and media around them where 'fair-skinned' is considered more attractive.

An honest and vulnerable piece in the *New York Times* parenting section by a mother, Norma Newton, who is darker than her young child offers a beautiful narrative of how children form a sense of beauty norms that create their biases and prejudices and so mean dark skin can become 'threatening' or 'ugly' for them. She writes how her mixed-heritage young child starts calling Newton's skin 'dirty', and expresses what many parents who have darker skin than their children, and who might have internalised the shame around their skin colour, must feel. We do not often hear stories like these publicly about how our mixed-heritage families form and develop a sense of self-esteem, tackling colourism and societal discomfort around darker hues of skin.

My three-year-old twins are the only multiracial children at their preschool in the small town where we live, the staff are all white Europeans with local accents, and I am the only brown person they ever meet and see on a regular basis. It is a very white community and I am very conscious of how the twins would see and understand race. We recently visited India for the first time since they were born, and their initial reaction to people there was one of fear. This is not a permanent bias or prejudice at this stage, merely a fear of novelty of someone who does not look like them. We sat next to an Asian-American family at Heathrow airport on the way back from India, and one of my twins could not stop staring at them. She was intrigued, and I could see that she was carefully observing me and her father, and our attitudes and behaviour towards this family, to take cues as to how she ought to feel about them. She wanted to get a sense of whether they were threatening or whether she could feel secure in their difference. This is where our nonverbal cues really mattered. It becomes our responsibility – as parents, teachers, educators – to teach our children racial socialisation, a strategy to understand race and racial difference, and of which societal messages to filter out and which ones to take on board. Busting implicit biases has to start young and has to be a consistent process throughout our adult lives. It isn't useful to ignore these differences; rather it is more crucial to understand how we respond when we make these racial distinctions.[*]

***

The 'post-racial' world-view is that racism has no value or place in today's world, with its liberal democracies, and decline in explicit racial prejudice and expression. Douglas Murray in his column in the *Spectator* in 2018 uses the marriage of Meghan Markle into the royal family to prove that racism in Britain is a 'myth'. It would also be easy to be fooled by Boris Johnson's 'diverse', virtue-signalling Cabinet

---

[*] I have discussed this in detail in an episode of BBC *Women's Hour* on Radio 4 in August 2019, in a *Huffington Post* article, and in a podcast episode of 'Outside the Boxes'.

with the most BAME representation in recent times: Sajid Javid, Priti Patel, Alok Sharma and Rishi Sunak. Thus, a post-racial illusion of the world is created where there is no structural racism or bigotry, and therefore any acts of racism are more aversive, less explicit, and seemingly 'non-racial'. Racism has not disappeared, but the nature of racism has changed – 'racism without racists' – and its expression and articulation is different. Dr Tina Patel, a sociologist from the University of Salford, says that 'in a "post-racial" context, concerns around immigration are reframed as legitimate and seemingly non-racial.' The notion of 'self' and 'other' (the foreigner or the immigrant) is becoming the cornerstone of modern forms of racism in this post-racial society, consolidating its hold on the societal subconscious by drawing upon primal fears and anxieties about place, identity and belonging. Eduardo Bonilla-Silva, Professor of Sociology at Duke University, in his 2018 paper talks about the threat of loss of white privilege, which is making white people feel threatened and marginalised, thereby resulting in implicit bias against those who are the source of this threat. This legitimises the hostility against anyone with a different skin colour on public forums (both in the real and the digital world), as it is perceived to be rooted in nationalistic pride and identity rather than in racial bias – an acceptable form of xenophobia. People precede their prejudicial comments with 'not meaning to sound racist' or that 'I'm not racist but,'* or

---

* Many of these incidents occur over Twitter but are also played out in workplaces and in academic institutions. Again much of my data comes from the anonymous surveys carried out online but also from informal comments from family and friends. My (white) husband tells me that his Sunday league football team has several people who routinely start their sentences with 'I'm not racist but' and finish them with vehemently racialised words against minority ethnic communities.

even justify through their affiliation and association in remarks such as 'I have many black [or Asian] friends' or 'My children are mixed-race', often exaggerating their closeness to those from a minority ethnic community to display their level of racial tolerance.

As the nature of racism and its form of articulation changes, being quiet and non-racist isn't enough anymore. Silence breeds prejudice. The only way to combat racism is to be actively anti-racist.

## CHAPTER NINE

# Swipe Right for a Match

There seems to be a bias even in the way bias is studied and talked about. Gender and race are hugely important, there is no doubt about it. But there are other biases that exist at the margins, sometimes far more prevalent but not acknowledged or recognised as prejudice and discrimination. They are far more normalised and part of prevailing social norms. You could say that there is a bias within the world of bias itself.

## In the eyes of the beholder

Since ancient classical Greece, there has been a cognitive heuristic that has placed both physical and moral beauty on a pedestal. In his *Tusculan Disputations*, Cicero highlighted the parallels between moral and physical beauty as this: 'And as in the body a certain symmetrical shape of the limbs combined with a certain charm of colouring is described as beauty; so in the soul the name of beauty is given to an equipoise and consistency of beliefs and judgements, combined with a certain steadiness and stability following upon virtue or comprising the true essence of virtue.' Robert FitzRoy, the *Beagle*'s[*] captain, believed in physiognomy, the idea that one can tell a

---

[*] HMS *Beagle* was a ship of the Royal Navy launched on May 1820. The second voyage of HMS *Beagle* is notable for carrying the naturalist Charles Darwin around the world.

person's character from their appearance, which was widely accepted during Charles Darwin's time.

We tend to be reluctant to talk about beauty bias because we all like to believe that we are not so shallow or superficial as to judge a book by its cover. What we consider beautiful is largely dependent on the unconscious decisions and the biases that we have internalised based on cultural and social norms and expectations woven into our perception. An assessment of attractiveness also shapes how we see the person as a whole and affects our cognitive heuristic. Two psychology studies in the 1970s showed the attractiveness halo or the beauty bias that shapes our view of the people we interact with. In one study, when participants were asked to assess photographs for a range of traits, they ranked those they deemed most attractive with the most positive traits. In the other study, two photographs – one attractive and the other not so much – were each linked to an essay, and two group of participants were asked to grade these essays. The essays were identical. However, you won't be surprised to hear that the person in the attractive photo was consistently evaluated to have written a better essay. When the researchers replaced the essays with truly awful essays, the difference was magnified. The people perceived as being attractive scored much higher, while the other person was penalised much more harshly, hence showing that we expect more from beautiful people but also forgive them more easily.

In an exclusive *Newsweek* poll in 2010, based on telephone interviews conducted with around a thousand adults aged 18 and over, nearly two-thirds of the Americans interviewed saw being good-looking as an advantage, with women being more affected by looks discrimination, and 72 per cent of the surveyed believed that attractive females have an advantage at a job interview. Stanford Law's Professor

Deborah Rhode asserts that 'Women who fail to meet conventional beauty standards are often passed up for promotions and suffer from the economic effects of people's perceptions of their attractiveness.' It is also important to consider here how much of the implicit biases were coming into play while responding to this question. Was it based on their own personal experience, showing recall bias, or something they'd read before, showing recognition bias?[*] In the same survey, 24 per cent of employed US adults said they knew someone in their workplace who had progressed because of their looks, and so their personal experience was impacting their judgements on this interview.

We might be told to not judge a book by its cover, but research has reliably proven that our faces are the first cues in how we judge and perceive other individuals. A fraction of a second is enough to assess beauty. Our first impressions are largely based on what we look like, and there's research to show that people's physical appearance has a huge impact on how others perceive and treat them. The physical-attribute stereotype is very easily accessible and so the assessment is fast and automatic and serves as the basis for inferences about other socially relevant personal traits. People who are assessed as physically attractive are also attributed other positive personal and interpersonal qualities such as trustworthiness, intelligence and competence. This can be explained by the halo effect or the 'physical attractiveness premium'. There is a well-documented relationship between attractiveness and intelligence, with attractive faces perceived to be more intelligent, and intelligent-looking faces perceived to be more attractive.

---

[*] Recall and recognition biases were discussed in further detail in Chapter 6.

A study in 1989 demonstrated that intelligence was the second most desired trait in a long-term partner for both males and females cross-culturally. Because of this, evolutionarily speaking, there is an implicit preference towards any visual cue that denotes intelligence since it is likely to confer certain advantages such as heritable intelligence for one's offspring. If the mate is clever, the offspring is more likely to be clever too, and according to mate-choice theory certain characteristics are more attractive in a partner that would ensure survival of the offspring. The benefits and social value that an individual or a group accumulates due to their looks was termed 'erotic capital' by British sociologist Catherine Hakim in the 2000s. She added erotic capital as a multifaceted interaction of perceived social and physical attractiveness as the fourth personal asset to the French sociologist Pierre Bourdieu's* economic, social and cultural capital. Beauty bias crosses class and caste and therefore is shown to be more subversive than the other three assets, overturning the traditional power structures, but it offers significant economic and social advantage. The reverse or the horn effect is also true in this case, whereby an assessment of 'ugliness' or unattractiveness also results in other negative associations or evokes fear and threat, which in turn create prejudice and discrimination.

The attractiveness bias bypasses conscious awareness, comes very early on in our assessment of an individual and is used as a perceptual anchor to form other associations. This stereotype and its associated bias are perpetuated by

---

* A French sociologist and anthropologist, Bourdieu's work was primarily concerned with the dynamics of power in society, especially the diverse and subtle ways in which power is transferred and social order is maintained within and across generations.

films where usually the goodies are beautiful, while the baddies are ugly.* Infants look longer at attractive faces within a week of being born, and the effects of attractiveness on infants' gaze generalise across race, gender, and age by six months. Our ideas of beauty are of course shaped by our cultural and social factors, but there seem to be certain standards that are similar across different cultures, and theories suggest that our brains are coded in a way to recognise these particular traits and consider them attractive, such as symmetry in faces. Facial attractiveness is one of the key determinants, and some of the facial attributes associated with attractiveness are even colouring, smooth and pliant skin, clear eyes and shiny hair, which are all signs of being healthy. A sense of a facial prototype is formed using the social and cultural norms and an average of the total population. A bias towards attractive faces results from their similarity to facial prototypes. Such faces are processed more fluently, resulting in increased positive effect in the viewer.

This implicit bias affects our decision-making and has been shown to affect judgement even in situations where people are trained and explicitly prohibited and discouraged from showing any differential treatment and discrimination, such as during salary negotiations, job interviews, school assessments and court sentences. Attractive individuals are often given more lenient sentences in mock trials. Judith Langlois and Lisa Kalakanis, along with colleagues from the University of Texas at Austin, showed that an assessment of physical beauty in candidates also influences voting behaviour. Electoral candidates who are deemed more attractive are seen as possessing more integrity, competence,

---

* Here I use 'beautiful' and 'ugly' as socially imposed labels and norms, and not my own personal opinion.

likeableness, open-mindedness, extraversion and fitness for
public office – factors all related to positive evaluations.
Physically attractive individuals are therefore rewarded
socially as well as biologically.* A study has found
recognition bias with attractiveness, hence showing that
individuals believe they remember that attractive individuals
have positive qualities and that unattractive individuals
have negative qualities, regardless of what information
actually occurred.

Attractive teachers are more effective in the classroom,
commanding more attention from students, and attractive
students tend to get higher grades. There is considerable
evidence that attractive people receive more attention than
unattractive people and are also considered possibly more
persuasive. The favourable impression of supposedly
attractive individuals creates a self-fulfilling prophecy
where the initial false belief creates a behaviour that then
makes the belief come true. In this case, beautiful people
are seen as more valuable members of the community,
which leads them to be given preferential treatment and
more opportunities, which in turn enables them to be more
successful.

There is, however, also some research in psychology to
show that the reverse might be an implicit bias resulting in
negative characteristics being attributed to attractiveness
associated with the 'what is beautiful is self-centred'
stereotype. Attractive people may be perceived as vain and
self-centred. Alice Eagly and colleagues showed that

---

* A recent example would be the largely conflicted opinions and
views towards Canadian prime minister Justin Trudeau when
images of him dressed in a Middle Eastern costume with his face
painted brown were revealed. Since he is considered good-looking,
people were quick to forgive him, finding excuses for this
behaviour.

attractive men were found to possess negative social attributes such as sternness and arrogance, and attractive women were associated with negative intellectual qualities. This can be equally harmful in situations where such implicit biases can negatively affect people who are perceived as attractive, for instance, attractive women not being considered as serious and academic. Women faced a penalty for attractiveness in certain male-dominated domains. Attractive businesswomen are seen as less trustworthy and honest, termed the 'femme fatale effect'. 'Highly attractive women can be considered dangerous,' says Leah D. Sheppard, an assistant professor of management at Washington State University. In the 2010 *Newsweek* survey, 12 per cent believed that good-looking men were at a disadvantage in getting a job, while 9 per cent believed that good looks negatively impact a woman's chances (much higher than compared to a 1990 *Times Mirror* body image survey).

The intersection of looks and gender makes a difference too in creating a bias. A study with 750 PhD students across 10 economics departments – typically a male-dominated environment in the US – showed that more attractive individuals publish more. For first job placements, appearance seems to affect only women: women get placed in a high-ranked academic institution if they are attractive but not too attractive. Moreover, this inverse U-shape between women's attractiveness and their placement success is stronger when the woman's research field has a higher share of males. Attractive academics were invited more to conferences, were seen as more confident and convincing while presenting, and more sought-after as co-authors. These results were heightened in male-dominated environments, hence making a case for sexual discrimination.

Ken Podratz from Rice University, in his study on the 'beauty is beastly effect', confirms this intersectionality of looks and gender bias, saying that 'physical attractiveness is related to perceived femininity' and so women who are perceived to be more attractive are less likely to be chosen for professions that are perceived as hyper-masculine. These include jobs such as truck driver and security guard, where it was felt that attractive women wouldn't be able to meet the physical demands of the job. The study also shows that men are keener to place women they perceive as attractive in positions that require more interpersonal contact, such as receptionist and public relations officer. The study highlights the masculine and feminine stereotypes that exist in our society, where certain traits are seen as prototypes for what a typical man and a typical woman looks like.

Dating in the techno-sexual age is based on photos and physical appearance. On some apps, people swipe right to 'like' a potential match based purely on looks and first impressions. Judgements are made in a flash. The Tinder app, launched in 2012 and still one of the most popular dating apps, is constantly updated to allow people to put more photos on their profile and to make photos display larger in the interface, and there is no real incentive to add much personal information. So any such judgements are made purely based on the photos, a superficial hot-or-not approach to dating based solely on the beauty bias. When this happens, there is not much time for rational decisions, and people tend to fall back on their subconscious implicit stereotypes and biases. The format encourages users to make rapid judgements based on physical attractiveness, a primary determinant in the early stages of mate selection. We know from evolutionary theories that attractiveness serves as an implicit cue to other evolutionary advantages such as dominance and social status. The anthropologist

Helen Fisher says that too many choices on such apps can cause cognitive overload and the human brain is not equipped to deal with it.* This is why, she says, it is important to stop after nine right swipes, because the brain can only handle nine choices at one time. The algorithm is also designed in a way that the more you swipe left, the choices become worse and less likely to be a good match, and people become increasingly stressed. We fall back on the social desirability bias, where we tend to go for the option that we feel would be more socially desirable.

Profile photos play a huge role in the sharing economy, and a more trustworthy photo leads to a higher-value association and increased chance of being liked. In a study in 2018, Bastian Jaeger and colleagues from universities in the Netherlands showed that beauty bias also affects online peer-to-peer networks such as Airbnb. From an analysis of 1,020 listings in New York, it is seen that hosts' appearance influences how trustworthy they are deemed and thereby the consumers' preferences.

Faces evoke trust. Back in 2014, Georgia Tech researchers analysed likes and comments in a set of a million Instagram images and found that selfies were 38 per cent more likely to receive likes and 32 per cent more likely to receive comments. A hashtag movement #ScientistsWhoSelfie showed that, by posting selfies on social media, scientists were able to garner more public engagement and trust. Scientists are traditionally seen as competent and clever but not necessarily warm and accessible, and showing the face behind a profile encouraged a feeling of familiarity, intimacy and trust. Dr William Skylark from the Department of Psychology at the University of Cambridge shows that

---

* We saw in Chapter 1 how when we are rushed and tired, we are more likely to fall back on cognitive shortcuts and our biases.

people were more interested in learning about the work of scientists who were physically attractive and who appeared competent and moral. Interest was also slightly stronger for older scientists, and slightly lower for females. There was no difference in interest between white and non-white scientists, so this particular study – with around 600 scientists from physics and biology departments in the US and the UK – did not highlight any racial bias. 'It seems that people use facial appearance as a source of information when selecting and evaluating science news,' says Dr Skylark, with participants more likely to choose research that was paired with a photo of an interesting-looking scientist.

This can be an issue in how people connect with and collaborate with people on networking sites such as LinkedIn. The design agency Beyond (BYND) recently came up with a Chrome extension app called Antibias. When installed it hides profile photos on the LinkedIn platform so that the first impressions – and the associated judgement and implicit bias based on race and gender – are minimised, giving people time to make more informed and rational decisions and judgements about the person concerned. A survey by Photofeeler of a million ratings of perceived competence, likeability and influence for 100,000 'business' profile photos in their database, found that males over 50 were scored most competent and influential. The perceived competence and influence increased with age, but this was shown to grow more rapidly in men (between 2.5 and six times faster) than women. Research shows that unlike men, likeability and competence are inherently linked for women. While men can be perceived to be competent even if they are not seen as very likeable, the women must be seen as likeable to be considered competent.[*]

---

[*] Related again to the double-bind bias discussed in Chapter 7.

Psychologists from Princeton University developed a measure of competence and a computational model based on the parameters extracted from a group of participants, which was then used to develop some composite faces. In this study, participants evaluated these faces on measures of attractiveness and competence. Faces that were assessed as competent were also perceived as attractive, thereby validating the 'attractiveness halo' hypothesis. They also found an inherent gender bias in the assessment of competence. As the 'masculinity' of a face increased, the perception of competence increased. Also, when asked to rate competent faces as male or female, they rated more competent faces as male and lesser ones as female. Competence and masculinity seems to be interlinked. While there is no evidence to show how accurate these perceptions of personality traits are, it has been suggested that they can turn into self-fulfilling prophecies, with expectations eventually leading people to conform to these overgeneralised assessments.

## Love doesn't come in sizes

In an informal discussion with a group of female academics, I heard numerous stories of how they were 'invisible' when they were above average weight, but suddenly garnered more attention at academic conferences and their opinions were taken more seriously when they lost weight. Women face obesity penalty. Men are less likely to do so. Rebel Wilson is a fierce body-positive activist and the film *Pitch Perfect* conveys this well. However, it also shows how Rebel's character 'Fat Amy' has to overcompensate for her weight through her character and personality; it isn't enough just to be herself.

There is a plethora of scientific literature that explicates the pervasive nature of weight bias and, as we know, discrimination closely follows bias. The World Health Organization asserts that weight bias and prejudice against people who are overweight can lead to an obesity stigma in society. People who are obese or overweight can be excluded and marginalised in the workplace or receive inadequate healthcare because weight is portrayed as a result of lifestyle and therefore controllable. The bias against excessive weight is formed primarily because this is seen as a personal responsibility issue, and people are often stereotyped as lazy, gluttonous, unattractive, intellectually slow, socially inept and lacking in self-esteem.

Among healthcare professionals, numerous studies show the implicit biases against people carrying excess weight. The cost to the NHS in the UK of treating obesity also creates the view that people who are carrying excess weight are a burden on society, with headlines such as 'Get serious about obesity or bankrupt the NHS'. Anti-fat attitudes abound and are usually being measured using the 'Attitudes Toward Obese Persons'(ATOP)* scale and the 'Beliefs About Obese Persons' (BAOP)† scale or the 'F-Scale'. A survey of more than 1,200 doctors in 1997 showed that doctors have less patience with such patients and even consider seeing them a 'waste of time'. There is more

---

* ATOP is a 20-item Likert rating scale that measures stereotypical attitudes about obese people. Each question asks respondents to indicate the extent of agreement or disagreement to a specific statement, such as 'Obese workers cannot be as successful as other workers.' Scores range from 0 to 120, where higher scores reflect more positive attitudes toward obese people.

† BAOP is an eight-item Likert rating scale that assesses beliefs about the causes of obesity. Each question asks individuals to indicate the extent of agreement or disagreement to a specific statement about the causes of obesity, such as 'Obesity is caused by a lack of willpower.' Scores range from 0 to 48, where higher scores indicate beliefs that obesity is not controllable.

ambivalence about treating them and recommending them to weight-management programmes.

Of course, age, gender and race all intersect with weight-related implicit bias and determine its salience. There are not enough large-scale cross-cultural and cross-racial studies testing whether biases and attitudes are different in other communities. The implicit weight bias has been seen to be highest in young white females. A report completed at Yale University, published in the *International Journal of Obesity*, showed that weight discrimination, particularly against women, is as common as racial discrimination. Women are more likely to face weight bias than men, and women face a discriminatory backlash at far lower weights, relative to body size, than men. The study showed that discrimination against women started at a BMI* of around 27, while for men it was more likely to happen at a BMI of around 35. There is evidence that women with obesity are less likely to seek recommended screening for some cancers, and are subject to derogatory and cynical humour from students training to be healthcare professionals. A 2013 study with 1,130 students in the UK demonstrated that the majority reported fat stigmatisation and carried strong beliefs that obesity is controllable. This 'controllability' belief is one of the basic causes of implicit bias and fat stigmatisation.

An article in the *British Journal of Obesity* reports that fat stigmatisation and implicit attitudes associated with weight are some of the most difficult to shift. Language continues to be a major factor shaping these attitudes, with media insistence on 'fat-shaming'. These media messages, especially focused on celebrities, can leave a 'private trace

---

* Body mass index is most commonly used as a measure of healthy weight range and has long been the yardstick to measure this.

in people's minds', and can lead to a spike in weight bias, says Jennifer Bartz of the psychology department at McGill University. In research looking at data from weight-implicit association tests between 2004 and 2015, the team focused on 20 body-shaming incidents in the popular media, such as Tyra Banks being shamed in 2007 while wearing a swimsuit on vacation and Kourtney Kardashian's husband fat-shaming her for not losing weight faster after her pregnancy in 2014. There were discernible spikes in weight bias just after each of these incidents, and a general increase in negative implicit bias against body weight. These provide scientific clues to the manner that popular culture, however transient it might be, shapes our psyche. Movies continue to use fatness as a source of light relief and humour, and perpetuate stereotypes that overweight people are jolly and happy, using them as props for people to laugh at. Ximena Ramos Salas, the managing director of the University of Alberta-based Obesity Canada, calls this discriminatory portrayal in the media as 'fattertainment'. An extrapolation of numerous studies carried out in the US in the last decade or so shows that weight bias is as serious a problem as racism, if not more so. Yet it remains more socially acceptable.

Where do these biases start forming? I had a sense of this recently when one of my three-year-old twins came back from nursery and told me that she had a 'fat little tummy'. On another occasion, I remember when my eldest child was attending a national children's orchestra residential music course and, as they were being measured for their uniforms, the seamstress was telling the girls they had obviously been eating 'too many biscuits' and 'being lazy' over the summer holidays as she had to adjust their skirts. These were growing children aged 12–13 years old, on the cusp of puberty. I was appalled and shocked.

These weight-related stereotypes start forming from a young age, and again verbal and nonverbal cues from caregivers and in media and books can influence how children see body shape and form, and the biases they form against those who do not conform to the kind of body shapes they see idealised. This is nothing new. Fortunately, the impact of visual cues, especially in this age of social media, is being talked about a lot. We mostly discuss and focus on body positivity in teenagers, and often believe that this is the age when such insecurities begin to surface. However, results from psychology studies showing that weight stigma and stereotypes start forming in children as young as five years old are quite startling. Janet Latner and Albert Stunkard discuss a range of studies demonstrating that when shown body silhouettes, boys as young as six years old said they would prefer to look like a mesomorphic* (muscular) silhouette and consistently assigned unfavourable adjectives such as 'sloppy' to endomorphic (overweight) silhouettes. Girls in the same age group also disliked silhouettes of girls with an endomorphic build. Even in primary school children, an aversion to 'chubbiness' is seen, and they are less likely to select an endomorphic silhouette as a playmate. Anti-fat attitudes in children as young as three

---

*William Sheldon was an American psychologist and physician who believed that the psychological make-up of humans had biological foundations. He constructed a classification system that associated physiology and psychology, proposing three main body types: endomorphs, who are rounded and soft; mesomorphs, who are square and muscular; and ectomorphs, who are thin and fine-boned. He also proposed the relationship of personality types with body shape, e.g. mesomorphs demonstrate more delinquent and criminal behaviour. His sample size was not representative and he mistook causation for correlation.

years old are evident as they categorise drawings of chubby children as 'mean' and possessing other negative characteristics. This bias had already doubled between 1961 and 2001. I could not find any recent comparative study, although a recent study published in the journal *Body Image* shows that body-size bias does indeed start as young as three. The researchers set up a study where 84 girls, 3–10 years of age, were asked to assign positive or negative traits to Barbie dolls that varied in size and shape (original, tall, petite, curvy). Participants also answered questions about their preferences for the dolls and completed measures of body dissatisfaction. Results generally demonstrated greater negative attitudes towards the curvy Barbie doll and more positive attitudes towards dolls with a thinner body size/shape (original and tall dolls). Girls identified the curvy Barbie as the doll they least wanted to play with.

While there is much more awareness and a trend towards body positivity in recent years, and the term 'body-shaming' has entered our common parlance, it is not evident that the implicit biases or our snap judgements associated with weight and obesity have reduced in any way. Even with a growing body-positivity movement, the implicit forms of this bias are rarely challenged. Measuring weight bias is tricky. Most studies use a combination of questionnaires, self-reported journal entries and scales such as the Stigmatising Situations Inventory, the Fat Phobia Scale, and the FAT subscale of the Universal Measure of Bias. These methods, however, do not capture implicit weight bias. A study published in the journal *Paediatrics* in 2017 and carried out at Duke University showed the implicit nature of these weight biases and the way they are reinforced with primacy. The study tested snap judgements made by youngsters

aged 9 to 11 years old right after they had seen pictures
of children with varied body shapes. Participants were
briefly shown pictures of older children who were
similar to each other in age, race and sex but of different
weights. After that, they briefly viewed images of
meaningless fractals and were asked to rate these abstract
geometric patterns as 'good' or 'bad'. These judgements
were made in a hurry. The children only saw pictures of
other children for 350 milliseconds, followed by an
image of a fractal for 200 milliseconds. After seeing
pictures of healthy weight children, the participants gave
64 per cent of the fractals a 'good' rating, compared
with just 59 per cent of the fractals they saw after looking
at overweight children, showing an implicit bias of
5.4%. This might appear to be a low number but it is
similar to that in studies of implicit racial bias among
adults.

The psychological and emotional consequences of being
overweight or obese, along with the stigmatisation, are
huge. These can include lowered self-esteem and anxiety,
and more serious disorders like depression and eating
disorders such as binge eating, bulimia and anorexia. Such
stereotypes continue to take the focus away from serious
mental health problems associated with being overweight.
Feeling stigmatised and being discriminated is very stressful
and can lead to further weight gain, when weight stigma is
internalised, further compounding the problem.

Three longitudinal studies between 2001 and 2009
involving more than 14,000 adults in the US and Britain
showed that perceiving oneself as overweight is counter-
intuitive and adults who thought of themselves as
overweight were more likely to gain weight over time.
The obese persons may internalise negative social weight-
based stereotypes and so discriminate against their in-group

members. In this way, this kind of bias differs from some of the other biases discussed here, where the in-group/out-group demarcation is hugely important in creating self-identity and self-concept. Here, there is likely to be a bias against the in-group members as the normative standards of anti-fat attitudes are internalised and projected onto one's self and others.

Weight bias is an implicit attitude that occurs when we categorise and identify people based on their body weight, and then attach certain characteristics to them without much conscious rational thought such as 'they must be lazy', or 'they're not very clever' or 'they lack willpower'. When these implicit biases and our perception of what their weight represents about their personality or intellect affects how we treat these individuals, such as fewer promotions in the workplace, lower salaries, lower expectations by teachers for children with obesity in school, then we are acting on our biases and turning it into weight prejudice and discrimination.

## The long and short of it

In a letter in the *New York Times* on 22 October 2017 Henry Salvi asserts that President Trump shows a height bias and has been discriminating according to height. Salvi notes that 'Mr Trump repeatedly insults opponents because of their height ('Liddle Corker,' 'Little Rocket Man,' 'Little Marco') and overlooked Senator Bob Corker for secretary of state reportedly because he was too short, at 5-foot-7, to be the country's top diplomat.'

The term 'heightism' was coined by sociologist Saul Feldman in 1971. Height has always been seen as a marker of good looks, although cultural parameters vary. Grounded theories of cognition pioneered by George Lakoff and

Mark Johnson[*] postulate that abstract concepts, such as power, are mentally associated with vertical spatial orientations. So 'up' is perceived as powerful while 'down' is perceived as powerless. This also aligns with common idioms of power and submission in the English language that are vertically positioned, such as 'high ranking'. Being tall has been associated with success and ability. Women like to date tall men, and its roots lie in evolutionary psychology where height has been a measure of 'fitness' and 'health', thereby influencing mate choice and selection. Fitter mates are equivalent to fitter (and thus more likely to survive) progeny.

Height is implicitly associated with greatness, leadership and communication skills. Statistics show that taller men and women make more money than their shorter counterparts (more than $750/inch over 5'6"). Taller presidential candidates have received more votes. Texas Tech University political scientist Gregg Murray's analysis concluded that the taller of the two major-party candidates from 1789 to 2012 won 58 per cent of presidential elections and received the majority of the popular vote in 67 per cent of those elections. Researchers in Canada studied whether this also impacts the orientation of selfies on Tinder to provide cues of physical height and position of power. They predicted that men would orient selfies more often from below to appear taller (i.e. more powerful) than the viewer, and women would use a from-above perspective to appear shorter (i.e. less powerful). A 2005 study that looked at 23,000 users in Boston and San Diego during a

---

[*] Their book *Metaphors We Live By* was like a bible to me during my PhD years. It is an influential treatise in how conceptual metaphors surround us and shape our communication and the way we act and behave.

three-month period found that men who were 6'3" to 6'4" received 60 per cent more first-contact emails than those who were 5'7" to 5'8". Meanwhile, tall women received fewer initial emails than women who were shorter or of average height.

There is overwhelming evidence that human stature is positively related to social status in both men and women in Western societies but, despite several different theories being proposed, it has been unclear as to how this implicit bias has been formed. From genetic advantage to height being used as a cue to signify parental involvement and social dominance in a confrontation, the theories have attempted to explain that height bias could be linked to a bias towards another factor and hence the correlation between height and social status is indirect. However, Gert Stulp and colleagues from the University of Groningen proposed that there is a direct correspondence between height and perceived social standing because height denotes dominance in social interactions and interpersonal confrontations. Taller people are also perceived as more competent, authoritative, intelligent, dominant and having better leadership qualities. This becomes a self-fulfilling prophecy as, when shorter-statured individuals believe this to be the case, they are more likely to easily succumb to taller individuals, thereby proving this perceived bias to be true. A study mapping out interpersonal interactions showed that taller individuals were more likely to take precedence when entering a narrow passage wide enough for only a single individual to pass, were less likely to collide with pedestrians than shorter ones, and were more likely to be given precedence with others giving way to them in a busy shopping street. This effect was independent of both sex and perceived age, and showed that height determines how others react to an individual. It also affects how an individual perceives themselves, with more self-esteem, confidence and self-assurance.

## The age-old question

Ageism is a hidden bias in our society. The 'old is gold' adage does not apply to the older population in our society. Jokes are made at the expense of the older population, showing them variously as grumpy or cuddly. Older people are teased about their cognitive abilities, ignored and not taken seriously, and there is a greater assumption that they have physical and mental impairments. Anti-wrinkle creams and treatments crowd the shelves. In a 2004 report by Age Concern in the UK, one in three people surveyed thought older people are 'incompetent and incapable'. Explicit discrimination and bias are illegal but also increasingly frowned upon. Yet implicit biases against age persist.

Much like with race and gender, it takes less than a second for age-based social categorisations to take place; they happen so quickly and automatically that it is difficult to make them thoughtful and deliberate. Variables might include cues such as wrinkled skin, grey hair, weight and posture, and when this categorisation based on age leads to stereotypes, prejudice and hence discrimination, it is called ageism.

Psychiatrist and gerontologist Dr Robert Butler coined the term 'ageism' in 1969. Research in bias has been slow to address issues of age-related bias and discrimination. Ageism is usually very subtle but there is evidence across a number of domains to show how it works in subversive ways. Much like racism and sexism, it counts on 'othering' but, unlike those two, ageism 'others' a group that once was not the out-group. Those who are biased will one day join the group against whom they target this bias and prejudice. Talk about life coming full circle. From Pope Francis criticising Europe as 'a "grandmother", no longer fertile and vibrant' to Homer Simpson telling Abe Simpson, 'Aw, Dad, you've done a lot of great things. But you're a very old man now, and old people are useless,' ageism is rife and pervasive. Anthropologist Margaret Mead once said that the elderly are 'immigrants in time, immigrants from an earlier world', and that the 'young are at home here.' It is especially pertinent as lifespans become longer; by 2020, for the first time, there will be more people on Earth over the age of 65 than under five.

Philip Roth in one of his later novels wrote that 'old age isn't a battle; old age is a massacre.' Our fairy tales are filled with characters fearful of growing old and stereotyped either as a wicked stepmother (in fairy tales such as Snow White and Cinderella) or a cuddly and helpless grandmother (as in Red Riding Hood). Shakespeare alludes to old age as 'second childishness and mere oblivion, / sans teeth, sans eyes, sans taste, sans everything.' As a society, we are used to dehumanising old people, seeing old age as a second childhood where the individual becomes dependent once again and loses their economic and social capital. The media is a place where age-related stereotypes are both created as well as perpetuated. Sociologist Mike Featherstone talks of 'pornography of old age' (a fascination with and disgust of old wrinkled flesh), Anne Karpf talks about old age as 'hideous ruin', and who can forget the witches in literature from *Macbeth* to the Wicked Witch of the West in *The Wonderful Wizard of Oz*? Intergenerational conflict has often been used as a motivator in election debates. Nancy Pelosi at 78 was criticised by younger activists and politicians such as David Hogg for not moving on and creating space for them.

'It's an incredibly prevalent and insidious problem,' said Alana Officer, who leads the World Health Organization's global campaign against ageism. 'It affects not only individuals, but how we think about policies.'* In particular, implicit rationing of medical resources and treatment towards older patients has been studied well both in the US and the UK. Ann Bowling, Professor of Health Services Research at the University of Southampton, shows that ageism in clinical medicine and health policy reflects in wider society, with many older Americans refused the same post-operative care and treatment for heart conditions as those offered to younger patients. David Hughes and Lesley Griffiths showed in 1999 that age was being used tacitly and implicitly to decide who to place on a waiting list for cardiothoracic surgeries. In the NHS, studies showed an underlying bias among healthcare practitioners against the aged, with surveys in 1999 and 2000 showing that lifestyle advice isn't offered to the elderly, and mental health problems in older people are often misdiagnosed or unrecognised. Also, 16 per cent of GPs had not referred older patients primarily because of their age, and cancer care in older people is disputed as many are not offered the same level of care and treatment as younger patients. Cancer trials have not been carried out on older patients and so the efficacy of treatment over age is not as well understood, and there is a stereotype that some of the aggressive treatments are not well handled by the older population. A number of US studies have shown, however, that most older patients would choose aggressive treatment if it improved survival and that they may cope better psychologically with a cancer diagnosis than younger patients. Some of these decisions have been backed up by

---

* *New York Times*, April 2019.

'intergenerational equity', with the perception that the older population has already had a 'fair innings' and so they should not have the same access to social and economic resources.

Economic activity is seen as a sign of active contribution and so older people are viewed as passive and a 'burden'. This can affect how ageing is perceived and the implicit biases that are formed against the aged. There is not, however, a one-size-fits-all stereotype, as two studies in 1986 and 1994 showed that there were seven subgroups of older people identified with a range of positive and negative traits. The out-group characterisation of older generations shows that they are grouped with developmentally delayed and disabled individuals, and stereotyped as low competence and high warmth. As we have already seen, stereotypes have the power to shape people's identity and behaviour in stereotype-consistent ways. Older people are framed in a negative light in print and media. There are not many older men or women on screens around us.

Gender plays a huge role in how the ageing process and aged are perceived. Women face more barriers as they grow older compared to men, often called the 'George Clooney effect', or what economists call the 'attractiveness penalty'. While older women are called 'hags', men are still virile and called 'silver fox' as they grow older. Grey hair gives men like Clooney, Tom Jones and Colin Firth an air of sophistication and distinction. By contrast, the internet erupted when the 50-year-old ex-model Helena Christensen stepped out in a lacy bustier. Former *Vogue* editor Alexandra Shulman wrote of the model, 'Something you wore at 30 will never look the same on you 20 years later. Clothes don't lie,' and called her 'tacky'. There are stereotypes as to how older women should act and behave. Madonna has spoken honestly about how ageism is rife in the music industry. 'I am punished for turning 60,' she says. Melora Hardin from *The Bold Type* says, 'The conversation of ageism goes both ways. It's important for people to recognize that youth and exuberance [are] valuable just as life experience is valuable.' Actress Amy Poehler has said that ageism is systemic in Hollywood, especially for middle-aged women. Anne Hathaway has spoken of the ageist bias against women, saying that 'I was always told that once I turned 35 I would turn into a pumpkin and never get a good part again. It makes me sad that the world tells me my skin is somehow less valuable than it used to be.' Maggie Gyllenhaal, at 37, was told she was 'too old' to play the love interest of a 55-year-old man. A study at the University of Southern California of the films nominated for Best Picture between 2014 and 2016 showed that only 11.8 per cent of the actors were 60 or older, but significantly 78 per cent of the films had no older female actors in leading or supporting roles. In 2016, The Pudding conducted an exhaustive study on film dialogue from screenplays of over 2,000 films across all genres. They found that the percentage of dialogue available to women decreased significantly with age compared to men. Men over 40 had more roles and spoken dialogue (55 million words for the 42–65 age group) compared to women in the same age group (11 million words).

Silicon Valley and tech start-ups have especially created and perpetuated a trope that 'Young people are just smarter'* and that 'people over 45 basically die in terms of new ideas'.† The median age at tech companies such as Facebook and Google is under 30. Paul Graham, co-founder of the

---

* Quote from Mark Zuckerberg, founder of Facebook, in 2007, when he was 23 years old.
† Attributed to venture capitalist Vinod Khosla.

Valley's leading start-up accelerator, Y Combinator, declared that 'the sweet spot is your mid-20s.'

Misogyny and ageism go hand in hand too at times, with older men shunning and discriminating against older women. The high-profile French author and television presenter Yann Moix, himself 50 years old, famously said in early 2019 that he would be 'incapable' of loving a woman aged over 50 as they were simply 'invisible' to him. 'The body of a woman of 50 is not extraordinary at all,' he said. In the UK, the newsreader Moira Stewart left the BBC in 2007 over an ageism row. Former *Countryfile* presenter Miriam O'Reilly won an age-discrimination case against the BBC in 2018 after she was dropped from the rural affairs show when it moved to a primetime Sunday-evening slot in 2009. Former newsreader Anna Ford accused the BBC of 'tokenism' in the debate over ageism on television, saying the broadcaster discriminated against anyone over 60. The sexist undertone in the ageism bias was evident when 68-year-old BBC newsreader Michael Buerk, who claimed it was 'fair enough' for TV bosses to axe older presenters, likened the process to 'pruning the raspberries to make way for new growth' and said that those given jobs 'because they look nice' should not protest if they later lost them. Olenka Frenkiel, a multi-award-winning broadcast journalist, said that after 30 great years with the BBC she found herself 'being rubbed out', with fewer opportunities to showcase her work. 'While I could see the guys of my age thriving, the women were gone,' she wrote in the *Guardian*. The newsreader Susan Osman moved to China, where she said 'experience was revered', unlike at the BBC, where she felt invisible because of her age and had staff asking her if she was menopausal.

Psychologist Becca Levy at Yale University says that 'older adults exposed to positive stereotypes have significantly better memory and balance, whereas negative self-perceptions contributed to worse memory and feelings of worthlessness.' Old-age stereotypes are self-fulfilling. Older people stereotype themselves, which tends to shape their own identities so they are likely to be much more explicitly biased against other people in the same age group compared to the younger people around them. In 2002 Mary Lee Hummert and her colleagues measured implicit age biases on an Age-based Implicit Association Test in a study that showed all participants irrespective of their age carried the implicit age biases and associated negative traits with older people. Older participants were stereotyping themselves and attributing these negative stereotypes to others in their own age group, and hence showing the most age-related explicit bias in favour of the younger population and against older people. They also tended to have lower confidence in their own abilities and to underperform on tasks, which in turn reinforced the stereotype. The stereotype threat affects mental health, with research revealing that those with more positive self-perceptions of ageing lived 7.5 years longer than those with negative self-perceptions of ageing, as shown from a longitudinal study carried out with more than 650 'over-50' individuals.

Culture and context play a role in shaping implicit biases against old age. In Greek, Indian and Native American cultures, old age is a sign of wisdom, revered and respected. In Korea, 60th and 70th birthdays are special occasions at which children celebrate their parents' transition into old age. In a study conducted by the Royal Society for Public Health (RSPH) including more than 2,000 questionnaires and focus groups, it was seen that people who identified as ethnically black did not recognise the negative stereotypes with old age that others had reported. Their attitudes towards ageing and older people are overwhelmingly more positive, an effect that proved statistically significant. In a study comparing Chinese and American attitudes and biases towards ageing, Becca Levy and the social psychologist Ellen Langer found that the older Chinese people – exposed to less ageism than their American counterparts – performed memory tests more like their younger compatriots. Among the Americans, however, there were significant memory differences between the old and young. Our culture gives us these messages about how life goes downhill once we start ageing, we see the prejudices against older people, and we believe in these messages and internalise them. This shapes our own biases, and our beliefs become self-fulfilling. Self-perception and performance are activated by stereotypes.

It is not entirely clear how these implicit biases towards old age develop but children as young as six have shown the age-related stereotypes of their culture. Children see negative attitudes around them, in films and on television. Adverts often show older people incapable of understanding technology or being frail and 'out of date'. The milestones around ageing are continuously shifting. We are told that '60 is the new 30' and I hear my friends moan about their wrinkles and grey hair. Youth is fetishized and their achievements celebrated. Forbes' annual 30 Under 30 list celebrates those who have made a positive impact before they turn 30. There is no '50 over 50' or even 'under 40'. The prodigies, the wunderkind, the whizz-kids perpetuate the cult of youth. This awe and wonder with the notion of young overachievers undervalues the hard work, persistence and grit that comes with experience and age. We are continuously getting the message that it is all doom and gloom after 30, which creates fear, anxiety, panic and negative age-related biases.

A study of 2,000 women conducted by Superdrug in 2012 found that women start to worry about the signs of ageing at 29. These messages do not have to be explicit; children pick up on casual remarks such as 'Grandpa is too old to walk that far' or seeing how older members of the family might be ignored and sidelined. They do not question these stereotypes as the older people do not conform to their 'in-group' membership while they themselves are forming and strengthening their own sense of self and identity and consolidating the in-group and out-group associations. Once these implicit stereotypes are formed, these biases are activated every time they encounter an older person, and strengthened over time, even when we see contradictory evidence. Such contradictory evidence (for instance, Nancy Pelosi as Speaker of the House at 78 or John Glenn as a 78-year-old astronaut) are merely seen as exceptions. Instagrannies – however horribly stereotyping a word it might be – have now become a phenomenon among Instagram users. These are a group of women who are disrupting the idea of what old looks like and what the rules and parameters around ageing, particularly for women, are. Their followers are mostly young, in the age range of 25–35. Yet I cannot stop wondering whether, in trying to disrupt the age-related stereotypes, they are displaying classic signs of stereotype threat, an implicit bias where they are trying so hard not to conform to the stereotype that they in some way are creating a stereotype of what a non-traditional older person ought to look like.

I have previously talked about how lack of contact can further strengthen stereotypes. In the context of information processing, research shows that we assign a positive or negative evaluation to a cue within a few seconds, and then we avoid any information that has been evaluated negatively (termed an approach-avoidance motivation). The old are automatically assigned a negative evaluation, which would then disincentivise younger people to interact and engage with the older population. The scarcity of contact further strengthens the negative implicit biases as there is a lack of opportunity for any negative stereotypes to be countered and for positive stereotypes to develop. Positive explicit and implicit attitudes, although complex and multidimensional, are also linked, so if no explicit positive attitudes can be developed it becomes very difficult to challenge the basis of the implicit ageist biases. The best way to address this implicit bias would be to create more intergenerational contact. We saw earlier how extended contact can help mitigate racial bias; similarly, the opportunity for younger and older people to assimilate and work together in spaces where they can mingle and benefit from each other would counter these negative age-related stereotypes.

Age-related stereotypes are unlike the ones shaped by gender or race. They are unique in the way that even the ones belonging to the in-group hold the same negative stereotypes. When over the course of the first 50-odd years of our lives we see and internalise the negative stereotypes associated with ageing, the implicit bias is so strong that we do not have the opportunity to develop a mechanism to then develop strong in-group bonds. We are often complicit in our own marginalisation too as we grow older through the implicit bias we ourselves carry against old age. This leads to an implicit out-group favouritism, where the old are seen to associate strongly with the younger group. When someone says 'you are only as old as you feel' or the phrase 'young at heart' or that they 'don't feel old' they are displaying some of these implicit biases and fears associated with ageing. Ageing is a highly salient and negative implicit bias, and most of the associations with ageing are those associated with anxiety and fear of 'losing our marbles' and then inevitable death. Unlike other stereotypes, there is no benefit in associating with our in-group. Instead, it is the out-group that affords the benefit of health and long life.

While negative, age-related implicit biases are shaped by subliminal priming – the processing of information at a subconscious level without the awareness of an individual – through seeing images of older people portrayed in a negative light, the effect can also be temporarily reversed by showing positive visual stimuli such as images of positive role models. But since this is a unique kind of bias, where out-group favouritism is significant as opposed to the usual in-group attachment and affiliations, it is important to address the implicit biases and negative stereotypes that older people have of themselves, and address stereotype threat that makes some individuals try to thwart the ageing process, using cosmetic procedures and interventions. Stanford University sociologist Doug McAdam calls it 'cognitive liberation', where people have to collectively (and individually) recognise and define their situation as unjust and one that can be changed by collective action.

Virtual embodiment – an illusion created in immersive virtual reality where a virtual body is seen as our own – has been used in a novel exploratory environment to address bias against old people. In this particular experiment, 30 young men were recruited at the University of Barcelona to see if having an older virtual body (in this case, that of Albert Einstein) can change people's perception against older people. While also enhancing the cognitive abilities of the participants, the embodiment of an older body altered their view of age and led to a reduction of implicit bias against the elderly. The participants did not have to imagine being old; they inhabited the body of an older person and experienced it directly. Since the transformed self is now similar to the out-group (older people in this case) the negative value associated with the out-group is disrupted, and out-group derogation therefore reduced. By remodelling the perceptions of self, the associated physiological characteristics could be transformed too. In this particular case, though, it is not clear whether this change in implicit bias was because of an association with a famous person (Einstein) or truly because of the virtual illusion of transformed self. There have been other experiments with white people given black virtual bodies that have shown a reduction in their implicit bias against black people that lasted at least a week. Literally 'stepping into someone else's shoes' can give us an important perspective on their experiences, and so minimise the biases that we carry.

Ashton Applewhite, author of *This Chair Rocks: A Manifesto Against Ageism*, says the words and language we use around ageing and with reference to old people matter because 'if we diminish our regard for the senior members of our society verbally, we are likely to do the same when it comes to the way we frame policy – removing their dignity and sense of agency in condescending generalisations that assume vulnerability and dependence instead of resilience and independence.' Ashton questions the binary young/old view of the world, and words such as 'the elderly' that suggest a homogenous group. If we view age as a spectrum, then we minimise the effects of overgeneralisation.

Although we primarily talk about ageism in the context of older people, the reverse is true too. There are many biases against teenagers and the younger population, created and perpetuated by the media. They are labelled as lazy, immature and reckless. Numerous explanations have been proposed: from raging hormones to neuroscience and psychology research showing an underlying scientific basis to some of the rash decisions that teenagers make due to the way their brain develops* or a recent theory that it is mainly due to lack of experience and a thirst for exploration. Whatever the reason might be, the way these pervasive stereotypes persist and are perpetuated creates a bias towards all young people. The way that language is used to project these multiple negative images of teenagers creates a mental negative image of a typical teenager, and it isn't flattering. But these biases are much more explicit and less insidious than the discrimination against older people.

In 1968 at the age of 85, the American-born playwright, suffragette and analyst Florida Scott-Maxwell wrote: 'Age puzzles me. I thought it was a quiet time. My 70s were interesting and fairly serene, but my 80s are passionate. I grow more intense as I age. To my own surprise, I burst out with hot conviction … I must calm down. I am far too frail to indulge in moral fervour.' Sociologist Anne Karpf writes in her book *How to Age* that the only way to overcome these deeply embedded unconscious biases is through a complete 'Gestalt switch', where when we see someone older than us, rather than being fearful of wrinkles and their failing facilities, we should try to imagine ourselves as an old person and feel empowered by it. Positive and empowering experiences of ageing show a humane side of ageing, capturing the multifaceted nature of getting older rather than the massive generalisations and dehumanising of old people who do not have a voice anymore.

---

* According to this theory, the prefrontal cortex, the centre of the brain's cognitive-control system, matures more slowly than the limbic system, which governs desires and appetites including drives for food and sex. This creates an imbalance in the adolescent brain that leads to even more impulsive and risky behaviour than seen in children.

The poet May Sarton wrote that she was more herself than ever as she turned 70. Her piece in the *New York Times*, 'Lighter with age', is a beautiful example of how implicit negative biases can be minimised: 'Old age is not an illness, it is a timeless ascent. As power diminishes, we grow more toward the light.'

## CHAPTER TEN

# I Hear You, I Say

‘ Think thou how that this is not our home in this world, in which we are strangers, one not knowing another's speech and language.' (*The Diary of Samuel Ward*, entry for 13 May 1595.)

My three-year-old has started speaking in a Liverpool accent since she started nursery a few months ago. It comes out in the way she pronounces 'bird' and 'book' and the way her sentences end with a particular intonation. I speak with traces of an Indian accent, my husband with a Scottish accent, and our eldest in Queen's English. 'Oh no, she is picking up a Scouse accent,' I sighed the first time I heard it. As I said this aloud – even when I meant it as a flippant remark – it made me wonder why I was dismayed. I love the Scouse accent and people, but before we moved to the area from further south three years ago I had heard numerous jokes about it, its harsh nasal tones, and how the linguist Fritz Spiel once described it as 'one-third Irish, one-third Welsh, and one-third catarrh'. The Scouse accent is consistently voted as the worst in the country, deemed unsophisticated and unintelligent. Online poll results from 5,000 participants in 2004 conducted by the BBC concluded that Asian, Liverpool and Birmingham accents were 'unpleasant to listen to and lacking in social status'. Perhaps I had internalised these external messages and stereotyped the Liverpool accent.

Besides faces, accents are the other thing we often notice immediately about people, and often the only thing if the facial cues are not significant enough. We can sometimes be so focused on accents that it shapes our perception of the content and often detracts from it. A female academic (who preferred to stay anonymous) told me: 'I gave a paper in a university in rural upstate New York. In my opinion, I completely smashed it. Strong argument, well researched. At the end I was super-ready for questions. No hands went up. I waited a while. Then someone piped up: "What part of Scotland are you from?"' Another offered this: 'After giving a lecture, I asked my supervising professor for feedback. His response? "I think they were amused by your accent."'

Rosina Lippi-Green, an American writer and author of *English with an Accent*, says that 'an accent is a loose reference to a specific way of speaking involving intonation, pitch, stress patterns, and rates of speaking.' An accent is the variation in pronunciation of the same language by different communities. Biological anthropologist Professor Helen Fisher says the human voice is like a second signature and reveals idiosyncrasies of character that can 'attract or repel a potential mate in moments.' Everyone has an accent, but we find some more attractive than others, with a preference for certain accents and bias against others. This can have huge implications but it is not usually given as much consideration as racial or gender-based bias. Although we are increasingly conscious and vocal about any prejudice based on people's race, ethnicity or gender, we still think jokes about people's accents are funny and just 'banter'. Even comedians rely heavily on accents to make people laugh. Science is beginning to lift the lid on how accents can hold us back and bring out our prejudices, where this bias comes from, and how it changes in different global settings.

The discrimination based on accent dates back to an excerpt in the Bible. In Judges 12:5–6 the following quote depicting the mass-killing of a people based on their accent appears:

> The Gileadites captured the fords of the Jordan leading to Ephraim, and whenever a survivor of Ephraim said, 'Let me cross over,' the men of Gilead asked him, 'Are you an Ephraimite?' If he replied, 'No,' they said, 'All right, say "Shibboleth".' If he said, 'Sibboleth', because he could not pronounce the word correctly, they seized him and killed him at the fords of the Jordan. Forty-two thousand Ephraimites were killed at that time.

Passing required a password – 'Shibboleth' with a 'sh' sound, but the Ephraimites did not have this sound in their dialect, and so pronounced the word with an 's' sound, and were therefore revealed as the enemy and slaughtered.

Most accent discrimination and prejudice does not have such a drastic life-threatening consequence, of course, but is more insidious. Accents are our way of defining ourselves and others. There have been studies showing that any accent that is not similar to our own is immediately characterised as foreign. Even with foreign accent syndrome, when people were asked what accent the person was speaking in, the responses varied widely. This means that when people listen to an accent they immediately characterise and label it, and if there are other aspects of the accent that don't correspond with this label, it is ignored. Speaking with a non-native accent can influence perceptions of the speaker's fluency, and expectations concerning performance abilities. Moreover, research suggests that speaking with a non-native accent may lead speakers to feel excluded and devalued at work. We tend to gravitate towards those with a similar accent to ours, also termed 'linguistic security'. Own-accent bias links to social identity theory, explaining how we are biased towards anything that signals in-group membership. As we know, anything out-group can be perceived as suspicious, unfamiliar, threatening or outright dangerous. Children show an understanding of nationality very early on, although the association American = speaks English (preferably with an American accent) comes before American = white, so language category association to nationality starts earlier for children than race. These findings support the argument that implicit social biases emerge early in life and do not need extensive experience or knowledge to develop. This is consistent with the development of inter-group theory, which argues that, in order to make sense of the world around them, children gather environment cues and organise stimuli into categories. In a 2009 study by Caroline Floccia and others, five-year-olds listened to recordings of several children from different racial backgrounds in a range of accents. They then chose playmates based purely on who had a more unaccented English, and results confirmed that they placed more emphasis on accent than race in guiding their social preferences.

Media, especially television and films, are also key influences in how children develop a sense of accents and their associated personality attributes. Rosina Lippi-Green analysed all animated Disney films released between 1938 and 1994. In the study, all characters who uttered more than just single words were included in the analysis. Some very distinctive systematic patterns emerged on how accents were used across the different roles. Lippi-Green found that most characters (91 per cent) spoke with a native English accent, particularly mainstream American English. The characters were then put into four groups based on their motivation and actions (i.e. positive, negative, mixed, unclear). Twice as many foreign accents compared to native-accented speakers were portrayed as negative characters. When the number of speakers was very low, all characters with African-American vernacular English accents appeared as non-human animals. Lippi-Green concluded that 'what children learn from the entertainment industry is to be comfortable with *same* and to be wary about *other*', and that language is a prime and ready diagnostic for this division between what is approachable and what is best left alone. The results show that, while being entertaining, these animated films are teaching children to stereotype and hold a low opinion of nonstandard English.

★★★

We are more likely to be biased against speakers who have accents that are markers for undesirable characteristics. Research has shown that it takes us less than 30 seconds to linguistically profile a speaker, and to make quick decisions – on their ethnic origin, socio-economic class and backgrounds – called 'linguistic first impressions'. People have linguicism or 'accenticism' without realising it. 'An accent is a basis on which it's easy to make judgements about a person's cultural affiliation or education,' says Ingrid Piller, a sociolinguist at Macquarie University in Brisbane, Australia. 'It's a springboard for a lot of heavy assumptions which may or may not be true.' When we impose our judgements about a specific person on the whole group or community this individual belongs to then we have a bias. We tend to unconsciously group people into a specific social class and prejudice against them based on their accents. By thinking that someone with a particular accent is not very smart or clever, we are showing our unconscious bias.

Professor Pear, a psychologist from the University of Manchester, was the first to study linguistic first impressions, as far back as 1931. In an experiment, he asked 200 listeners to a radio show to provide personality profiles of a variety of voices heard. He noticed that a speaker's voice and accent could dramatically affect the perception of the person. In a later study, he had nine different speakers (including children and individuals from different social classes) read a short text about a skating incident. The BBC broadcast the same text nine times over three days, and the *Radio Times* published a personality questionnaire to be completed and sent back to the BBC. Several thousand listeners responded to questions about voice gender, age and profession of the speaker. Age and gender were accurately judged, as well as an estimate of the geographical background and their professions, suggesting that speech variations and accents can provide detailed hints to a speaker's age, gender, geographical background and social class, and are often used in this manner too. Entire stereotypes can be built around accents: British accents are sexy,[*] New Yorkers are rude, British Received Pronunciation (RP) or 'Queen's English' speakers are educated, Yorkshire speakers are trustworthy, Southern Americans are pleasant, and Birmingham speakers – depending on who you ask – either sound melodic or like criminals.

We are also naturally inclined to trust those who sound like us, as our conformity biases come into play and our brain makes the split-second decision to assign them an in-group or out-group status. Psychologists Morteza Dehghani and Peter Khooshabeh found that 'bi-culturals'

---

[*] Although many baddies have British accents in American films!

and 'mono-culturals'* change their interpretive framework based on the accent they hear. In an experiment where the subjects heard the same statement repeated in a Chinese-American accent and then in a standard American accent, it was found that all the subjects had their social identity reinforced when they heard someone who sounded like them. The foreign accent made the mono-culturals more aware of their own social norms and consequently more protective of their self-concept and identity. In another related experiment, Shiri Lev-Ari, a psycholinguist at the Max Planck Institute of Psycholinguistics in Nijmegen, asked non-native speakers of Polish, Turkish, Austrian-German, Korean and Italian to record statements such as 'Ants don't sleep' in English. Native English speakers recorded the same too. When native English speakers rated the recordings for their accuracy, they rated the speakers with the heaviest accents as least true, while native speakers were rated most true.

This lack of trust may be one reason why a foreign accent is discriminated against and can be a barrier to career progression in the modern workplace. The venture capitalist Paul Graham admitted in an interview that 'a strong foreign accent' counted against entrepreneurs when he was considering admitting them to his programme because of 'the practical difficulty of getting a start-up off the ground when people can't understand you'. These comments were symptomatic of the wider bias that foreign and even regional accents face.

---

* Psychologists termed those with only white American national identity as 'mono-culturals' in this study while those with two racial or national identities were termed 'bi-culturals', a much better term in my opinion than 'mixed-race'.

Shiri Lev-Ari believes the tendency to mistrust statements in foreign accents is due to the additional effort and increase in cognitive load that means 'we are less likely to believe that which is said in a foreign accent.' Additionally, people have an implicit bias that non-native speakers would be less proficient, thereby shaping our perception of what they have to say when they speak and making us less likely to remember what was being said. Stereotypes shape our view of foreign speakers, and hence their accents, and this can determine a speaker's credibility. By contrast, says Guy Winch, a psychotherapist from Britain now based in the US, sometimes 'People tend to think a foreign accent is more interesting and more sexy because in general we tend to value what's less common.' Americans associate a British accent with someone being more intelligent, more sophisticated and more competent – all qualities that a lot of people find attractive.

Perception of what we find attractive is also related to social acceptability and norms. A standard higher accent is, therefore, selected by social processes. Higher-status groups (as determined in social hierarchies, either self-imposed or through social dynamics) impose their ideas of what is standard and their own view of what is more acceptable on others. We form a hierarchical view of accents as per societal and cultural acceptability, and assign values such as pleasantness and prestige but also intelligence. Rosina Lippi-Green refers to this as the 'standard language ideology', where many people believe the dialect with the highest social prestige is also the only correct and valid form of the language. When an accent is assigned higher status, people speaking in that accent are given more importance, seen more favourably and their views are taken more seriously. Assigning a higher status to one accent over another is also linked to prototype theory in cognitive psychology. Sometimes a particular member of a category is deemed to be more central than others, as per prototype theory. If this is applied to the notion of how some accents are seen as better or higher in status than others, it is easy to understand how some accents become exemplars of a category because of history, tradition, their familiarity and availability for recall. The more we see and hear a particular accent, the more likely we are to assign it a prototype status. Other accents are then judged on the basis of their distance from this prototype accent.

In England, the north–south divide still plays a big role in what is an accepted accent, and research has shown that it determines job prospects. Various studies have now shown that the RP accent is equated with competence, high social prestige and more intelligence in comparison to other regional accents, while regional accents score higher on friendliness, trust and sincerity. In a 1970 paper, William Cheyne, a researcher at the University of Strathclyde, showed that both English and Scottish subjects rated speakers with a Scottish accent lower on a scale primarily concerned with status, while on scales concerned with friendliness they were rated to have warmer personalities. BBC reporter Steph McGovern reported in 2018 that she was paid less than her counterparts because of her distinct north-east accent. A report by the government's Social Mobility and Child Poverty Commission found that entry into elite firms continues to be dominated by people from more privileged socio-economic backgrounds, as they were more likely to have an RP accent. A survey of recruitment processes at 13 top law, accountancy and financial companies found that 70 per cent of jobs offered by those firms in 2014 went to applicants from private or selective schools, using criteria such as 'personal style, accents and mannerisms'. Radio and TV dramas, and movies, create characters through accents. In the long-running British drama *The Archers*, class, prestige and status are reinforced through characters' RP accents, while the 'country bumpkins' who are friendly and trustworthy but not as high up the social pecking order have a generalised, non-RP accent.

This is also perhaps the reason that elocution lessons are growing in popularity as people try to remove any traces of their regional accents. George Bernard Shaw's *Pygmalion* is a classic story of accents: association of class and status to particular dialects, the social acceptance of a flower-girl only when she 'poshed' it up, and her magical transformation from working class to upper crust of society thanks to elocution lessons. A recent research project by Alex Baratta from the University of Manchester showed that trainee teachers – particularly those from the north and the Midlands – were instructed to modify their accents by their mentors.

A social hierarchy of accents exists in other countries too. One of the most exhaustive studies in the US, by Diane Markley from the University of North Texas, showed a distinct preference for Californian and Minnesota accents. The New Jersey and Georgia accents were ranked lowest. Non-black Americans tend to judge African American Vernacular English (AAVE) as coming from ignorance or stupidity because of a lack of education. Latino-accented English speakers were seen to be less competent and judged to be of a lower socio-economic status than native standard American English speakers. Attitudes towards southern American English have also been shown to be more negative than attitudes towards more neutral accents. A study by Howard Manns from Monash University showed that this was also the case in Australia, where there has historically been a clear social distinction between Cultivated (British-oriented) and Broad or General, distinctly Australian ways of speaking. Even in a large country like India, hints of regionality such as that from South India can be looked down upon, and people take elocution lessons to 'neutralise' their accents.

With the growth of outsourced call centres, the bias and prejudice against Indian accents has increased in recent years. As the clients in the UK and the US become more sensitive to the political issue of outsourcing of jobs to India, racist abuse has also increased, and this has been primarily associated with the accent. 'Locational masking' is focused on removing any local inflections that would mark the accent as Indian, and this has also included anglicising names to avoid any name-related stereotypes and biases. The staff at these call centres used to be trained in generalised British or American accents, but increasingly they are being encouraged to adopt a more neutral global English accent so that they appear to be citizens of everywhere and nowhere – possibly so that people cannot make any assumptions around them or the business based on their accent, and so speakers will not be alienated by anyone with bias towards a particular accent. Indian accents also became somewhat synonymous with the character Apu in *The Simpsons*, and people think it is perfectly OK to do a caricature impression of them as a joke. This is not a laughing matter. In a 2016 interview with NPR, the American-Indian comedian Hari Kondabolu said, 'I think some people are used to accents in comedy because that's how they see immigrants: immigrants are funny voices. Immigrants are foreign, strange experiences.' The linguist Adrian Holliday calls this 'native-speakerism', which reflects the everyday stereotyping and leads to the belief that anyone who is not a native speaker is not as good at English, and thereby not as clever, which leads to discrimination. Native-speakerism is therefore not linked to just language but also to ethnicity and race. When I was doing my PhD and looking for part-time teaching positions, I found that most of these were only open to 'native' English speakers. My English, both written and spoken, was good but, since I came from India, I was automatically classed as a non-native speaker. My nationality and my accent automatically 'othered' me, and even when I was offered a job I was offered a much lower salary than 'native' speakers. When we discuss the ethnicity pay gap in the UK today, this is a point worth considering.

Accents can have a huge implication in criminal trial settings, where trust plays a role in assessing the credibility of the speaker. Studies show that participants perceive an eyewitness who delivers their testimony with an accent as less favourable – even when the text of the testimony is identical and the witness is the same person. Also, independent of evidence presented and crime type, a regional-accented suspect is evaluated as more typically criminal and more likely to be re-accused of a crime than a standard-accented suspect. In 1983, a study assessed the effects of three accents – RP, broad Australian, and Asian – on Australian participants' attributions of guilt. Participants listened to a recorded conversation in which an alleged criminal pleaded his innocence and were then asked to assess his guilt. The results showed that the suspect's accent significantly influenced the responses, but it also varied according to the nature and severity of the crime. For instance, more guilt was attributed to the Australian accent when the suspect was accused of assault whereas more guilt was attributed to the RP accent when the suspect was accused of theft. Therefore, a highly significant correlation was shown between accent and the guilt associated with having committed a crime. More recently, in 2014 John

Dixon and Bere Mahoney in the *Journal of Language and Social Psychology* confirmed the relation of accent and suspected crime, which was in turn indicative of perceived superiority and social attractiveness. In this experiment, 119 participants listened to a recorded exchange between a British male criminal suspect and a male policeman, and the exchange was varied to produce Birmingham*/RP standard, black/white, and blue collar/white collar groups. The results suggested that the suspect was rated as significantly more guilty when he employed a Birmingham rather than a standard RP accent.

Neutral accents with no hint of a specific social group association make people relatable – and trustworthy – to a larger population. Because we tend to gravitate towards the people who are more like us, and tend to trust them more, politicians and leaders have used the science of implicit biases and cognitive heuristics to appeal to as wide a demographic as possible. Language is a powerful force that has been long used to forge a connection. The late theorist Kenneth Burke wrote that speaking your audience's language is the *sine qua non* of this. There have been numerous instances of politicians changing their accents according to the context. It is not always clear whether they are pandering to their audience or mimicking the people around them. What is clear is that accents have long been a way that we assess people's personality and intelligence. Humans also have a tendency to subconsciously imitate accents that we like, termed 'linguistic accommodation' or the 'chameleon effect'. In linguistics, accommodation is the

---

* The Brummie or Birmingham accent has been featured in accent-evaluation research since the early 1970s and has been considered a 'third-class' urban accent. It has generally been evaluated more negatively than either rural regional or RP accents, and so was deployed in this particular study.

process by which participants in a conversation adjust their accent in line with that of the others around them. Howard Giles from the University of California showed that this could be 'convergence', where speakers may modify their speech in order to sound more like others they talk with to achieve greater social integration with them, or 'divergence', where deliberate differences can be employed to assert and maintain a distinct identity. There is record of Hillary Clinton's accent having changed throughout her political career to appeal to different regional audiences. The former British prime minister Tony Blair neutralised his accent to appeal to a wider demographic, and even Prince William has used slang terms such as 'missus' for his wife. The tendency is to sound as neutral and classless as possible and, in a country as obsessed with class as the UK, it is advisable for politicians to dial down their poshness or to 'posh up' their working-class accent.

In a 2015 interview with the comedian Russell Brand, politician Ed Miliband chose to adopt Brand's noted mockney accent – rather than his normal clipped accent – in a bid to win common support. 'It ain't gonna be like that,' the Oxford-educated Miliband told Brand. 'Yes' became 'yeah', 'going to' became 'gonna', and glottal stops were used throughout the interview. This modification of his accent to sound more 'urban' was widely branded as a desperate bid for Miliband to woo younger voters since they were likely to empathise and relate with him more if he sounded like them.[*] But this could be also a case of linguistic mimicry, where – in a stressful situation and with the rush of adrenalin – Miliband resorted to cognitive shortcuts and his unconscious bias to copy Brand's accent in order to build an affinity with him.

---

[*] *Daily Telegraph*, 30 April 2015.

Changing accents is often about social mobility. The former British prime minister Margaret Thatcher is believed to have had elocution lessons to change her regional Lincolnshire accent to RP. The former England footballer David Beckham had a very pronounced cockney accent that has now changed to something akin to RP. Being attracted to a certain accent can be 'a bit of subconscious, aspiring social-climbing', according to Glenn Geher, a psychology professor at the State University of New York at New Paltz who looks at evolutionary studies and mating in his work, with specific reference to why Americans find the British accent most attractive. Professor Geher shows that Americans associate a British accent with someone more intelligent, attractive, sophisticated and competent, bringing up visions of the monarchy, boarding schools, castles, country manors and James Bond. In a 2009 study, participants listened to one of three versions of a taped interaction between a customer and a bank employee, with the only difference in the three versions being the accent of the employee as Indian, American or British. Results showed that, even when the interactions followed identical scripts, participants rated their customer satisfaction as significantly higher when the employee had a British accent.

Deliberate attempts to target voters' unconscious bias can backfire as well. Joe Biden, vice-president of the United States between 2009 and 2017 and a presidential candidate for 2020, was mocked after he adopted a comically over-the-top Southern drawl during one rally in the US.* On 5 April 2019 New York representative

---

* This video and reference to it has since disappeared from YouTube and elsewhere online, possibly in an attempt to clean up Biden's image for the presidential elections.

Alexandria Ocasio-Cortez spoke at a National Action Network convention comprised largely of African-Americans. 'I'm proud to be a bartender. Ain't nothing wrong with that,' she said, also stretching 'wrong' out a bit and intoning in a way sometimes referred to as a 'drawl', which is also part of the Black English toolkit. She was criticised widely and termed a 'racist' for putting on a 'fake African-American accent' or a 'faux Southern accent', 'affecting an accent' and trying to sound more black. Ocasio-Cortez retaliated to the accusations of 'verbal blackfacing' by defending her 'flexible' accent developed while growing up in the Bronx, where she navigated and straddled different cultures and environs. Linguists call this code-switching. Many of us living and moving across borders and cultures are doing so: when I move seamlessly between English and Hindi in the same sentence, my English has an RP accent in the UK but slips back into the Indian nuances, drawl and twang when in India or when speaking to my parents. This is code-switching or bi-dialecticism. The rules in different dialects are perfectly clear, and the native dialect is not substandard to the standard language, but rather a nonstandard or an alternative dialect of the same language. Bi-dialecticism is also a form of unconscious bias that compels us to adopt a cognitive shortcut to try and fit in; in this case our identity is shaped by membership of two distinct social groups. It is not a deliberate act of misleading anyone or 'faking' or deception. So there remains a distinct possibility that Ocasio-Cortez heightened one aspect of her accent to appeal to the audience and appeal to their confirmation bias. Or perhaps, when stressed and tired, she resorted to cognitive heuristics and adopted the part of her identity that helped her identify with the people around her.

Accent bias becomes more heightened when gender stereotypes intersect to form a compound bias.[*] Although very few studies exist where different genders have been directly assessed, and most participants in research studies have been male, there have been some informal discussions that show this gender bias. The Australian accent with its upspeak and vocal fry has been called 'ditzy', 'childlike' and 'unintelligent', particularly for women. Californian women have a similar experience, being labelled as 'too sexy' or sounding like 'sorority girls at a bar'. In an experiment, women with an RP accent were judged as 'too masculine', cold and calculating, aggressive, and 'possibly too intimidating to work with', which was not the case for their male counterparts.

A person with an accent cannot, according to the Equality and Human Rights Commission, be discriminated against if they are able to communicate and be understood effectively in English. An employer may base an employment decision on accent only if that accent materially interferes with effective spoken communication required for performing professional duties, which may have a real-terms business impact. However, these are still vague parameters and we continue to hold hidden personal and cultural biases against certain accents, organising them in hierarchical order, and making decisions based on our perception of a speaker's linguistic background. We need much more awareness of accent bias in the workplace and everyday life, and this can only be done through active intervention and bias training and management. When you listen to a speaker with a foreign accent, do you find yourself making assumptions about their education, their religious beliefs, their intellect or

---

[*] More evidence of intersectional effect in social categorisation.

even their extremist views? Ask yourself: 'If this person had a different accent, would I still think the same about them?'

## What's in a name?

Quite a lot, it seems. Much like accents, names are not something that are biologically predetermined in a person; they are a social and cultural construct, but nevertheless a critical aspect of a person's identity, forming their sense of self. In the age of digital communication, often we do not even meet a person face-to-face and only know them by the name they use on their social media profiles and in email communication. Names are an important part of culture, and hugely significant to those who receive them and to the society and culture that gives an individual their name.

Names are rich sources of information. They can signal gender, class and race, and can evoke a feeling of comfort and familiarity, and create a glow of warmth. Descriptive food names can also cause a change in sensory perception. They evoke a lot of semantic information, even about personality, age and intellectual competence, and are therefore cues for stereotypes too. In a *New York Times* article, Sendhil Mullainathan wrote about a study that he had co-authored in 2003. In this study, he and Marianne Bertrand, at the University of Chicago, mailed thousands of identical résumés to employers with job openings and measured which ones were called back for interviews. They randomly used stereotypically African-American names (such as Jamal) on some and stereotypically white names (like Brendan) on others. They were shocked to find that roughly 50 per cent were more likely to result in a call-back for an interview if it had a 'white' name. Because the résumés were statistically identical, any differences in outcomes could be attributed only to the one factor that was changed: the name.

In 2009, government researchers in the UK sent nearly 3,000 job applications under false identities. They used names recognisably from three different communities: Nazia Mahmood, Mariam Namagembe and Alison Taylor, created with similar experience and qualifications. Every false applicant had British education and work histories. The results showed that an applicant who appeared to be white would send nine applications before receiving a positive response of either an invitation to an interview or an encouraging telephone call. Minority candidates with the same qualifications and experience had to send 16 applications before receiving a similar response.* Similarly, the BBC programme *Inside Out* sent out CVs from two candidates, Adam and Mohamed, who had identical skills and experience, in response to 100 job opportunities. Adam was offered 12 interviews and Mohamed four. Similar results were shown in France in 2016, when job applicants with North African names faced discrimination. A consulting firm commissioned by the labour ministry sent out 3,000 applications for 1,500 jobs advertised by 40 companies in six cities. It found that 47 per cent of candidates with traditional French names got interviews, compared with 36 per cent of those with North African names. Another experiment, which focused on exposing the 'leaky pipeline' in academia, where academics with minority ethnic names and of specific gender fail to get hired for a postdoctoral position in natural sciences, was investigated and reported in the journal *Sex Roles*. Identical CVs for a hypothetical PhD graduate were sent to biology

---

* The *Guardian*, 18 October 2009.

and physics professors at eight large public US research universities, and the only difference in the eight CVs sent out were the names used for the candidates: Bradley Miller, Claire Miller, Zhang Wei, Wang Li, Jamal Banks, Shanice Banks, José Rodriguez and Maria Rodriguez. The research found that physics academics rated men as being significantly more competent and hireable, and that they preferred white and Asian candidates over black and Latinx applicants. Physics traditionally has a masculine culture. Black women and Latinx men and women were rated as having the lowest hireability in physics. Women were rated as being more likeable than their male counterparts but ultimately less hireable, showing double-bind bias. This research shows the racial and gender prejudice and bias that is created purely on the basis of names. As a consequence of this bias and prejudice, there is a lack of role models and equal representation in the sciences, with women across all science and engineering fields making up 42.5 per cent of assistant professors and 24.5 per cent of full professors at four-year universities in the US, and African and Latinx Americans accounting for less than 1 per cent of the STEM faculty.

In a study in 2012, 6,500 professors at top US universities drawn from 89 disciplines and 259 institutions were contacted by fictional prospective students to discuss research opportunities before applying to a doctoral programme. Names of students were randomly assigned to signal gender and race (Caucasian, black, Hispanic, Indian, Chinese) – categories assigned on the basis of a previous research experiment – but messages were identical. Twenty different names in 10 different race/gender categories were used. Professors were more responsive to those who had names that sounded white male than to female, black, Hispanic, Indian or Chinese students in almost every discipline and across all types of universities, but particularly in higher-paying disciplines and in private institutions. The response rates depended on students' race and gender identity, also showing same-race and same-gender bias in institutions and disciplines that have a higher representation of women and minority candidates in general. In this case, in-group bias was overridden by the stereotype bias. Or it is likely that the inherent need to 'belong' and identify with the group that we associate ourselves with changes, and so professors who were women and from a minority background, were showing association bias, discriminating against certain names because of association with the wider academic community that they were part of. It is important to note that the email recipients had no other information but names of the students. Names acted as cues to racial and gender stereotypes, and the underlying implicit bias was activated at the intersectionality of these two domains. This implicit bias can therefore affect career progressions and opportunities on offer to individuals, even before they come face-to-face and other normative stereotypes can be activated.

I decided to check this for myself, albeit on a smaller scale. In 2015, while looking for a new academic position, I applied for 12 vacancies, identical in nature, at the same salary scale and in similar kinds of academic departments. I sent the same résumé to all these places, but on six I used my maiden surname (which I use professionally and which is clearly a foreign name), while on the other five I used my double-barrelled surname combining my husband's (very European) surname with mine. I received a call for interviews from all six places where I had used the double-barrelled surname, but from only one of the six places where I had just used my own Indian surname. Clearly, this is a small dataset and other variables are obviously in play, but perhaps the results do hint at something. Was my anglicised surname giving me more professional respectability? If so, why? On each occasion, I received the names of the members of the recruitment committee. A quick survey of the university websites revealed that all recruitment committees were white. It is therefore highly likely that they were choosing people who sounded like themselves,* and it is likely they are doing so without being explicitly prejudiced against foreigners in any way. Nevertheless, the name acts as a priming mechanism for other dimensions where stereotypes can be activated.

Familiarity bias also plays a role in how we react to certain names. Those with unique and unusual names are less likely to be hired. A 2008 study where respondents were asked to rate names on a uniqueness and likeability scale showed that common names were seen as least unique, best liked, and these people most likely to be hired. Unusual names were seen as most unique, least liked, and these people least likely to be hired.

Name bias also has a wider impact on systemic social inequality. A study in 2018 showed the continuing existence of discrimination in the housing market against applicants whose surnames suggest that they are minority ethnic individuals, and who on average have to send out more applications than those whose last names suggest they are of the majority white population. Merely on the basis of a typical minority ethnic surname, the landlord often infers that an applicant is likely to be in a weaker financial position than other applicants. The level of discrimination decreased when information about social status and income levels was included to counter this implicit bias. In a similar vein, three Harvard researchers

---

* A confirmation bias, discussed in detail in Chapter 5.

found that 'black-sounding' names were discriminated against by Airbnb hosts.* The researchers sent housing requests to roughly 6,400 hosts across five cities: Baltimore, Dallas, Los Angeles, St Louis and Washington. Fictional guests set up by the researchers with names like Lakisha or Rasheed were roughly 16 per cent less likely to be accepted than identical guests with names like Brent or Kristen. Renters with names that sounded African-American got a positive reply about 42 per cent of the time, compared with roughly 50 per cent for white guests, and the researchers say that 'white people were discriminating against blacks, blacks discriminating against blacks, and both male and female users displayed bias.' The results across all these different studies were remarkably persistent, and consistent, showing an unequivocal bias against names that sound 'non-white'.

Names are, therefore, subject to stereotype bias. People associate certain stereotypes to certain names and fall back on their implicit biases associated with these stereotypes when they hear a name. In a 1973 study, it was first shown that teachers' evaluations of student performance were linked with stereotypical perceptions of the first names. Short essays actually written by fifth-grade students were presented for evaluation to 80 female teachers (aged 20–45) and 80 female undergraduates. Authorship of the essays was randomly linked with boys or girls, and with common, popular and attractive names or rare, unpopular and unattractive names. The quality of the essay was judged to be better when authored by names associated with positive stereotypes. This stereotype bias was more pronounced for

---

* Since this study was published, Airbnb has increased the proportion of hosts who offer 'Instant Book' (letting guests book instantly, without the host first seeing the guest's picture or name).

experienced teachers than for inexperienced undergraduates, and the effect was clearer for boys' names than for girls' names. Again, much like many other unconscious biases, names also intersect with gender and race to create compound biases. Intersectionality is hence an important consideration here.

★★★

A woman academic, Nila, wrote to me with this story:

> Today one of my female course mates told me her tutor told her to use a different 'professional name' when submitting to journals because it is more masculine and if she uses her name she's more likely to be rejected, i.e. instead of using her name Stephanie, she should use Stevie (a nickname she goes by sometimes). Apparently, it's pretty common and he even pointed to people in the department who do the same thing (Alexandra to Alex, Charlotte to Charlie, etc.) because they're more likely to be taken seriously.

Similarly, the story of Catherine Nichols, an author who tested the gender bias in the publishing industry, illustrates the same gender-biased association with names. Catherine sent out a book proposal to 50 publishers including several women, and had only two noncommittal responses. She then sent the same proposal under an assumed male name, and immediately heard back from more than 17 publishers, with several even offering to mentor him (her).

How we use names can be symptomatic of inherent gender bias. Have you ever considered why we call Darwin by his second name, while Marie Curie by her full name? The same applies to authors too. Shakespeare but Mary Shelley? Research in sociology suggests that sports commentators are more likely to refer to male (vs female) players by surname. In research published in 2018 in the *Proceedings of National Academy of Sciences* by Melissa Ferguson, a professor and the chair of psychology in the College of Arts and Sciences at Princeton University, and her doctoral student Stav Atir, it was seen that men and women were, on average across eight studies, more than twice as likely to describe a male professional by surname than a female professional. Similar results were seen across science, politics and literature academic domains. Beyond the academic domain, the researchers coded data from transcripts of American political television shows such as *All Things Considered, Fresh Air, Morning Edition, The Rush Limbaugh Show* and *The Sean Hannity Show,* where they found that speakers were more than twice as likely (126.42 per cent) to use a surname when speaking about a man than when speaking about a woman. This might seem like a seemingly minor detail, but the results show that this use of surname vs full name is directly correlated to association of eminence and professional recognition.

When people are addressed by their surnames alone, they are perceived to have a more significant status. This can hamper the recognition of women on a similar par to men and explain the gender gap in eminence. It could also explain why the media landscape is so gendered, with more male professionals called upon as experts to give their opinions or making up panels. (There is now even a word to describe this phenomenon: manels.) Women are less likely to be seen in scientific and technological domains, and the default representative category is always male, so it is likely that the first name is used to mark the atypical gender in such male-dominated professions. Researchers admitted that they hadn't yet looked at female-dominated professional domains[*] to investigate whether similar gender bias would exist for men, who would be the atypical category in that situation. But while the use of first name is intended to implicitly commend and highlight a woman's contribution and participation in a domain, at the highest level of professional achievement, in turn what it does is diminish the perception of their eminence and status. A positive stereotype implies and signposts that a negative stereotype exists, that there is difference between the two sexes, that the default category is male, and that women are encroaching upon a domain they are not intended to be in. The use of the first name for women signals that they are not as well known as men.

A study presented at the Cognitive Society Conference in Chicago in 2004 showed that the sound of a name – especially the vowel sounds, and its perceived masculinity and femininity – also influences how attractive an individual is viewed and rated. Linguist Amy Perfors showed that front vowel sounds are often perceived as 'smaller' than

---

[*] It is an interesting consideration as to what such female-dominated domains would be and how such niches are created. I asked this question in a Facebook group of women academics, and the answers ranged from psychology, art history, nursing and education to critical and human geography. It was interesting that many of the gender studies departments are dominated by men, although I admit that my sample size (75) is not extensive. Why are these niches created? As per a very recent study, in Chapter 12, even when women are considered as intelligent and competent as men, they are seen in more nurturing and social roles rather than in those domains that require more agency, authority and leadership. This could be something to do with the way different academic disciplines are perceived and the skills that are required for success. Or is this more social and cultural in that, once a department/discipline becomes gendered, it attracts more people of the same gender as there is a natural tendency for people to recruit those who are more like them?

back vowel sounds, and men with such names, such as Matt or Ben, were rated as more attractive, while women with round-sounding names, such as Laura, tended to score higher than those with smaller vowel sounds. Professor Perfors proposed that perhaps women were subconsciously seeking 'sensitive' or 'gentle' men – traits often considered 'feminine'. Perfors said she also noted that men with 'women's names' were rated least attractive of all. The cultural connotations of a name also influenced how masculine and feminine, and attractive, people found those with such names. This was a small sample study with lots of caveats, and so the results were statistically significant but not representative of the whole population.

A research study of hurricane names and corresponding fatalities, published in the Proceedings of the National Academy of Sciences of the US in 2014 showed that even in the case of a natural disaster, an association with a certain sex in its assigned name resulted in the hurricane being judged as per the social biases and expectations for that sex. The researchers did a historical analysis of 92 actual hurricanes that made landfall in the US from 1950 to 2012, and showed that the death toll for severe hurricanes with more feminine names was higher than that for hurricanes with masculine names. They took the storms' names and gave them to a group of participants (who didn't know that they were hurricane names) and asked them how masculine or feminine each one was. Over six experiments, researchers showed that hurricanes that had explicitly female names were judged to be less risky by people than those that had male names. Kiju Jung and his collaborators at the University of Illinois at Urbana-Champaign and Arizona State University also conducted experiments asking people to predict the intensity and riskiness of a hurricane. When asked about a male hurricane, like Alexander, people predicted a more violent storm than when asked about a female hurricane, like Alexandra. They were also more willing to evacuate to avoid Hurricane Victor than when it was Hurricane Victoria. The more masculine the name, the more respect the hurricane drew. People assumed the hurricanes randomly given feminine names to have less violent impact, and therefore prepared less for the severity of the impact, which was a likely reason for more fatalities from hurricanes with feminine names. The robustness and statistical validity of this study was debated, but another follow-up archival study demonstrated that category labels may influence responses to natural hazards and other events. The participants were being led by their unconscious bias to equate masculine names with strength and aggression and feminine names with warmth and gentleness. How many times have we read or watched a crime thriller, especially one with violent serial killings, and just automatically assumed that the murderer was a man? These are the traditional masculine and feminine frameworks that our society operates under, which create these implicit biases. When we see anything labelled with other categories, our responses to such an event or entity are informed by our mental representation associated with this category, and then it is likely that these mental representations will influence our reactions. For example, if a hurricane was named after a flower, we would naturally assume it to be gentler than one that is named after a reptile.

We know that names shape people's views of others. Leonard Newman at Syracuse University in New York and his colleagues asked 500 college students to rate 400 popular male and female names, and asked questions such as 'Imagine that you are about to meet Samantha. How competent/warm/old do you think she is when you see her name?' We have already seen how familiarity can create a glow of warmth, and we link accents to competence too. In this experiment, results reflected gender bias and stereotypes. Female names such as Melody and Hannah were associated with low competence and high warmth, while names associated with high competence and low warmth tended to be male, like Howard and Lawrence – typically 'manly' names. In the same experiment, some names were associated with age, such as Joan and Betty. An experiment conducted in the 1960s famously showed that identical essays that were labelled 'John' or 'Joan' were graded differently, and Joan's essay tended to be marked lower. Newman proposes that this could have been gender or age bias, as Joan is an older-generation name. And the intersectionality of these two parameters is likely to generate a deeper implicit bias.

For as long as I can remember, I have felt an acute pang of anxiety any time I have to introduce myself to someone or my name has to be announced in a public setting. I have groaned internally, as I hear people falter over my name and inevitably mispronounce it. Some look uncomfortable as they see this unfamiliar name, and some chuckle awkwardly after reading the name out aloud. 'Oh, I am no good at foreign names,' some would say or, as the dean said out loud at my doctoral degree ceremony, 'I think I am going to get this wrong.' While I should have felt no guilt, I did so because I felt responsible for creating such awkward encounters and uncomfortable situations for others. When I started my PhD, some people asked me if they could just shorten my name to 'Prags' as my name was just difficult to pronounce. I went along with it and just introduced myself as such for a long time to any new person because it felt more convenient and sociable. Barack Obama used 'Barry' while he was growing up, and I know several Chinese friends who have an 'English' (or anglicised) name while maintaining their traditional name for family and friends. What exactly is it that triggers this discomfort with unfamiliar names, and why do people feel compelled to change their names to more easy and familiar names?

Ease of name pronunciation affects the perception of the named individual. Across five studies it was shown that easy-to-pronounce names (and consequently the people bearing them) are evaluated more positively than difficult-to-pronounce names. This stems from the processing fluency theory,[*] which states that there is subjectivity in the level of difficulty associated with a cognitive process. According to the hedonic marking hypothesis,[†] some words are processed very fluently, and fluency elicits a positive response. Those words elicit a positive emotion, and so in turn the object with which these words are related is perceived more favourably. Objects (or persons) to whom such positive emotions are attached can be perceived more vividly and easier than others, and would be remembered more easily. Familiar words are processed more easily and fluently, and so are familiar names, which is one reason why people unconsciously prefer names that are familiar to them. Easy-to-perceive stimuli, such as familiar names and accents, were not only judged more positively but increased activation in the zygomaticus major muscle, the so-called 'smiling muscle'. Familiarity evokes a glow and warmth, and the positive state reduces sensitivity to negative characteristics, while the opposite is true for those that are relatively unfamiliar and not as immediate in a person's memory.

---

[*] The ease with which information is processed in the human mind.
[†] There is also some debate as to whether bias against foreign (unfamiliar) accents is because of the lack of fluency and difficulty in processing these accents rather than a bias against particular ethnicities.

Most people take care to make sure they pronounce another person's name correctly, especially in introductions. People generally – and rightly – resent the mispronunciation of their name because it amounts to a distortion of their identity. Sometimes this is done carelessly and ignorantly, and on other occasions it can be done maliciously and intentionally. In both cases, the effect is to 'other' the person by attacking an important aspect of their self-identity; this is explicit bias in the latter case, and implicit bias in the former. Names bring stories of generations gone by, and in many first- and even second-generation immigrants this could be their only link to their heritage. Downplaying the significance of getting someone's name right or not taking adequate care to learn the correct pronunciation is yet another form of microaggression (discussed in Chapter 8). We have seen how such microaggressions can affect mental health, and this has now been proven by research in 2012 that showed failure to pronounce a name correctly impacts the world-view and social emotional well-being of students, and has a direct consequence on their learning.

Getting a name wrong is not an offence in itself; rather it creates a distancing effect. Microaggressions are important because they can easily turn into macro-aggressions as they become cumulative, and they can often aversively communicate a larger social message that is offensive. It is not an acceptable excuse to say that you are just bad with names or that you get everyone's names wrong. Mispronouncing a name in the workplace can negate the experience of a colleague and give them the message that they or their culture is not as important or is an inconvenience. It isn't about getting it right the first time; instead, it is about giving a name, its associated culture and social values, and the associated person due importance.

When we talk about biases and consequently discrimination established through accents or names, we are largely spurred on by our social and cultural archetypes. These act as cues, activating the implicit stereotypes. These are learned behaviours, ones that are formed sometimes due to the fear of the unfamiliar and the unknown, and often due to the messages that we see around us, those implicit and explicit cues from our parents, teachers, social media tribes, friends and media.

'A rose is a rose, no matter what name you call it,' said William Shakespeare. But, apparently not.

# MORAL CONUNDRUM

## CHAPTER ELEVEN

# I'd Blush If I Could

Peggy Johnson, executive vice president of business development at Microsoft, told an audience at the New Rules Summit, hosted by the *New York Times* in 2010, about Kinect for Microsoft's Xbox gaming system. Kinect allowed users to play with gestures and spoken commands rather than using a controller. It was revolutionary and ready to go to market. But just before it did, a woman who worked for the company took the game home to play with her family and something strange happened. The motion-sensing devices worked just fine for her husband, but not so much for her or her children. The system had been tested on men aged 18–35 and did not recognise the body motions of women and children as well. This error could be attributed to the inherent bias in the data that was used to train the automated system. It could also be attributed to the implicit bias within the design team, which was no doubt composed of a certain demographic and not diverse enough. This is not an isolated incident. When Microsoft's Kinect was finally released and shipped with Spanish voice recognition, it did not recognise Castilian Spanish. Not a great advocate for diversity and inclusivity!

If human cognitive facilities are inherently biased, should we resort to machines, and can Artificial Intelligence (AI)\*

---

\* The *MIT Technology Review* defines AI: 'In the broadest sense, AI refers to machines that can learn, reason, and act for themselves. They can make their own decisions when faced with new situations, in the same way that humans and animals can.'

bring objectivity and bust these biases? AI and technology in general are being touted as a panacea for all of society's ills. We are increasingly reliant on automated technology, powered by data and algorithms. But is it really helping us create a bias-free world?

Much of what we see and hear of AI in our systems is based on machine learning. These algorithms use statistics from previous actions to find patterns in gigantic datasets. They then use these patterns to make predictions and give recommendations, such as things you would like to watch on Netflix based on your previous viewing history, or things you might like to purchase on Amazon based on your previous shopping behaviour. It is also built into online systems, face-recognition software, and diagnostic tools such as the ones used to predict the possibility of cancer based on biopsy results. In her book *Weapons of Math Destruction*, data scientist Cathy O'Neil writes about the rise of the new WMDs: widespread, mysterious and destructive algorithms that are infiltrating more facets of society. It is even suggested that at a hypothetical future point in time this technological growth will becomes uncontrollable and irreversible, resulting in unimaginable changes to human civilisation. This has been called technological singularity.[*] More and more algorithms are being used in situations

---

[*] Philosophers and computer scientists have suggested that, although the notion of AI singularity has been discussed for the last few decades, it is likely that in the imminent future (i.e. the next 30–70 years) there may not be such an alarming rise of AI that our existence will be threatened. However, a long-term view should recognise the possibility of artificial general intelligence posing an existential threat to mankind and should require us to work towards a responsible AI future (from: https://medium.com/datadriven investor/some-thoughts-on-artificial-intelligence-singularity-3f16db2ae8ae).

where any decision impacts real life. Technological biases have real-world consequences, and so it crucial to understand, acknowledge and address them.

There are two primary facets to implicit bias in technology: how the data and design reflect and mirror biases existing in the real world; and how technology in turn contributes to biases in the real world. The datasets that AIs are trained on reflect ingrained biases, and AIs incorporate these biases as they 'learn'. An algorithm can be only as good as the data it learns from. Discrimination can be an artefact of the data itself, even if it isn't intentional. By the mere fact of it being a representative sample, no matter how large this dataset is, it will always have some implicit bias in it. We can ask if machines are sexist and racist, but the fact remains that these algorithms are being trained on 'bad' data. This bias can be at the data-collection stage, where either the way it has been collected is biased or it is not a complete representation of reality. Alternatively, the way it has been structured can reflect existing prejudices. It could be a systematic omission of certain groups of people, as people who live on the margins of society and are invisible and under-represented are more likely to be missed. These groups are unlikely to be participating in the formal capital-generating activities and economy, and they might not be considered as important. Larry Bartels, an American political scientist, talks about representative democracy being a myth, where the views and interests of the poor are relatively less well represented in the political process. Unequal access to technology and lack of fluency in the use of such data-generating platforms and tools is likely to create a skewed dataset. Study after study shows that data-mining techniques further obfuscate marginalised groups and legitimise these biases and social disparities.

Bias can also creep in while the problem that the algorithm is designed to solve is being framed, or when it is being decided which attributes are significant in the dataset during the preparation stage for training. In framing the problem and the goal of the machine learning, the designers have to set some statistical parameters. Their primary goal is, of course, always to optimise the search rather than to be fair and indiscriminate. Blind spots, known as 'unknown unknowns', can occur, and they are hard to spot. This is especially true for words that might be implicitly gendered or racist and that could sneak in even when the designers have explicitly removed any gendered language. Often identifying the implicit gendered language is only possible retrospectively once the behaviour of the algorithm is much clearer. For instance, in 2018 it was reported that Amazon had developed an experimental hiring tool to help rank job candidates. The model was 'taught' to recognise some 50,000 terms that showed up on past candidates' résumés. The algorithms learned to assign less significance to skills that were common across all IT applicants, such as the ability to code in different languages, instead looking for a unique set of skills. Amazon anticipated that the résumé-scanning tool, by learning from its past preferences, would be able to efficiently identify qualified applicants by comparing their applications to previous hires. The system quickly began to downgrade résumés from candidates who attended all-women's colleges, along with any résumés that included the word 'women' (or 'women's', as in women's netball team captain). This bias wasn't identified for a while, but eventually it was reported by Reuters, and Amazon had to abandon the tool because gender-based discrimination was built too deeply within the system. Implicit bias during recruitment and hiring has recently been the subject of much discussion and it has been proposed that AI could help resolve it. But, as this case demonstrated, when the data and the system were trained based on Amazon's past hiring practices, it inherited the unconscious biases and prejudices that were a part of the inherently sexist culture. Even when the programmers noted the bias, and removed any gendered words such as 'women', other words that were more often seen on male CVs such as 'executed' and 'captured' (proven by studies as typically 'masculine' words) were then used to favour male candidates.

'The idea of bias in technology depends on the context,' Professor Nisheeth Vishnoi of Yale University told me. Most algorithms suffer from this 'portability trap' because, although most computer programmes are designed to work across a range of contexts, the idea of fairness is not the same across different domains, whether it be geographic or a social and cultural construct. For instance, the idea of what is fair and what is biased is not the same in the automotive industry and in the criminal justice system, and what is fair in India might not be the same as in the UK. Computer systems are based in a deterministic reality, and the human conception of what is fair and just is tricky to model in this way. While the concept of fairness is more flexible and can change in the real world, it is more black and white in the world of tech where it has to be modelled in mathematical terms. There is inevitably a trade-off between predictive accuracy of the model and fairness, and in certain contexts such as criminal justice or healthcare, where it is a matter of life and death, the predictive accuracy is really critical.

More and more of the decisions in the real world are being taken away from humans in order to minimise the possibility of human errors. Often this is done through supervised learning, where the data is tagged and labelled and told exactly what to look for – a situation rife for biases to creep in unnoticed. Or to reduce time and resources, it can be unsupervised learning, which is increasingly used in cybersecurity, or reinforcement learning where the algorithm learns through trial and error (much like a star chart used for children to train them to do the right thing). Bias can creep in at so many stages in this process, and even before the data is collected. The machine-learning researcher Stephen Merity said in 2017, 'Bias is not just in our datasets, it's in our conferences and community.' When the people designing the systems and services do not understand cognitive biases, how can they design something that combats it? Designers and software architects bring their own biases to the table. They fall foul to 'pattern bias', where they only see the patterns they want to see. Yael Eisenstat, a former Facebook employee, gives an example of how ads are often mischaracterised based on the individual's own biases. For instance, an associate mistakenly categorised a pro-LGBT ad run by a conservative group as an anti-LGBT ad. They had let their assumptions about conservative groups' opinions on LGBT issues lead to incorrect labelling. Such mischaracterisations are then incorporated into manuals that train both human reviewers and machines. Systems therefore mimic the bias from the real world that they are designed and trained to emulate, and this creates more bias in return. It is a vicious cycle.

Dr Elisa Celis from Yale University has been studying bias and fairness in algorithms, and most recently working on how personalised news feeds can be polarised and create bias. In Chapter 5 we saw how social media algorithms – and the inherent algorithmic bias – mean that all of us can exist in echo chambers. The algorithms control what we see by personalising our social media feed, and gradually the points of view that we see become increasingly limited and narrow. When you click on one link rather than another, the algorithms used by social media platforms like Facebook learn what your preferences are and provide more and more content that matches your interests. 'By ever more carefully selecting what we see, these algorithms are distorting reality. Social media platforms effectively become echo chambers in which opinions can become increasingly extreme,' Dr Celis told me. The technology then also 'learns' users' bias and employs these patterns to train the algorithm. Companies using Facebook ads for recruitment use targeted posting based on previous patterns. If the algorithm 'thinks' that in the past men have been the target audience, they are less likely to show future job ads to women, thereby reinforcing and perpetuating gender inequity. For example, between October 2017 and 2018 ads by Nebraska Furniture Mart of Texas were seeking staff members to 'assemble and prepare merchandise for delivery' and the ad was targeted to reach 'men 18 to 50' who lived in or were recently near Fort Worth, actively choosing to filter out women. Several companies such as Facebook, IKEA and Amazon are also discriminating against jobseekers in their 50s and 60s through targeted job ads. The Communications Workers of America, a labour union representing 700,000 media workers across the country, added the companies to a class-action lawsuit in 2018. Known as the 'Bradley v. T-Mobile case', this has major implications for US employers who routinely buy job ads on Facebook to reach users. The Facebook business model is based on allowing advertisers to target or exclude specific groups using a huge database of personal attributes that the company has collected from its users. This kind of microtargeting is designed to tap into the implicit biases and prejudices existing in our society. The Brexit vote was won in this way, and this is how advertisers reach niche

SWAY

audiences, such as swing-state voters concerned about climate change.

In fact, Facebook came under fire in 2016 when a ProPublica investigation showed that companies could buy ads that screened out users based on their race, which is potentially illegal in the context of housing and employment advertising. This is basically akin to the Jim Crow* of social media, where certain ads are only shown to white people. LinkedIn and Google also generally allow advertisers to exclude men or women from receiving ads, although LinkedIn said in a statement that it would take down job ads that exclude a gender, and Google said it would remove ads that discriminated against a protected class. Facebook said it generally did not take down job ads that exclude a gender. The social media platform acknowledged that this form of microtargeting, which capitalises on the implicit biases of the various communities, was used as an important tool in Russia's efforts to influence the 2016 election, when 126 million people saw Russia-linked content, some of which was aimed at particular demographic groups and regions.

Deep learning is an even more powerful form of machine learning and underpins advances such as facial recognition, hyper-realistic photo and voice synthesis. It has many more layers and computational nodes, and hence has the ability to find the tiniest of patterns from enormous amounts of data. 'Deep fake',† a term coined in 2017, has recently

---

* The 'separate, but equal' racial segregation mandate known as Jim Crow laws were implemented in the southern United States until 1965.
† Developed primarily in machine vision research communities, the 'Synthesizing Obama' programme, published in 2017, modified video footage of Barack Obama to depict him mouthing the words contained in a separate audio track. The Face2Face programme,

surfaced prominently in the news as we see fake videos of celebrities and politicians distributed maliciously and contributing to the phenomenon of fake news. This is also based in a deep-learning technique known as 'generative adversarial network'. In June 2019, a downloadable application called DeepNude was released that used neural networks (specifically, generative adversarial networks) to remove clothing from images of women. The app had both paid and unpaid versions, with the paid version costing $50, and is touted to become a mass phenomenon. It is, of course, capitalising on the inherently misogynistic tendencies of its users, but in doing so it is also reinforcing the gender biases by creating systems that will make it easier to target, humiliate and control women.[*] Besides celebrity 'porn videos' that first surfaced on Reddit in 2017, these neural networks are now being used to misrepresent well-known politicians. In May 2019, Nancy Pelosi was the subject of two viral videos: one where the speed had been slowed down to 75 per cent and another that edited together parts of her speech at a news conference. Both were intended to make Pelosi appear as though she was drunk and slurring her speech. These videos were viewed more than 2 million times on Facebook, even though it was a fake. This is what is being now known as a 'dumbfake',

---

published in 2016, modifies video footage of a person's face to depict them mimicking the facial expressions of another person in real time. Both demonstrated how audio and video files could be synthesised to mouth shapes and facial expressions to create photo-realistic imagery.

[*] On 27 June 2019, after a huge media outrage against this app, which went viral in just four days after launch, the founder 'Alberto' took to Twitter to announce DeepNude's end, saying the chances of people abusing the app were too high and that: 'The world is not yet ready for DeepNude.'

SWAY

as it does not even require sophisticated technology but can be easily created by varying speed or with quite amateurish editing. This makes them even more dangerous.

Bots accelerate the spread of true and false news at the same rate, while a recent MIT study found that it takes true stories about six times as long as false ones to reach 1,500 people, demonstrating that false news spreads because humans are more likely to share it. A photograph of Trump where he was saving a flood victim on a raft in Texas after Hurricane Harvey appeared online in August 2017. It was a digitally altered image using an original image from 2015 before Trump became president. Trump was not even present in the original photo. There were some indications and telltale signs, such as Trump wearing a suit and not a life jacket while out on flood waters and the fact that it is not customary for presidents to go out on rescue operations. However, this image was shared many thousands of times on Twitter and Facebook without people questioning its authenticity.

This constant threat of misinformation and the way technology is enabling creation and distribution of fake media is making people trust news less.* A Stanford University study in late 2016 based on more than 7,800 responses from middle school, high school and college students in 12 states found that students were consistently unable to determine the credibility of an online news source. A Pew Research Center study in June showed that 63 per cent of Americans surveyed said that altered videos

---

* A year-long report (commissioned by the Knight Foundation and published by the non-profit Project Information Literacy) analysed posts from 135,000 college-aged Twitter users to learn more about their media consumption habits. Researchers found that students often cross-reference their news with several different sources because of the possibility of misinformation.

and images were creating a great deal of confusion around the facts of current issues. Yet we also tend to share and consume content without checking sources and credibility, so there is an inherent dichotomy in how we behave in response to this threat. The overwhelming information overload created by social media contributes to the way we let our unconscious cognitive biases take over our rational mind.

★★★

How do we know the difference between reality and fake, and how can we rely on our cognitive processes to assess reliability and trust? When we can no longer do this, it becomes even more imperative that we slow down the decision-making process and don't blindly trust the first thing we see in our social media feeds, instantly sharing and retweeting it so that it becomes viral. Before we know it, such fake news is easily available, vivid in our memories, and then becomes so familiar that we instinctively trust it. People are less likely to be motivated to spot a fake video or headline if it aligns with their own world-view and confirms their beliefs and biases. When people are angry, stressed and anxious about misinformation, they are more likely to fall back on their biases and trust any information that validates their feelings, and such technology, which is enabling disinformation, is likely to play a key role in even further political polarisation.

Melinda Gates said, 'men who demean, degrade or disrespect women have been able to operate with such impunity – not just in Hollywood, but in tech, venture capital, and other spaces where their influence and investment can make or break a career. The asymmetry of power is ripe for abuse.' As we saw with the development of Kinect, we have to talk about how the lack of diversity in AI and technology makes the design teams skewed. Tech is a very male-dominated but also a 'masculine' workforce and workplace culture, where traditional forms of toxic masculinity and swagger still persists. Recent studies found only 18 per cent of authors at leading AI conferences are women and more than 80 per cent of AI professors are men. Women comprise only 15 per cent of AI research staff at Facebook and 10 per cent at Google. There is no public data on trans workers or other gender minorities. Only 2.5 per cent of Google's workforce is black, while Facebook and Microsoft are each at 4 per cent.* So the issue of the bias and lack of diversity within the AI and tech sector intersects with the bias that is being inbuilt into these systems. These two issues are not distinct anymore. The tech industry is being acknowledged as a space where gender and racial discrimination, and exclusion, has been allowed to exist.

Since Apple launched Siri in 2013, voice assistants and smart speakers have exploded in popularity; industry researchers forecast that there will be more voice-activated assistants than people by 2021. Google reports that 20 per cent of their searches are made by voice query today – a number that's predicted to climb to 50 per cent by 2020. In 2017 Google announced that their speech recognition had a 95 per cent accuracy rate. But this figure does not tell us that the voice-activated searches still carry racial and gender bias. Meredith Whittaker, a founder and a director of the AI Now Institute at New York University, noted that voice-recognition tools that rely on AI often do not recognise higher-pitched voices. As these more often belong to women, the systems are not as well equipped to

---

* From publicly available Google, Facebook and Microsoft reports.

interact with women as with men. Research by Rachael Tatman from the University of Washington published in 2017 by the North American Chapter of the Association for Computational Linguistics (NAACL) indicated that Google's speech recognition is 13 per cent more accurate for men than it is for women. There are also dialect issues. For instance, Indian English has been shown to have a 78 per cent accuracy rate and Scottish English a 53 per cent accuracy rate. I could take it personally that Siri finds it very difficult to understand me, even when I have attempted to train the voice-recognition tool numerous times. The repeated refrains of 'could you repeat that' have meant that I have stopped using it now.

Most of the voice assistants are female[*] because psychology research shows how we associate authority and care with different pitch of voices. Voices of lower pitch are perceived as more authoritative by both men and women, while higher-pitched voices are associated with submissive, helpful and caring characters. These are all impressions that make the voice assistants more often female. In the late 1990s, BMW had to withdraw the satnav system in one of its models because a huge proportion of German drivers – largely men but also some women – complained that they did not want to take instructions from a female voice. They felt it was demeaning to do so. They also could not trust 'her' to know the correct information. The automated call centres for brokerage firms in Japan give stock quotes in a female voice, but confirm transactions in a male one,

[*] As of September 2019, Apple and Google now allow the user to make Siri or Google Assistant male, while Amazon has kept the assistant's persona as female, repeatedly referring to the technology as 'she' in their documents and presentations.

showing inherently how the technology conforms to societal norms of gender roles and then reinforces them.

Titled 'I'd blush if I could', a report from UNESCO says the almost exclusive market of largely female voice assistants* fuels the stereotype that women are 'obliging, docile and eager-to-please helpers'. The report also shows that the gender bias is deeply ingrained, with people preferring male voices when they need someone with authority and female voices for a more 'helpful' role. This kind of stereotypical representation in the digital space allows for biases to take hold and spread. At the current moment, technologies such as Siri and Alexa are designed to create empathy and connection with the users, which leads to them being anthropomorphised. Hence, any gender stereotype and bias that is built into the system reflects the wider societal bias in the real world, while in turn also enabling the spread and reinforcement of such biases. Another issue raised by this report is how technology is reflecting not only societal biases but also perpetuating and reinforcing the sexual dynamics, where Siri responds to the statement 'You're a slut' with 'I'd blush if I could.'† In addition to indifference to harassment, female voice assistants are programmed to be non-confrontational and respond with submissiveness to blunt commands. Alexa used to respond to insults with 'Thanks for the feedback.' Due to lobbying and pressure from various groups, Amazon have since introduced a 'disengage' mode, so that Alexa now responds to statements such as 'You are a slut' with a passive 'I am not going to respond to that.' The most recent feature introduced on 25 September 2019 is for Alexa to

---

* While the British version of Siri is male by default, it is female by default in 17 of 21 languages.

† This has recently been updated to 'I won't respond to that'.

recognise the voice tonality and emotion. This is going to be launched completely in the US in 2020. Called the 'frustration detection', it enables the voice-recognition technology to recognise when the user is frustrated and then respond with a suitable apology. Emotion recognition has many advantages – especially in health monitoring for elderly people and Alzheimer's patients, where these technologies might require more patience – but such passivity and submissiveness when challenged or insulted is dangerous, as it then contributes to and normalises this treatment of women in the real world and amplifies the gendered power imbalance.

Although these technologies are reflecting the gender biases in society, they are also reflecting the lack of diversity in the design teams. As we have seen in previous chapters, there is a dearth of women in the technology and computer programming sectors, which face a 'leaky pipeline' whereby women who enter these domains are less likely to reach a position where they have influence and decision-making powers. This means that many of these systems are being designed by men, whose world-view is possibly one where women are submissive and coy.

★★★

AI bias is not limited to gender. A 2017 ProPublica report found that an American computer algorithm used by courts to predict reoffending rates among criminals labelled black defendants as 'high-risk' twice as often as white defendants, and mislabelled white defendants as 'low-risk' more often than black defendants. Risk assessments using scores to inform decisions about who can be set free at what stage of the criminal justice system are increasingly common in courtrooms across the US. In Arizona, Colorado, Delaware,

Kentucky, Louisiana, Oklahoma, Virginia, Washington and Wisconsin, the results of such assessments are given to judges during criminal sentencing. In 2014, then US attorney general Eric Holder warned that the risk scores might be injecting bias into the judicial system: 'Although these measures were crafted with the best of intentions, I am concerned that they may inadvertently undermine our efforts to ensure individualized and equal justice.' ProPublica studied the bias within these as part of a larger examination of the effect of algorithms in American life. They obtained the risk scores assigned to more than 7,000 people arrested in Broward County, Florida, in 2013 and 2014. They then checked to see how many were charged with new crimes over the next two years, the same benchmark used by the creators of the algorithm. The score proved remarkably unreliable in forecasting violent crime, as the study found that only 20 per cent of the people predicted to commit violent crimes actually went on to do so. The algorithm also showed huge racial disparity in the way the risk of reoffending was calculated. In forecasting who would reoffend, the algorithm made mistakes with black and white defendants at roughly the same rate but in very different ways. Using a tool called COMPAS (Correctional Offender Management Profiling for Alternative Sanctions), it was found that the algorithm was particularly likely to falsely flag black defendants as future criminals, incorrectly labelling them this way at almost twice the rate as white defendants. White defendants were mislabelled as 'low-risk' more often than defendants from other minority communities. To rule out the possibility that this bias was a reflection of the type of crime that was committed or taken into account, the team looked at more than 10,000 criminal defendants in Broward County, Florida, and compared their predicted reoffending rates with the rate that actually occurred over a two-year period. The analysis clearly showed that – even when controlling for prior crimes, actual future reoffending, age and gender – black defendants were 45 per cent more likely to be assigned higher-risk scores than white defendants for committing a future crime of any kind, and as much as 77 per cent for committing a violent crime. These are shocking statistics, and truly a reflection of the racial bias existing in the real world. They also create further racial disparity and inequity by choosing to exclude some and not others based entirely on their race.

As I read reports of AI tools that detect sexuality from headshots, or predict 'criminality' based on facial features, and even check for competence via 'micro-expressions', I am hugely concerned that these systems are replicating historical notions of stereotypes based on physical appearance, and that using physical cues for determining character will only perpetuate implicit biases and the historical structural inequalities existing in society.

Joy Buolamwini, the founder of the Algorithmic Justice League, has referred to the phenomenon of 'coded gaze' in her work at MIT Media Lab, where the robots that she worked with did not recognise her dark skin and she had to wear a white mask in order to be recognised. Buolamwini has talked extensively about how calls for tech inclusion often miss the bias that is embedded in written code. Programmers and graduate students often use libraries of pre-existing collections of code. Instead of writing everything from scratch, it is widely acceptable to just borrow code from a face-detection library to get started. Although this saves time and resources, it creates a cycle of bias as the bias inbuilt into any of these libraries will just be carried forward and propagated in any future work. When people talk about using AI to increase diversity or minimise bias, they often do not seem to understand that these algorithms, apps and software are trained using existing datasets. They have a sense of 'normal' built into them so that anything that doesn't conform with this is seen as an outlier. For instance, when uploading photographs to online visa-application systems, often my daughter's photograph was rejected as it was too dark for their system. I also read about the experiences of a man of Asian descent who had his eyes registered as closed by the facial-recognition software analysing his photo during an interaction with an automated passport-renewal system. He received an error message saying 'The photo you want to upload does not meet our criteria because the subject's eyes are closed.' Automated systems are (or can be) racist because they imitate the bias and prejudice in society or the designers of these systems, and the dataset on which the system algorithms are trained. If the training dataset is not diverse, the algorithm will fail to recognise anything that does not meet the 'criteria' set by it. As a result, algorithmic bias, much like human bias, can create social inequity and unfairness.

Buolamwini and Timnit Gebru, a scientist at Microsoft Research, working on its Fairness Accountability Transparency and Ethics in AI group, studied the performance of three leading face-recognition systems – by Microsoft, IBM and Megvii of China (whose Face++ software is widely used for identification in online payments and ride-sharing services) – by classifying how well they could guess the gender of people with different skin tones. These companies were selected because they offered gender-classification features in their facial analysis software, and also because their code was publicly available for testing. The researchers built a dataset of 1,270 faces, using faces of lawmakers from countries with a high percentage of women in office. The dataset included three African nations with predominantly dark-skinned populations, and three Nordic countries with mainly light-skinned residents. Then the faces were scored as per a six-point labelling system used by dermatologists to classify skin types. The analysis of software from Microsoft showed an error rate for darker-skinned women was 21 per cent, while IBM's and Megvii's rates were nearly 35 per cent. They all had error rates below 1 per cent for light-skinned males.

This is hugely concerning, as facial-recognition software is increasingly being used across a broad range of retail environments. In 2018, Cali Group in the US piloted facial-recognition software for its in-store loyalty programme. The software could identify registered customers, activate their loyalty accounts and display their favourite meals from the West Coast restaurant. The store was even planning face-based payments instead of credit cards. This might seem like some sort of dystopian futuristic vision but it is very much the immediate future, if not the present. Companies such as Samsung and AT&T are launching facial-recognition software to calculate demographics and store traffic and to send store associates the names of incoming shoppers. The supermarket Walmart has been working on patenting facial-recognition software that can detect a shopper's mood, where the goal is to identify how customers are feeling when something catches their eye enough to buy it. Heralding a new era in personalised shopping and lowering shoplifting threats, this also raises concerns about privacy and, more importantly, about 'Big Brother' kind of monitoring, what racial and gender bias this will perpetuate, and how this will affect people of colour. Facial-recognition software is not free of error. For white men, facial recognition technology is reported to work correctly 99 per cent of the time; for women of colour, it has 35 per cent more errors. For instance, in 2015 Google had to apologise after its image-recognition photo app initially labelled African-Americans as 'gorillas'. Furthermore in 2017, the iPhone Face ID[*] unlock system came under fire when it was realised that it could not tell the Chinese users apart. Many users in China reported that they could unlock each other's phones even when they had vastly different features and haircuts. Apple had bragged that it was the most sophisticated and advanced system they had created. During set-up, the user is required to move the phone in a semi-circular motion around their face to record as many angles as possible, similar to rolling the fingerprint around on Touch ID. When a face-owning human holds up the locked phone, the front-facing TrueDepth camera projects 30,000 invisible dots onto it, creating a depth map that is converted into a mathematical representation, which is compared with the detailed facial data on file. When such an 'advanced' programme fails to differentiate people of a certain minority ethnicity, it is once again symptomatic of the pervasive problem of diversity in the tech and design industry, and we must ask whether the algorithms were ever even designed and trained to recognise Asian facial features. It is symptomatic of the racial bias within society, where certain communities are marginalised and continue to be so even via technology.

Facial-recognition software employing machine learning is being used by police departments across the US. The Perpetual Line-up Project by the Center on Privacy and

---

[*] Face ID, Apple's follow-up to Touch ID, allows users to unlock their phone with a mathematical representation of their facial structure.

Technology at Georgetown Law showed that one in two adults in the US (that is, 117 million people) have their images in a facial-recognition network. Currently, police departments can search these faces without regulation using algorithms that have not been audited for accuracy. Although facial recognition is an important tool and highly beneficial, it also raises important questions about privacy, regulation and consent, and about bias. In 2016, the Government Accountability Office revealed that close to 64 million Americans do not have a say in the matter, as 16 states let the FBI use face-recognition technology to compare the faces of suspected criminals to their driver's licence and ID photos, creating a virtual line-up of their state residents. Historically, FBI fingerprint and DNA databases have been primarily or exclusively made up of information from criminal arrests or investigations. By running face-recognition searches against 16 states' driver's licence photo databases, the FBI has built a biometric network that primarily includes law-abiding Americans. This is unprecedented. Here, in the line-up, it is an algorithm rather than a human being that points to the suspect. We know that face recognition as a technology is not accurate. It is less accurate than fingerprinting, particularly when used in real-time or on large databases, and it is likely to affect those who have darker skin because of their ethnicity. Many police departments do not realise that. In a 'Frequently Asked Questions' document, the Seattle Police Department says that its face-recognition system 'does not see race'. As many of these systems are being trained on previously existing datasets, systems that rely on mug-shot databases are likely to include a disproportionate number of African-Americans in the US due to a disproportionate number of previous arrests skewed in their direction. FBI co-authored research suggests that these systems may be least accurate for African-Americans, women, and young people aged 18–30. Despite these findings, there is no independent testing regime for racially biased error rates. In interviews the Perpetual Line-up researchers found that, despite this evidence of bias, two major face-recognition companies admitted they did not run these tests to make sure that their systems are robust and bias-free.

In the UK, the Metropolitan Police has been testing a version of facial-recognition software, claiming that it could help hunt down wanted offenders and reduce violence. These trials have so far cost more than £222,000 in London. Eight trials carried out in London between 2016 and 2018 resulted in a 96 per cent rate of 'false positives' – where software wrongly alerts police that a person passing through the scanning area matches a photo on the database. It has misidentified members of the public as potential criminals and exhibited racial profiling, which was brought to attention when a 14-year-old black schoolboy was fingerprinted after being misidentified. A parliamentary debate was told that South Wales Police and Leicestershire Police have also used live facial recognition, while other forces use software to compare new images of suspects to their databases. A report from Big Brother Watch* shows that 91 per cent of facial-recognition matches made by South Wales Police led to incorrect identification of innocent people. Facial recognition was introduced in 2014 on the Police National Database (PND), which includes around 13 million faces. The BBC reported that documents from the police, Home Office and university researchers show that police are aware

---

* An independent non-profit organisation leading the protection of privacy and civil liberties in the UK.

ethnicity can have an impact on such systems and cause errors because of embedded bias, but have failed on several occasions to test this. At an April 2014 meeting, Durham Police Chief Constable Mike Barton noted 'that ethnicity can have an impact on search accuracy', and asked the Canadian company managing the police's facial image database to investigate the issue, but subsequent minutes do not mention a follow-up, indicating that this has been ignored. An assessment by Cardiff University researchers found that the effect of racial discrimination was not tested during the trial evaluation period, and an interim report of the Biometrics and Forensics Ethics Group Facial Recognition Working Group in February 2019 (an advisory group to the government) highlighted concerns about the lack of ethnic diversity in datasets. There is an under-representation of a diverse range of faces from different ethnic communities in the database, meaning the bias towards such faces, the bias resulting from the exclusion of certain communities, and the preferential inclusion of others all 'feed forward' into the use of the technology.

While this debate rages in the UK, with protestors claiming that such technologies are an invasion of our basic human rights, there are 170 million CCTV cameras across China. In March 2018, as part of the nationwide monitoring programme 'Skynet', cameras in 16 parts of China were upgraded with automated facial-recognition software, enabling the identification of millions of citizens within a second by the cameras. A Big Brother Watch report from May 2018 states that Chinese developers have even successfully integrated facial recognition into 'smart' sunglasses, enabling the police to patrol Beijing's outskirts and check travellers' identities independently from surveillance cameras. A Human Rights Watch report in

February 2018 warned that this technology isn't limited to catching criminals, as had been claimed. People from minority ethnic backgrounds and dissidents are frequently being targeted. For example, the north-west province Xinjiang has cynically been called a 'Frontline Laboratory for Surveillance', targeting the province's Muslim Uighur minority who can be arrested for suspected political disloyalty or simply expressing their religious and cultural identity. Since around April 2016, Human Rights Watch estimates, Xinjiang authorities have sent tens of thousands of Uighurs and other people from minority ethnic backgrounds to 'political education centres' with the use of such technologies.

The default settings for digital cameras have a tradition of privileging lighter skin. Colour film was built for white people. Professor Lorna Roth, whose work we considered in Chapter 8, has also looked at how there has been a light-skin bias embedded in digital camera design. She quotes Jan Kasoff, former cameraman for NBC New York, from her personal communication in 20 November 1994: 'a good VCR person will have a colour girl stand in front of the cameras and stay there while the technicians focus on her flesh tones to do their fine adjustments to balance the cameras. This colour girl is always white.' The sensitivity of film emulsions and dynamic ranges, i.e. the difference between the lightest and the darkest of colours, has been problematic in the digital media sphere to capture darker skin, especially when there is a very dark-skinned person sitting next to a very pale-skinned person. The reason for this is the global assumption of 'whiteness' that has been embedded in the film chemistry, photo lab procedures, video screen colour-balancing practices, and digital cameras in general, and in the expected ensemble of practices. Thierry Le Brun, an independent cinematographer, calls this a sign of 'technological unconscious', which is an apparent lack of awareness of the dominance of whiteness in the cognitive patterns of people, impacting the design of technology.

Self-driving cars are believed to be the next big thing. The last time I was in California, everyone was talking about them and they were being trialled along the West Coast. But algorithmic bias means that these cars are more likely to hit people with darker skin, due to racial bias in their object-detection system. Georgia Institute of Technology researchers have shown that the sensors and cameras of such vehicles detect lighter-skinned pedestrians more easily. The algorithms are trained on real-life datasets, and they learn from the information they are given. So if they are not shown images of women with darker skin during the learning and training phase, they are less able to recognise them. The object-detection models had mostly been trained on examples of light-skinned pedestrians, and the models didn't place enough weight on learning from the few examples of dark-skinned people that were included. This means a self-driven automated car potentially carries a violent bias to accidentally run over disadvantaged minority groups more than other socially advantaged racial groups.

Besides racial and gender bias, the need for more stratified validation of such systems also surfaced in a study showing that YouTube's automated captioning system was unable to recognise certain dialects as well as others. A linguistic study by Rachael Tatman from the University of Washington across two genders and five linguistic variations of spoken English revealed lower accuracy for women and for speakers from Scotland, even though the overall accuracy of automatic speech recognition (ASR) has increased substantially over the past decade with a word error rate (WER) of just 6.3 per cent on the Switchboard

corpus, compared to an ASR error rate of 27 per cent just
a decade ago. A total of 80 speakers were sampled for this
project. Videos for eight men and eight women from each
dialect region were included: California, Georgia, New
England (Maine and New Hampshire), New Zealand and
Scotland. These regions were chosen based on their high
degree of geographic separation from each other, distinct
local regional dialects and (relatively) comparable
populations. It is possible that the reason for errors between
genders was the way the automated system was trained for
a particular pitch. As we have seen in Chapter 10, pitch
differences are one of the most reliable and well-studied
perceptual markers of gender in speech. There is no distinct
difference between the various linguistic dialects in terms
of intelligibility, so one of the reasons for this error-rate
difference is that any bias in the training data will be
embedded in a system trained on it. Much like many other
AI and automated systems, the system behind YouTube's
automatic captions is propriety – a 'black box' – and
impenetrable, so it is not possible to validate this theory.
However, knowing what we know about the bias in
technology, and the notion of coded gaze, it is possible to
reliably propose that the problem lies with the lack of
stratified validation of these systems across a diverse
population.

In a video that went viral in 2017, a soap dispenser was
shown as unable to recognise a darker-skinned hand. The
soap dispenser was created by a company called Technical
Concepts, and this simple technology shows the endemic
problem where no one at the company thinks it relevant to
test their products on darker skin. This results in a
discriminatory soap dispenser, which demonstrates the
inherent culture of 'whiteness' in the tech industry and the
racial bias, but also makes people with darker skin feel

excluded and 'othered', reinforcing that they are not the norm.

★★★

We know that technology can be racist and sexist. Using technology and AI isn't the panacea to resolving or bypassing our implicit biases. Instead, they imitate the biases of the design team and wider society, they inherit the biases in the dataset they have learned and trained on, and they bring these biases to the decision-making process. If the design team is not diverse, they have cognitive blind spots. The team is unlikely to even consider the lack of inclusivity or the bias they are embedding in the technology they are creating. One of the solutions could be to focus on collecting unbiased socially stratified samples for training the datasets. Most of AI technology is like a black box. Besides replicating biases by reusing previously existing models and algorithms, many of these systems have such complicated and convoluted sets of algorithms that humans have little to no understanding of how they work. Both Nisheeth Vishnoi and Elisa Celis told me that in order to ensure the AI systems we create do not replicate our biases, we need to understand how AI systems work and arrive at their decisions. The problem remains that there is still little understanding as to how we can tackle and combat cognitive biases in a systematic and methodical way. Speaking to many in the tech industry, and those working in Silicon Valley, I hear stories of urgent deadlines and move-fast culture where, much like the space-war between the US and Russia in the 1960s, investment depends on turning ideas into operational products before a competitor does. This kind of culture does not permit the pauses needed for us to combat some of our cognitive biases. The industry is also overtly reliant on data that is easily available – an example of 'availability bias' discussed in Chapter 5.

There have been some recent attempts in the academic domain to de-bias the algorithms. For instance, a team from Boston University and Microsoft research looked at word embeddings, the framework used to represent text data as vectors in machine leaning and then used as a sort of dictionary for the computer programme. Any gender bias in these word correlations – such as the word 'computer programmer' being more semantically related to a 'man' – reflects the gender bias in the society but is then amplified through its use in a machine-learning algorithm. The team used real people to identify the types of word connections that are appropriate (brother/sister, king/queen) and those that should be removed from the huge datasets used to train the AI systems (such as woman/homemaker). Using these human-generated distinctions, they then set the parameters for removing any such biased relationships and found that the algorithm no longer exhibited blatant gender stereotypes. This approach was carried out only for English terms, and the team is investigating how it can be extended to other languages as well as to racial and cultural stereotypes. While there has been much debate in the AI community about whether there is really a need to de-bias algorithms since they inevitably reflect the bias in the society, the researchers here agree that 'At the very least, machine learning should not be used to inadvertently amplify these biases.' The scalability of such approaches is still under consideration and, while this is a significant step forward, it does not absolve the individual organisations who apply and develop the machine-learning technology from taking necessary steps to guard against any bias.

Technological organisations need to make a commitment to equality and fairness in their teams and in their processes.

Social media platforms have to take responsibility and accountability for mitigating societal biases, abusive behaviour and language, and for the algorithmic bias that results in partisan echo chambers. And there has to be more transparency in the design of systems and services that rely on machine learning and AI. For instance, IBM has been looking at dataset bias pertaining to not only gender and skin type but also to age groups, ethnicities and factors such as pose, illumination, resolution, expression and decoration (from IBM report, February 2018). They have been creating a million-scale dataset of face images annotated with attributes and identity, with geo-tags from Flickr images to balance data from multiple countries to minimise sample-selection bias.

It might appear to be a bleak picture, but it is crucial that we understand that technology doesn't exist in a silo. It cannot be a black box. I am not a technophobe; I am exactly the opposite. I am hugely concerned by the socio-technical responsibility of tech and AI, and the notion of fairness and discrimination within these systems. How can we trust AI systems, and how do we engender true diversity and inclusivity? Face recognition is a long-standing challenge, and with the recent advances in neural networks, it is becoming more accurate. However, it is still failing to capture the diversity in faces. Faces are so personal, and faces are unique, but we do not have systems to capture and then parameterize this uniqueness and variation. Much of our technology is still data-driven. Bad training data can lead to higher error rates and biased decision-making. Data is a mere snapshot of the real world. It is one single story, and we know that when we only listen to one story, we are more prone to succumb to the stereotypes deeply entrenched in our society and to fall back on our implicit biases. But the problem also lies in how we expect technology to solve our problems, including that of the implicit biases affecting our decision-making, and in how we trust technology to make rational decisions on our behalf, eliminating any human errors. Yet, as technology explodes, we are lagging behind in having a considered discussion about the ethics and moralistic implications of the use of technology and AI. And, in doing so, we are missing an opportunity to create interventions that would truly make a difference in addressing and mitigating human biases.

CHAPTER TWELVE
# Good Intentions

As we arrive at the final chapter, I am sure you will agree that unconscious biases are even more pervasive than we thought.

Study after study, and deep-dives into various datasets, show overwhelming evidence of racial and gender disparities in health, wealth, policing, education, employment and virtually every measurable index of aggregated well-being. Yet the refrain that there is no bias persists. Someone recently sent me a strongly worded message to prove that there is no inequality and therefore no need to consider implicit bias. In this they quoted a recent research study,* which shows that now '*most* of Americans' think that women are '*as* competent as men'. How wonderful that we are celebrating women being 'almost' as equal 'as men'! This cross-temporal meta-analyses of US public opinion polls from 1946 to 2018 shows that belief in women's competence has increased from 35 per cent to 86 per cent, and these stats are being used across media to represent the leaps we have made in addressing any gender bias. The study shows that, despite

---

* Alice Eagly and her colleagues at Northwestern University examined public opinion polls representing the views of more than 30,000 adults from 1946 to 2018, looking specifically at how they rated communion (compassion, sensitivity, warmth); agency (ambition, aggression, assertiveness); and competency (intelligence, organisation, creativity) along gender lines.

this change in attitude, women are still pushed in certain niches such as communal and service-based roles, and their agency or the perception of them as leaders has not changed much. Even as women have more choice of profession, and as they step into traditional male-dominated domains such as lawyers and managers, they are still constrained to lower-level positions. Women are being rewarded and celebrated for their competence but not for their leadership. Alice Eagly calls this the emergence of 'female ghettos', where women are restricted to jobs with lower authority, where primarily social skills are rewarded, and with low promotability (for instance, serving on committees, which is not seen to bring any rewards in terms of career advancement). This study does not consider intersectionality at all, in terms of race, ethnicity, disability and sexual preferences, so such stereotypes could not be investigated. No doubt this will have a huge impact on how competence and leadership potential is perceived within and between the groups. While maintaining men as the norm against which women's competence is compared ('as competent as men'), we are also still focusing on gender binaries and not even beginning to collect detailed data on or have an in-depth discussion about the prejudice and discrimination that non-binary or gender-queer people face in everyday life. So, though it is a dramatic shift and we should celebrate this change in attitudes, we should not rejoice just yet.

In this closing chapter, I address some of the critiques of implicit biases in recent years, and discuss our moral and ethical responsibility about something that is 'beyond our conscious control', before finally proposing some ways in which implicit bias can be minimised.

One of the criticisms people make of implicit bias is that the social inequalities it attempts to explain just do not exist. I hear this argument a lot – from people who tell me there is no racism because the society is so multicultural or that they have so many friends from different ethnic communities. I hear that we cannot be sexist because women have more freedom than ever, women are leading organisations and companies and working side by side with men everywhere, they are free to move, and they have financial freedom. We don't need to talk about implicit biases, I've been told. There may be people who believe all the systemic inequities discussed in this book are just incidental. Some also assert that, although there are inequalities in that some people are taller or prettier than others, there is no injustice due to this difference and it does not create any inequity; rather it is a matter of perception. However, as we know, diversity simply does not equate to inclusivity or equality, and merely having an equal representation does not give everyone an equal opportunity. Giving everyone a seat at the table is not enough; their voice has to be heard too.

Since the election of President Trump and the growth of far-right political movements in Europe, some critics assert that we don't need implicit bias to explain contemporary discrimination and inequality, as explicit bias can do the explaining. For example, science blogger Jesse Singal points to the Justice Department's report that the Ferguson[*] police and court officials engaged in widespread intentional

---

[*] Michael Brown, an unarmed black teenager, was shot and killed on 9 August 2014 by Darren Wilson, a white police officer, in Ferguson, a suburb of St. Louis in Missouri. The shooting prompted protests. On 24 November, the St. Louis County prosecutor announced that a grand jury had decided not to indict Mr Wilson. The announcement set off another wave of protests. In March, the Justice Department called on Ferguson to overhaul its criminal justice system, declaring that the city had engaged in constitutional violations.

race-based discrimination. He wrote in 2016, 'It might be advantageous to various people to say implicit bias rather than explicit bias is the most important thing to focus on, but that doesn't make it true – a point driven home, perhaps, by the fact that the United States just elected one of the more explicitly racist presidential candidates in recent history.' Fair point, but would people who voted for Trump admit to being racist? I don't believe many would, and Trump recently said that accusations of him being a racist are biased, claiming 'I am the least racist president ever.' Either he is saying things to evoke a reaction, creating partisan out-group behaviours by capitalising on herd mentality, primal fears and biases, or he is completely unaware that his behaviour is in fact discriminatory and biased. Recently, we were witness to videos of a Trump rally in the arena of East Carolina University where loud aggressive chants of 'send her home' rang out as Trump singled out Somali-born Representative Ilhan Omar. This racially charged rally cry is not the first of its kind. There has been an anti-immigrant rhetoric resonating from the White House since Trump's presidential election, and he made immigration the centre point of his campaign. The racist behaviour this has led to was also recently seen in the El Paso shootings in August 2019. Although it is an explicit bias seen through words and actions, and it is increasingly being normalised, the fact remains that these messages are now undoubtedly seeping into the unconscious of those who previously believed themselves to be fair and just.

As I write this, the Netherlands has just announced a ban on face-covering in government buildings, hospitals and public transports, including the hijab – the Muslim veil. The Netherlands has a population of around 17 million, of which 900,000 are Muslims or of Muslim origin. Critics of the law stated that it was motivated by anti-Muslim sentiment and was racially driven, but advocates of the law maintain it was not directed towards Muslims in particular and argue that it is purely politically motivated. These are not mutually exclusive. In either case, it is pandering to the whims of the far right and reeks of Islamophobia. It is a clear indication of the racial bias so endemic in society that authorities justify policing some communities more than others. While some might (correctly) argue that this is explicit prejudice and discrimination, it also definitely comes from an implicit bias that Muslims' rituals and beliefs are not of as much value and that they do not have a place in society. It does not meet with larger societal norms and can therefore be stigmatised. We could go into a wider discussion concerning the oppression associated with the veil in certain cultures, but these are systemic and cultural gendered norms that are not relevant to this public ban, as the veil is a choice for many women (even if, for some people, it might seem to be a manifestation of centuries of cultural oppression). The ban will no doubt 'other' a specific community and it will make them feel isolated and marginalised. This will also limit their involvement and engagement in public life, which constrains the contribution that they can make to society, consequently affirming the perception that they are not of as much value to society. It will also perpetuate the implicit biases and stereotypes of Muslim women, and those who choose to wear the hijab, bringing both race and gender into this discourse. Moreover, this law predominantly affects women, thereby creating more gender inequity, and allows women to be policed. This is why talking about and understanding the intersectionality in unconscious bias is so crucial. And, while an act of discrimination is explicit, it is grounded in an implicit bias and its repercussions are far-reaching. As we have repeatedly seen, this is a self-fulfilling prophecy whereby, once this cycle of disadvantage is established, it creates more bias and discrimination against those who have been marginalised. It can also lead to their disenfranchisement, which can confirm their isolation and peripheral status.

Racism is a card that is increasingly being played whether we admit it or not, and not just in this unequivocally explicit manner but also in more subversive forms in real and virtual interactions. Results from an anonymous internet survey I conducted in early 2019 were startling: almost 150 people of colour from across the UK responded to this online survey, and 98 per cent of these had faced some sort of racially motivated verbal or physical attack in the last 12 months in the UK. People from minority communities – especially those who stand out because of their skin colour in predominantly white spaces – are hyper-aware of their presence, mindful of their actions and interactions, and conscious of the looks, glances and glares that tell them often without words that they do not belong. Someone spelling or saying their name incorrectly or someone making fun of their dress or religion – while making excuses and justifying it as humour – are some of the many micro-incivilities that are being played out across workplaces and public settings. Needless to say, this is reinforcing the divisions and intra-group hostilities. It isn't of value to debate whether implicit bias is more important than explicit bias, but what is crucial to acknowledge is that it exists, and that it can be more dangerous and harmful than overt forms of discrimination because often people who claim to be unbiased can also partake in discriminatory behaviour without sometimes even being aware of it or considering it to be discriminatory. For instance, making fun of someone's accent, height or ethnicity is not a joke. The intention might not be malicious, and it is often borne out of ignorance, but such comments tend to reinforce the differences and the non-conformity of any minority community from the majority demographic. Language is a powerful medium through which unconscious bias and prejudice against certain nationalities are reinforced. These jokes alienate people and make them feel isolated and different. As we become more aware and prohibitive of explicit forms of bias and prejudice, aversive forms of discrimination are becoming more rife. People talk about the huge numbers of people of all races who co-exist, without considering their own privilege that they bring with them to this discussion.

There is a long-standing debate in social science research about whether societal outcomes are caused by social institutions and structures or by the psychological make-up and behaviour of individuals within society. Some people would argue that, although inequalities exist, they can be easily explained by structural bias. The structuralists – those who are anti-individualists – believe that implicit bias results from social inequalities rather than explains them.[*] I personally don't agree that only social norms, and not individually biased minds, are the cause of injustices and inequalities in the world. For instance, it has been suggested that the only cause of racial discrimination in the United States is racial segregation followed by accumulation of privilege (in the form of wealth and property) along racial lines. Some people even claim that 'black culture' is the cause of this racial inequality. But, as we have seen, numerous studies and datasets have shown that disparity and inequality exist, and it is difficult to explain this from a purely structural point of view without considering

---

[*] While it is an important critique, there is no space in this book to discuss this stream of thought from Marx to situationists.

implicit bias and prejudice. I believe that psychological bias and societal norms and practices interact to create inequities, and neither is more significant than the other; rather they act together to create outcomes that are different in different contexts. Michael Brownstein, a philosopher based in the United States, provides an example of this:

> If you wanted to combat housing segregation, you would want to consider not only problematic institutional practices, such as 'red-lining' certain neighbourhoods within which banks will not give mortgage loans, and not only psychological factors, such as the propensity to perceive low-income people as untrustworthy, but the interaction of the two. A low-income person from a red-lined neighbourhood might not be perceived as untrustworthy when they are interviewing for a job as a nanny, but might be perceived as untrustworthy when they are interviewing for a loan.

Individual implicit biases, as we have seen, can underlie large-scale social and structural inequalities. The social norms might be the same for all, but when an individual does not meet these normative standards, they can be stigmatised. Also, these norms can be applied to different people in different ways to create entirely different outcomes.

★★★

There has been criticism of the way implicit bias is measured and of the reliability of such tests, and assertions that implicit bias is 'false science' because it cannot be measured accurately. There is continuing debate around whether the results of cognitive measurements (such as the many discussed in this book involving sequential priming tasks) really show us an individual's inner attitudes and beliefs or whether they are instead the products of the cultural environment. Within implicit bias research, the Implicit Association Test (IAT) is considered an integral psychometric tool that can be used to measure implicit attitudes, and most people who deliver unconscious bias training promote this as part of their educational programmes. IAT has also been hyped up in the media and by business professionals, garnering attention worldwide. There have been many adaptations and versions of IAT measuring body bias and gender, but the first was a race IAT focusing primarily on black–white race relations.* In a basic sense, IAT measures our cognitive association between different terms and how closely our brains link concepts such as 'blacks and bad' and 'women and passive'. As we have repeatedly seen, the science underlying cognitive associations indicate that people are quicker and more fluent with those concepts that are higher in their cognitive hierarchy and to which they assign more importance. So, if a person is quicker to associate good words with white faces than good words with black faces, the IAT test shows that the person has a slight, moderate or strong 'preference for white faces over black faces', depending on the time taken to react to the images on the computer screen.

Although the developers caution against certain interpretations of the test, the research that has been carried out evaluating IAT and highlighting its weaknesses isn't widely available or understood, so coverage of the test often

---

* There have been other versions in different racial contexts. German researchers have used IAT to test how ethnic Germans respond to German-sounding names vs Turkish-sounding ones, since Turks are the largest minority ethnic group in Germany and face various challenges to fair treatment. Here much of the literature critiquing IAT refers primarily to the original version of IAT focusing on black vs white race attitudes.

states that if a person gets a high IAT score it means they are implicitly biased against a minority group. But what IAT measures is a reaction time and there can be various physiological and environmental effects on this in real time. Furthermore, there is no indication of why this reaction time tells us anything more about our automatic cognitive biases, or how they could – or would – impact our actions and behaviour. Meta-analysis of numerous studies and datasets has shown that the power of IAT to predict some specific behaviour is, on average, not very significant. The analysis also show that the test is too noisy (it includes data distortions) to gauge usefully and accurately people's likelihood of engaging in discrimination. IAT results do not correlate reliably with related behavioural outcomes. Other critics of IAT say the test is measuring external attitudes rather than internal automatic and implicit ones. There is no reliable empirical and statistical evidence to show that IAT is really measuring our implicit biases. Also, IAT does not show test-retest reliability,* which means that if you took an IAT test today and then again in a few weeks' time, your results would not be

---

* Hypothetically, if the IAT had a test-retest reliability of $r = 1$, and you administered the test to five people over and over and over, they'd be placed in the same order (least to most implicitly biased) every time. At the other end of the spectrum, when $r = 0$, the ranking shifts every time the test is administered, completely at random. Surprisingly the developers have not published this data for the IAT even though it is a crucial parameter for most psychological tests. Some studies indicate that $r = .32$ in a study consisting of four race IAT sessions conducted with two weeks between each; $r = .65$ in a study in which two tests were conducted 24 hours apart; and $r = .39$ in a study in which the two tests were conducted during the same session. Yoav Bar-Anan and Brian Nosek reported a race IAT test-retest reliability of $r = .4$. This is much lower than any standards and shows that the test is not reliable.

identical. The test measures speed of association (such as how quickly one relates a positive or negative association to African-Americans as compared to European-Americans) and gives a score on a scale of -2.0 to +2.0, with anything above +0.65 or below -0.65 indicating a 'strong' link. The test results are used to give feedback on your implicit attitudes. The problem is in how this feedback is worded so, rather than using it merely as another diagnostic tool with probabilistic measurements, people are likely to use it as a conclusive outlook on the implicit biases they carry, especially in workplace discrimination settings and legal proceedings. The test depends on our social settings and the way we have been primed, so any information around us in our environment can affect our decisions too. The test has been used and promoted heavily and considered as the most reliable measure of implicit bias. Consequently, any rigorous critiques of the test – and even admissions from the developers that it was not tested rigorously before it was released to the public – have not gained much attention.

IAT is contributing to the discussion, and admittedly it can still be used to indicate the level of bias in society rather than individual level measurements accurately. It is also a good indicator of how our cognitive associations might reflect our unconscious biases, and it is 'better than a self-report at predicting behaviour', as the IAT developers claim, but it is not a reliable measure of implicit bias. It does not give us an insight into the unconscious biases that we carry. I want to include this here because it pains me to see reports and articles talking about IAT as some sort of magic wand that will 'cure' individuals of their implicit biases and prejudices. It worries me that IAT can be used to set anti-discrimination laws and standards in organisations without an understanding of what the test is really showing or its reliability. We have to take IAT and its results with a pinch of salt. There is so much to uncover in the way IAT is designed and the misinformation around its efficacy that it is impractical to cover it all here. What is important for anyone interested in implicit bias training and mitigation is that the use of IAT will not help you bust or eradicate any biases. Its use as an educational tool is also debatable, it is not a panacea to all of society's biases, and it will not help 'train' people in addressing their unconscious biases.

★★★

Last, but not in any way least, we turn to a discussion of unconscious bias from a moral and ethical perspective. If we don't know about it, are we really morally responsible for actions that are based on our unconscious beliefs and biases? Michael Brownstein and I discussed whether having negative associations makes us wicked. Some people believe that just because people have negative biases against others does not necessarily make them prejudiced. Philosophers and cognitive psychologists have debated the issues of knowledge and control in the formation of implicit bias. Keith Payne and Bertram Gawronski from the University of North Carolina consider this as a matter of understanding virtue, and the roots of this debate can be traced back as far as ancient Greece. Plato argued that virtue is about developing the right inclinations or motives, so a virtuous person has good inclinations, whereas a wicked person has evil inclinations. By contrast, in the Aristotelian tradition it is believed that both good and bad people sometimes have wicked impulses, and that virtue is a measure of how well these can be regulated and channelled. As per Natalia Washington and Daniel Kelly, philosophers based at Purdue University, an individual agent is morally responsible for an action if they have knowledge of what they are doing and have the ability and agency to choose an alternative action. In the case of explicitly held beliefs, these are both true. However, in the case of implicit biases, it is tricky to assign culpability of action as this is 'opaque to introspection' and operates automatically without the conscious control of the individual.

Even as we debate the nature and extent of this moral responsibility, Brownstein says that most philosophers will agree that all individuals bear some moral responsibility for actions that result from these beliefs, even when they explicitly claim to have no racist or sexist beliefs. Again, the context matters a lot, which Natalia Washington and Daniel Kelly refer to as 'responsibility externalist', where the extent of societal discourse around biases and equality must determine an individual's responsivity and their role. The social knowledge that individuals gain from such discussions and information is called their 'outside of head' knowledge, which is also a factor in determining the extent and nature of their responsibility. This is why discourse occurring in this domain is important: in examining it, a knowledge framework is being created within which we start holding people morally responsible and accountable for their implicitly held beliefs and any prejudicial and discriminatory actions resulting from this bias. We can do this while not attributing bias to these individuals, so that the focus remains on the harmful effect of their actions rather than the focus being primarily on making the biased individual feel guilty or legally responsible for their unconscious biases. Then again, as soon as we become aware of our beliefs and stereotypes but do nothing to minimise them, we are completely morally responsible for any actions that result from such stereotypical beliefs.

Clea Rees, a researcher at Cardiff University, proposes that bias can be changed by developing 'automatised egalitarian commitments', where a focus on virtue can reliably guide cognitive processing. I am sceptical that this approach alone can solve the problem, but it is worth a try. There is a broad agreement among academics and philosophers that the moral responsibility concerning implicit bias varies according to context. It also depends more on harm rather than intention. For me, personal intention matters because the assessment of harm can often be subjective. It will vary depending on the perception of the harmed individual as opposed to that of the person inflicting harm. But the intention is one that can manifest in numerous ways, and this is what underlies the issues surrounding stereotype threat that we have discussed at length.

Unconscious bias works in perplexing ways. Recently, while out with my children, we had an encounter with an elderly couple who screamed at them for being too loud and at us to keep them under control. My three-year-olds were completely taken aback and stunned into silence. I felt my face burning and my eyes filling up with tears as this woman stared at me with contempt. It is impossible to say whether race played a role and if this (white) woman would have behaved any differently if I was white. Did she feel entitled to judge me and my parenting, did she feel some kind of supremacy over me, and did it annoy her more because I was a 'foreigner' – an outsider – due to my skin colour (even though I am British and so are my kids)? I posted about this on Twitter, and there was a show of support, with several parents telling me that their (white) children were 'feral' and loud but had never had this kind of reaction from anyone in a public place. Many assumed that I and my children weren't British and were just visiting the UK, and reassured me that I was welcome in this country (*my* country, I might add!). While supportive and kind, their messages were also rooted in many assumptions created as a result of stereotypes they imposed on me merely from my profile picture on social media (brown skin = a foreigner). One woman told me that American (white) children are taught to be quiet, while her many Afghan friends brought up their children to be quite 'wild'. She could not understand why it was inappropriate to draw this conclusion even when it was gently explained to her by several people. This was a cultural assumption and a racist trope, drawn from a very limited sample size of a few non-white 'Afghan' acquaintances that she had. Here, several different kinds and layers of implicit attitudes were revealed. Are non-white individuals policed to different standards in public spaces and predominantly white spaces? Does their skin colour set some specific parenting standards and expectations? And do people feel justified in judging women more easily for their parenting, especially if they are non-white?

★★★

This book looks at the past and the future, at how evolution might have shaped our biases, and at how tech can further perpetuate these biases. As we move increasingly towards a tech- and data-driven society and communicate largely via social media channels, an understanding of our echo chambers, groupthink and filter bubbles becomes crucial. This will help us understand how our implicit biases shape the way information is now being shared, what information we trust, and how the way we create content and spread it reinforces the systemic biases that are entrenched in our society. This book also shows how the collection and design of data, and the way it is mined in machine-learning algorithms, can demonstrate the implicit biases that exist in our society, with some communities and groups better represented than others. A better understanding of the biases that exist within our technology and the way that tech can contribute towards creating these discriminations will be very helpful in campaigning for better technology and non-biased social media platforms. Tech companies and social media channels have to take as much responsibility for societal injustices as individuals. This is becoming an urgent concern, especially as we are now in a world where deep-fake technology is creating an alternative reality so that the lines between 'what really happened' and 'what we believe happened' are blurring further and faster than ever before.

Understanding more about unconscious bias is not going to magically fix all the injustices in the world. But, if we start becoming more aware of our unconscious bias and what triggers when we are most vulnerable to it, we will become more attuned to the consequences of externalising our unconscious biases in the form of behavioural outcomes. And if we actively exercise strategies to mitigate and counter our unconscious biases, we can hopefully finally put a dent in them.

Hopefully this book has done what it set out to do, explaining these multiple levels of inequality from a scientific as well as a social perspective, and highlighting some of the myriad ways these injustices manifest in the form of prejudice and discrimination. What I have also attempted to focus on is the intersectionality of these implicit biases that affect every walk of life, and how it creates privilege and opportunities for some but not for others due to an associated attribute that is considered less socially normative or desirable. This intersectionality of inequities in gender, sexuality, class, race, education, age, appearance, accent and so on has often been ignored in implicit bias research and discourse. The goal of intersectional analysis is not an inter-category comparison but more of a focus on intra-category heterogeneity, its origins and its consequences.

The focus on implicit bias might seem like a risk. It can be seen as muddying the structural and systemic issues by placing a larger emphasis on individual agency. What we ought to remember is that unfair biases can reflect institutionally constructed reality, and any discriminatory attitudes are confirmed by implicit biases. There is a continuing debate about the nature of implicit bias in whether any training or measure reveals an error in our memory representations or whether they are situation and context dependent, and whether any such prejudices are cultural artefacts or personal attributions. Researchers are grappling with the issue of whether our implicit beliefs tell us something about the individual or about their environment. I would say both.

# De-biasing 101

## So how do we tackle unconscious bias?

Unconscious bias is not just a 'trend', although there is a real danger of it becoming so. It is crucial that we use any understanding of implicit bias, training and measurement of our implicit attitudes as the foundation for further interventions in actively denigrating harmful stereotypes. Training does not work without a change of attitudes and addressing systemic inequalities, which are often the result of stereotypes too. Taking our time with important decisions can help us de-automatize. This means that we do not fall back on our unconscious biases, but instead activate our logical and rational thinking and actively bust any biases that can affect our decisions.

Being aware of how our own implicit biases are shaped by our own upbringing and our life experiences can help us minimise these in our roles as parents, carers, friends and educators. This is crucial so that parents and educators can limit the transmission of bias. One way that I encourage adults to break this cycle of gendered norms and stereotypes is via the moderation of information related to social categories in their language. So rather than using generic language such as 'boys like dinosaurs' or 'girls like pink', they could signify that a particular attribute is associated to an individual rather than to their whole group, such as '*This* boy is good at maths.' In the first case, the words signify that such attributes are enduring properties of the whole group, and highlights group differences while also

SWAY

signifying to children that such group distinctions are meaningful and important. In the second case, essentialist tendencies and stereotypes can be reduced and the formation of rigid social group boundaries avoided. This will minimise in-group and out-group behaviour as well as the need and expectation to conform to any pre-existing and normative standards.

It is important to create safe, non-judgemental spaces in an organisation to discuss this. It is also important to criticise the microaggression rather than the microaggressor so that the focus remains on how that statement has made the other person feel rather than apportioning blame. If you are the microaggressor, use empathy and do not get defensive. Try to acknowledge and recognise your unconscious biases, reflect on them and the hurt your words might have caused. For others, it is important to act as an ally rather than speaking out for someone else who has suffered microaggression, since this is an act of aggression itself, dehumanising them and indicating that they do not have their own voice and cannot stand up for themselves. Microaggressions are causes and symptoms of larger systemic and structural problems. Calling out microaggressions can serve as a deterrent. Accountability and empathy together can help to create more thoughtful and inclusive communication across all the divides of race, gender, sexual orientation and gender identity. Overall, it is important to recognise that jokes about anyone's race, gender, ethnicity or sexual orientation are never OK. They perpetuate the racism and sexism that exists in this society and, even though they might seem harmless, they reinforce discrimination and prejudice.

To avoid confirmation bias during hiring and recruitment, write an inclusive job description – language matters. Use gender-neutral descriptions and avoid gender-coded words. Research has also shown that women are less like to apply for jobs that have a very long list of 'desirable' qualities, as they do not wish to waste the employer's time if they are not perfectly suited to the role. Women are also less likely to shout about their achievements and to negotiate salaries. To avoid bias, name- and gender-blind reviewing of résumés has shown to be most effective. Researchers from Harvard and Princeton found that blind auditions increased the likelihood that women musicians would be hired by an orchestra by 25 to 46 per cent.

In terms of unconscious bias training, I like to follow a 'prejudice-breaking' approach, adapted from a workshop that was first designed by Patricia Devine and colleagues to address gender bias in STEM and technology. The workshop operates on the principle that formation of stereotypes is a habit and, much like any other habit, it needs active intervention to break it. It works on a three-pronged approach of de-automatization, perspective-taking and active denigration. This includes a conscious attempt to visualise another person's viewpoint and can be particularly effective in reducing implicit bias in social interactions. In a related study, nurses were shown pictures of either white or black patients with genuine expressions of pain and asked how much pain medication they recommended. Nurses told to use their best judgement recommended significantly more pain medication for white than black patients, whereas nurses instructed to imagine how the patient felt recommended equal treatment regardless of race. In the second case, the nurses were being trained to see the problem from a patient's perspective.

Role models and representation matter because when we see them we can begin to individuate, question pre-existing stereotypes, and visualise from another person's perspective. Invisibility contributes to marginalisation and stigmatisation of a group. However, diversity should never be merely a box-ticking exercise. True inclusivity happens when people are given equal voice. And sometimes, to overturn the tide of oppression and marginalisation through history, positive discrimination might be necessary. Equality is not equity. People have to start from the same place for them to be equal.

Finally, unconscious bias is never an excuse for discriminatory behaviour. Not every bias is unconscious and outside the control of the person. There are biases that we can control once we are aware of the way they influence our decisions. Unconscious bias training does not exonerate an individual from taking responsibility for their actions and their role in creating inequities and amplifying injustice.

# Appendix

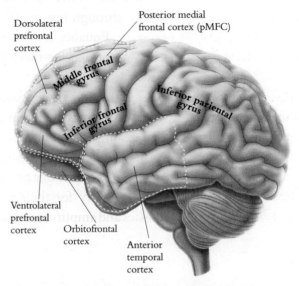

Dorsolateral prefrontal cortex

Posterior medial frontal cortex (pMFC)

Middle frontal gyrus

Inferior frontal gyrus

Inferior parietal gyrus

Ventrolateral prefrontal cortex

Orbitofrontal cortex

Anterior temporal cortex

**Gross Topography of the brain**

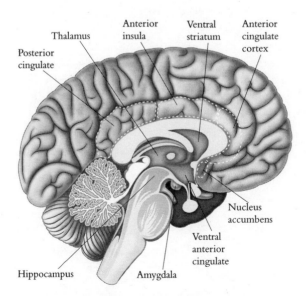

Thalamus

Anterior insula

Ventral striatum

Anterior cingulate cortex

Posterior cingulate

Nucleus accumbens

Ventral anterior cingulate

Hippocampus

Amygdala

**Medial Section of the brain**

# References

Several hundreds of scientific studies, research papers and books, social media feeds and more mainstream publications were referred to while writing this book. Where possible, I have included names and details within the text. For reasons of space, I am unable to catalogue the complete list of references and include only a few that I refer to in most detail.

## Chapter 1

Allport, G.W. (1954). *The Nature of Prejudice*. Reading, MA: Addison-Wesley.

Chabris, C. F., and Simons, D.J. (2010). *The invisible gorilla: And other ways our intuitions deceive us*. New York: Harper Collins.

Cialdini, R.B., and Goldstein, N.J. (2004). Social influence: Compliance and conformity. *Annual Review of Psychology*, 55, 591–621.

Gadenne, V., and Oswald, M. (1986). 'Entstehung und Veränderung von Bestätigungstendenzen beim Testen von Hypothesen [Formation and alteration of confirmatory tendencies during the testing of hypotheses]'. *Zeitschrift für Experimentelle und Angewandte Psychologie*, 33: 360–374 via Oswald & Grosjean 2004, p. 89.

Greenwald, A.G., & Banaji, M.R. (1995). Implicit social cognition: Attitudes, self-esteem, and stereotypes. *Psychological Review*, 102, 4–27.

Greenwald, A.G., Banaji, M.R., Rudman, L.A., Farnham, S.D., Nosek, B.A. and Rosier, M. (in press). Prologue to a unified theory of attitudes, stereotypes, and self-concept. In: Forgas, J.P. (Ed.), *Feeling and thinking: The role of affect in social cognition and behavior*. New York: Cambridge University Press.

Greenwald, A.G., McGhee, D. and Schwartz, J.L.K. (1998). Measuring individual differences in implicit cognition: The Implicit Association Test. *Journal of Personality and Social Psychology*, 74, 1464–1480.

Newstead, S. (2003). 'Peter Wason (1924–2003)'. *Thinking and Reasoning*, 9 (3): 177–184.

Popper, K.R. (1959). *The logic of scientific discovery*. London: Hutchinson.

Sanderson, C. A. (2010). *Social psychology*. Hoboken, N.J.: Wiley.

Simon, Herbert A. (1990). Invariants of Human Behavior. *Annual Review of Psychology*, 41:1, 1–20.

Wason, P.C. and Johnson-Laird, P.N. (1968). *Thinking and reasoning*, (Eds.), Harmondsworth, UK.

## Chapter 2

Bar-Tal, D., and Labin, D. (2001). The effect of a major event on stereotyping: Terrorist attacks in Israel and Israeli adolescents' perceptions of Palestinians, Jordanians, and Arabs. *European Journal of Social Psychology*, 31, 265–280.

Chakraborty, R. (2017). A Short Note on Accent–bias, Social Identity and Ethnocentrism Department of Communication Disorders, *Advances in Language and Literary studies*, Vol. 8. No. 4.

Fiske, S.T., Cuddy, A.J.C., and Glick, P. (2006). Universal dimensions of social perception: warmth, then competence, *Trends in Cognitive Science*. Vol. 11, No. 2.

Haselton, M.G., and Buss, D.M. (2009). Error management theory and the evolution of misbeliefs. *Behavioral and Brain Sciences*, 32 (6): 522–523.

Henrich, N., and Henrich, J. (2007). *Why humans cooperate: A cultural and evolutionary explanation*. Oxford: Oxford University Press.

Kahneman, D., Slovic, P., and Tversky, A. (1982). *Judgment under uncertainty: Heuristics and biases*. New York: Cambridge University Press.

Kinzler, K.D., Dupoux, E., Spelke E.S. (2007) The native language of social cognition. The *Proceedings of the National Academy of Sciences of the United States of America*, 104: 12577–12580.

Kurzban, R. and Leary, M.R. (2001). Evolutionary origins of stigmatization: The functions of social exclusion, *Psychological bulletin* 127 (2), 187.

Nesse, R. M. (2001). The smoke detector principle. Natural selection and the regulation of defensive responses, *Annals of the New York Academy of Sciences*, 935: 75–85.

Pelham, B.W., Mirenberg, M.C., and Jones, J.T. (2002). Why Susie Sells Seashells by the Seashore: Implicit Egotism and Major Life Decisions. *Journal of Personality and Social Psychology*, Vol. 82, No. 4, 469–487.

Pfeifer, J.H., Ruble, D.N., Bachman, M.A., Alvarez, J.M., Cameron, J.A., & Fuligni, A.J. (2007). Social identities and intergroup bias in immigrant and nonimmigrant children. *Developmental Psychology*, 43(2), 496–507.

Sumner, W.G. and Albert G.K. (1906). *Folkways: A Study of the Sociological Importance of Usages, Manners, Customs, Mores, and Morals*. Boston; New York [etc.]: Ginn and Company.

Torney, Colin J., Lorenzi, Tommaso, Couzin, Iain D. and Levin, Simon A. (2015). Social information use and the evolution of unresponsiveness in collective systems. *Journal of the Royal Society*, Interface/the Royal Society, 12.

## Chapter 3

Amodio, D.M. and Frith C.D. (2006). Meeting of minds: the medial frontal cortex and social cognition. Nature Reviews, *Neuroscience*, 7: 268–277.

Aron, A.R., Robbins, T.W. and Poldrack, R.A. (2004). Inhibition and the right inferior frontal cortex. *Trends in Cognitive Sciences*, 8, 170–177.

Afdile, M., Jääskeläinen, J.P., Glerean, E., Smirnov, D., Alho, J., Äimälä, A. and Sams, M. (2019) Contextual knowledge provided by a movie biases implicit perception of the protagonist, *Social Cognitive and Affective Neuroscience*, Vol.14, Issue 5, May 2019, pp.519–527.

Belin, P., Fecteau, S. and Bedard, C. (2004). Thinking the voice: Neural correlates of voice perception. *Trends in Cognitive Sciences*, 8, 129–135.

Bestelmeyer, P., Belin, P. and Ladd, D.R. (2015). A Neural Marker for Social Bias Toward In-group Accents. *Cerebral Cortex*, Vol. 25, Issue 10, October 2015, 3953–3961.

Bohland, J.W. and Guenther, F.H. (2006). An fMRI investigation of syllable sequence production. *Neuroimage*, 32, 821–841.

Campbell-Meiklejohn, D.K., Bach, D.R., Roepstorff, A., Dolan, R.J. and Frith, C.D. (2010). How the opinion of others affects our valuation of objects. *Current Biology*. 20, 1165–1170.

Casado-Aranda, L-A., Venkatraman, V., Sánchez-Fernández, J., Luque-Martínez, T. (2019). Does Partisan Bias Modulate Neural Processing of Political Information? An Analysis of the Neural Correlates of Corruption and Positive Messages. *Political Psychology*, Vol. 40, No. 2. Wiley.

Crocker, J. and Luhtanen, R. (1990). Collective self-esteem and ingroup bias. *J. Pers. Soc. Psychol.*, 58, 60–67.

Eriksson, E., Sullivan, K., Zetterholm, E., Czigler, P., Green, J. and Skagerstrand, A., (2010). Detection of imitated voices: Who are reliable earwitnesses? *International Journal of Speech Language and the Law*, 17, 25–44.

Festinger, L. (1957). *A Theory of Cognitive Dissonance*. Stanford, CA: Stanford University Press.

Freeman, J.B. Schiller, D., Rule, N.O. and Ambady, N. (2010) The neural origins of superficial and individuated judgments about ingroup and outgroup members. *Hum. Brain. Mapp.*, 31 pp.150-159.

Gabrieli, J.D., Chiao, J.Y. and Eberhardt, J.L. (2001). Differential responses in the fusiform region to same-race and other-race faces, *Nat. Neurosci.*, 4, 845–850.

Harris, L.T., and Fiske, S.T. (2007). Social groups that elicit disgust are differentially processed in mPFC. *Social cognitive and affective neuroscience*, 2(1), 45–51.

Harrison, L.A., Hurlemann, R., and Adolphs, R. (2015). An Enhanced Default Approach Bias Following Amygdala Lesions in Humans. *Psychological Science*, 26(10), 1543–1555.

Hart, A.J., Whalen, P.J., Shin, L.M., McInerney, S.C., Fischer, H. and Rauch, S.L. (2000). Differential response in the human amygdala to racial outgroup vs ingroup face stimuli. *Brain Imaging.* 11:2351–5.

Izuma, K. (2013). The neural basis of social influence and attitude change. *Curr. Opin. Neurobiol.* 23, 456–462.

Jenkins, A.C., Macrae, C.N. and Mitchell, J.P. (2008). Repetition suppression of ventromedial prefrontal activity during judgments of self and others. *Proceedings of the National Academy of Sciences*, US, 105(11), 4507–4512.

Kurth, F., Zilles, K., Fox, P.T., Laird, A.R. and Eickhoff, S.B. (2010). A link between the systems: Functional differentiation and integration within the human insula revealed by meta-analysis. *Brain Structure & Function*, 214, 519–534.

Lamm, C. and Singer, T. (2010). The role of anterior insular cortex in social emotions. *Brain Structure & Function*, 214, 579–591.

Levine, J.M. and Tindale, R.S. (2015). Social influence in groups, in *APA Handbook of Personality and Social Psychology*, Vol. 2: Group Processes, M. Mikulincer, P.R. Shaver, J.F. Dovidio, and J.A. Simpson (Eds.), (Washington, DC: American Psychological Association), 3–34.

Lieberman, M.D., Hariri, A., Jarcho, J.M., Eisenberger, N.I. and Bookheimer, S.Y. (2005). An fMRI investigation of race-related amygdala activity in African-American and Caucasian-American individuals. *Nat. Neurosci.*, 8, 720-722.

McGettigan, C., Eisner, F., Agnew, Zarinah K., Manly, T., Wisbey, D. and Scott, S.K. (2013). T'ain't What You Say, It's the Way That You Say It – Left Insula and Inferior Frontal Cortex Work in Interaction with Superior Temporal Regions to Control the Performance of Vocal Impersonations. *Journal of Cognitive Neuroscience*, 25:11, 1875–1886.

Molenberghs, P. (2013). The neuroscience of in-group bias. *Neurosci. Biobehav. Rev.* 37, 1530–1536.

Price, C. J. (2010). The anatomy of language: A review of 100 fMRI studies published in 2009. *Annals of the New York Academy of Sciences*, 1191, 62–88.

Rongjun Yu, Mobbs, D., Seymour, B. and Calder, A.J. (2010). Insula and Striatum Mediate the Default Bias. *Journal of Neuroscience*, 30 (44), 14702–14707.

Santos, A., Meyer-Lindenberg, A. and Deruelle, C. (2010) Absence of racial, but not gender stereotyping in Williams syndrome children, *Current Biology*, Vol. 20, Issue 7, 13 April 2010.

Shestakova, A., Rieskamp, J., Tugin, S., Ossadtchi, A., Krutitskaya, J., and Klucharev, V. (2013). Electrophysiological precursors of social conformity. *Soc. Cogn. Affect. Neurosci.*, 8, 756–763.

Simmonds, A.J., Wise, R.J.S., Dhanjal, N.S. and Leech, R. (2011). A comparison of sensory-motor activity during speech in first and second languages. *Journal of Neurophysiology*, 106, 470–478.

Telzer, E.H., Humphreys, K.L., Shapiro, M., and Tottenham, N. (2013). Amygdala sensitivity to race is not present in childhood but emerges over adolescence. *J. Cogn. Neurosci.*, 25, 234–244.

Vaes, J., Cristoforetti, G., Ruzzante, D., Cogoni, C. and Mazza, V. (2019) Assessing neural responses towards objectified human targets and objects to identify processes of sexual objectification that go beyond the metaphor. *Scientific Reports*, Vol. 9, Article number: 6699.

Wheeler, M.E. and Fiske, S.T. (2005). Controlling racial prejudice: social-cognitive goals affect amygdala and stereotype activation. *Psychological Science*, 16: 56–63.

Wise, R.J., Greene, J., Buchel, C. and Scott, S.K. (1999). Brain regions involved in articulation. *Lancet*, 353, 1057–1061.

## Chapter 4

Banaji, M.R. and Hardin, C.D. (1996). Automatic stereotyping. *Psychological Science*, 7(3), 136–141.

Banaji, M. and Greenwald, A.G. (1995). Implicit gender stereotyping in judgments of fame. *Journal of Personality and Social Psychology*, 68, 181–198.

Bar-Tal, D. (1989). Delegitimization: The extreme case of stereotyping and prejudice. In: Bar-Tal, D., Graumann, C., Kruglanski, A. and Stroebe, D., (Eds.) *Stereotyping and Prejudice: Changing Conceptions*. NY: Spinger-Verlag, 169–182.

Belkin, L. (2003). The opt-out revolution. *New York Times Magazine*, October 26.

Bem, S. L. (1994). *The lenses of gender: Transforming the debate on sexual inequality*. New Haven, CT: Yale University Press.

Ben-Zeev, T., Fein, S. and Inzlicht, M. (2005). Stereotype Threat and Arousal. *Journal of Experimental Social Psychology*, 41 (2): 174–181.

Bonilla-Silva, E. (2000). 'This is a White Country': The racial ideology of the Western nations of the world-system. *Sociological Quarterly*, 70, 188–214.

Bruch, Elizabeth E. and Newman, M.E.G (2019). Structure of Online Dating Markets in US Cities. *Sociological Science*, 6: 219–234.

Collins, P.H. (1999). Moving beyond gender: Intersectionality and scientific knowledge. In: M.F. Ferree (Ed.), *Revisioning gender* (261–284). Thousand Oaks, CA: Sage.

Crenshaw, K.W. (1995). Mapping the margins: Intersectionality, identity politics and violence against women of color. In: K. Crenshaw, N. Gotanda, G. Peller and K. Thomas (Eds.), *Critical race theory: The key writings that formed the movement* (357–383). New York: New Press.

Cuddy, A.J.C., Fiske, S.T. and Glick, P. (2007). The BIAS map: Behaviors from intergroup affect and stereotypes. *Journal of Personality and Social Psychology*, 92, 631–648.

Devos, T. and Banaji, M.R. (2005). American = white? *Journal of Personality and Social Psychology*, 88, 447–466.

Eagly, A.H. and Kite, M.E. (1987). Are stereotypes of nationalities applied to both women and men. *Journal of Personality and Social Psychology*, 53, 451–462.

Eagly, A.H. and Mladinic, A. (1994). Are People Prejudiced Against Women? Some Answers From Research on Attitudes, Gender Stereotypes, and Judgments of Competence. *European Review of Social Psychology*, 5:1, 1–35.

Epstein, C.F. (1973). Black and female: The double whammy. *Psychology Today*, 89, 57–61.

Fein, S. and Spencer, S.J. (1997). Prejudice as self-image maintenance: Affirming the self through derogating others. *Journal of Personality and Social Psychology*, 73(1), 31–44.

Fiske, S.T. (1998). Stereotyping, prejudice, and discrimination. In: Gilbert, D.T., Fiske, S.T., Lindzey, G. (Eds.), *Handbook of Social Psychology*. 4th edn. Vol. 2. New York: McGraw-Hill, 357–411.

Gonzales, P.M., Blanton, H. and Williams, K.J. (2002). The effects of stereotype threat and double-minority status on the test performance of Latino women. *Personality and Social Psychology Bulletin*, 28, 659–670.

Hancock, A.M. (2007). When multiplication doesn't equal quick addition: Examining intersectionality as a research paradigm. *Perspectives on Politics*, 5, 63–79.

Hess, U., Senécal, S., Kirouac, G., Herrera, P.D., Philippot, P., and Kleck, R.E. (2000). Emotional expressivity in men and women: Stereotypes and self-perceptions. *Cognition and Emotion*, Vol. 4, Issue 5.

Hess, U., Adams Jr., R. and Robert, K. (2005). Who may frown and who should smile? Dominance, affiliation, and the display of happiness and anger. *Cognition and Emotion*, 19:4, 515–536.

Inzlicht, M., McKay, L. and Aronson, J. (2006). Stigma as ego-depletion: How being the target of prejudice affects self-control. *Psychological Science*, 17 (3): 262–269.

Jenkins, A.C., Macrae, C.N. and Mitchell, J.P. (2008). Repetition suppression of ventromedial prefrontal activity during judgments of self and others. *Proceedings of the National Academy of Sciences*, US, 105 (11), 4507–4512.

Kawakami, K., Dovidio, J.F., Moll, J., Hermsen, S. and Russin, A. (2000) Just say no (to stereotyping): effects of training in the negation of stereotypic associations on stereotype activation. *Journal of Personality and Social Psychology*, 78: 871–888.

King, E.B. (2008). The effect of bias on the advancement of working mothers: Disentangling legitimate concerns from inaccurate stereotypes as predictors of career success. *Human Relations*, 61, 1677-1711.

Krieglmeyer, R., and Sherman, J.W. (2012). Disentangling Stereotype Activation and Stereotype Application in the Stereotype Misperception Task. *Journal of Personality and Social Psychology*, August, 103(2): 205–224.

Livingston, G. (2014). Opting out? About 10% of highly educated moms are staying home. Pew Research Foundation. Retrieved online: www.pewresearch.org/fact-tank/2014/05/07/opting-out-about-10-of-highly-educated-moms-are-staying-at-home/.

Maddox, K.B. (2004). Perspectives on racial phenotypicality bias. *Personality and Social Psychology Review*, 8, 383–401.

Pendry, L.F. and Macrae, C.N. (1994). Stereotypes and Mental Life: The Case of the Motivated but Thwarted Tactician, *Journal of Experimental Social Psychology*, Vol. 30, Issue 4, 303–325.

Purdie-Vaughns, V. and Eibach, R.P. (2008). Intersectional Invisibility: The Distinctive Advantages and Disadvantages of Multiple Subordinate-Group Identities. *Sex Roles*, 59: 377.

Reid, P.T. and Comas-Diaz, L. (1990). Gender and ethnicity: Perspectives on dual status. *Sex Roles*, 22, 397–408.

Reuben, E., Sapienza, P. and Zingales, L. (2014). How stereotypes impair women's careers in science. *Proceedings of the National Academy of Sciences*, 111, 4403-4408.

Saleem, M. (2016). Why bad news for one Muslim American is bad news for all Muslims. *The Conversation*, 24 June.

Schmader, T. and Johns, M. (2003). Converging Evidence That Stereotype Threat Reduces Working Memory Capacity. *Journal of Personality and Social Psychology*, 85 (3): 440–452.

Sidanius, J. and Pratto, F. (1999). *Social dominance: An intergroup theory of social hierarchy and oppression*. New York: Cambridge University Press.

Siy, J.O. and Cheryan, S. (2013). When Compliments Fail to Flatter: American Individualism and Responses to Positive Stereotypes. *Journal of Personality and Social Psychology*, 87–102.

Smith, D.G., Rosenstein, J.E. and Nikolov, M.C. (2018). The Different Words We Use to Describe Male and Female Leaders. *Harvard Business Review*, May 25.

Sue, S. (1999). Science, ethnicity, and bias: Where have we gone wrong? *American Psychologist*, 54, 1070–7077.

Sumner, W.G. (1906). *Folkways: A study of the sociological importance of usages, manners, customs, more, and morals.* Boston, MA: Ginn & Co.

Tsunokai, G.T., McGrath, A.R. and Kavanagh, J.K. (2014). Online dating preferences of Asian Americans. *Journal of Social and Personal Relationships*, 31(6), 796–814.

Turner, J.C. (1985). Social categorization and the self-concept: A social cognitive theory of group behaviour. In: Lawler, E. J. (Ed.), *Advances in group processes*. Greenwich, CT: JAI Press, 77–122.

Woodzicka, J.A. and LaFrance, M. (2001). Real versus imagined gender harassment. *Journal of Social Issues*, 57, 15–30.

## Chapters 5

Allison, P. (1993). The cultural evolution of beneficent norms. *Social Forces*, 71:279-301

Bandura, A. (1971). *Social Learning Theory.* New York: General Learning Press.

Campbell, J.D. and Tesser, A. (1983). Motivational interpretations of Hindsight bias: An individual difference analysis, 51 *Journal of Personality*, 605, 613–615.

Cihon, P., and Yasseri, T. (2016). A Biased Review of Biases in Twitter Studies on Political Collective Action. *Frontiers in Physics*, vol. 4, 34.

Clementson, D. E. (2018). Truth Bias and Partisan Bias in Political Deception Detection. *Journal of Language and Social Psychology*, 37(4), 407–430.

De Brigard, F. (2010). 'If you like it, does it matter if it's real?' *Philosophical Psychology*, 23: 1, 43–57.

de Vries, M., Holland, R.W., Chenier, T., Starr, M.J. and Winkielman, P. (2010). Happiness cools the warm glow of familiarity: psychophysiological evidence that mood modulates the familiarity-affect link. *Psychological science*, 21(3), 321–328.

Delaney, K. J. (2017). Filter bubbles are a serious problem with news, says Bill Gates. *Quartz*, Retrieved from https://qz.com/913114/bill-gates-says-filter-bubbles-are-a-serious problem-with-news/, February 22.

Fleming, S.M., Thomas, C.L. and Dolan, R.J. (2010). Overcoming status quo bias in the human brain. *Proceedings of the National Academy of Sciences of the United States of America*, 107(13), 6005–6009. doi:10.1073/pnas.0910380107.

Freud, S. [1922] (1959). *Group Psychology and the Analysis of the Ego.* London: Norton.

Furnham, A. (1983). Contagion. In: Harre, R. and Lamb, R. (Eds.) *The Encyclopaedic Dictionary of Psychology*, 119.

Green, L., Fry, A.F. and Myerson, J. (1994). 'Discounting of delayed rewards: A life span comparison'. *Psychological Science*, 5 (1).

Knetsch, J.L. and Sinden, J.A. (1984). Willingness to Pay and Compensation Demanded: Experimental Evidence of an Unexpected Disparity in Measures of Value. *The Quarterly Journal of Economics*, 1984, Vol. 99, Issue 3, 507–521.

Lindzey, G. and Aronson, E. (Eds.) (1985). *Handbook of Social Psychology: Group Psychology and the Phenomena of Interaction* (3rd Ed.), New York: Random House.

Lynch, A. (1996). *Thought Contagion. How Belief Spreads Through Society. The New Science of Memes.* New York: Basic Books.

Murphy, M. (2018). Twitter creates filter bubbles, and 'we need to fix it,' says Jack Dorsey. Retrieved from www.marketwatch.com/story/twitter-creates-filterbubbles-and-we-need-to-fix-it-says-jack-dorsey-2018-10-15, October 16.

Pitkin, H.F. (1967). *The Concept of Representation.* Los Angeles: University of California Press, 323.

Wien, C. and Deutz, D.B. (2019). What's in a tweet? Creating Social Media Echo Chambers to inflate 'the donut'. *LIBER Quarterly*, 29(1), 3.

Wollebæk, D., Karlsen, R., Steen-Johnsen, K. and Enjolras, B. (2019). Anger, Fear, and Echo Chambers: The Emotional Basis for Online Behavior. *Social Media + Society*, Jun 32(3), 257–273.

Zuckerman, H. (1965). 'Nobel Laureates: Sociological Studies of Scientific Collaboration' (PhD. diss.), Columbia Univ., 1965.

## Chapter 6

Johnson, E.J. and Goldstein, D. (2003). Medicine. Do defaults save lives? *Science*, 302: 1338–1339.

Kahneman, D. and Tversky, A. (1979). 'Prospect Theory: An Analysis of Decision under Risk' (PDF). *Econometrica*, 47 (2): 263–291.

Knetsch, J. (1989). The Endowment Effect and Evidence of Nonreversible Indifference Curves. *The American Economic Review*, 79 (5), 1277–1284.

O'Donoghue T. and Rabin, M. (2001). Choice and Procrastination. *The Quarterly Journal of Economics*, Vol. 116, No. 1 (Feb. 2001), 121–160.

Roese, N.J. and Vohs, K.D. (2012). *Hindsight Bias*, Vol. 7, Issue 5, 411–426.

Samuelson, W. and Zeckhauser, R. (1988). Status Quo Bias in Decision Making. *Journal of Risk and Uncertainty*, 1: 7–59.

Shavitt, S. (2018). A New Version of Loss Aversion: Introduction to Research Dialogue. *Journal of Consumer Psychology*, 28, 3, 495-496.

Vazire S. (2017). Our obsession with eminence warps research. *Nature*, 547:7.

Yechiam, E. (2018). Acceptable losses: the debatable origins of loss aversion. *Psychological* Research, 10.

Young, A.I., Ratner, K.G. and Fazio, R. H. (2014). Political Attitudes Bias the Mental Representation of a Presidential Candidate's Face. *Psychological Science*, 25(2), 503–510.

Zajonc, R.B. (2001). Mere exposure: A gateway to the subliminal. *Current Directions in Psychological Science*, 10: 224–228.

Zeng, J., Wang, Y., Zeng, J., et al. (2019). Predicting the behavioural tendency of loss aversion, *Sci. Rep. 9*, 5024.

## Chapter 7

Aries, E. (1998). Gender and communication. In: Shaver, P. and Hendrick, C. (Eds.), *Review of Personality and Social Psychology*, Vol. 7, 149–176. Beverly Hills, CA: Sage.

Bauer, L. and Trudgill, P. *Language Myths*. London & New York: Penguin Books, 208.

Brescoll, V.L. (2012). Who Takes the Floor and Why: Gender, Power, and Volubility in Organizations. *Administrative Science Quarterly*, Vol. 56, Issue 4, 2011.

Calogero, R.M. (2004). A test of objectification theory: The effect of the male gaze on appearance concerns in college women. *Psychol. Women Q.*, 28(1), 16–21.1 (2004).

Calogero, R.M., Tantleff-Dunn, S. and Thompson, J.K. (2011). Self-objectification in women: Causes, consequences, and counteractions. (American Psychological Association, 2011).

Carnes, M., Bartels, C.M., Kaatz, A., and Kolehmainen, C. (2015). 'Why is John More Likely to Become Department Chair Than Jennifer?' *Transactions of the American Clinical and Climatological Association*, 126: 197–214. PMC 4530686. PMID.

Ceci, S.J. and Williams, W.M. (2010). Sex differences in math-intensive fields. *Current Directions in Psychological Science*, 19(5), 275-279.

Cimpian, A., Arce, H.-M.C., Markman, E.M. and Dweck, C.S. (2007). Subtle linguistic cues affect children's motivation. *Psychological Science*, 18(4), 314–316.

Dasgupta, N. and Asgari, S. (2004). Seeing is believing: Exposure to counterstereotypic women leaders and its effect on the malleability of automatic gender stereotyping. *Journal of Experimental Social Psychology*, 40(5):642–658.

Ditonto, T. (2016). A High Bar or a Double Standard? Gender, Competence, and Information in Political Campaigns. *Political Behavior*, Vol. 39, Issue 2, 301–325.

DongWon Oh, Buck, E.A. and Todorov, A. (2019). Revealing Hidden Gender Biases in Competence Impressions of Faces. *Psychological Sciences*, Vol. 30: Issue 1.

Eagly, A.H. and Karau, S.J. (1991). Gender and the emergence of leaders: A meta-analysis. *Journal of Personality and Social Psychology*, 60, 685–710.

Eagly, A.H. and Steffen, V.J. (1984). Gender stereotypes stem from the distribution of men and women into social roles. *Journal of Personality and Social Psychology*, 46, 735–754.

Eagly, A.H. and Wood, W. (1991). Explaining sex differences in social behavior: A meta-analytic perspective. *Personality and Social Psychology Bulletin*, 17, 306–315.

Eagly, A.H., Makhijani, M.G. and Klonsky, B.G. (1992). Gender and the evaluation of leaders: A meta-analysis. *Psychological Bulletin*, 111, 3–22.

Eagly, A.H. and Mladinic, A. (1993). Are people prejudiced against women? Some answers from research on attitudes, gender

stereotypes, and judgments of competence. In: W. Stroebe &
M. Hewstone (Eds.), *European review of social psychology*. New
York: John Wiley. 1994; 5(1): 1–35.

Falk, E. (2008). *Women for President: Media Bias in Eight Campaigns*.
Urbana, IL: University of Illinois Press.

Fredrickson, B.L. and Roberts, T.A. (1997). Objectification theory.
*Psychol. Women Q.*, 21(2), 173–206.

Gallup, G.H. (1996). The Gallup poll. Wilmington, DE: Scholarly
Resources.

Glick, P. and Fiske, S.T. (2011). Ambivalent Sexism Revisited.
*Psychology of women quarterly*, 35(3), 530–535.

Glick, P., Diebold, J., Bailey-Werner, B. and Zhu, L. (1997). The
two faces of Adam: Ambivalent sexism and polarized attitudes
toward women. *Personality and Social Psychology Bulletin*, 23,
1323-1334.

Hancock, A.B. and Rubin, A.B. (2014). Influence of
Communication Partner's Gender on Language, *Journal of
Language and social psychology and group composition. American
Sociological Review*, 54, 424–435.

Harris, L.T. and Fiske, S.T. Social groups that elicit disgust are
differentially processed in mPFC. *Soc. Cogn. Affect. Neurosci.*
2(1), 45–51 (2007).

Henderson-King, D., and& Stewart, A.J. (1997). Feminist
consciousness: Perspectives on women's experience.
*Personality and Social Psychology Bulletin*, 23, 415–426.

Hill, C., Corbett, C. and Rose, S.A. (2010). *Why so few? Women in
Science, Technology, Engineering, and Mathematics*. Washington,
DC: American Association of University Women.

Holland, E., Koval, P., Stratemeyer, M., Thomson, F. and Haslam,
N. (2017). Sexual objectification in women's daily lives: A
smartphone ecological momentary assessment study. *Br. J.
Soc. Psychol.*, 56(2), 314–333.

Holme, J. (1992). Women's Talk in Public Contexts. *Discourse and
Society*, Vol. 3, Issue: 2, 131–150.

Horowitz, M.C. (1976). Aristotle and women. *Journal of the History
of Biology*, 9(2), 183–213.

Huber, K. (2016). *Everybody's a Little Bit Sexist: A Re-evaluation of
Aristotle's and Plato's Philosophies on Women*. Department of
History, Lake Forest College, Lake Forest, Illinois.

Ito, T.A. and Urland, G.R. (2003). Race and gender on the brain:
Electrocortical measures of attention to the race and gender

of multiply categorizable individuals. *J. Pers. Soc. Psychol.*, 85(4), 616.

Jarreau, P.B., Cancellare, I.A., Carmichael, B.J., Porter, L., Toker, D., and Yammine, S.Z. (2019). Using selfies to challenge public stereotypes of scientists. *PLoS ONE*, 14(5).

Jeffreys, S. (2014). *Beauty and misogyny: Harmful cultural practices in the West.* East Sussex, UK: Routledge

Johnson, P. (1976). Women and power: Toward a theory of effectiveness. *Journal of Social Issues*, 32, 99–110.

LaFrance, M. (1992). Gender And Interruptions Individual Infraction or Violation of the Social Order. *Psychology of Women Quarterly*, Vol. 16, Issue 4, 1992.

Leaper, C. and Smith, T. E. (2004). A Meta-Analytic Review of Gender Variations in Children's Language Use: Talkativeness, Affiliative Speech, and Assertive Speech. *Developmental Psychology*, Vol. 40(6), Nov 2004, 993–1027.

Leslie, S.-J., Cimpian, A., Meyer, M., and Freeland, E. (2015). Women are underrepresented in disciplines that emphasize brilliance as the key to success. *Science*, 347, 262–265.

Meyer, M., Cimpian, A. and Leslie, S.-J. (2015). Women are underrepresented in fields where success is believed to require brilliance. *Frontiers in Psychology*, 6, Article ID 235.

Morsink, J. (1979). Was Aristotle's biology sexist? *Journal of the History of Biology*, 12(1), 83–112.

Moss-Racusin, C.A., Dovidio, J.F., Brescoll, V.L., Graham, M.J. and Handelsman J. (2012). Science faculty's subtle gender biases favor male students. *Proceedings of the National Academy of Sciences*, 109(41), 16474–16479.

Orcutt, J.D. and Harvey, L.K. (1985). Deviance, rule breaking and male dominance in conversation. *Symbolic Interaction*, 8, 15–32.

OSCE (2003) Bosnia and Herzegovina General Elections 5 October 2002: OSCE/ODIHR Final Report. Warsaw: OSCE. [Google Scholar], 18.

Peradotto, J. and Sullivan, J.P. (1983). Women in the ancient world: The Arethusa papers. Albany, NY: SUNY Press.

Plato. (2008). The republic. (Jowett, B.). Retrieved from http://www. gutenberg.org/files/1497/1497-h/1497-h.htm.

Reis, H.T., Wilson, I.M., Monestere, C., Bernstein, S., Clark, K., Seidl, E., et al. (1990). What is smiling is beautiful and good. *European Journal of Social Psychology*, 20(3): 259–267.

Rudman, L. and Kilianski, S. (2000). Implicit and Explicit Attitudes Toward Female Authority. *PSPB*, Vol. 26, No.11, November, 1315–1328.

Sanchez, D.T., Chaney, K.E., Manuel, S.K., Wilton, L.S. and Remedios, J.D. (2017). Stigma by Prejudice Transfer. *Psychological Science*, Racism Threatens White Women and Sexism Threatens Men of Color. *Psychological Science*, 28(4), 445–461.

Shenk, J.W. (2014). The end of 'genius'. *The New York Times*.

Smith-Lovin, L. and Brody, C. (1989). Interruptions in group discussions: The effects of gender. *American Sociological Review*, Vol. 54, No. 3, 424–435.

Steffens, M.C., Jelenec, P. and Noack P. (2010). On the leaky math pipeline: Comparing implicit math–gender stereotypes and math withdrawal in female and male children and adolescents. *Journal of Educational Psychology*, 102(4): 947.

Storage, D., Horne, Z., Cimpian, A. and Leslie, S.J. (2016). The Frequency of 'Brilliant' and 'Genius' in Teaching Evaluations Predicts the Representation of Women and African Americans across Fields. *PLOS ONE*, 11(3).

Whaley, L.A. (2003). *The classical debate: Can women do science? Women's history as scientists: A guide to the debates*. Santa Barbara, CA: ABC-CLIO.

Willis, M. and Jozkowski, K.N. (2018). Ladies First? Not So Fast: Linguistic Sexism in Peer-Reviewed Research. *The Journal of Sex Research*, 55:2, 137–145.

Williams, B. (2018). Media coverage of the UK's female prime ministers. London: King's College London.

## Chapter 8

Albert, M.A., Cozier, Y., Ridker, P.M., Palmer, J.R., Glynn, R.J., et al. (2010). Perceptions of race/ethnic discrimination in relation to mortality among black women: results from the Black Women's Health Study. *Arch. Intern. Med.* 170: 896–904

Angre, K. (2015). Sharad Yadav Unapologetic After Comments on 'Dusky South Indian Women'. NDTV, March 13, 2015.

Bar-Haim Y., Ziv T., Lamy D. and Hodes R. (2006). Nature and Nurture in Own-Race Face Processing. *Psychological Science*, 17:159–163.

Bertrand, M. and Mullainathan, S. (2004). Are Emily and Greg more employable than Lakisha and Jamal? A field experiment on labor market discrimination. *The American Economic Review*, 94(4): 991–1013.

Cleeland, C.S., Gonin, R., Baez, L., Loehrer, P. and Pandya K. (1997). Pain and treatment of pain in minority patients with cancer. The Eastern Cooperative Oncology Group Minority Outpatient Pain Study. *Ann. Intern. Med.* 127(9): 813–816.

Cole, K.R. et al., (2014). *The Color Complex: The politics of skin color in a new millennium*. US: Anchor books.

Cosmides, L., Tooby, J. and Kurzban, R. (2003). Perceptions of race. *Trends in Cognitive Sciences*, 7:173–178.

Eberhardt, J., Goff, P. and Purdie-Vaughns, V. (2004). Seeing Black: Race, crime, and visual processing. *Journal of Personality and Social Psychology*, 87(6): 876–893.

Farinella, G. and Dugelay, J-L. (2012). Demographic classification: Do gender and ethnicity affect each other? In Informatics, Electronics & Vision (ICIEV), 2012.

Gaertner, S. and Dovidio, J.F. (1986). The aversive form of racism. In: Dovidio, J.F., Gaertner, S., (Eds.), *Prejudice, discrimination, and racism*. Orlando: Academic Press, 61–89.

Garari, K. (2014). Skin Whitening Isn't Right, Experts Reveal. *Deccan Chronicle*, 26 May.

Gelman, A., Fagan, J., and Kiss, A. (2007). An analysis of the New York city police department's 'stop-and-frisk' policy in the context of claims of racial bias. *Journal of the American Statistical Association* 102(479): 813–823.

Goff, P., Lloyd, T., Geller, A., Raphael, S., Glaser, J. (2016). The science of justice: Race, arrests, and policy use of force. New York, NY: Center for Policing Equity, John Jay College of Criminal Justice.

Green, A.R., Carney, D.R., Pallin, D.J., Ngo, L.H., Raymond, K.L., Iezzoni, L.I. and Banaji, M.R. (2007). Implicit bias among physicians and its prediction of thrombolysis decisions for Black and White patients. *Journal of General Internal Medicine*, 22:1231–1238.

Greenwald, A., Smith, C., Sriram, N., Bar-Ana, Y. and Nosek, B. (2009). Implicit race attitudes predicted votes in the 2008 US Presidential election. *Analyses of Social Issues and Public Policy* 9(1): 241–253.

Hall, R. (1995). The Bleaching Syndrome: African Americans' Response to Cultural Domination Vis-a-Vis Skin Color. 26 *J. Black Stud.*, 172, 179.

Heard-Garris, N.J., Cale, M., Camaj, L., Hamati, M.C. and Dominguez, T.P. (2018). Transmitting trauma: a systematic review of vicarious racism and child health. *Soc. Sci. Med.*, 199: 230–240.

Jones, J.M. (1997). *Prejudice and Racism.* New York: McGraw Hill. 2nd ed.

Kang, J., Bennett, M., Carbado, D. and Casey, P. (2012). Implicit bias in the courtroom. *UCLA Law Review*, 59: 1124–1186.

Levinson, J. and Young, D. (2009). Different shades of bias: Skin tone, implicit racial bias, and judgments of ambiguous evidence. *West Virginia Law Review*, 112: 307–350.

Mishra, N. (2015). India and Colorism: Finer Nuances. *Washington University Global Studies Law Review*, Vol. 14, Issue 4, Global Perspectives on Colorism (Symposium Edition).

Patel, R.K. (2014). A Conjoint Analyses Of Consumer Preferences For Fairness Creams Among Small Towns Located Near Ahmedabad City. *2GIRJ* Giirj3, Vol. 2 (3), March, 12, 13–14.

Rachlinski, J., Johnson, S.L., Wistrich, A. and Guthrie, C. (2009). Does unconscious racial bias affect trial judges? *Notre Dame Law Review*, 84: 1195–1246.

Rice, D., Rhodes, J.H. and Nteta, T. (2019). Racial bias in legal language. *Research & Politics*, Vol. 6, Issue 2.

Singh, R. (2013). Fairness Creams' Segment Slows Down: Has The Nation Overcome Its Dark Skin Complex? *The Economic Times*, 18 August 2013.

Spark Outrage, NDTV NEWS (13 March, 2015 23:49 IST).

Staub, E. (1989). *The Roots of Evil: The Origins of Genocide and Other Group Violence.* NY: Cambridge University Press.

Tidyman, P. (1826). A sketch of the most remarkable disease of the negroes of the southern states. *Phila. J. Med. Phys. Sci.* 12:306–338.

Washington, H.A. (2006). *Medical Apartheid: The Dark History of Medical Experimentation on Black Americans from Colonial Times to the Present.* New York: Doubleday.

Wickremesekera, C. (2002). *Best Black Troops In The World?: British Perceptions And The Making Of The Sepoy 1746–1805.* Manohar Publishers, 95–97.

# Chapter 9

Agerström, J. and Rooth, D.O. (2011). The role of automatic obesity stereotypes in real hiring discrimination. *Journal of Applied Psychology*, 96, 790–805

Audit Commission. (1995). Dear to our hearts? Commissioning services for the treatment and prevention of coronary heart disease. London: HMSO.

Blaker, N.M., and Van Vugt, M. (2014). The status-size hypothesis: How cues of physical size and social status influence each other. In: Cheng J.T., Tracy J.L., Anderson C., (Eds.), *The Psychology of Social Status*. New York: Springer, 119–137.

Blaker, N.M., Rompa, I., Dessing, I.H., Florijn Vriend, A., Herschberg, C., et al. (2013). The height leadership advantage in men and women: testing evolutionary psychology predictions about the perceptions of tall leaders. *Gr. Process. Intergr. Relations,* 16: 17–27.

Brody, J. (2017), Fat Bias Starts Early, *New York Times*, 21 August 2017.

Byrski, L. (2014), On turning 70. *Sydney Morning Herald*, 3 August 2014.

Carnegie Institute. (1993). *Life, work and livelihood in the third age: final report of the Carnegie Inquiry into the Third Age.* Dunfermline: Carnegie United Kingdom Trust.

Carrigan, M. and Szmigin, I. (2000). Advertising and older consumers: image and ageism. *Business Ethics: A European Review*, 9. 10.1111/1467-8608.00168.

Choplin, J. M. (2010). I Am "Fatter" Than She Is: Language-Expressible Body-Size Comparisons Bias Judgments of Body Size. *Journal of Language and Social Psychology*, 29(1), 55–74.

Cinnirella, F. and Winter, J. (2009). Size matters! Body height and labor market discrimination: A cross-European analysis. CESifo Working Paper No. 2733.

Dudley, N.J. and Burns, E. (1992). The influence of age on policies for admission and thrombolysis in coronary care units in the United Kingdom. *Age and Ageing*, 21:95–98.

Eagly, A.H., Ashmore, R.D., Makhijani, M.G. and Longo, L.C. (1991). What is beautiful is good, but...: A meta-analytic review of research on the physical attractiveness stereotype. *Psychological Bulletin*, 110, 109–128.

Ferla, R. (2018). Instagram Grandmas, *New York Times*, 20 June.

Gurwitz, J.H., Col, N.F. and Avorn, J. (1992). The exclusion of the elderly and women from clinical trials in acute myocardial infarction. *JAMA*, 268:1417–1422.

Hughes, D. and Griffiths, L. (1996). 'But if you look at the coronary anatomy…': risk and rationing in cardiac surgery. *Sociology of Health and Illness*, 18: 172-197. 19 Health Advisory.

Judge, T.A. and Cable, D.M. (2004). The effect of physical height on workplace success and income: Preliminary test of a theoretical model. *J. Appl. Psychol.* 89: 428–441. doi: 10.1037/0021-9010.89.3.428 PMID: 15161403.

Langlois, J.H., Kalakanis, L., Rubenstein, A.J., Larson, A., Hallam, M. and Smoot M. (2000). Maxims or myths of beauty? A meta-analytic and theoretical review. *Psychological Bulletin.* 126(3):390. pmid:10825783.

Langlois, J.H., Kalakanis, L., Rubenstein, A.J., Larson, A., Hallam, M. and Smoot M. (2000). Maxims or myths of beauty? A meta-analytic and theoretical review. *Psychological Bulletin*, 126, 390–423.

Latner, J.D. and Stunkard, A.J. (2003). Getting Worse: The Stigmatization Of Obese Children. *Obes Res*, 11:452–456.

Locher, P., Unger, R., Sociedade, P., and Wahl, J. (1993). At first glance: Accessibility of the physical attractiveness stereotype. *Sex Roles*, 28, 729–743.

Malinen, S. and Johnston, L. (2013). Workplace ageism: discovering hidden bias. *Exp. Aging Res.,* 39(4), 445–465.

Marsh, A.A., Yu, H.H., Schechter, J.C. and Blair, R.J.R. (2009). Larger than life: humans' nonverbal status cues alter perceived size. *PLoS One.* 4: e5707. doi: 10.1371/journal.pone.0005707 PMID: 19479082.

Montepare, J. M., Kempler, D., and McLaughlin-Volpe, T. (2014). The Voice of Wisdom: New Insights on Social Impressions of Aging Voices. *Journal of Language and Social Psychology*, 33(3), 241–259.

Puhl, R. M., Moss-Racusin, C.A., Schwartz, M.B. and Brownell, K.D. (2008). Weight stigmatization and bias reduction: perspectives of overweight and obese adults. *Health Education Research*, Vol. 23, Issue 2, April, 347–358.

Re, D.E., Dzhelyova, M., Holzleitner, I.J., Tigue, C.C., Feinberg D.R., et al. (2012). Apparent height and body mass index influence perceived leadership ability in three-dimensional faces. *Perception*, 41: 1477–1485.

Royal College of Physicians. (1991). Cardiological intervention in elderly patients. A report of a working group of the Royal College of Physicians. London: RCP.

Sabin, J.A., Marini, M., and Nosek, B.A. (2012). Implicit and explicit anti-fat bias among a large sample of medical doctors by BMI, race/ethnicity and gender. *PLoS ONE*, 7(11): e48448.

Skinner A.C., Payne, K., Perrin, A.J., et al. (2017). Implicit Weight Bias in Children Age 9 to 11 Years. *Pediatrics*, 140(1).

Stulp, G., Buunk, A.P., Verhulst S. and Pollet T.V. (2013). Tall claims? Sense and nonsense about the importance of height of US presidents. *Leadership Quarterly*, 24: 159–171. doi: 10.1016/j.leaqua.2012.09.002.

Turner, N., et al. (1999). Cancer in old age – is it inadequately investigated and treated? *BMJ*, 319: 309–12.

Tsukiura, T. and Cabeza, R. (2010). Shared brain activity for aesthetic and moral judgments: implications for the Beauty-is-Good stereotype. *Social cognitive and affective neuroscience*, 6(1):138–148.

Watson, S. (2019). The bustier bust-up: where do you stand on over-50s style? *Telegraph*, 1 May.

Wenger, N.K. (1997). Coronary heart disease: an older woman's major health risk. *BMJ*, 315:1085–1090.

Young, T.J. and French, L.A. (1996). Height and perceived competence of US presidents. *Percept. Mot. Skills*, 82: 1002. PMID: 8774043.

Zhang, Y.B., Harwood, J., Williams, A., Ylänne-McEwen, V., Wadleigh, P.M. and Thimm, C. (2006). The Portrayal of Older Adults in Advertising: A Cross-National Review. *Journal of Language and Social Psychology*, 25(3), 264–282.

## Chapter 10

Birney, M.E., Rabinovich, A., Morton, T.A., Heath, H. and Ashcroft, S. (2019). When Speaking English Is Not Enough: The Consequences of Language-Based Stigma for Nonnative Speakers. *Journal of Language and Social Psychology*. First Published online November 6.

Cantone, J.A., Martinez, L.N., Willis-Esqueda, C. and Miller, T. (2019). Sounding guilty: How accent bias affects juror judgments of culpability. *Journal of Ethnicity in Criminal Justice*, 17:3, 228-253.

Devine, P.G., Forscher, P.S., Austin, A.J. and Cox, W.T. (2012). Long-term reduction in implicit race bias: A prejudice habit-breaking intervention. *Journal of experimental social psychology*, 48(6), 1267–1278.

Gluszek, A. and Dovidio, J. F. (2010). Speaking With a Nonnative Accent: Perceptions of Bias, Communication Difficulties, and Belonging in the United States. *Journal of Language and Social Psychology*, 29(2), 224–234.

Holbrooka, C., Daniel, M.T., Fesslera, C. and Navarreteb, D. (2016). Looming large in others' eyes: racial stereotypes illuminate dual adaptations for representing threat versus prestige as physical size. *Evolution and Human Behavior*, Vol. 37, Issue 1, January 67–78.

Klein, A. (2018). Names evoke biased stereotypes in all of us, *New Scientist*, Vol. 238, Issue 3179, 26 May, 9.

Lindemann, S. (2005). Who speaks "broken English"? US undergraduates' perception of nonnative English. *International Journal of Applied Linguistics*, 15, 187-212.

Lippi-Green, R. (1997). *English with an accent: Language, ideology, and discrimination in the United States*. New York: Routledge.

McDavid, J. and Harari, H. (1966). Stereotyping of Names and Popularity in Grade-School Children. *Child Development*, 37(2), 453-459.

Monteith, M.J., Voils, C.I. and Ashburn-Nardo, L. (2001). Taking a look underground: Detecting, interpreting, and reacting to implicit racial biases. *Social Cognition*, 19:395–417.

Munro, M. J. and Derwing, T. M. (1995). Processing time, accent, and comprehensibility in the perception of native and foreign-accented speech. *Language and Speech*, 38, 289-306.

Paluck, E.L. and Green, D.P. (2009). Prejudice reduction: What works? A review and assessment of research and practice. *Annual Review of Psychology*. 2009; 60:339–367.

Pitts, M., and Gallois, C. (2019). Social Markers in Language and Speech. *Oxford Research Encyclopedia of Psychology*, May 23.

Plant, E.A. and Devine, P.G. (1998). Internal and external motivation to respond without prejudice. *Journal of Personality and Social Psychology*, 75:811–832.

Plant E.A. and, Devine P.G. (2009). The active control of prejudice: Unpacking the intentions guiding control efforts. *Journal of Personality and Social Psychology*, 96:640–652.

Redheadab, D., Cheng, J.T., Driver, C., Foulsham, T. and O'Gorman, R. (2019). On the dynamics of social hierarchy: A longitudinal investigation of the rise and fall of prestige, dominance, and social rank in naturalistic task groups. *Evolution and Human Behavior*, Vol. 40, Issue 2, March, 222–234.

Ryan, E.B. (1983). Social psychological mechanisms underlying native speaker evaluations of non-native speech. *Studies in Second Language Acquisition*, 5, 148-159.

Spencer-Rodgers, J. and McGovern, T. (2002). Attitudes toward the culturally different: The role of intercultural communication barriers, affective responses, consensual stereotypes, and perceived threat. *International Journal of Intercultural Relations*, 26, 609-631.

## Chapter 11

AI Index 2018. (2018). Artificial Intelligence Index 2018. Retrieved from http://cdn.aiindex.org/2018/AI%20Index%202018%20Annual%20Report.pdf.

Angwin, J., Larson, J., Mattu, S. and Kirchner, K. (2016). There's software used across the country to predict future criminals. And it's biased against blacks. ProPublica, 23 May 2016.

Buolamwini, J. (2019). Face: The Final Frontier of Privacy – Full Spoken Congressional Testimony. *Medium*, 22 May.

Buolamwini, J. (2019). Response: Racial and Gender bias in Amazon Rekognition – Commercial AI System for Analyzing Faces. *Medium*, 24 January.

Buolamwini, J. and Timnit Gebru, T. (2018). Gender Shades: Intersectional Accuracy Disparities in Commercial Gender Classification. *Proceedings of Machine Learning Research*, 81:1–15, 2018 Conference on Fairness, Accountability, and Transparency.

Celis, E., Mehrotra, A. and Vishnoi, N. K. (2019). Toward Controlling Discrimination in Online Ad Auctions. ICML 2019, 4456-4465.

Element AI. (2019). *Global AI Talent Report 2019*. Retrieved from https://jfgagne.ai/talent-2019/.

Face++ Terms of Use. a. Accessed: 2018-12-13.

Faception, Facial Personality Analytics. www.faception.com/, b. Accessed: 2018-10- 06.

Garvie, C., Bedoya, A. and Frankle., J. (2016). *The Perpetual Line-Up: Unregulated Police Face Recognition in America.* Georgetown Law, Center on Privacy & Technology, October 18.

Gershgorn, D. (2019). *Here's How Amazon Alexa Will Recognize When You're Frustrated.* OneZero, Medium, 27 September.

Ifeoma A., S., Friedler, Scheidegger, C. and Venkatasubramanian, S. (2016). Hiring by algorithm: predicting and preventing disparate impact. Available at SSRN.

Jonathon P., Jiang, F., Narvekar, A., Ayyad, J., and O'Toole, A.J. (2011). An other-race effect for face recognition algorithms. *ACM Transactions on Applied Perception (TAP)*, 8(2):14.

Klare, B., et al. (2012). Face Recognition Performance: Role of Demographic Information, 7 IEEE Transactions on Info. Forensics and Sec. 1789, 1789 (Dec.), MITRE Technical Reports. https://assets.documentcloud.org/documents/2850196/Face-Recognition-Performance-Role-of-Demographic.pdf.

Larson, J., Mattu, S., Kirchner, L., and Angwin, J. (2016). How We Analyzed the COMPAS Recidivism Algorithm. ProPublica, 23 May.

Lohr, S. (2018). Facial Recognition is Accurate if you are a white guy. *New York Times*, February 9.

Nalini Ratha, M.M., Feris, R., Smith, J.R. (2019). Diversity in Faces, IBM AI research.

O'Neil, C. (2017). *Weapons of math destruction: How big data increases inequality and threatens democracy.* Broadway Books.

Obermeyer, Z., Powers, B., Vogeli, C. and Mullainathan, S. (2019). Dissecting racial bias in an algorithm used to manage the health of populations. *Science*, 25 Oct: Vol. 366, Issue 6464, 447-453.

OGS (2019). Ethical issues arising from the police use of live facial recognition technology Interim report of the Biometrics and Forensics Ethics Group Facial Recognition Working Group, February.

Plunkett. L. (2010). Report: Kinect Doesn't Speak Spanish (It Speaks Mexican). *Kotaku*. January 9.

Mukudi, P.B.L. and Hills, P.J. (2019). The combined influence of the own-age, -gender, and -ethnicity biases on face recognition *Acta Psychologica*, Vol. 194, March, 1–6.

Rhue, L. (2018). Racial Influence on Automated Perceptions of Emotions. Retrieved from https://papers.ssrn.com/sol3/papers.cfm?abstract_ id=3281765.

Roth, L. (2009). Looking at Shirley, the Ultimate Norm: Colour Balance, Image Technologies, and Cognitive Equity. *Canadian Journal of Communication*, Vol. 34:1.

Shahani, A. (2015). Now algorithms are deciding whom to hire, based on voice. All Tech Considered: *Tech, culture and connection*, March 30.

Simonite, T. (2018). AI is the future – but where are the women? WIRED. Retrieved from www.wired.com/story/artificial-intelligence-researchers-gender-imbalance/.

Smith, N. (2019). Make Your Smart Devices Easy to Setup, Use, and Maintain with Frustration-Free Setup, New Smart Home Skill API Features, and the Alexa Connect Kit. Amazon Alexa Developer Blog, 25 September.

Stefanos, Z., Zhang, C. and Zhang, Z. (2015). A survey on face detection in the wild: past, present and future. *Computer Vision and Image Understanding*, 138:1–24.

Tatman, R. (2017). Gender and Dialect Bias in YouTube's Automatic Captions. *Proceedings of the First Workshop on Ethics in Natural Language Processing*, Valencia, Spain, 4 April, 53–59.

Wang, Y., and Kosinski, M. (2017). Deep neural networks are more accurate than humans at detecting sexual orientation from facial images. *Journal of Personality and Social Psychology*, 114(2):246-257.

Wu, X. and Zhang, X. (2016). Automated Inference on Criminality using Face Images. Retrieved from https://arxiv.org/pdf/1611.04135v2.pdf.

Wen, Y., Zhang, K., Li, Z., and Qiao, Y. (2016). A discriminative feature learning approach for deep face recognition. In: *European Conference on Computer Vision*, 499–515. Berlin: Springer.

## Chapter 12

Bartlett, T. (2017). Can we really measure Implicit Bias? Maybe not. *The Chronicle of Higher Education*, January 5.

Brownstein, M. and Michaelson, E. (2015). Doing without Believing: Intellectualism, Knowledge-How, and Belief-Attribution. *Synthese*, 193(9), 2815-2836.

Brownstein, M. (2016). Context and the Ethics of Implicit Bias. In Brownstein, M. and Saul, J. (Eds.) *Implicit Bias and Philosophy: Volume 2, Moral Responsibility, Structural Injustice, and Ethics.* Oxford: Oxford University Press.

Greenwald, A.G., Banaji, M.R. and Nosek, B.A. (2015). Statistically small effects of the Implicit Association Test can have societally large effects. *Journal of Personality and Social Psychology*, 108, 553–561.

Greenwald, A.G., Poehlman, T.A., Uhlmann, E.L. and Banaji, M.J. (2009). Understanding and using the implicit association test: III. Meta-analysis of predictive validity. *Journal of Personality and Social Psychology*, 97, 17–41.

Greenwald, A.G., Poehlman, T.A., Uhlmann, E.L. and Banaji, M.R. (2009). Understanding and using the Implicit Association Test: III. Meta–analysis of predictive validity. *Journal of Personality and Social Psychology*, 1, 17–41.

Greenwald, A.G., McGhee, D.E. and Schwartz, J.L.K. (1998). Measuring individual differences in implicit cognition: The implicit association test. *Journal of Personality and Social Psychology*, 74, 1464–1480.

Jost, J.T. (2019). The IAT Is Dead, Long Live the IAT: Context-Sensitive Measures of Implicit Attitudes Are Indispensable to Social and Political Psychology. *Current Directions in Psychological Science*, 28(1), 10–19.

MacDonald, H. (2017) The False 'Science' of Implicit Bias, Wall Street Journal, October 9.

Olson, M.A. and Fazio, R.H. (2003). Relations Between Implicit Measures of Prejudice: What Are We Measuring? *Psychological Science*, 14(6), 636–639.

Oswald, F.L., Mitchell, G., Blanton, H., Jaccard, J. and Tetlock, P.E. (2013). Predicting ethnic and racial discrimination: A meta-analysis of IAT criterion studies. *Journal of Personality and Social Psychology*, 105, 171–92.

Sie, M. and van Voorst Vader-Bours, N. (2016). *Stereotypes and Prejudices: Whose Responsibility?* In: Implicit Bias Volume 2. Saul, J. and Brownstein, M. (Eds.). Oxford: Oxford University Press.

Singal, J. (2017). Psychology's Favorite Tool for Measuring Racism Isn't Up to the Job. *The CUT*, January.

Tierney, J. (2008). In Bias Test, Shades of Gray. *New York Times*, November 17.

Washington, N. and Kelly, D. (2016). Who's Responsible for This? Moral Responsibility, Externalism, and Knowledge about Implicit Bias. In: J. Saul and M. Brownstein (Eds.), *Implicit Bias and Philosophy, Volume 2: Moral Responsibility, Structural Injustice, and Ethics*. Oxford: Oxford University Press.

# Acknowledgements

First and foremost, I want to thank my husband, Paul. He has seen me agonise and obsess over this book, humoured me even when I have been in the foulest of moods, and celebrated my victories with me, no matter how small. His calm mind has kept me grounded, he has been my sounding board, and he has done more than half his share of the household work. You really are my better half.

I am hugely indebted to Jim Martin at Bloomsbury Sigma for taking a chance on me and for his unwavering support throughout the process, and to Anna MacDiarmid, my editor at Bloomsbury, for her superlative editing powers. You both believed in me and in this book, even when I couldn't see the wood for the trees.

There are too many scientists and researchers to name here who shared their time and expertise with me, but you know who you are. Thank you. You are doing incredible work, and I am just grateful that I had an opportunity to shine some light on it through this book. All the errors are, of course, mine alone.

Thank you also to so many of you who spoke with me and shared your personal experiences during the last year or so, and to the community on Instagram, Facebook and Twitter who shared my frustrations and my journey. You were my echo chamber and my tribe, which is what I most needed at times.

I will always be eternally grateful to my parents, Sudha and Nand Kishore, who let me spread my wings in a world that was not designed for women. You taught me generosity and compassion, and to never judge a book by its cover.

I cannot not thank Taylor and Belle, my four-legged companions, although they will never read this book. They have kept me company through the long solitary hours of writing during the day and through the night, although that might just have been the temptation of the biscuit crumbs. You got a good deal out of it, but I did better!

And, finally, I dedicate my book to my children. To India and April, who have shared me with this book and let me hide away with my thoughts. Thank you for loving me unconditionally during this process, and for all the cuddles and giggles. And, to Prishita, who first made me a mother and a much better person in the process. You have always been my moral compass, and my north star.

# Index